Contemporary
Law Office
Management

ASPEN COLLEGE SERIES

Contemporary Law Office Management

Second Edition

Lori Tripoli

Wolters Kluwer

Law & Business

Copyright © 2014 CCH Incorporated.

Published by Wolters Kluwer Law & Business in New York.

Wolters Kluwer Law & Business serves customers worldwide with CCH, Aspen Publishers, and Kluwer Law International products. (www.wolterskluwerlb.com)

To contact Customer Service, e-mail customer.service@wolterskluwer.com, call 1-800-234-1660, fax 1-800-901-9075, or mail correspondence to:

Wolters Kluwer Law & Business
Attn: Order Department
PO Box 990
Frederick, MD 21705

Printed in the United States of America.

1 2 3 4 5 6 7 8 9 0

ISBN 978-1-4548-3880-7

Library of Congress Cataloging-in-Publication Data

Tripoli, Lori, 1963-author.
  Contemporary law office management / Lori Tripoli.—Second edition.
    p. cm.—(Aspen college series)
  Includes bibliographical references and index.
  ISBN 978-1-4548-3880-7 (alk. paper)
 1. Law offices—United States. I. Title.

KF318.T75 2014
340.068—dc23
                                                    2013043164

About Wolters Kluwer Law & Business

Wolters Kluwer Law & Business is a leading global provider of intelligent information and digital solutions for legal and business professionals in key specialty areas, and respected educational resources for professors and law students. Wolters Kluwer Law & Business connects legal and business professionals as well as those in the education market with timely, specialized authoritative content and information-enabled solutions to support success through productivity, accuracy and mobility.

Serving customers worldwide, Wolters Kluwer Law & Business products include those under the Aspen Publishers, CCH, Kluwer Law International, Loislaw, ftwilliam.com and MediRegs family of products.

CCH products have been a trusted resource since 1913, and are highly regarded resources for legal, securities, antitrust and trade regulation, government contracting, banking, pension, payroll, employment and labor, and healthcare reimbursement and compliance professionals.

Aspen Publishers products provide essential information to attorneys, business professionals and law students. Written by preeminent authorities, the product line offers analytical and practical information in a range of specialty practice areas from securities law and intellectual property to mergers and acquisitions and pension/benefits. Aspen's trusted legal education resources provide professors and students with high-quality, up-to-date and effective resources for successful instruction and study in all areas of the law.

Kluwer Law International products provide the global business community with reliable international legal information in English. Legal practitioners, corporate counsel and business executives around the world rely on Kluwer Law journals, looseleafs, books, and electronic products for comprehensive information in many areas of international legal practice.

Loislaw is a comprehensive online legal research product providing legal content to law firm practitioners of various specializations. Loislaw provides attorneys with the ability to quickly and efficiently find the necessary legal information they need, when and where they need it, by facilitating access to primary law as well as state-specific law, records, forms and treatises.

ftwilliam.com offers employee benefits professionals the highest quality plan documents (retirement, welfare and non-qualified) and government forms (5500/PBGC, 1099 and IRS) software at highly competitive prices.

MediRegs products provide integrated health care compliance content and software solutions for professionals in healthcare, higher education and life sciences, including professionals in accounting, law and consulting.

Wolters Kluwer Law & Business, a division of Wolters Kluwer, is headquartered in New York. Wolters Kluwer is a market-leading global information services company focused on professionals.

For Michael Ciavardini, who is accompanying me to the finish;
for Victor Laino, just for being; and for Kenneth Laino, who
helped me get my start.

Summary of Contents

Contents

Chapter 1

Introduction: What Do Law Office Managers Do?

Chapter 2

The Changing Structure of Law Firms from Solo to Mega

Chapter 3

Clients

Chapter 4

Ethics

Chapter 5

Human Resources

Chapter 6

The Physical Law Office

Chapter 7

Communications

Chapter 8

Marketing

Chapter 9

Money Management

Chapter 10

File Management

Chapter 11

Docket Management

Chapter 12

Knowledge and Records Management

Chapter 13

Law Firm Library Management

Chapter 14

Technology and the Law Firm of the Future

Preface

The legal field is more exciting—and providing more opportunities for more people—than ever before. I note this even as the industry, in recent years, has had to adjust to shrinking legal budgets, to downward pressures of recession and slowdown, and to heightened competition from a variety of sources, thanks to the growth of the Internet and technological advances. Rather than hesitating about entering the legal field, I say "jump in." Entrepreneurial opportunities abound as technological advances and ethical restrictions evolve to allow broader access to the law and to legal help by many who might not otherwise be able to afford it or to understand it. Certainly, the market has changed since I graduated from law school, but so too has every other market in every other industry. The law has never been static, and those working in the field should appreciate that the way they do business is unlikely to be either.

The opportunities that will be available in the future aren't quite the same ones that were available when I was a little girl and dreamt about becoming a lawyer, just as they aren't the same as the ones available when I actually graduated from law school, took the bar exam, and became a lawyer. What is quite clear, both about the present legal industry and its future directions, is the focus on the business of providing legal services. Effectiveness will continue to be measured in new and more accurate ways. Efficiencies will need to be enhanced. Everyone involved in the legal industry needs to be a competent business person. Everyone—lawyer, paralegal, law office manager, or other—needs to apply law office management principles to their work. There's no pretending that the legal services industry is anything other than a business.

No matter what size or type of legal services provider you plan to work for, you will be involved, to a greater or lesser degree, in law office management. Even if you are not a full-time law office manager, you will likely be filling out time sheets or filing documents or writing memos or interacting with clients, and you will be doing so in a certain way because your organization has established procedures to help it function smoothly. Whether you plan to pursue law office management as a career, or you just want to have a strong understanding of law office management principles, this textbook will help you. Taking a college-level course in law office management—for which this textbook is designed—will provide you with an essential understanding of how law offices function. If you plan to attend law school, this foundation will serve you well. Too often, the business aspects of a law practice are overlooked as law students focus their energy on learning the law and how to think like lawyers.

Any prospective lawyer who ignores law office management while obtaining his legal education does so at his peril. Asking a lawyer what she does for a living will invariably lead to an answer like *litigate, corporate transactional work, IP,* or *entertainment law.* It's the rare lawyer who admits to making a run to Costco to buy air freshener for the office bathrooms or who concedes to having been at the office late trying to get wireless Internet access working again. No matter what profession we are talking about—doctor, lawyer, rocket scientist—someone has to mind the store. In very small firms, law office management tasks may be shared between lawyers and their staff. In large ones, they are likely to be divvied up among numerous specialists, from accountants to marketing folks to techies.

Too often, lawyers fail because they do not fully understand how to operate a law practice. Evidentiary support is evident in the legal and general-interest publications that cover lawyers and law firms that have taken a fall. It needn't be this way. This book is designed to help people employed in the legal services industry succeed.

Inevitably, running a business is far more exciting than learning how to run one. While certain foundations are necessary, this book emphasizes the real-world dilemmas that lawyers and those who work with them regularly confront. Yes, ideal scenarios are described here—as are grittier, more perplexing, and stressful situations that may well arise in any law firm, of any size, at any time. The time to learn how to deal with difficult situations is the present. With a solid background in law office management, legal staff and practicing lawyers can avoid many prospective disasters. With a willingness to implement the solid business practices described here, lawyers, their staff, and their firms will be on surer footing as they negotiate what can too often be very challenging times.

Enjoy this work. Follow your own curiosity and pursue the suggestions offered at the end of each chapter in the section "If You Want to Learn More." Ponder the scenarios described in the case studies in each chapter, and consider how you would handle each situation if you found yourself in a similar one. Take the career preparation tips offered in every chapter to heart, and began plotting your career path now—take steps to realize your goal. *Instructors*, take advantage of supporting materials that are available on our companion Web site. Teachers and students, feel free to stay in touch with this author, via Facebook (https://www.facebook.com/ContemporaryLawOfficeManagement), LinkedIn, Twitter (@LegallyLori), or on my blog (http://contemporarylawofficemanagement.blogspot.com/).

Acknowledgments

It's fitting that Aspen/Wolters Kluwer would publish my first textbook because it was Aspen/Wolters Kluwer editors who, in large part, gave me my start. Thanks to Larry Smith, then editor of *Inside Litigation* and *Of Counsel*, for picking my résumé out of the pile, and to Christine Housen, formerly with the *Almanac of the Federal Judiciary*, for fostering my work for so many years. I would not know nearly so much about the legal business were it not for you two. Working in the legal field, and then covering it for a number of different publications, has been a privilege and a pleasure. I'd immediately sign up for coffee-fueled all-nighters and adrenaline-charged writing marathons if I had my life to live over again. I have been fortunate to meet many lawyers passionate about their work who were also willing to share their expertise.

I am also grateful to Kara VanDam for giving me the opportunity to teach at Kaplan University. I am also grateful to Kara VanDam for giving me the opportunity to teach at Kaplan University a number of years ago. I've very much enjoyed participating in the advancement of online legal education. I couldn't ask for better guidance from Penny Lorenzo and very much appreciate her help and that of my fellow academic department chairs. The students themselves have been a delight, and sharing my knowledge with them has been rewarding in ways I hadn't anticipated.

Those who know me well are aware how time-consuming this project has been. Working, researching, and writing took more than a few late nights and weekends, but the result is a product that I am very proud of. I am appreciative that Aspen/Wolters Kluwer's David Herzig and Betsy Kenny were willing to coax this project along.

To the few who placed obstacles in my path over the years: thank you for the learning experiences. I am a better writer—and a better person—for them.

For those who read this work, I hope you become as engaged in the topic of law office management as I have been, and I hope you take away knowledge that you couldn't gain elsewhere. The legal business is a vibrant field and would benefit from the addition of people who appreciate its strengths and know how to compensate for its weaknesses.

—Lori Tripoli

Contemporary Law Office Management

1

Introduction: What Do Law Office Managers Do?

Chapter Outcomes

By the end of this chapter, a student will be able to:

- Describe the changing role of the law office manager
- Identify the members of a legal team
- Distinguish between the practice of law and the business of law

As the world has changed in the last century, as customs have evolved, as technology has advanced, as communications and travel have become easier, faster, and less expensive, as economies have declined and risen again, lawyers have all along been doing pretty much the same activity they've always done: They help clients solve problems. How they do it, of course, has changed a lot over the decades, and the team that lawyers hire to help them run their business has evolved as well. Despite shifts in the legal market, despite automation, and despite ease of access to legal materials, lawyers still practice law, and they still need someone to focus on running their business so that they themselves can counsel their clients. That's where the law office manager becomes vitally important.

To determine what a **law office manager** does, envision a lawyer sitting in her office writing a legal brief. Is the lawyer using a pen? A computer? A law office manager procured them. Does the lawyer know when the brief is due? A law office manager made sure the firm calendar specified the deadline. Are the lights in the office on? The law office manager saw that the electric bills were paid. Can the lawyer access the Internet from her computer? Print documents? Access firm records? The law office manager made these tasks possible.

law office manager:
A lawyer or hired nonlegal professional employee who handles the business aspects of a law firm's operations.

Is the lawyer sitting at a desk? On a chair? The law office manager procured the furniture, the filing cabinets, the supplies—and made arrangements to pay for them. The law office manager might have screened the first set of résumés submitted when the lawyer was applying for her job, might have set up the interviews, might have helped conduct background checks and obtained transcripts, and might have had a hand in setting up the firm's benefits. Is the lawyer drinking a cup of coffee while she focuses on the intricacies of her brief? The law office manager made sure that the firm has a kitchen, someone to clean it, and coffee, milk, and sugar to stock it. Is the office clean? Are business cards displayed in a holder on the lawyer's desk? Does someone pick up the mail in the attorney's outbox? Has a client been billed for the work the lawyer is doing? The law office manager had a hand in making sure that all of these jobs are done. Now consider what the law office manager typically does not do: practice law. The law office manager does pretty much everything else.

In very small law firms that have fewer than ten attorneys, some of the lawyers might divide up the tasks of a law office manager. One might be responsible for ordering supplies, another for paying the firm's bills each month, and a third for hiring. Paralegals and legal secretaries might be called on to perform some of these functions. Larger firms can afford to hire a dedicated law office manager. Even larger firms might have individuals or entire staffs that handle specific functions, such as technology, firm finances, marketing, and so on.

A.   Handling the Business Side of a Law Practice

Everything lawyers need to know about running a legal practice was not actually taught in law school. Yes, law students learn how to think like lawyers. They learn how to pick apart the elements of a contract, they master civil procedure, they read the Constitution and every single one of its amendments. But most do not learn much about how to run their own business. They might take a single elective on law office management, or they might not.

Traditionally, the business side of a law practice was not covered in law school at all. Law was considered a very genteel practice. It was a "learned profession" practiced by those with advanced training:

> Learned professions "are characterized by the need of unusual learning, the existence of confidential relations, the adherence to a standard of ethics higher than that of the market place, and in a profession like that of medicine by intimate and delicate personal ministration. Traditionally, the learned professions were theology, law and medicine; but some other occupations have climbed, and still others may climb, to the professional plane. . . . Dentistry, a branch of medicine, has done so within modern times."
> *Commonwealth v. Brown*, 20 N.E.2d 478, 480 (Mass. 1939) (citations omitted).

Even into the 1960s, law firms might send clients a very basic bill—even months after the legal work was completed—listing only a dollar amount due "for services rendered."

In the last 40 years or so, though, the legal business has really changed. It has become much more competitive. In keeping with fluctuating economies, law firms have actually laid off lawyers—and others—or even gone into bankruptcy. There has been a lot of consolidation among law firms. Clients are more inclined to shop around for good rates.

In law school, students traditionally were taught to be adversarial; business management skills were not necessarily intuitive to them. Unlike in business schools, where students often work together on group projects, law students are taught to pierce a legal argument, jab holes in it, work it over, and basically knock it to pieces. When they do this in an office setting, however, their coworkers might not be pleased. A law firm, in and of itself, does not necessarily have a collaborative atmosphere. Lots of lip service may be paid to being a good "team player," but a lawyer is always competing against class members—those who joined the firm as new associates at the same time the lawyer did—for coveted partner positions. Associates need to make themselves look good. Even partners can be competitive. They need to bring in business—for themselves as well as for associates. Lawyers in branch offices might try to poach clients from their own colleagues within the firm. Lawyers are competitive by nature, working in a competitive atmosphere where they're somewhat unsupervised. Some experts have likened managing lawyers to herding cats. Highly individualistic and independent, both cats and lawyers often like to go off in their own directions no matter what anyone else is telling them to do.

When lawyers are subject to professional discipline, they have often slipped up in some way with respect to their own law office management practices, whether botching court dates, mishandling client funds, or making some other mistake or error in judgment. "History has largely excluded *business practices* from any definition of professionalism, but it is apparent that many malpractice and ethical claims come more from inappropriate client management and inappropriate relationships with other attorneys than from a recurrent lack of professional competence as this term has been historically defined," writes one practitioner.[1] Lawyers historically were left on their own to discover good business management practices, such as incorporating accounting practices into their billing, providing prompt client service, and developing systems to manage their workflow.

Lawyers have had to devote more time and effort to law office management as the practice of law has evolved over the last several decades. Some courts presiding over attorney disciplinary actions have gone so far as to order lawyers to take law office management classes. In one case, a lawyer who "consistently placed the blame for his failure to appear, the scheduling difficulties encountered on these motion[s], and the 'odd' timing involved in filing papers after the return date of the motion, on his office manager or a previously employed associate" was ordered to attend a law office management seminar.[2] A number of bar associations have set up law office management assistance programs to help lawyers manage their businesses before they run into trouble.[3]

B. The Changing Role of the Law Office Manager

Clearly, someone at any law firm must be responsible for handling basic business operations, such as accounting, billing, collection, client records management, facilities management, procurement. Someone has to buy supplies, from Post-it notes, legal pads, and staplers to computers, copiers, desks, chairs, and even art. Similarly, someone must make sure that clients are billed and that they pay those bills promptly. The firm's money must be managed, payroll must be made, the firm's own bills must be paid, support staff must be hired and supervised—these are all duties for which a law office manager can be responsible.

The precise responsibilities of a law office manager vary by firm. When a law office manager is hired, the law firm's leadership should clarify the responsibilities of the law office manager, ideally in a written description of the position. At very small firms, a lawyer might handle office management tasks and even make runs to Costco on weekends to purchase supplies. After all, someone needs to make sure that the restrooms have toilet paper and soap. The lawyer responsible for law office management might delegate some tasks to her secretary or to a paralegal. As the firm grows, a dedicated employee whose sole responsibility is to manage the business side of the office might be hired. Law office managers are also called legal administrators or administrative managers. Their basic job is the same, though: to make sure that the law firm functions as a business.

A thrifty law office manager can yield significant savings for a firm by drafting a budget, issuing requests for proposals to vendors for major outlays, contacting vendors and performing product due diligence, and negotiating prices. A law office manager should also review invoices to make sure that the law firm is charged appropriately (for instance, were ten computers, as specified in an invoice, actually delivered, or were there only eight?) and to ascertain that services are delivered as specified in a contract. A law office manager might also solicit feedback from users of the purchased product to make sure the product ultimately met their needs.

In addition to handling the firm's finances and procuring appropriate products, law office managers tend to be involved in human resources management. They might recruit new staff, review incoming résumés, schedule initial interviews, conduct background and reference checks, and even make some hiring decisions. They might coordinate holiday schedules, develop a policy and procedures manual, ensure compliance with federal and state employment laws, and organize performance appraisals of employees. Law office managers might also oversee work assignments given to nonlegal staff members.

Law office managers may also have a hand in developing a firm's marketing materials. This could involve ordering firm stationery and business cards; handling the development and printing of firm brochures, newsletters, and other marketing materials; and overseeing the design and content of the firm's Web site. Advertising might also be a component of marketing. Where will the firm advertise, if anywhere? In legal newspapers? In general-interest magazines? In mainstream newspapers? In trade publications? Online? Law office managers might also be responsible for coordinating the firm's information technology needs. What computer programs will the firm be using? Will it develop its own software? Buy software off the shelf? How will computers be networked? How will firm computers interact with lawyers' mobile devices such as smartphones and tablets?

Law office managers at law firms that have more than one office must coordinate activities with their counterparts in other offices.

At large law firms with 150 lawyers or more, law office management roles might be divided among a number of people, such as a chief operating officer, a chief financial officer, a recruiting director, a marketing director, a library services director, a human resources director, a business development manager, and an information technology manager. The responsibilities of each of these individuals vary by firm. These people might have their own staff members to assist them, and the staff members probably work in different offices.

Some firms **outsource** certain law office management functions to specialists.[4] Firms may hire consultants to manage law office technology, to develop and maintain the firm's Web site, to develop office procedures, and even to undertake certain human resources tasks, such as conducting background checks on applicants. Even more mundane matters are sometimes outsourced. For instance, some law firms hire outside companies to handle their mail rooms. "Outsourcing menial jobs works . . . because there are not a lot of upward career paths within a small firm if you're not a lawyer. . . . Someone working for an outsourcing company, however, can proceed up the career track by, for example, being promoted to oversee several mailrooms."[5] Law firms can also outsource their word processing to companies like LawDocsXpress (http://www.lawdocsxpress.com). Increasingly law firms are also outsourcing even legal work.[6]

No matter who oversees law office management, the job is of the highest importance. Bungling it can even jeopardize an attorney's ability to practice law.[7]

Opportunities for law office managers and for nonlegal staff can be expected to expand as law firms increasingly shape their practices around a business model. At one large law firm, a manager with an M.B.A., not a law degree, was put in charge of a 250-lawyer practice group. The firm "was looking for professional management help, because as the firm continues to grow, the firm wants decisions driven by business rationale and understanding," the new manager told the press.[8]

outsource:
The practice of retaining a third party to perform a portion of a business's activities.

C.   Membership on the Legal Team

The law office manager, to perform her job well, typically interacts with all the personnel at a law firm. Law offices at other businesses, such as corporations, and in government agencies will be covered in Chapter 2.

A law firm's team consists of both lawyers and nonlegal staff members.

1.   Partner

Not all lawyers are created equal. There are two main categories of lawyers at a firm: **partners** and **associates.** Partners supervise lower-level attorneys known as associates. Historically, law firms were organized as partnerships, with partners sharing in the profits of the firm. **Profits** are revenue, or income, minus expenditures. Associates who joined the firm were on a **partnership track** to be promoted to partners, typically after seven to ten years. Today, most law firms are organized as limited liability corporations, limited liability partnerships, or professional corporations. Lawyers with an ownership interest in the firm may be called *shareholders* instead of partners.

partner:
A lawyer who jointly owns and runs a law firm with other lawyers.

associate:
A lower-level attorney, typically with only a few years of practice.

profits:
Revenue less expenditures.

partnership track:
The path of a newly hired attorney who is expected to be promoted to partner after serving as an associate for a requisite number of years.

nonequity partner:
A junior partner who does not have an ownership interest in the firm.

equity partner:
A partner with an ownership interest in a firm.

draw:
An advance taken by an equity partner against her share of the firm's profits.

After becoming a partner, a junior partner will probably be a salaried or **nonequity partner** for a few years before "buying in" to the partnership by making a capital contribution to it. The partner is then an **equity partner** with full voting power. Equity partners do not earn salaries but instead share in the profits of the firm. To manage their own income stream, equity partners typically "draw" an advance from their share of firm profits periodically (so the **draw** is akin to a paycheck) rather than waiting for the end of the year to receive their share of those profits.

Partners, as the most experienced members of the legal team, charge more than junior lawyers do for their services. The average billing rate for partners was $536 per hour in 2012.[9] Associates billed out at an average of $370 per hour in 2012.[10]

How Much Money Do Lawyers Make?

- In 2012, the average revenue per lawyer in the top 100 law firms in the United States was $844,245.[11]
- A lawyer's average compensation at firms of all sizes was $295,010 in 2012.[12]
- Midlevel partners earned, on average, $194,036 in 2012.[13]
- The median compensation for first-year associates at firms of all sizes was $125,000 in 2012.[14]

2. Associate

Newly minted lawyers who have recently graduated from law school and taken the bar exam are hired as associates. A lawyer working in her first year on the job is called a "first-year associate." In her second year, she is a "second-year associate." The group of new associates a law firm hires each year is called a "class." At large law firms, junior associates are often mentored by more senior associates who help them learn the legal business and their way around the firm. Typically, associates on the partnership track work seven to ten years before being elevated to partner.

summer associate:
A law student hired to work at a law firm during the summer with the understanding that the student will be considered for an associate position at the firm.

The median salary for first-year associates at law firms was $125,000 in 2012.[15] The amount a new lawyer will earn depends somewhat on the size of the firm she joins. Whereas the median salary for a first-year at a small firm with 25 or fewer attorneys was $70,750 in 2012, the median salary for first-years at megafirms with more than 700 lawyers was $145,000,[16] down from $160,000 two years earlier.[17] Law firms often hire second- and third-year law students to work at the firm during the summer when they are not in school. These summer hires are referred to as **summer associates.** At the end of the summer, the firm often makes an offer to these summer associates for permanent employment following graduation from law school. Summer associates typically are compensated at a rate approaching the salary of a first-year associate.

"I won't see you in court!"

Many lawyers never go to court at all.

The legal field today is highly specialized. In a large law firm, if a matter starts heading toward litigation, an attorney from the litigation department might be called in to work on the case. That person is an expert on jurisdiction, court filings, and civil procedure—not necessarily knowledgeable about substantive areas of the law.

Even litigators may not go to court all that often. They might have a big trial every few years. Many matters are settled before they actually get to court.

Some lawyers just draft contracts for the development of energy sources, like pipelines or nuclear power plants. Other lawyers just represent clients before federal agencies, working on regulations, obtaining permits for their clients, or registering products.

In the past, a lawyer hired as an associate at a law firm often stayed at the firm for his entire career, moving up from associate to partner. Today, associates and even partners might switch to different law firms several times during their careers. Lawyers who join a law firm after practicing elsewhere are referred to as **lateral hires.** Lawyers switch firms for any number of reasons: because pay scales at another firm are higher, because the hours worked are more tolerable, because there's more opportunity in a certain practice area, or even because a lawyer is more drawn to the **firm culture.** Some law firms have reputations for employing cutthroat litigators; others are considered a more genteel place to work.

Nowadays not all associates become partners. The New York law firm Cravath, Swaine & Moore is credited with being the first law firm to hire lawyers with the stated understanding that many would not be elevated to partner.[18] Law firms often have an **"up or out"** policy, meaning that an associate who is not promoted to partnership status must leave the firm. Today, some firms hire **permanent associates** who are not on the partnership track.

Generally, a law firm seeks to retain more associates than partners, because the firm makes a profit on the work of those associates (but the firm shares profits among the partners). **Leverage** is the ratio of nonequity lawyers (associates, permanent associates, of counsel, nonequity partners) to equity partners. A highly leveraged firm has a high nonequity lawyer-to-partner ratio. Some law firms have as many as eight associates for every partner. During the challenging economy associated with the Great Recession that began in 2007, some law firms reduced the number of associates given the diminished amount of work that was coming in. With a reduced workload, fewer associates were necessary. Although partners are often a greater expense to a firm, some law firm partnership agreements provide that partners can only be removed "for cause." Associates, as at-will employees, can be easier to lay off.

lateral hire:
A lawyer who joins a different law firm after practicing law elsewhere.

firm culture:
The personality and tradition of behavior at a law firm.

"up or out":
The policy that an associate passed over for partnership is expected to leave the firm.

permanent associate:
An associate who is not on the partnership track at a law firm.

leverage:
The ratio of nonequity lawyers to equity partners.

3. Of Counsel

of counsel:
A salaried attorney, typically one with more experience than an associate, who is not on the partnership track at a firm.

Some attorneys who are not elevated to the partnership level instead become **"of counsel"** to their firm. This position is more senior than that of an associate but below the rank of partner. Lawyers who are of counsel are typically salaried attorneys. Some are older partners who opt to work reduced hours and to forgo the responsibilities of partnership. A number of women become of counsel at larger law firms. Even if they are highly experienced attorneys, they might not want to put in the long hours required of a partner.

4. Staff Attorney

staff attorney:
An attorney hired with the understanding that he is not on the partnership track at a firm.

Similar to the of counsel position is the staff attorney. **Staff attorneys** are hired with the understanding that they are not on the partnership track at a law firm. Staff attorneys may be hired to conduct more routine legal work. They might work fairly standard hours (associates and partners, in contrast, often have very long workdays) and generally are not compensated as well as associates are.

5. Contract Attorney

contract attorney:
A lawyer hired temporarily by contract for a specified period of time.

Similar to a staff attorney is a **contract attorney**, who may be hired to work for a specified period of time. Contract attorneys are not permanent employees of a law firm, but are hired on a per-project basis. When the project is finished, so is their work at the firm. Contract attorneys often undertake document review work.

6. Legal Secretary

Legal secretaries perform much of the work a conventional secretary does (such as answering the telephone, typing, filing, scheduling meetings, and making travel arrangements), although the documents they prepare while working for a lawyer tend to be specialized legal papers, such as motions, complaints, summonses, responses, and subpoenas, among other things.

A legal secretary may be assigned to work for several lawyers—for instance, one partner and two associates. A legal secretary with 7 to 11 years' work experience could expect to earn between $49,250 and $61,750 in 2013, according to one legal recruiting firm.[19]

7. Paralegal

paralegal:
A person who assists a lawyer in completing certain legal tasks but is not trained as an attorney.

The use of legal assistants, or **paralegals,** started becoming a common practice in the 1960s as the American Bar Association and other organizations tried to make legal services more affordable. In 1967, the American Bar Association recognized the appropriateness of delegating legal work to nonlegal staff,[20] today referred to as legal assistants or paralegals.

As salaries rise for first-year associates, law firms increasingly turn toward parale-gals for help. Paralegals do not expect to have an ownership interest in their firm because they cannot be promoted to partner, their salaries are significantly lower than those of associates, and they are generally cheaper to replace than an associ-ate is.[21]

Paralegal salaries vary greatly depending on the size of the firm, the job responsibilities, and the location of the firm. The median salary for a paralegal in 2010 was $46,680.[22] A paralegal with four to six years' experience working at a midsize law firm could expect to earn between $53,500 and $66,000 in 2013.[23]

Paralegals assist lawyers by performing legal research, drafting documents and correspondence, gathering information, and interacting with clients. They have varied responsibilities. At some firms, paralegals are involved in basic clerical tasks. At other firms, a paralegal might be much more engaged at an intellectual level and work side by side with lawyers in handling cases:

> Paralegals who are seeking to reach the upper echelon of a firm's non-lawyer ranks need to know not only how to do their job but also how to work the system in their favor. Admittedly, "a lot of times, assignments can be very basic," [Lauren Stiller] Rikleen [a partner at Bowditch & Dewey's Framingham, Mass. office] acknowl-edges. But "a paralegal who takes an interest in the underlying matter may be able to generate opportunities to contribute in other ways," she explains. Paralegals "who show initiative and interest in the case" are the ones who do well, Rikleen maintains.[24]

While some paralegals are recent college graduates who want to work in the legal field for a year or two before proceeding to law school, others are "career parale-gals" intending to work in the legal field as nonlawyers.

Most paralegals work for law firms. The rest typically work in corporate legal departments or for federal, state, or local government agencies.[25] Some paralegals are freelancers and not on the permanent staff of a firm. They might work for temporary employment agencies or be independent contractors.

8. Law Clerk

Law clerks are usually law students who work on a part-time basis at a firm while attending school. They generally are not as well compensated as summer associates.

law clerk:
A law student who works at a law firm, typically on a part-time basis, while attending law school.

9. Marketing Director

As law firms have evolved and begun to run their practices as businesses, many firms have hired **marketing directors** to help produce marketing materials, develop advertisements, draft marketing plans, handle publication relations, and coordinate efforts to obtain new business. One survey conducted in 2012 found that the average salary of law firm media professionals was $130,391.[26] Large firms might have a separate marketing department headed by a chief marketing officer.

marketing director:
A person who oversees the development and implementation of a firm's marketing initiatives.

10. Other Nonlegal Staff

Depending on the size of a firm, any number of nonlegal staff members might be employed in addition to a law office manager, such as information technology staff, word processors, receptionists, filing clerks, copy room attendants, mail room staff, proofreaders, investigators who look for evidence in a case, messengers, process servers, information managers, and law librarians.

Law librarians are an indispensable resource for anyone conducting legal research. In addition to maintaining a firm's library, a law librarian is available to advise lawyers and staff about pertinent legal materials and research techniques.

As law firms evolve, so do the positions in them. For example, some law firms have begun referring to their human resources directors as **chief talent officers,** a development that has been praised by some for elevating the position of human resources director to the **C-suite.** Others dismiss the title as merely a new buzzword. As law firms have become more cognizant of diversity, they increasingly are hiring **diversity managers** to promote awareness of diversity issues within a law firm and to help the firm reach its diversity goals. As clients and firms themselves increasingly seek to minimize their impact on the environment and to conserve resources, some law firms are appointing **chief sustainability officers.**[27] Sustainability is often described as development that "meets the needs of current generations without compromising the ability of future generations to meet their own needs."[28]

D. Educational Requirements

Although there are no formal education requirements for law office managers, they typically have college degrees. Some might have advanced degrees such as an M.B.A. or even a J.D. **J.D.** stands for *Juris Doctor,* which is the legal degree that most law students earn. Some students might go on to obtain a Masters of Laws degree, or an **LL.M.**

At small firms, a partner might assume some of the responsibilities of a law office manager while maintaining her legal practice on at least a part-time basis. A full-time law office manager who happens to have law degree is a nonpracticing lawyer.

Large law firms may have entire office management teams with any number of specialists, such as a chief financial officer, a chief marketing officer, a chief technology officer, and so on. Employees who have reached these ranks may have specialized degrees in finance, marketing, technology, and the like.

Some universities now have certificate and masters programs emphasizing law office administration. For instance, the University of Denver offers a Master of Science in Legal Administration degree (http://www.law.du.edu/msla/), a certificate in legal administration, and a joint J.D./Master of Science in Legal Administration degree. Similarly, the George Washington University offers a Master of Professional Studies and a graduate certificate in law firm management (http://cps.gwu.edu/lfm.html).

chief talent officer:
A new title for the head human resources director, who focuses on recruiting employees and managing their performance.

C-suite:
The chief officer positions in an organization, such as chief executive officer, chief operating officer, and chief financial officer.

diversity manager:
A person who promotes awareness of diversity issues and helps an organization achieve its diversity goals.

chief sustainability officer:
A new job description in some law firms for a person who promotes the conservation of resources and seeks to minimize the impact of the firm and its clients on the environment.

J.D.:
Juris Doctor, or Doctor of Laws, degree earned by most graduates from law school today.

LL.M.:
Masters of Laws degree.

E. Skills

A successful law office manager must bring a wide variety of skills to her job, from leadership skills to organizational skills to decision-making skills to communication, team-building, and process-management skills. A competent law office manager needs to be flexible, to be able to delegate, and to get along well with attorneys! While lawyers typically recognize the need for a law office manager, they sometimes have difficulty working with one. Many lawyers are accustomed to working on their own and to making their own decisions. If a law office manager attempts to limit their actions, such as by asking lawyers to submit their timesheets by a deadline, lawyers might bristle. Law office managers need to learn to work with the "lawyer personality" and not take rebuffs personally.

A law office manager might be a "jack of all trades" or might work in a specialized area within law office management, such as technology. The job depends on the exact requirements of a given position at a law office.

To get a better sense of the job responsibilities of a law office manager, see Figure 1-1.

F. Compensation

A law office manager's salary depends on the law firm's size, the job responsibilities of the position, the educational level of the law office manager, the region in which the law firm is located, and the law office manager's ability to negotiate a reasonable level of compensation. Law office managers can earn anywhere from $28,000 a year at small firms to $74,000 or more at large ones.[29]

G. How to Succeed As a Law Office Manager

To be effective at their jobs, law office managers must be knowledgeable about the legal field and keep abreast of best law firm practices that might work well for the manager's own firm. Clearly, initiative is required—this is not a position for shrinking violets! If a manager notices that billables are down, that accounts receivable are slowing, or that nonlegal support staff are disgruntled, the law office manager needs to alert his supervisor to the problem and propose a plan for improving the firm's performance. How a law office manager goes about informing appropriate partners about developments depends on the firm's culture, the structure of management at the firm, and the practical working relationships the law office manager has developed with the lawyers with whom he works.

FIGURE 1-1
Sample Job Description for a Law Office Manager

Workplace Alaska Job Class Specifications

Law Office Manager I

. . . .

Class Definition:

Under general direction, supervise the support staff and coordinate and facilitate administrative activities to ensure efficient and consistent operation of a midsized urban law office.

This is a supervisory class with substantial responsibility for the exercise of independent judgment in appointing, promoting, evaluating, transferring, suspending, discharging, and adjudicating the grievances of subordinate personnel.

Distinguishing Characteristics:

Law Office Manager I is a member of the office management team and, as a second-level supervisor, has substantial authority for the supervision and coordination of the legal support staff and office administrative needs. Typically, Law Office Managers I directly supervise two or more Law Office Assistant II subordinate supervisors. This class is distinguished from the Law Office Assistant II in that the duties and responsibilities do not routinely include providing direct legal support to attorneys and by the greater scope of supervisory and administrative authority.

Law Office Manager I is distinguished from Law Office Manager II by the smaller size of the law office operations and the physical location, and the number and composition of the support staff directly and indirectly supervised. These characteristics of the office environment when compared to the Law Office Manager II limit the nature, variety, and complexity of the work, nature of supervision received by the incumbent, initiative and originality required, and the nature and extent of supervision over the work of other employees. In addition, Law Office Manager I incumbents are more directly involved with the day-to-day work assigned to subordinate staff, provide training, and may occasionally perform the work.

The Law Office Manager series is distinguished from the Administrative Manager series in that the duties and responsibilities are focused on the supervision and management of the program support staff as well as the day-to-day administrative needs of the law office, primarily as they relate to the support staff operations. Generally, there are no higher-level administrative specialists or managers in the same geographic location. Any administrative responsibilities in addition to the supervision and management of the support staff extend only to the office assigned, are of a coordinative or facilitative nature and are not the primary purpose of the work. Incumbents ensure that required administrative paperwork is completed correctly, appropriate processes and procedures are followed, and information and requests are appropriately forwarded for action to other administrative specialists and managers elsewhere in the agency. Incumbents are not substantially involved in the long-range planning, management, and control of the agency's overall administrative needs as is typical of the Administrative Manager series. The Law Office Manager performs more of a "program" than a "line" function.

Examples of Duties:

Manage, coordinate, and supervise the office administrative and legal support activities and employees, set priorities and work schedules, assign and distribute work, complete and review or approve performance evaluations and leave. Discuss assignment of work and completion of projects with attorneys and shift projects between sections or units and between offices as necessary to ensure deadlines and priorities are met. Recommend, approve, and coordinate overtime. Provide and recommend training for support staff. Prepare or review position descriptions.

(continued)

Serve as liaison between attorneys and support staff to resolve employee conflicts and complaints. Counsel employees on performance problems. Initiate and participate in disciplinary actions and respond to grievances. Conduct meetings with employees and union representatives. Investigate and prepare factual reports on disciplinary actions, grievances, and terminations. Receive and perform initial investigation of affirmative action, harassment, and human rights complaints.

Request hiring approval and initiate recruitment efforts. Independently or as a hiring team member, screen applicants, interview selected applicants. Make appointments and complete disposition for hire. Monitor and provide guidance to the hiring manager or supervisor, and act as approving authority upon completion of the recruitment effort.

Provide new employee orientation, obtain and submit new hire paperwork to the Human Resources Office. Provide advice and guidance to employees and supervisors concerning staff problems, personnel and payroll, benefits and recruitment matters or refer to appropriate staff or agency. Supervise time and attendance reporting and maintain leave schedule for the office. Responsible for compliance with Federal Medical Leave Act (FMLA) and Alaska Family Leave Act (AFLA), monitor absences and notify both the employee and personnel section of potential family leave situations. Prepare requests for personnel actions and submit personnel forms to effect employee changes. Track employees' merit anniversary dates and request timely completion of performance evaluations. Maintain personnel files for all office employees. May act as certifying officer for leave slips, time sheets, and payroll batches for the office. May act as the office Americans with Disabilities Act (ADA) Coordinator.

Inventory and maintain office supplies and equipment, prepare inventory lists and supply orders. Obtain comparative quotes from vendors, approve or arrange for purchase of minor equipment. Determine availability and suitability of office equipment and furniture. Make recommendations on major purchases. Project equipment needs. Arrange transfer or disposal of surplus equipment, maintain storage area and property control.

Control and reconcile petty cash disbursements and account for expenditures. Act as certifying officer for the issuance, approval, and control of field warrants up to delegated limits. Calculate and prepare travel advances; review travel authorizations for accuracy and completeness. Verify and approve office invoices for payment and allocate costs to correct accounting codes. Monitor cost performance reports for reimbursable service agreements. Resolve billing discrepancies with vendors or contractors. Obligate funds for administrative and case-related costs. Receipt and forward monies received. Maintain files and account records for administrative transactions.

Arrange repair and maintenance of office equipment and furniture. Perform initial analysis of problems and, if unable to repair, contact appropriate repairperson. Troubleshoot computer problems, install software updates, install printers, receive and install new computers. Serves as computer liaison with department information technology staff. Provide office training in utilizing information systems and equipment such as the Internet, email, and multimedia projector. Set up and break down personal computers for training.

Administer the records management systems. Participate in the design, development, acceptance, implementation, training, and management of the system.

Responsible for the maintenance and control of the building security system, phone system, building passes, and general maintenance. Ensure that lessor adheres to the building lease agreement regarding safety, janitorial services, maintenance, and parking. Work with department's contracting section on lease problems. Coordinate and arrange office and equipment moves and rearrangements.

Serve as terminal security officer and operator for criminal records networks (e.g., APSIN and NCIC). Train staff as operators.

(continued)

During legislative session, open and maintain new bill files, cross-reference previous sessions' bills; index, track bill progress, and file all related bill information. Type fiscal notes, bill analyses, position papers, and memos to legislators with information related to specific bills. Act as the liaison with Commissioner's office.

May provide backup and assistance to Law Office Assistants and higher-level administrative positions.

Knowledge, Skills, and Abilities:

Working knowledge of supervision and training practices and techniques.

Working knowledge of computer systems and applications and hard-copy filing systems.

Working knowledge of legal terminology and forms, judicial system rules, procedures, and requirements.

Some knowledge of administrative and personnel rules, policies, and procedures and processes.

Some knowledge of governmental organization, structure and function, and the legislative process.

Strong communication skills, both oral and written.

Skill in investigating and solving problems.

Skill in organization and time management.

Developed keyboarding skills.

Ability to supervise, motivate, train, and objectively evaluate employees.

Ability to resolve personnel and disciplinary problems.

Ability to effectively negotiate with a variety of people.

Ability to give clear and effective oral and written instructions.

Ability to establish and maintain cooperative working relationships.

Ability to anticipate problems and find creative solutions to avoid future occurrences.

Ability to independently balance and establish changing priorities to ensure consistent and efficient office operations.

Ability to compile and analyze information.

Ability to exercise tact and discretion in dealing with others.

Ability to exercise good judgment in interpreting and applying complex rules and regulations.

Ability to effectively deal with people who are under stress by remaining calm and professional.

Ability to prepare and explain policies and procedures.

Ability to use data and word processing equipment and software.

Ability to remain abreast of changes in office technology, personnel, legal issues and keep staff informed.

(continued)

Minimum Qualifications:

High school diploma or the equivalent;

AND

One year of supervisory experience;

AND

One year of experience in a legal or law enforcement environment preparing and processing legal documents and correspondence.

OR

One year of experience performing a variety of administrative functions for an office.

The required supervisory and legal or administrative experience may be earned concurrently.

Special Note:

"High School Equivalent" includes a G.E.D., or completion of any basic education course of 480 class hours (16 weeks at 30 hours per week), or six months of work experience performing duties related to the job class, or 12 months of work experience involving some routine tasks related to the job in question or highest grade of school completed plus amount of work experience which totals 12 years.

Some positions may require incumbents to be able to obtain a Notary Public Bond and to pass a criminal background check. If this requirement is present, it will be stated in the vacancy announcement.

Other Information:

ADDENDUM TO LAW OFFICE MANAGER I

Contacts include any individual, internal and external to the department, who provides the office with goods and services. The purpose of the contacts is to provide information that is readily understandable; to collect facts in order to solve problems, errors, or complaints when the issues or results are not known; and to advise and guide the direction taken to resolve complaints or problems and influence or correct actions and behaviors.

Examples of Commonly Used References: Administrative Code and Manual, Alaska Family Leave Act, Americans with Disabilities Act, Barron's Law Dictionary, Black's Law Dictionary, Blue Book—A Uniform System of Citation, case law, Case Management Manual, computer software and hardware manuals, Contract Award Manual, Department Style Manual, Drafting Manual for Administrative Regulations, equipment maintenance and operation manuals, Federal Medical Leave Act, Internal Policies/Procedures, lease agreements, Legislation Preparation Information Packet, Legislative Handbook, Network User's Manual, OSHA Standards, Personnel Rules, Procurement Manual, Rater's Guide to Performance Appraisals, Records Management Manual, Rules of Court, Supervisor's Manual, union contracts, Webster's Legal Speller, Workplace Alaska Guideline.

Source: State of Alaska Department of Administration Workplace Alaska, Job Class Specifications for a Law Office Manager, *available at* http://agency. governmentjobs.com/alaska/default.cfm?action=viewclassspec&ClassSpecID=8 91228 (last visited July 28, 2013).

A law office manager should oversee various aspects of the firm's business and be sure to give a heads-up to appropriate partners about any difficulties the firm is experiencing. Depending on the nature of the problem and the job responsibilities of the law office manager, the manager might be able to resolve a difficulty on her own before it spirals into a larger problem.

H.   Professional Associations

Law office managers are fortunate to be able to join professional associations that can provide information and foster career growth. One such organization is the Association of Legal Administrators, which was formed in 1971 and has some 10,000 members.[30] Information about the association is available at http://www.alanet.org.

The College of Law Practice Management (http://www.colpm.org) is a nonprofit corporation formed to promote law practice management. Members include administrators, lawyers, judges, professors, consultants, and others dedicated to improving law practice management.

Some bar associations allow law office managers to join if they are sponsored by an admitted lawyer. For example, the Indiana State Bar Association offers affiliate membership to legal administrators.[31]

Checklist

- Historically, lawyers did not learn about the business aspects of a legal practice while in law school.
- Good business practices help lawyers avoid claims of professional misconduct.
- Law office managers handle business operations at a law firm.
- Equity partners have an ownership interest in a law firm.
- Partners supervise more junior attorneys, known as associates.
- Associates at a law firm are salaried employees.
- Firms have created other positions for lawyers who are not on a partnership track.
- Some universities offer master's programs in law office management.

Vocabulary

associate (p. 5)

C-suite (p. 10)

chief sustainability officer
  (p. 10)

chief talent officer (p. 10)

contract attorney (p. 8)

diversity manager (p. 10)

draw (p. 6)

equity partner (p. 6)

firm culture (p. 7)

J.D. (p. 10)

lateral hire (p. 7)

law clerk (p. 9)

law office manager (p. 1)

leverage (p. 7)

LL.M. (p. 10)

marketing director (p. 9)

nonequity partner (p. 6)

of counsel (p. 8)

outsource (p. 5)

paralegal (p. 8)

partner (p. 5)

partnership track (p. 5)

permanent associate (p. 7)

profits (p. 5)

staff attorney (p. 8)

summer associate (p. 7)

"up or out" (p. 7)

Career Preparation Tips

Just as the practice of law is a business, so too is a career. Begin thinking about where your ideal career will fit in to the legal industry. What is your ideal job? What are the educational qualifications for that job? Research salaries for that job in the region where you would like to work. Look up the ideal employers, and research the people who already hold the position that you are seeking. What has been their career trajectory? How might you ascend to their position more expeditiously? Open a file on prospective employers and one on background research for the position you are interested in. Begin compiling helpful articles, links to pertinent Web sites, and information about professional associations. Consider using social media to research your ideal job further. LinkedIn groups, Facebook pages, Twitter, and Pinterest might all provide pertinent information that can be helpful to job seekers.

If You Want to Learn More

The Legal Management Resource Center, run by the Association of Legal Administrators, offers helpful information on law firm management questions. http://www.alanet.org/research/

The Law Practice Management Section of the American Bar Association offers nonmembers some free content on law firm management matters. http://www.lawpractice.org

Information about sustainable law firms is available at the American Bar Association site, too. http://www.americanbar.org/groups/law_practice_management/resources/resources_sustainable_law_firm.html

The Florida Bar has been running a Law Office Management Assistance Service since 1979. Helpful materials and forms are available on its Web site. http://www.floridabar.org/tfb/TFBMember.nsf/840090c16eedaf00 85256b61000928dc/2ce4258d54fcadcb85256fd5005c36d9?OpenDocument

The Texas Bar has made "how to" brochures on subjects such as setting billing rates, drafting employee handbooks, and documenting client expenses and attorney fees available online. http://www.texasbarcle.com/CLE/LMHowToBrochures.asp

Information about paralegal careers is available from the American Bar Association Standing Committee on Paralegals http://www.americanbar.org/groups/paralegals.html

The American Association of Law Libraries is a membership organization for law librarians and related professionals. http://www.aallnet.org/default.aspx

Paralegal managers might find membership in the International Paralegal Management Association to be useful. http://www.paralegalmanagement.org

The National Association of Legal Assistants, a membership organization for legal assistants and paralegals, has more than 18,000 members. http://www.nala.org

The National Federation of Paralegal Associations, founded in 1974, offers information on paralegal education and issues facing paralegals in the workplace. http://www.paralegals.org/default.asp?page=33

The American Association for Paralegal Education promotes quality in legal education. http://www.aafpe.org

Marketing information for law firms is accessible on the Legal Marketing Association's Web site. http:// www.legalmarketing.org

Although membership in the Managing Partners' Forum is limited to leaders of professional firms, helpful materials on management issues are available on the group's Web site. http://www.mpfglobal.com

Information about prospective law firm employers is available on the Web site of the Association for Legal Career Professionals, known as NALP because the group was founded as the National Association for Law Placement, Inc. Members of NALP are recruiters and professional development administrators from law firms and career placement professionals from law schools. http://www.nalp.org

Much pertinent information is available via social media, such as Facebook (https://facebook.com), LinkedIn (http://www.linkedin.com), Twitter .com (https://twitter.com), and Pinterest (http://pinterest.com).

Reading Comprehension

1. Why do law firms focus more on standard business practices now than previously?
2. How do the responsibilities of a law office manager at a small law firm differ from those at a large firm?
3. Why do law firms outsource certain activities?
4. What is the advantage to a lawyer of becoming a partner at a law firm?
5. What is the difference between a lawyer who is of counsel at a firm and one who is a permanent associate?
6. What are the most challenging aspects of a law office manager's job?
7. Partners at law firms bill clients at higher rates than associates do. Why, then, do law firms seek to have a high associate-to-partner ratio?
8. Suppose that you are a partner at a law firm and have advertised for a law office manager. Two equally qualified candidates have applied for the position, one with a J.D. and the other with an M.B.A. Who would be better suited for the job? Does your answer depend on the size of the law firm?

Discussion Starters

1. Search for a case where an attorney was directed to take law office management classes. What was the attorney accused of? Why did the court direct the attorney to take law office management classes?
2. Find your state's bar association online. What sort of material, if any, does it offer on law office management?
3. A prospective client at your firm has inquired about its sustainability activities. As the firm's law office manager, you haven't really been active in this area. Where would you seek information about sustainability policies in law firms? Might all clients appreciate a law firm's sustainability efforts?
4. What promotion potential does a law office manager have?
5. As a paralegal, would you rather work for an associate or for a partner?
6. Search legal news articles for an example of a law firm outsourcing some aspect of its business. What was the result of the outsourcing effort? Did the firm save money? Were clients pleased? Were clients even aware that certain tasks had been outsourced?
7. If offered a job at a law firm, how would you decide whether to accept the position? What factors would you consider?

Case Studies

1. Consider this scenario: A senior paralegal who has the biggest workstation *and* a window view is retiring. Who should get that paralegal's workstation? In formulating your answer, address the following questions:
   a. How should workstation assignments be made? Should there be some "system" in place?
   b. Should the decision be based on the proximity of the paralegal to his or her practice group?
   c. Should the workstation be assigned to the managing partner's favorite paralegal?
   d. Should the workstation go to the paralegal who bills the highest number of hours?
   e. Should the decision be based on paralegal seniority?
   f. What does *seniority* mean? The number of years in the profession? The number of years since graduating from college? The number of years with the firm? Age?
   g. Should workstation assignments be based on performance? Should the paralegal with the best performance appraisals get the spot?

h. What if the paralegal assigned to the workstation telecommutes from home three days a week, in which case that workstation is unused for part of the time? Should the workstation go to someone else instead?

i. Should the workstation simply be raffled off?

2. A large Chicago firm recently raised its first-year associates' salaries. Suppose you're a partner at a competing law firm. Your firm currently pays first-years $20,000 less per year. Should you increase salaries? In formulating your response, consider the following questions:

   a. What would be the advantage of increasing associates' salaries?

   b. Who would pay for these higher salaries? Partners? Clients?

   c. How could the firm raise salaries for first-years without reducing partner profits?

   d. Suppose you raised salaries in your firm's Chicago office. Should first-years in Washington, D.C., be paid the same amount? What about first-years in Louisville, Kentucky? What about first-years in Hong Kong?

   e. If you keep your salaries at the same level in Chicago, how could you hope to recruit top law school graduates? How would you persuade them to join your firm rather than the higher-paying one?

   f. What will you do if your firm does not raise salaries for associates and suddenly the firm starts losing more associates than usual to other firms that are paying more?

   g. Suppose you're a client of this firm. How do you feel about being billed for the legal services provided by an inexperienced lawyer who is only 25 years old? Would you continue to use the services of the firm if billing rates rose? Would you switch firms? What would be a disadvantage to switching firms?

3. An eighth-year associate at a firm will be considered for partnership next year. In evaluating the associate's candidacy, what should the partners consider?

4. Why might partners who passed over an associate for partnership status consider retaining that associate in some lesser capacity?

Endnotes

1. John W. Frost, II, *President's Page: Professional Competence and Legal Excellence Enhanced by Sound Business Management*, 70 Fla. B.J. 6 (1996) (emphasis original).

2. *Oxfurth v. Siemens A.G.*, 142 F.R.D. 424, 424 (D. N.J. 1991).

3. *See, e.g.*, Raphael Gonzalez, *Annual Report of Florida Bar Committees: LOMAS*, 81 Fla. B.J. 30 (2007).

4. Paul Sullivan, *Outsourcing Law Office Management to an Expert*, 92 Ill. B.J. 317 (2004).

5. Lori Tripoli, *Improve Productivity Without Micromanaging*, Small Firm Bus., Apr. 27, 2006.

6. Thomas S. Clay, *2013 Law Firms in Transition: An Altman Weil Flash Survey* (2013), available at http://www.altmanweil.com/LFiT2013/.

7. *See, e.g.*, Jan Lewellyn-Davidson, *Law Office Management*, 5 Nev. Law. 8 (1997).

8. Martha Neil, *MBA Manages 250-Lawyer Practice Group*, A.B.A. J., (Sept. 11, 2007), http://www.abajournal.com/news/article/mba_manages_250_lawyer_practice_group /print/.

9. Debra Cassens Weiss, *Average Hourly Billing Rate for Partners Last Year Was $727 in Largest Law Firms*, A.B.A. J. (July 15, 2013), http://www.abajournal.com/mobile /article/average_hourly_billing_rate_for_partners_last_year_was_727_in_largest_law_f.

10. *Id.*

11. NewsRx.com, The American Lawyer Reports 2012 Growth of Am Law 100 Firms Modest, Spotty (May 13, 2013), *available at* http://www.businesswire.com/news /home/20100429005683/en/American-Lawyer%E2%80%99s-Law-100-Issue-Baker-Mckenzie.

12. Leigh Jones, *Revenues Up at Larger Law Firms, Nat'l L.J. (July 29, 2013), available at* http://www.law.com/jsp/nlj/PubArticleNLJ.jsp?id=1202612599398&Revenues_Up_ at_Larger_Law_Firms&slreturn=20130631051033.

13. *Id.*

14. Press Release, National Association for Law Placement, Median First-Year Big-Law Associate Salary Slumps to $145,000 in 2012, a Median Last Seen in 2007 (Sept. 20, 2012), *available at* http://www.nalp.org/2012_associate_salaries.

15. *Id.*

16. *Id.*

17. Press Release, National Association for Law Placement, Some Associate Salaries Retreat from Their High but Remain Far Ahead of Salaries for Public Service Attorneys (Sept. 9, 2010), *available at* http://www.nalp.org/assoc_pi_sal2010?s=2010%20associate%20 salary%20survey.

18. Janet Ellen Raasch, *Making Partner—Or Not: Is It In, Up or Over in the 21st Century?*, Law Prac., June 2007, at 32, 33.

19. Press Release, Robert Half Legal, Robert Half Legal Releases Annual Salary Guide: Starting Salaries for Legal Professionals Projected to Rise 3.0 Percent in 2013 (Oct. 30, 2012), *available at* http://legal.rhi.mediaroom.com/2012-10-30-ROBERT-HALF-LEGAL-RELEASES-ANNUAL-SALARY-GUIDE-Starting-Salaries-for-Legal-Professionals-Projected-to-Rise-3.0-Percent-in-2013.

20. Susan Mae McCabe, *The Paralegal Profession: A Brief History of the Paralegal Profession*, 86 Mich. B.J. 18, 18 (July 2007).

21. D. Jeffrey Campbell, *Associates Versus Paralegals: The Shifting Balance of Profitability*, SCOLA Update (Fall 2001).

22. *U.S. Bureau of Labor Statistics, Occupational Outlook Handbook, 2012-13 Edition, Paralegals and Legal Assistants (March 29, 2012), available at* http://www.bls.gov /ooh/legal/paralegals-and-legal-assistants.htm.

23. Press Release, Robert Half Legal, supra note 19.

24. Lori Tripoli, *How to Find and Groom the Practical—and Practiced—Paralegal*, Of Counsel, Mar. 2007, at 12, 13.

25. *See, e.g.*, U.S. Bureau of Labor Statistics, *Estimates from the Occupational Employment Statistics Survey, Paralegals and Legal Assistants* (May 2009), http://www.bls.gov.

26. Larry Bodine, *How Much Law Firm Media Professionals Earn* (June 18, 2012), *available at* http://blog.larrybodine.com/2012/06/articles/money/how-much-law-firm-media-professionals-earn/.

27. Lori Tripoli, *Sustainability: What Law Firms Have at Stake*, Of Counsel, May 2012, at 19.

28. See United National Economic Commission for Europe, *Sustainable development—concept and action* (n.d.), *available at* http://www.unece.org/oes/nutshell/2004-2005/focus_sustainable_development.html.

29. *Salary Snapshot for Office Manager, Law Firm Jobs*, Payscale.com (data last updated on July 26, 2013), *available at* http://www.payscale.com/research/US/Job=Office_Manager%2c_Law_Firm/Salary/by_Company_Size, Feb. 2006, at 3, 4.

30. Association of Legal Administrators, *FAQ*, http://www.alanet.org/about/faq.aspx (last visited July 28, 2013).

31. Indiana State Bar Association, *Affiliate Application: Legal Administrator*, https://www.inbar.org/LinkClick.aspx?fileticket=mNBZ3M4jMNs%3d&tabid=93 (last visited July 28, 2013).

2

The Changing Structure of Law Firms from Solo to Mega

Chapter Outcomes

By the end of this chapter, a student will be able to:

- Compare and contrast various law firm structures
- Discuss the evolution of the legal business
- Distinguish between the authorized and unauthorized practice of law
- Describe the difference between multidisciplinary practice and multijurisdictional practice

Lawyers might find themselves working in a firm with thousands of lawyers and dozens of offices in locations around the world. Or they might work in a street-front office in a shabby neighborhood. Lawyers work in law offices in corporations, in government agencies, in lobbying firms, and elsewhere. Some lawyers opt not to formally practice law at all, although they might still rely on their legal expertise in conducting their work. These lawyers might work as consultants or in fields where a law degree is helpful but not required. A variety of work options are available in the legal marketplace today.

A. The Evolution of the Legal Business

1. The Twentieth Century

Law firms, throughout the last century, served as training grounds for lawyers fresh out of law school. Newly minted attorneys schooled in the art of "thinking

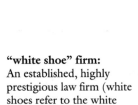

like a lawyer," a skill learned in law school, were unlikely to know a lot about the rigors of an actual law practice. Young lawyers served an apprenticeship of sorts as, mentored by partners, they learned to practice law, to provide client service, and to build a business.

Traditionally, law firms were organized as partnerships of lawyers who practiced law together and shared profits, risks, and clients. Young lawyers moved up the ranks of the firm from associate to partner, and they often stayed with a single firm for their entire careers. Firms were generally fairly small. Fewer than 40 law firms in the late 1950s had more than 50 lawyers.[1] The legal profession itself, with its **"white shoe" firms,** was fairly elitist. Plenty of barriers to entry into the law "club" existed:

> Looking back to the legal profession circa 1950, it is easy to see features of club organization. Membership in the bar required graduation from college and law school, passage of the bar examination, and approval by the relevant committee on character and fitness. Family connections were often a ticket into a good college, and graduation from a good college was a significant factor improving chances for admission to a top law school. To get set up in a firm, it paid to know someone who could introduce you, and to obtain clients, it was desirable to have personal connections. Lawyers in a community would be members of the same country clubs and civic organizations as the business leaders, and they would socialize together in all sorts of different settings. Almost all elite attorneys—and almost all senior managers of corporate clients—were men of European backgrounds. Jews could and did practice law, but tended to do so in firms characterized by ethnicity; "white shoe" firms had few Jews, no women, and no African-Americans.[2]

In the "golden era" of law practice, the profession was not particularly competitive, clients were loyal, and limitations on advertising made competition difficult. Start-ups and novices faced an uphill battle trying to get market share held by established firms with respected reputations.

Developments toward the end of the twentieth century, however, triggered changes in the industry. The 1970s, 1980s, and 1990s were characterized by increased competition as the numbers of lawyers entering the profession increased, advertising became permissible, and clients themselves started beefing up their in-house legal departments, diversified the firms they used, and began negotiating fee agreements. The marketplace started changing, and law firms had to change with it. Globalization, technological advances, and competition from unanticipated sources, such as tax and accounting firms, all had an impact on law firms. The legal industry experienced slowdowns at certain times in the 1970s, 1980s, and 1990s.[3] Some attorneys were laid off and law firms dissolved. During that time period, one of the largest law firms in the United States went bankrupt:

> Finley, Kumble, Wagner, Heine, Underberg, Manley, Myerson & Casey . . . was once the fourth largest law firm in the United States. It had approximately 700 attorneys, of whom some 200 were partners. The firm, which had offices in fifteen cities in the United States and an office in London, England, terminated its operations at the end of 1987. By the time the Debtor closed its doors, the partners had been split apart by factional feuding over responsibility for the firm's $83 million bank debt.[4]

At the very moment that law firms were experiencing business troubles, their business became open to public discussion. Specialized newspapers started covering

"white shoe" firm:
An established, highly prestigious law firm (white shoes refer to the white bucks worn by members of the upper class in the northeastern United States).

the business of law, ranking law firms, and reporting on tensions, defections, mergers, and messes. Publications such as *Legal Times* and the *National Law Journal* were chronicling the business of law. Lawyers didn't necessarily like these developments, but they did enjoy reading about their competition. *American Lawyer*, a magazine focusing on the legal industry, was founded by Steven Brill in the late 1970s.[5] Described by some as "the *People* magazine of the legal field," the magazine covered salaries, disputes between lawyers and law firms for which they once worked, and other previously unreported aspects of the legal business.[6]

In the 1980s, Steven Brill purchased a handful of regional legal newspapers, and then he started Court TV. Legal newspapers had existed before, but now the news had much more pizzazz. Partner profits and associate salaries appeared in print.

Clearly, the legal market, to be competitive, had to respond.

2. Twenty-First-Century Merger Trend

As the legal industry was being compelled to adopt a business model to remain competitive, more lawyers began entering the field. In 1974, 27,756 students earned J.D.s or LL.B.s (Bachelor of Laws, the standard law degree that was once conferred by U.S. law schools but has now been replaced by the J.D.); by 1978, the number of students earning law degrees topped 30,000, and those figures increased steadily every year, topping 40,000 in 1998.[7] By 2012, there were 1,268,011 licensed lawyers in the United States.[8]

As more lawyers entered the field, more of them started moving around rather than staying at the same law firm for their entire legal careers:

> In the classical big firm, almost all hiring was at the entry level; the firm recruited partners from the ranks of associates. Those who left went to corporations or smaller firms, not to similar large firms, because these adhered to the same no-lateral-hiring norm. But starting in the 1970s, lateral movement became more frequent, soon developing into a systematic means of enlarging the specialties and localities a firm could service and acquiring rainmakers who might bring with them or attract new clients. Eventually the flow of lateral movement widened out from individual lawyers, to whole departments and groups within firms, and finally to whole firms. Mass defections and mergers became common, enabling firms in one stroke to add new departments and expand to new locations.[9]

In the 1980s, law firms began to expand by increasing the number of lawyers in their offices and by opening more branch offices, some of them in remote worldwide locations. Often, a firm's leadership remained in the **home office,** or headquarters, where the firm had originally been based. Lawyers in the **satellite offices,** or branches, sometimes resented this long-distance supervision.

home office:
The headquarters of a law firm.

satellite office:
A branch office of a firm.

As time went on, law firms saw that it might be easier to expand their business into new locations by merging with previously existing law firms. By joining forces in this way, a firm could increase its market share and improve its ability to provide an array of services to clients without undertaking the risk of starting up an entirely new office in a new location. Mergers have remained attractive to law firms, even during challenging economic times.[10]

Successful mergers take considerable effort on the part of the lawyers and employees in the firms being merged. Before a merger is undertaken, lawyers conduct due diligence assessments that focus on the financial strength of the firm and the ability of the firms to merge without losing clients due to conflicts of interest.

To ease the transition process and the melding of different firm cultures and ways of doing business, law firms often hire outside consultants. Law firm personnel tend to experience a fair amount of anxiety during a merger. After all, will the new firm need only one director of paralegals instead of two? How will the one director be selected? Which head librarian will become the head librarian of the merged firm? Mergers can, of course, actually create opportunities for staff members to advance their careers; where an employee may have been the head of a small office outfit, she may supervise many more people in a much larger office, or even be appointed to a firmwide position, such as firmwide director of paralegals.

3.   The Impact of the Great Recession

The legal business, like other industries, felt the effects of the Great Recession that began in December 2007 that have lingered long after the recession ended in June 2009.[11] The economic downturn yielded a slowdown in business for many, combined with a renewed client interest in driving down legal costs. Pay cuts occurred at some firms.[12] Layoffs occurred at others.[13] Dwindling business meant that some law firm graduates were challenged to find employment as lawyers after graduating from law school. Employment for law school graduates in the class of 2012 was 84.7 percent in the February following graduation.[14] In 2007, before the onset of the Great Recession, employment of new graduates was 91.9 percent.[15] Yet, not all new graduates managed to obtain a job for which bar passage was necessary. Only 64.4 percent of law school graduates from the class of 2012 obtained jobs that required that they be admitted to practice law.[16] These less-than-impressive employment statistics led some to question the viability and affordability of legal education.[17] Was the marketplace simply flooded with too many lawyers and too little legal work?

The economic downturn provided an opportunity for law firms and other organizations to change the way they do business. Administrators at some law schools began to reassess the educational methods by which law students traditionally have been taught. Historically, law students learn how to think like a lawyer. What they really need to do, however, might be to learn how to run a legal business, how to get new clients and keep them, how to interact well with the judges, clerks, and others—in short, how to do all of the things that lawyers need to do. They don't just "think."

Some law firms began providing more training to lawyers on the business aspects of legal practice.[18] Some law firms moved toward new billing methods. Some law firms hired more nonlawyers with expertise in business, management, and marketing to help them refine their business methods. These and other responses to business challenges are explored in the remainder of this book. Many of the responses to economic challenges that law firms developed were aided by technology.

4.   *The Global Legal Marketplace*

The growth in technology is often said to have contributed to "shrinking borders" between countries. Today, it's easy to travel to foreign countries, to make international phone calls, and to communicate with people in faraway places. The growth in international trade and the increase in the number of law firms with overseas offices mean that more and more lawyers are participating in cross-border transactions. A lawyer who works for a U.S. company that is taking over a foreign company might perform a due diligence investigation of properties owned in foreign locations. Another might find himself working on a deal between U.S.-based investors and a foreign-owned energy company to build a facility in a foreign location. These sorts of opportunities are endless.

This development, however, has raised the issue of the **unauthorized practice of law** by lawyers who are not admitted to practice in a given jurisdiction. If, for instance, a client based in California calls its New York–based law firm with a legal problem, must the lawyer in New York be admitted to the bar in California in order to answer?

Initially, a California court seemingly answered *yes* to that question in *Birbrower, Montalbano, Condon & Frank, P.C. v. Superior Court of Santa Clara County*, 17 Cal. 4th 119 (1998). The California Supreme Court determined that an out-of-state law firm, not admitted to practice law in California, violated California's unauthorized practice of law statute when the firm performed legal services in California for a California-based client. In a world becoming smaller, where lawyers and clients at different locations could communicate by e-mail, phone, and fax, this decision was troubling.

> In Birbrower, Montalbano, Condon & Frank, P.C. v. Superior Court, the California Supreme Court denied a New York law firm any fee for work its lawyers did for a California company on an impending California arbitration (which never occurred) when the work was performed physically in California (the lawyers traveled there three times for a few days each time) and when the work was done physically in New York but "virtually" in California by email, fax, or phone. The court described the lawyer's work "in" California as "extensive," citing the trips, the fact that the client was a California company, and the fact that the arbitration would occur in the state under California law. ("In" is also a key word in the world of unauthorized practice.) The court did not say whether any single factor was decisive or identify their relative weights, making planning nearly impossible. But the court also said that the very same work, even the lawyers' advice on California law, could be compensated if done while the lawyers were physically in New York and not "virtually" in California.
>
> The Birbrower decision, by focusing on the physical or virtual location of the lawyers, was so misguided, and so unclear in explaining when the nexus with California was great enough for the work to be deemed "in" California and therefore the unauthorized practice of law, that it had to be quickly undone. Lawyers were spurred into action because here was a living casualty of a dated idea and even more so because other lawyers could easily see themselves in the same predicament. The California Supreme Court had elsewhere been enlightened about modern practice—and if it could happen there, it could happen anywhere.[19]

Since the *Birbrower* decision was rendered, the law, in California and elsewhere, has evolved to accommodate contemporary aspects of legal practice. Now, in California, the rules governing attorney conduct are somewhat more permissive if the out-of-state attorney will not be litigating a matter in California but merely providing advice. See Figure 2-1.

unauthorized practice of law:
The practice of law by someone not admitted to practice in a given jurisdiction.

FIGURE 2-1
2013 California Rules of Court

Rule 9.48. Nonlitigating attorneys temporarily in California to provide legal services

(a) Definitions

The following definitions apply to terms used in this rule:

(1) "A transaction or other nonlitigation matter" includes any legal matter other than litigation, arbitration, mediation, or a legal action before an administrative decision-maker.

(2) "Active member in good standing of the bar of a United States state, jurisdiction, possession, territory, or dependency" means an attorney who meets all of the following criteria:

(A) Is a member in good standing of the entity governing the practice of law in each jurisdiction in which the member is licensed to practice law;

(B) Remains an active member in good standing of the entity governing the practice of law in at least one United States state, jurisdiction, possession, territory, or dependency other than California while practicing law under this rule; and

(C) Has not been disbarred, has not resigned with charges pending, or is not suspended from practicing law in any other jurisdiction.

(Subd (a) relettered effective January 1, 2007; adopted as subd (h) effective November 15, 2004.)

(b) Requirements

For an attorney to practice law under this rule, the attorney must:

(1) Maintain an office in a United States jurisdiction other than California and in which the attorney is licensed to practice law;

(2) Already be retained by a client in the matter for which the attorney is providing legal services in California, except that the attorney may provide legal advice to a potential client, at the potential client's request, to assist the client in deciding whether to retain the attorney;

(3) Indicate on any Web site or other advertisement that is accessible in California either that the attorney is not a member of the State Bar of California or that the attorney is admitted to practice law only in the states listed; and

(4) Be an active member in good standing of the bar of a United States state, jurisdiction, possession, territory, or dependency.

(Subd (b) relettered effective January 1, 2007; adopted as subd (a) effective November 15, 2004.)

(c) Permissible activities

An attorney who meets the requirements of this rule and who complies with all applicable rules, regulations, and statutes is not engaging in the unauthorized practice of law in California if the attorney:

(continued)

(1) Provides legal assistance or legal advice in California to a client concerning a transaction or other nonlitigation matter, a material aspect of which is taking place in a jurisdiction other than California and in which the attorney is licensed to provide legal services;

(2) Provides legal assistance or legal advice in California on an issue of federal law or of the law of a jurisdiction other than California to attorneys licensed to practice law in California; or

(3) Is an employee of a client and provides legal assistance or legal advice in California to the client or to the client's subsidiaries or organizational affiliates.

(Subd (c) relettered effective January 1, 2007; adopted as subd (b) effective November 15, 2004.)

(d) Restrictions

To qualify to practice law in California under this rule, an attorney must not:

(1) Hold out to the public or otherwise represent that he or she is admitted to practice law in California;

(2) Establish or maintain a resident office or other systematic or continuous presence in California for the practice of law;

(3) Be a resident of California;

(4) Be regularly employed in California;

(5) Regularly engage in substantial business or professional activities in California; or

(6) Have been disbarred, have resigned with charges pending, or be suspended from practicing law in any other jurisdiction.

(Subd (d) amended and relettered effective January 1, 2007; adopted as subd (c) effective November 15, 2004.)

(e) Conditions

By practicing law in California under this rule, an attorney agrees that he or she is providing legal services in California subject to:

(1) The jurisdiction of the State Bar of California;

(2) The jurisdiction of the courts of this state to the same extent as is a member of the State Bar of California; and

(3) The laws of the State of California relating to the practice of law, the State Bar Rules of Professional Conduct, the rules and regulations of the State Bar of California, and these rules.

(Subd (e) amended and relettered effective January 1, 2007; adopted as subd (d) effective November 15, 2004.)

(f) Scope of practice

An attorney is permitted by this rule to provide legal assistance or legal services concerning only a transaction or other nonlitigation matter.

(Subd (f) relettered effective January 1, 2007; adopted as subd (e) effective November 15, 2004.)

(continued)

(g) Inherent power of Supreme Court

Nothing in this rule may be construed as affecting the power of the Supreme Court of California to exercise its inherent jurisdiction over the practice of law in California.

(Subd (g) amended and relettered effective January 1, 2007; adopted as subd (f) effective November 15, 2004.)

(h) Effect of rule on multijurisdictional practice

Nothing in this rule limits the scope of activities permissible under existing law by attorneys who are not members of the State Bar of California.

(Subd (h) relettered effective January 1,2007; adopted as subd (g) effective November 15, 2004.)

Rule 9.48 amended and renumbered effective January 1, 2007; adopted as rule 967 by the Supreme Court effective November 15, 2004.

Source: Cal. Ct. R. 9.48 (2013), *available at* http://www.courts.ca.gov/cms/rules/index.cfm?title=nine&linkid=rule9_48.

State ex rel. York v. West Virginia Office of Disciplinary Counsel
744 S.E.2d 293 (W. Va. 2013)

OPINION

WORKMAN, Justice:

Mr. Olen York (hereinafter "the petitioner") seeks a writ of prohibition to prevent the West Virginia Office of Disciplinary Counsel (hereinafter "ODC") and the West Virginia Lawyer Disciplinary Board (hereinafter "LDB") from proceeding against him in an attorney disciplinary matter. During the relevant time period, the petitioner was registered to practice as a patent attorney before the United States Patent and Trademark Office (hereinafter "PTO") and was affiliated with the Waters Law Group in Huntington, West Virginia. The petitioner contends that the ODC and LDB lack jurisdiction over him because he was not a licensed member of the West Virginia State Bar and was not practicing law in West Virginia. Upon a thorough review of the briefs, arguments of counsel Joint appendix, and applicable precedent, we deny the relief sought by the petitioner.

I. FACTUAL AND PROCEDURAL HISTORY

The petitioner, the ODC, and the LDB stipulate to certain pertinent facts, including the petitioner's admission as a licensed member of the Ohio Bar in July 2002 and his admission to practice law before the PTO[1] in January 2003. The parties also stipulate that the petitioner is a resident of Milton, West Virginia, and was associated as an independent contractor with the Waters Law Group in Huntington, West Virginia, during the relevant time period. As also stipulated by the parties, the petitioner is not a member of the West Virginia State Bar, and his practice was limited to patent and trademark issues before the PTO while associated with the Waters Law Group. The petitioner represented clients from West Virginia, but he did not appear in the state courts of West Virginia.

On September 24, 2012, a Statement of Charges was issued against the petitioner by the Investigative Panel of the LDB. The LDB alleged that the petitioner violated Rules 1.15(a), 1.15(b), 1.15(d), 8.4(c), and 8.4(d) of the West Virginia Rules of Professional Conduct by improperly processing payments for patent work performed for clients in Poca, West Virginia, and Spencer, West Virginia, while associated with the Waters Law Group. This Statement alleged that the petitioner failed to maintain a separate client account; failed to notify the Waters Law Group of funds received from clients; failed to maintain an IOLTA account; and commingled, misappropriated, and converted funds for his own use.

On November 29, 2012, the petitioner filed a writ of prohibition with this Court, contending that the ODC and LDB lack jurisdiction to prosecute the alleged violations against him, under Rule 1 of the West Virginia Rules of Lawyer Disciplinary Procedure and federal preemption principles, because he was not licensed to practice law in the State of West Virginia and was not practicing law in this state.

. . .

III. DISCUSSION

The sole issue in this case is whether the ODC and LDB have jurisdiction to investigate and potentially prosecute the petitioner for alleged violations of the West Virginia Rules of Professional Conduct. The petitioner presents two primary arguments: first, he contends that the ODC and LDB lack jurisdiction under the rules and precedent of this state; second, he contends that federal law preempts state law regulation of this disciplinary matter. There is convergence of those two issues within the decisions addressed herein; to the extent possible, however, this Court evaluates those two arguments independently.

A. The Authority of This Court to Control the Practice of Law in This State

With specific reference to this Court's ultimate authority to regulate the practice of law in this state, we noted in syllabus point one of *State ex rel. Askin v. Dostert,* 170 W.Va. 562, 295 S.E.2d 271 (1982), that "[t]he exclusive authority to define, regulate and control the practice of law in West Virginia is vested in the Supreme Court of Appeals." . . .

The obligation of this state's disciplinary authorities to investigate issues of alleged attorney misconduct is enunciated in Rule 1 of the West Virginia Rules of Lawyer Disciplinary Procedure, providing that the LDB shall

> investigate complaints of violations of the Rules of Professional Conduct promulgated by the Supreme Court of Appeals to govern the professional conduct of those admitted to the practice of law in West Virginia *or any individual admitted to*

the practice of law in another jurisdiction who engages in the practice of law in West Virginia. . . .

W.Va. R. Law. Disc. P. 1 (1994). The petitioner contends that Rule 1 does not authorize the ODC and LDB to investigate his conduct because he is neither licensed to practice law in West Virginia nor does he practice law in West Virginia. It is undisputed that the petitioner is not admitted to the practice of law in West Virginia; thus, this Court's resolution of the jurisdictional question hinges upon a determination of whether the petitioner's practice of patent law in an office located in Huntington, West Virginia, constituted the "practice of law in West Virginia," subjecting him to the disciplinary authority of the ODC and LDB. This Court has not had occasion to decide whether the practice of patent law in this state constitutes the "practice of law in West Virginia," as that phrase is used in Rule 1 of the West Virginia Rules of Lawyer Disciplinary Procedure.

This Court, in the exercise of its constitutionally-granted power to promulgate rules regulating the practice of law, formulated a thorough "Definition of the Practice of Law" on March 28, 1947, and later amended on June 1, 1961. That definition provides that "[i]n general, one is deemed to be practicing law whenever he or it furnishes to another advice or service under circumstances which imply the possession or use of legal knowledge and skill." Further, that definition provides:

> More specifically but without purporting to formulate a precise and completely comprehensive definition of the practice of law or to prescribe limits to the scope of that activity, one is deemed to be practicing law whenever (1) one undertakes, with or without compensation and whether or not in connection with another activity, to advise another in any matter involving the application of legal principles to facts, purposes or desires; (2) one undertakes, with or without compensation and whether or not in connection with another activity, to prepare for another legal instruments of any character; or (3) one undertakes, with or without compensation and whether or not in connection with another activity, to represent the interest of another before any judicial tribunal or officer, or to represent the interest of another before any executive or administrative tribunal, agency or officer otherwise than in the presentation of facts, figures or factual conclusions as distinguished from legal conclusions in respect to such facts and figures.

Michie's West Virginia Code Annotated State Court Rules, Definition of the Practice of Law, in part, at 983 (2013).

In *State ex rel. Frieson v. Isner,* 168 W.Va. 758, 285 S.E.2d 641 (1981), a case involving allegations of unauthorized practice of law, this Court explained that courts have uniformly expressed difficulty in articulating a precise definition of the practice of law and have emphasized "that the practice of law is not limited to the conduct of cases before courts, but also includes services rendered outside court . . . ." *Id.* at 768, 285 S.E.2d at 650.

In *Lawyer Disciplinary Board v. Allen,* 198 W.Va. 18, 479 S.E.2d 317 (1996), this Court addressed the issue of whether attorney conduct occurring "outside of our State" could be subject to discipline under the West Virginia Rules of Professional Conduct. *Id.* at 25, 479 S.E.2d at 324. In *Allen,* ethics charges had been filed against Ohio and District of Columbia attorneys who were not licensed members of the West Virginia State Bar *and* did not practice law from a geographic location within this state. This Court found that the out-of-state attorneys who solicited clients from West Virginia for cases that could be filed in West Virginia courts were subject to discipline in West Virginia, "even if the conduct constituting a violation occurs outside of our State." *Id.*

. . .

The petitioner in the present case contends that the *Allen* decision supports his position that only attorneys capable of practicing law in state courts located in West Virginia are subject to the jurisdiction of the ODC and LDB. We disagree. In *Allen,* the attorneys were not operating their legal practices from a location in West Virginia; thus, only the *potential* for a West Virginia practice existed. This Court examined the effect of crossing state lines to obtain clients and determined that the attorneys' actions in *Allen* constituted the practice of law in West Virginia. The petitioner's situation is clearly distinguishable from the *Allen* scenario. His legal undertaking, albeit it federal in nature, was performed from an established West Virginia location for West Virginia clients. Consequently, the decision in *Allen,* while illuminating with regard to this Court's power to regulate the conduct of attorneys practicing law outside the state boundaries, does not provide direct guidance on resolution of the present case.

. . .

The provisions of the ABA Model Rules, adopted verbatim or in modified form in most states, address the realities of modern practice in which attorneys are admitted or practicing in multiple state and/or federal jurisdictions. The most recent revisions to the ABA Model Rules, not yet adopted in West Virginia, were formulated subsequent to the ABA's consideration of proposals submitted by the ABA Commission on Multijurisdictional Practice. In an effort to guarantee a host state's ability to discipline an out-of-state attorney who practiced law in a host jurisdiction, the commission revised Model Rule 8.5 to provide that a lawyer practicing in a jurisdiction in which that lawyer is not admitted is subject to that jurisdiction's disciplinary rules.

The paucity of authority on the precise issue presented in the case sub judice requires this Court to formulate a reasoned approach to resolution of this matter. Rule 1 of the Rules of Lawyer Disciplinary Procedure clearly provides that this state's disciplinary authorities have jurisdiction over an "individual admitted to the practice of law in another jurisdiction who engages in the practice of law in West Virginia." In applying the principles established in this state regarding precisely what constitutes the practice of law in West Virginia, we hold that pursuant to Rule 1 of the West Virginia Rules of Lawyer Disciplinary Procedure, the West Virginia Rules of Professional Conduct govern the conduct of an attorney who practices law in this state or provides or offers to provide legal services in this state, even where such attorney's practice consists entirely of federal matters. In such circumstances, the ODC and LDB have jurisdiction to investigate the alleged misconduct and recommend disciplinary action against the attorney regardless of whether the attorney is a member of the West Virginia State Bar.

. . .

B. Federal Preemption of State Law

The petitioner also argues that the jurisdictional authority of the ODC and LDB under Rule 1 of the Rules of Lawyer Disciplinary Procedure must be limited by recognition of federal supremacy on this disciplinary issue. In his brief, the petitioner argues that the disciplinary authorities' "attempt to impact Petitioner's ability to practice law directly contradicts the authority he has been granted by the [PTO] and thus, is preempted by federal law." In response, the ODC and LDB argue that the exercise of jurisdiction over the petitioner does not create a conflict between federal and state law and is not in any manner preempted by federal law.

Although the Supremacy Clause of the United States Constitution provides that federal law preempts any conflicting state law, the United States Supreme Court has recognized the broad authority of states to discipline attorneys violating state law and has been circumspect in addressing issues of alleged conflict. In *Sperry v. Florida,* 373 U.S. 379, 83 S.Ct. 1322, 10 L.Ed.2d 428 (1963), for example, the United States Supreme Court addressed an unauthorized practice of law case in which the Florida bar had issued an injunction against a *non-lawyer* patent agent who was licensed to practice before the PTO. The United States Supreme Court, acknowledging that "[t]he preparation and prosecution of patent applications for others constitutes the practice of law," concluded that the non-lawyer was authorized to practice before the PTO and that the State of Florida had no power to enjoin a lay person licensed by the PTO from the practice of patent law. *Id.* at 383, 83 S.Ct. 1322. The *Sperry* Court explained that "[t]he State maintains control over the practice of law within its borders *except to the limited extent* necessary for the accomplishment of the federal objectives." *Id.* at 402, 83 S.Ct. 1322 (emphasis supplied). . . .

The ODC and LDB contend that their exercise of jurisdiction in this case is not violative of the principles of *Sperry* or other federal law. They further maintain that their investigation of the alleged violations in this case would neither interfere with nor affect the federal investigation under the disciplinary rules and regulations of the PTO. The ODC and LDB do not dispute the petitioner's right to represent patent clients before the PTO and explain in their brief that they do not seek "to suspend or expel Petitioner from practicing before the [PTO.]" The PTO Office of Enrollment and Discipline regulations specify that "nothing in this part shall be construed to preempt the authority of each State to regulate the practice of law . . . ." 37 C.F.R. § 10.1 (2012). The PTO regulations also contemplate reciprocal discipline and require a practitioner to notify that office of any discipline imposed by another jurisdiction. 37 C.F.R. § 11.24 (2012). According to the regulations, a "final adjudication in another jurisdiction or Federal agency or program that a practitioner, whether or not admitted in that jurisdiction, has been guilty of misconduct shall establish a prima facie case by clear and convincing evidence that the practitioner violated [PTO disciplinary regulations]." 37 C.F.R. § 11.24(e) (2012). The ODC and LDB argue that because they will not seek to suspend or expel the petitioner from his federal practice, there is no conflict presently existing in the simultaneous federal and state disciplinary investigations. Based upon the foregoing, this Court agrees and finds that federal law does not preempt this state's disciplinary proceedings in this matter.

IV. CONCLUSION

For the reasons stated above, this Court denies the petitioner's request for a writ of mandamus to compel the ODC to cease further investigation and a writ of prohibition to prevent the LDB from prosecuting the alleged violations.

Writ denied.

Some have suggested that a national bar, rather than a state-by-state bar, should be created so that lawyers don't run into problems when their clients work out of state. The American Bar Association's *Model Rules of Professional Conduct* governing the unauthorized practice of law and **multijurisdictional practice** now do allow out-of-state lawyers to provide advice to clients on a temporary basis. For instance, consider Model Rule 5.5, available on ABA's Web site. States use these rules in creating their own ethics rules. Still, variations among states occur, and attorneys and others still need to take precautions to avoid even unintentionally violating another jurisdiction's unauthorized-practice-of-law statute.

> **multijurisdictional practice:**
> The practice of law in more than one state or country.

4. Multidisciplinary Practices

As law firms grew, other sorts of businesses were expanding as well. Notable for the discussion of law office management is the growth of large accounting firms. There are fine distinctions among accounting, tax, and law practices. After all, is a tax accountant who is applying the tax code to a tax problem actually practicing law?

Accounting firms, as they grew, began hiring significant numbers of lawyers. Some consulting firms started helping corporate clients with mergers and acquisitions and other tasks that had traditionally been handled by lawyers. Some sectors in the legal and accounting professions began calling for the approval of **multidisciplinary practices,** those that involve more than one profession. Many foreign jurisdictions are not so restrictive as U.S. jurisdictions are. Some members of the legal profession advocated changing the ethical rules that limited the ability of lawyers to share fees with nonlawyers:

> **multidisciplinary practice:**
> A practice that involves more than one profession, such as law and accounting.

> Advocates urged their approval, saying "one-stop" shopping was consumer-friendly and would enable a single firm to satisfy all of a client's needs by providing legal, accounting, architectural, and engineering services within one MDP [multidisciplinary practice] entity. At the time, the largest law firm in France was one of the big four accounting firms. The same was true in Australia.
>
> Critics were concerned that MDPs would erode the core values of the legal profession—values such as independence of the attorney, client protection, client loyalty, confidentiality of client communications, and avoidance of conflicts of interest.[20]

The American Bar Association's *Model Rules of Professional Conduct,* however, limit the sharing of legal fees between lawyers and nonlawyers. Consider Model Rule 5.4, available on ABA's Web site. In addition, Model Rule 5.7 subjects lawyers who provide law-related services to the Rules of Professional Conduct unless the lawyer assures clients that they are not being provided with legal services and that lawyer-client protections do not apply.

B.   Types of Law Firms

megafirm:
A law firm that has hundreds, or even thousands, of attorneys.

The majority of lawyers work in firms that have 50 or fewer lawyers. Indeed, despite the mergers of many law firms and the development of so-called **megafirms** with hundreds or even thousands of lawyers, most lawyers historically have worked for relatively small firms or as sole practitioners.

1.   Solo Practices

sole practitioner:
A lawyer who practices law on his own, without partners.

The percentage of **sole practitioners** practicing law in the United States has remained fairly steady over the years, moving from 49 percent of private practitioners in 1980 to 49 percent in the year 2005.[21]

Being your own boss can seem attractive to a lawyer, but "going solo" carries risks. Having to pay bills, including monthly rent on office space, and other overhead costs, such as utility bills and insurance bills, can be overwhelming to a sole practitioner, who also is solely responsible for purchasing computers and other equipment, for keeping up with technology, and for paying staff salaries. Managing a single lawyer's workload can be challenging, as the number of legal matters a lawyer is working on at any given time tends to ebb and flow in any practice. Sole practitioners are often confronted with cash-flow problems as they wait for clients to pay their bills.

Nevertheless, many lawyers are drawn to a solo practice because they can have more independence and avoid the conflicts of interest found in large law firms that have many clients. Working as a solo lawyer can also provide more flexibility in scheduling workdays and in telecommuting.

2.   Shared Office Space

To minimize costs, some lawyers opt to share office space, even while working as sole practitioners. Lawyers who share an office can save money by splitting the costs of rent, business machines, utilities, and staff. In addition, there may be overflow work, or work that one attorney cannot handle because he is busy, has a conflict of interest, or experiences some other problem. That attorney might then refer the matter to one of the lawyers with whom he shares office space.

3.   Small Firms (2 to 50 Lawyers)

Small law firms, those that have 50 or fewer lawyers, are also attractive to many lawyers. Small firms often have a collegial atmosphere because all the lawyers working at the firm know one another and typically work in a single office. Young lawyers are often drawn to small firms because they can get a great deal of job responsibility at an early point in their careers.

4. *Midsize Firms (51 to 150 Lawyers)*

A midsize firm, one with 51 to 150 lawyers, might have several offices and a strong regional presence.

5. *Large Firms (151-Plus Lawyers)*

Large law firms with more than 150 lawyers are likely to have a half-dozen or more offices, typically in major cities. A 2013 survey of the 350 largest law firms in the United States found that the biggest firm was DLA Piper with 4,036 lawyers in 2012.[22] In contrast, number 350 was Looper Reed & Mcgraw, with 117 lawyers.[23]

Megafirms such as DLA Piper are those that have several hundred or even thousands of lawyers who typically work in offices around the globe. These sorts of firms have the ability (both the resources and the expertise) to take on major cases. A criticism of firms of this size, though, is that both lawyers and clients can get lost in the crowd. The amount of attention provided to a client who is not, say, a Walmart or General Motors is likely to be significantly less than that provided to major clients. Similarly, lawyers who are not bringing in "big fish" clients may not get the in-firm recognition they deserve for their contributions. Because a large law firm has so many clients, there are increased chances for a conflict of interest between a current client and a potential one. Lawyers in large law firms are often limited in their ability to represent a potential new client because of these conflicts.

6. *Law Firm Subsidiaries*

In the 1980s and 1990s, law firms, in an effort to increase revenue, expanded into **law firm subsidiaries** or affiliate businesses, such as lobbying businesses, consulting services, or wealth management companies.

law firm subsidiary: An affiliate business, such as lobbying or consulting, of a law firm.

For instance, Philadelphia-based Duane Morris has more than half a dozen independent affiliates, including Duane Morris Government Strategies LLC, which assists clients with government relations; Selvam Corporate Services Pte. Ltd., a business advisory firm based in Singapore; Wescott Financial Advisory Group LLC, a financial planning organization; and Wescott Healthcare LLC, a healthcare services company (see http://www.duanemorris.com/site/affiliates.html). Philadelphia-based Drinker Biddle & Reath started an e-discovery subsidiary, Drinker Discovery Solutions, to process data for clients.[24]

The growth in affiliate businesses was spurred in part by the growth of accounting firms that hired lawyers. Law firms responded to market pressure to offer a variety of professional services by setting up affiliate companies. After a major accounting firm, Arthur Andersen, broke up after being implicated in the demise of its client Enron,[25] the legal market felt less pressure to offer such a variety of services.[26]

7.   Virtual Law Offices

Thanks to the Internet, laptops, cell phones, and computerized databases, lawyers need not be chained to their desks all day. They can conduct legal research and talk to clients from just about any location. It is even possible that, thanks to technology, a client and a lawyer may never speak at all—they might conduct all of their transactions, from engaging the attorney through paying the attorney, via the Internet.

Whether and to what extent virtual law offices are permissible given the professional code of conduct that is applicable to attorneys has been a matter of some discussion. In addressing the viability of a virtual law office, the California State Bar Standing Committee on Professional Responsibility and Conduct described a virtual law office

> also variously known as Digital Law, Online Law, eLawyering and Lawfirm 2.0, may take many different forms. For the purposes of this opinion, "VLO" shall refer to the delivery of, and payment for legal services exclusively, or nearly exclusively, through the law firm's portal on a website, where all of the processing, communication, software utilization, and computing will be internet-based.[27]

virtual law office:
A law office for which there is no formal, centralized office; instead, lawyers and staff work at remote locations (often their home offices) and generally communicate electronically rather than face-to-face.

In addressing this subject, the California State Bar Standing Committee on Professional Responsibility and Conduct observed that the same rules that apply to lawyers in traditional offices apply to those working in virtual law offices, but lawyers who maintain such law offices might need to take on additional members to confirm that they are addressing ethical matters raised by working in such a virtual law office.[28] "States that require residency, a physical office address, and accessibility of the lawyer and the lawyer's files restrict the ability of lawyers to use VLPs [virtual law practices]."[29]

Clearspire Law Co. (http://www.clearspire.com/contact) is one firm that is made up largely of virtual law offices combined with some brick-and-mortar locations.[30]

C.   Other Law Offices

1.   Government

Besides private-sector opportunities, lawyers have a wealth of choices if they opt to work for a government law office. Government legal offices exist at the federal, state, and local levels, where lawyers practice criminal law, civil law, administrative agency law, legislative advocacy, and other types of law. Often, people think of government lawyers as prosecutors, and many are (such as lawyers in the U.S. Department of Justice and district attorneys in counties), but government lawyers also handle civil matters for the government. Government lawyers are not necessarily litigators; they might draft policy and write regulations for an agency.

For example, the Department of Law in Westchester County, New York, consists of four bureaus and employs about 60 lawyers, supervised by the county attorney. The county attorney is appointed by the county executive with the approval of the board of legislators. The department is charged with conducting all of the civil law of the county. In other words, the department's lawyers give advice to county officials, review county contracts and legislation, and represent the county in legal proceedings.[31]

Public-sector salaries tend to be lower than those in the private sector, but some lawyers prefer the benefits and relatively reasonable working hours associated with a government job. For a sample job description for an attorney at the federal level, see Figure 2-2.

FIGURE 2-2
Sample Help-Wanted Ad

ATTORNEY VACANCY ANNOUNCEMENT

U.S. DEPARTMENT OF JUSTICE

TRIAL ATTORNEYS, GS-12 THROUGH GS-15
CIVIL DIVISION, FEDERAL PROGRAMS BRANCH
WASHINGTON, DC

Who May Apply: Applications will be accepted from all qualified U.S. citizens.

About the Office: The Federal Programs Branch specializes in defending Federal Government agencies and officials in high-profile civil litigation. Trial Attorneys litigate in federal district courts across the country on behalf of over 100 Federal agencies, the President and Cabinet officers, and other Government officials. Cases often involve challenges to the constitutionality of Federal statutes and attacks on significant Government policies, programs, and decisions. Trial Attorneys in the Branch are generalists and participate in a broad range of practice areas, including challenges to national security policy, the Patient Protection and Affordable Care Act, and personnel practices and policies of the Government. The Branch also engages in a limited amount of affirmative litigation to enforce statutes and regulations and to challenge state and local laws that are preempted by federal law. The most significant recent example is the Federal Government's challenge to Arizona's immigration law.

Opportunity Offered: The Federal Programs Branch is seeking experienced attorneys for permanent positions.

Qualifications: Applicants must possess a J.D. degree, be duly licensed and authorized to practice as an attorney under the laws of a state, territory or the District of Columbia, and have at least one year post-J.D. legal experience. Applicants should have a strong interest in district court work, strong research, writing and advocacy skills, and a strong academic background. Judicial clerkship experience is highly desirable.

Travel: This position requires some travel.

Salary Information: The salary for this position is at the GS-12 through the GS-15 level ($73,100.00 to $153,200.00 per year), depending upon experience.

(continued)

Location: Washington, DC

Relocation Expenses: Relocation expenses are not authorized.

Submission Process and Deadline Date: Applicants must submit a resume or current OF-612 (Optional Application for Federal Employment), a cover letter (highlighting relevant background) and a writing sample (no more than 12 pages) to:

U.S. Department of Justice
Civil Division, Federal Programs Branch
P. O. Box 883
Ben Franklin Station
Washington, D.C. 20044
Attn: Arthur R. Goldberg

or e-mail application materials to FederalPrograms.Vacancies@usdoj.gov

Application materials must be submitted no later than Friday, Feb. 22, 2013.

Please specify that the application is for the "Trial Attorney, Federal Programs" position in the subject line. No telephone calls, please. These positions are open until filled.

Internet Sites: For more information about the Civil Division and the Federal Programs Branch, visit the Justice Department web site at: http://www.usdoj.gov/civil/index.html.

Other attorney vacancy announcements can be found at: http://www.justice.gov/careers/legal/attvacancies.html

Department Policies: Assistant United States Attorneys generally must reside in the district to which he or she is appointed. See 28 U.S.C. § 545 for district-specific information.

The U.S. Department of Justice is an Equal Opportunity/Reasonable Accommodation Employer. Except where otherwise provided by law, there will be no discrimination because of color, race, religion, national origin, political affiliation, marital status, disability (physical or mental), age, sex, gender identity, sexual orientation, genetic information, status as a parent, membership or non-membership in an employee organization, on the basis of personal favoritism, or any nonmerit factor. The Department of Justice welcomes and encourages applications from persons with physical and mental disabilities. The Department is firmly committed to satisfying its affirmative obligations under the Rehabilitation Act of 1973, to ensure that persons with disabilities have every opportunity to be hired and advanced on the basis of merit within the Department of Justice. This agency provides reasonable accommodation to applicants with disabilities where appropriate. If you need a reasonable accommodation for any part of the application and hiring process, please notify the agency. Determinations on requests for reasonable accommodation will be made on a case-by-case basis.

It is the policy of the Department to achieve a drug-free workplace and persons selected for employment will be required to pass a drug test which screens for illegal drug use prior to final appointment. Employment is also contingent upon the completion and satisfactory adjudication of a background investigation. Only U.S. citizens are eligible for employment with the Executive Office for Immigration Review and the United States Attorneys' Offices. Unless otherwise indicated in a particular job advertisement, non-U.S. citizens may apply for employment with other organizations, but should be advised that appointments of non-U.S. citizens are extremely rare; such appointments would be possible only if necessary to accomplish the Department's mission and would be subject to strict security requirements. Applicants who hold dual citizenship in the U.S. and another country will be considered on a case-by-case basis.

(continued)

There is no formal rating system for applying veterans' preference to attorney appointments in the excepted service; however, the Department of Justice considers veterans' preference eligibility as a positive factor in attorney hiring. Applicants eligible for veterans' preference must include that information in their cover letter or resume and attach supporting documentation (e.g., the DD 214, Certificate of Release or Discharge from Active Duty and other supporting documentation) to their submissions. Although the "point" system is not used, per se, applicants eligible to claim 10-point preference must submit Standard Form (SF) 15, Application for 10-Point Veteran Preference, and submit the supporting documentation required for the specific type of preference claimed (visit the OPM website, www.opm.gov/forms/pdf_fill/SF15.pdf for a copy of SF 15, which lists the types of 10-point preferences and the required supporting document(s). Applicants should note that SF 15 requires supporting documentation associated with service-connected disabilities or receipt of nonservice-connected disability pensions to be dated 1991 or later except in the case of service members submitting official statements or retirement orders from a branch of the Armed Forces showing that his or her retirement was due to a permanent service-connected disability or that he/she was transferred to the permanent disability retired list (the statement or retirement orders must indicate that the disability is 10% or more).

The Department of Justice cannot control further dissemination and/or posting of information contained in this vacancy announcement. Such posting and/or dissemination is not an endorsement by the Department of the organization or group disseminating and/or posting the information.

Source: U.S. Department of Justice, http://www.justice.gov/careers/legal/jobs/civil-dc.htm (last visited Aug. 3, 2013).

2. *Corporate*

Businesses, especially large ones, often hire their own in-house lawyers who might either handle legal matters for the company themselves or supervise outside counsel. The "client" of a corporate law department is the corporation itself. Some in-house legal departments handle routine contracts, real estate transactions, insurance matters, and the like, but others handle litigation themselves and farm out the more mundane work to private law firms.

Although private law firms tend to be highly specialized, in-house counsel often find that they can work on a number of different legal issues. Some lawyers are drawn to in-house work because they like working for a single client and don't miss the pressure to constantly market themselves and to find new clients.

3. *Nonprofit*

Like other businesses, nonprofit organizations must address legal matters, such as contracts, real estate transactions, and insurance coverage. Some nonprofits are too small to afford in-house legal counsel, but larger ones have their own lawyers. Although the salaries at these organizations might not be comparable to those in the private sector, some lawyers are attracted to nonprofit organizations so that they can work for "the good guys."

D. Practice Specialties

Nowadays the law is highly focused, and many lawyers have become interested in becoming specialists in certain areas of the law. In the past, though, lawyers were discouraged from holding themselves out as specialists for fear that doing so would be misleading to potential clients.

For instance, the *Illinois Code of Professional Responsibility* at one time specified: "A lawyer or law firm may specify or designate any area or field of law in which he or its partners concentrates or limits his or its practice. Except as set forth in Rule 2-105(a), no lawyer may hold himself out as 'certified' or a 'specialist.' "[32] After a disciplinary action was brought against a lawyer whose letterhead specified that he was a "Certified Civil Trial Specialist By the National Board of Trial Advocacy," the lawyer challenged the validity of the rule. The Supreme Court of the United States, in *Peel v. Attorney Registration and Disciplinary Commn. of Illinois*, 496 U.S. 91 (1990), held that states may not impose a blanket prohibition on a truthful communication by a lawyer that she is certified as a specialist.

In 1993, the American Bar Association amended *Model Rules of Professional Conduct* Rule 7.4 to allow certification by programs that meet rigorous standards of integrity and competence.

Various groups offer certification programs to lawyers. To obtain certification, a lawyer typically must establish that he or she has substantial involvement in the practice area, provide references from other lawyers and judges, take a written test, and take continuing legal education courses in the specialty area.[33] In addition, the lawyer typically must be recertified in the specialty every three to five years.

As of 2011, 37,090 lawyers had been certified as specialists,[34] up from a little more than 19,000 lawyers in 1995.[35]

Even if a lawyer does not obtain certification in a specialty, many lawyers concentrate their practices in certain areas of the law. For instance, they might focus solely on environmental law, insurance law, intellectual property law, or some other subject.

1. General Practices

general practice:
A legal practice that offers a range of legal services, from business to personal.

Although specializing is an option for lawyers, some prefer to be a "jack of all trades" and to practice a little bit in many different areas of the law. These lawyers are referred to as **general practitioners.** If a client approaches a general practitioner with a legal problem that is beyond that lawyer's abilities, the lawyer can refer that client to a specialist.

2. Full-Service Practices

full-service practice:
A legal practice sufficiently large and with a depth of expertise to accommodate the vast majority of clients' legal problems.

Law firms that are sufficiently large and have the depth of expertise to accommodate the vast majority of clients' legal problems are referred to as **full-service practices.** Offering "one-stop shopping" to clients, large firms such as these can respond well to cyclical changes. If, for instance, the economy slows down and a full-service firm's mergers and acquisitions practice slows down with it, the firm can bolster its bankruptcy practice and its restructuring practice to accommodate the changing legal market.

3. Specialty and Boutique Practices

Law firms that focus on a highly specialized area of the law, such as intellectual property, are referred to as **boutique practices.** Clients are drawn to these sorts of firms because of the high level of expertise the lawyers can provide.

Similar to a boutique law firm, a **captive law firm** is made up of lawyers who are employees of an insurance company and who thus practice primarily in one area: insurance law. Lawyers at captive law firms typically defend policyholders pursuant to the insurer's liability policies.

> In 1892 in New York City, Travelers Insurance Company began a staff counsel program to defend policyholders. A century later, more than 300 lawyers work in-house for Travelers.
>
> A number of other insurance companies have followed Traveler's lead by employing lawyers to work in the insurance companies' **captive law firms** to defend their policyholders against covered claims. Insurance companies have increasingly been using **captive law firms** as a means to reduce the large expense of defending its policyholders. Insurance companies cite many benefits to **captive law firms. Captive law firms** offer less risk, and have no client development, law firm management or compensation issues. Insurance companies perceive that outside law firms pass on the cost of client development, inefficient office management, and partner profits to the insurance companies through higher hourly rates.[36]

Although lawyers in a captive law firm might provide more cost-effective legal service than lawyers in a traditional private-sector law firm, some industry observers wonder whether these lawyers really act in the best interest of the insured, since they are, after all, paid by the insurer.[37]

boutique practice:
A practice that focuses on only one particular area of the law.

captive law firm:
A law firm in which the lawyers are employees of an insurance company.

E. Firm Structure

Historically, law firms were structured as partnerships. As the practice of law evolved to become the business of law, lawyers became interested in other business forms for their law practices. Concerns about personal liability and the tax consequences of various business structures led lawyers to consider alternative models. Laws for establishing these different business organizations vary by state.

1. Professional Corporations

One option is setting up shop as a professional corporation rather than as a partnership. Typically, shareholders can only be liable for corporate debts up to the amount of their investment in the corporation. Shareholders are analogous to a partner in a partnership; they have an ownership interest in the organization. An advantage of organizing a law practice as a professional corporation is that shareholders are not personally liable for the debts of the corporation. They might, however, still be personally liable for their own negligence (see Figure 2-3).

As with other corporations, professional corporations must have a board of directors, officers, bylaws, and annual meetings.

2.   Limited Liability Corporations

Limited liability corporations (LLCs) started appearing in the 1970s.[38] A limited liability corporation has attributes of both a partnership and a corporation. A member of an LLC is protected from personal liability, as is a shareholder in a corporation. Like a partnership, income can pass directly to members in an LLC without being taxed at the corporate level.

An operating agreement, rather than a partnership agreement, must be drafted for a limited liability corporation. LLCs are often run by "managers" rather than by a board of directors and corporate officers.

3.   Limited Liability Partnerships

Limited liability partnerships (LLPs) allow partners to limit their personal liability for losses of the partnership while still sharing in firm profits. Texas was the first state to enact a law limiting the vicarious liability of partners for malpractice claims arising from the acts of other partners.[39] Some state statutes also limit partners' personal liability for all debts and obligations of the partnership.

Some states require LLPs to be registered.

FIGURE 2-3
New York's Professional Service Corporation Law

N.Y. Bus. Corp. Law §1505 (2013)
§1505. Professional relationships and liabilities

(a) Each shareholder, employee or agent of a professional service corporation and a design professional service corporation shall be personally and fully liable and accountable for any negligent or wrongful act or misconduct committed by him or by any person under his direct supervision and control while rendering professional services on behalf of such corporation.

(b) The relationship of an individual to a professional service corporation or a design professional service corporation with which such individual is associated, whether as shareholder, director, officer, employee or agent, shall not modify or diminish the jurisdiction over him of the licensing authority and in the case of an attorney and counsellor-at-law, the other courts of this state.

4. *Partnerships*

In a general partnership, each partner is jointly and severally liable for the partnership's liabilities, and partners can be held personally liable for debts of the law office. Given the risks inherent in setting up a business as a partnership, one wonders why lawyers would opt for partnership at all. But some see the newer forms of business organization as a disincentive for lawyers to assume leadership roles:

> Although many firms jumped on the limited liability bandwagon, some firms resisted, questioning the long term effect of firms operating as limited liability firms. One concern relates to the negative effect on monitoring within law firms. Most obviously, the elimination of vicarious liability destroys the most powerful incentive for firm partners to invest in monitoring. In addition to eliminating vicarious liability, limited liability statutes that impose supervisory liability can actually undermine principals' willingness to act as supervisors and monitors. Such statutes effectively shift liability exposure from all firm equity holders to those lawyers who graciously act in some supervisory capacity. Clearly, this can contribute to lawyers' reluctance or refusal to accept supervisory and management responsibilities, including service on such oversight committees as opinion review committees.[40]

5. *Sole Proprietors*

A sole proprietor is personally liable for the debts of the law office. Sole proprietorships are easily formed, however, and typically do not have any filing requirements with a state.

F. Firm Governance

1. *Structure*

As with any organization, the larger the law firm, the more hierarchical (and even bureaucratic) the organization will be. Small law firms might have a managing partner who practices law while overseeing the day-to-day business operations of the firm on a part-time basis. The partnership as a whole might vote on any significant business decisions.

Large law firms, in addition to having a managing partner, might have a management committee or an executive committee that makes business decisions for the firm. Other tasks might be delegated to advisory committees, such as an associates committee, a conflicts committee, a lawyer hiring committee, a client satisfaction committee, an engagement committee, and so on.

Comparable positions are found in firms organized as professional corporations. The chief executive officer is akin to the managing partner. There might also be a chief operating officer, a chief financial officer, a chief marketing officer, and so on. A board of directors is similar to an executive committee.

Large law firms traditionally were divided into two departments, corporate and litigation. Today, firms tend to be more striated and feature any number of departments, such as antitrust, bankruptcy, financial services, insurance, international transactions, labor and employment law, mergers and acquisitions, trusts and estates, real estate, and government relations, to name a few.

2. Firm Culture

Lawyers often refer to the firm culture, which is the personality of a firm. Attorneys tend to be fond of describing their firm's culture as collegial and that of others as cut-throat. Usually the reality tends to fall somewhere between the two extremes.

In some measure, law firms developed a "sink or swim" culture, meaning that a new lawyer, or even a new paralegal or secretary, was on his own. No one showed the new hire around, explained where the coffeemaker is, suggested a good place to go for lunch—or even told the new hire when or if he can leave for lunch, whom he has to check in with, and so forth.

As law firms have modeled themselves after businesses, greater attention has been paid to management and to incorporating team-building exercises.

To some, law firms seemed a bit like a college fraternity, with partners being members of the "club." Nonpartners sometimes felt very much outside of the inner circle of the firm. Part of a firm's culture is indicated by how that firm treats its staff. Is there an "us" and "them" attitude? Do lawyers encourage and foster the careers of staff? Do secretaries pick up their bosses' dry cleaning? Do secretaries fetch lunch for the partners? Fix their coffee? Are members of the staff included on firm committees? Do they participate in making decisions, such as the procurement of technology—since, after all, they probably use it more?

Firm culture can contribute to retention. Although employees are very concerned about their salaries, they also develop loyalty to an organization based on how they are treated. Expressing appreciation for well-done work, even sending an e-mail message or note, can go a long way toward fostering loyalty. But do partners at the firm even make the effort? All of these factors are a part of a firm's culture.

Some firms have a "work hard/play hard" attitude, and some partners reward their secretaries with expensive vacations at the end of the year.

In discerning a firm's culture, pay attention to how the firm treats the weaker players. If a partner has cancer, how does the firm react? Is its first concern maintaining the partner's client base? Is it making sure that the partner is taken care of even if he's less productive that year? Of course, it might seem cold-hearted to focus on business when real-life issues intervene, but a firm's reluctance to rid itself of underproductive partners can lead to its ruin.

G. Dissolving a Law Firm

1. Why Do Law Firms Break Up?

Law firms break up for the same reasons many marriages do: The partners aren't really getting along and then money starts to get tight. There might be fighting and tense conversations behind closed doors, practice groups might begin to leave the firm and go to another one, and, ultimately, the firm itself might combust. Rather than dissolving quietly, some firms have been driven into bankruptcy.

In 2003, the creditors of California-based Brobeck, Phleger & Harrison LLP filed a Chapter 7 involuntary bankruptcy petition a little more than a year after Tower Snow, a former chairman of the firm, and more than a dozen other lawyers departed for a different law firm, Clifford Chance. That firm ended up being drawn into litigation concerning the dissolution of Brobeck:

> On or about October 7, 2003, a group of retired Brobeck partners commenced an action against Clifford Chance and Tower Snow, in the Superior Court of California, . . . (the California state court action), asserting one cause of action against Tower Snow for breach of fiduciary duty, and two causes of action against Clifford Chance for unfair competition and intentional interference with prospective business relationships. . . . According to the California state court complaint, Tower Snow, at the request of, and with substantial assistance from Clifford Chance, orchestrated the exodus of the sixteen other former Brobeck partners, knowing that the departure of so many partners from Brobeck would trigger automatic default provisions in loan agreements that Snow negotiated for Brobeck during the time that he was Brobeck's Managing Partner. Plaintiffs in the California state court action alleged that activation of the automatic default provisions caused Brobeck's creditors to file the involuntary bankruptcy petition, and that Brobeck's involuntary bankruptcy substantially interfered with Brobeck's agreement to pay them retirement benefits.
>
> On the motion of Clifford Chance and Tower Snow, the California state court action was removed to the Bankruptcy Court, which rejected the first two attempts to settle the consolidated matters. Parties to the Settlement, which ultimately was approved by the Bankruptcy Court, include the Bankruptcy Trustee, the plaintiffs in the California state court action, Clifford Chance, and the seventeen former Brobeck partners that defected to join Clifford Chance, including Tower Snow. In accordance with the Settlement, Clifford Chance paid $5.5 million to the Bankruptcy Trustee in exchange for a general release of all claims that could be asserted against it, and against the defecting Brobeck partners by Brobeck.
>
> Clifford Chance paid an additional amount under the Settlement which, pursuant to stipulation, would not be disclosed, to the plaintiffs in the California state court action, in exchange for a release of all claims that were or could have been asserted in that action. Clifford Chance alleges that it also paid $2,259,660 in legal fees and expenses in connection with the Settlement and California state court action.[41]

In 2006, New York-based Coudert Brothers, LLP, which had been founded in 1853, opened its Paris office in 1879, and had, at one point, some 600 lawyers working in 28 offices, filed for bankruptcy:[42]

> [T]he firm faced a crossroads in the late 1990s when it realized that its niche, international law, was under attack by a multitude of new competitors. . . . [T]he firm could have decided then to focus on building domestic practices, possibly focusing on the New York metropolitan area or the Northeast Corridor, while also maintaining its strongest practices in Paris, Moscow, London and Beijing. . . . [T]he firm was perhaps too wedded to the idea of international expansion.[43]

Some news reports indicated that the firm was forced into bankruptcy after losing a $2.5-million malpractice and professional negligence action.[44]

Even some large law firms have dissolved in recent years. For instance, Washington, DC-based Howrey, a law firm founded in the 1950s, voted to dissolve in 2011.[45] Philadelphia-based Wolf Block, a 300-lawyer firm, dissolved in 2009.[46] Dewey & LeBoeuf LLP, which, following the merger of Dewey Ballantine and LeBoeuf, Lamb, Green & MacRae, had about 1,450 lawyers, petitioned for bankruptcy protection in 2012.[47]

2. Procedures

The method by which a law firm dissolves is determined by terms specified in the firm's ownership operating agreement. In some instances, a court might order the dissolution of a law firm.

Checklist

- Most lawyers work in small law firms.
- Law firms experience competition from tax and accounting firms.
- The legal industry is consolidating.
- Increasingly, lawyers find themselves working on cross-border transactions involving business in more than one country.
- Law has become increasingly specialized, and many lawyers are becoming certified as specialists.
- A law firm might be structured as a professional corporation, a limited liability corporation, a limited liability partnership, a partnership, or a sole proprietorship.
- Law firms sometimes dissolve, or go out of business.

Vocabulary

boutique practice (p. 45)

captive law firm (p. 45)

full-service practice (p. 44)

general practice (p. 44)

home office (p. 27)

law firm subsidiary (p. 39)

megafirm (p. 38)

multidisciplinary practice (p. 37)

multijurisdictional practice (p. 37)

satellite office (p. 27)

sole practitioner (p. 38)

unauthorized practice of law (p. 29)

virtual law office (p 40)

"white shoe" firm (p. 26)

Career Preparation Tips

Just as any prospective employer will research potential hires, conduct background checks, and consult references, so too should any potential hire do his or her due diligence to find out about the financial viability of the prospective employer. If you have identified potential workplaces, research information about their financial situation. Have these employers been subject to lawsuits or to trade publication coverage of their finances? What are bloggers saying about your selected organization? What are firm revenues and per-partner profits? How is the health of any subsidiaries?

In researching prospective employers, think about how you can add value to that employer. What skills do you have that the employer needs? What skills should you acquire before approaching this employer?

If You Want to Learn More

The American Bar Association *Model Rules of Professional Conduct* are accessible online. http://www.americanbar.org/groups/professional_responsibility/publications/model_rules_of_professional_conduct/model_rules_of_professional_conduct_table_of_contents.html

The American Bar Association has a Standing Committee on Specialization. http://apps.americanbar.org/legalservices/specialization/

The Association of Corporate Counsel, formerly the American Corporate Counsel Association, is a bar association for in-house lawyers who work in corporate legal departments and other organizations. Founded in 1982, the association has more than 30,000 members in roughly 75 countries. http://www.acc.com

The magazine *American Lawyer* covers the business of law. www.AmericanLawyer.com

The U.S. Department of Justice employs lawyers. Learn about "The DOJ Experience" at https://www.avuedigitalservices.com/ads/jobsatdojoarm/index.jsp

The International Bar Association, founded in 1947, has more than 50,000 members. http://www.ibanet.org

The Union Internationale des Avocats was created in 1927 by European lawyers who saw the need for lawyers to have international contacts. http://www.uianet.org

Reading Comprehension

1. What effect has media coverage of the business of law firms had on the firms themselves?
2. How can lawyers risk being accused of the unauthorized practice of law?
3. Why are so many law firms consolidating via merger?
4. Why can't lawyers engage in multidisciplinary practice?
5. Why are law firms motivated to develop subsidiary businesses?
6. What must a lawyer do to become a specialist in a certain area of the law?
7. Why do some clients turn to boutique practices for legal help?
8. What advantages do alternative forms of business organization have over a traditional law partnership?
9. Why do law firms sometimes dissolve?

Discussion Starters

1. Search for your state's unauthorized practice of law statute. Does your state law require lawyers to be physically present in the state when they give advice to clients?
2. Compare Cal. Ct. R. 9.47 (2013), *available at* http://www.courts .ca.gov/cms/rules/index.cfm?title=nine&linkid=rule9_47, with Cal. Ct. R. 9.48 (see Figure 2-1) and rules in your state on the practice of law by out-of-state attorneys. Which rules are more restrictive? Why? How do the rules protect clients? How might a client, dissatisfied with the outcome of a matter, use the rules against his or her lawyer? Do the rules sufficiently protect attorneys from disgruntled clients?
3. Consider law firm size from the perspective of a client. What sort of client would be drawn to a sole practitioner, to a small firm, to a megafirm?
4. Why might a major client still choose a midsize firm for some legal work?
5. What are your state's rules on specialization? In researching your answer, visit the American Bar Association Standing Committee on Specialization Web site at http://apps.americanbar.org/legalservices/specialization /directory/. How do your state's rules compare to the rules pertaining to lawyers in neighboring states?
6. Research a legal specialty, such as environmental law, energy law, or immigration law. What sort of legal work is involved? What kinds of clients do lawyers who work in the field represent?
7. Some commentators on the legal industry stress the need for lawyers to exercise independent judgment and assert that lawyers should work for

"independent" law firms. In 1990, L. Harold Levinson, a law professor at Vanderbilt University, wrote:

> By the term independent law firm, I mean one that comes close to having all of the following attributes: (1) the firm's only business is the practice of law; (2) the firm is owned exclusively by one or more lawyers who are engaged actively in the firm's practice (with narrow exceptions); (3) the firm requires its lawyers to exercise independent professional judgment (or, if the firm consists of one lawyer, that person exercises independent professional judgment); (4) the firm does not have any significant financial involvement with any of its clients other than cost reimbursements and fees payable in money; and (5) the firm does not expect to receive a major percentage of its fees from any one client.[48]

Do law firms meet this definition today? How has the introduction of affiliates affected the independent judgment of lawyers? How could a law firm's judgment be influenced by working for a single client?

8. Research your jurisdiction's rules on virtual law offices. Are they permissible? What ethical rules must lawyers practicing in virtual law offices take care not to violate? Why might virtual law offices appeal to both lawyers and to clients? Are clients at any disadvantage by hiring a lawyer who has a virtual law office?

Case Studies

1. A group of five friends from law school is planning to go into practice together after graduation. What form of business organization should they consider? What are the advantages and drawbacks of each form? Will the same sort of organization work as well for the friends after they have been in business for ten years? What sort of protections should the friends employ in case their legal business does not succeed?
2. A ten-lawyer firm in Philadelphia that focuses on family law is interested in merging with another firm. What firms should it consider, and why? What would be the advantages of merging with a like-sized firm? With a firm that is larger? What would be the disadvantages?
3. A junior lawyer is interested in obtaining more litigation experience. What types of law offices should she consider? Where is she likely to obtain the most courtroom experience in the shortest amount of time?
4. Research attorney job listings in your area. How do pay rates and job responsibilities vary?
5. Find one recent case involving the dissolution of a law firm. What form of business organization did the firm employ? Why did the firm break up? Was the dissolution voluntary, or involuntary?

Endnotes

1. Marc Galanter & Thomas M. Palay, *Why the Big Get Bigger: The Promotion-to-Partner Tournament and the Growth of Large Law Firms*, 76 Va. L. Rev. 747, 749 (1990).
2. Geoffrey Miller, *Colloquium: Ethics in Corporate Representation: From Club to Market: The Evolving Role of Business Lawyers*, 74 Fordham L. Rev. 1105, 1112 (2005) (citations omitted).
3. Michael M. Boone & Terry W. Conner, *Into the New Millennium: Change, Change, and More Change: The Challenge Facing Law Firms*, 63 Tex. B.J. 18, 21 (2000).
4. *In re Finley, Kumble, Wagner, Heine, Underberg, Manley, Myerson & Casey*, 85 B.R. 13, 14 (Bankr. S.D.N.Y. 1988).
5. Judson Hand, *Love It or Hate It, Law Journal Is Must Reading*, Star-Ledger (Newark, N.J.), June 14, 1998, at Business 4.
6. *See, e.g.*, Laura Mansnerus, *As Brash Publisher's Empire Ends, Quest Begins for Another*, N.Y. Times, Mar. 3, 1997, at D1.
7. American Bar Association, *Enrollment and Degrees Awarded, 1963-2005 Academic Years*, http://www.abanet.org/legaled/statistics/charts/stats%20-%201.pdf.
8. American Bar Association, *Lawyer Demographics* (2013), *available at* http://www.americanbar.org/content/dam/aba/migrated/marketresearch/PublicDocuments/lawyer_demographics_2013.pdf-3k-2013-04-30.
9. Galanter & Palay, *supra* note 1, at 750.
10. *See* Sara Randazzo, *Law Firm Merger Activity Up in 2013, Report Says*, Am Law Daily (April 4, 2013), *available at* http://www.americanlawyer.com/PubArticleALD .jsp?id=1202594853322&Law_Firm_Merger_Activity_Up_in_2013_Report_ Says&slreturn=20130701182550. *See also* Press Release, Hildebrandt Baker Robbins, Law Firm Merger Activity Back on Track, Says Hildebrandt Baker Robbins MergerWatch Report (July 1, 2010), *available at* http://www.hbrconsulting.com /mergerwatch-q2-2010.
11. For information on the recession itself, see U.S. Bureau of Labor Statistics, *BLS Spotlight on Statistics: The Recession of 2007–2009* (Feb. 2012), *available at* http://www.bls.gov /spotlight/2012/recession/pdf/recession_bls_spotlight.pdf.
12. *See, e.g.*, Zach Lowe, *Seyfarth Latest to Cut First-Year Associate Pay*, Law.com (Nov. 23, 2009), *available at* http://www.law.com/jsp/article.jsp?id=1202435728710&Seyfarth_ Latest_to_Cut_FirstYear_Associate_Pay; Julie Triedman, *Associate Pay Cuts Here to Stay, Say Firms, Analysts*, Law.com (Dec. 11, 2009), *available at* http://www.law.com/jsp /article.jsp?id=1202436246170&Associate_Pay_Cuts_Here_to_Stay_Say_Firms_ Analysts; Debra Cassens Weiss, *Median Starting Pay for Associates Is No Longer in the Six Figures; Figure Drops 35% in Two Years*, ABAJournal.com (July 12, 2012), *available at* http://www.abajournal.com/news/article/median_starting_pay_for_associates_is_no_ longer_in_the_six_figures_figure_d/.
13. Peter Lattman, *Big Law Firm to Cut Lawyers and Some Partner Pay*, N.Y. Times DealBook (June 24, 2013), *available at* http://dealbook.nytimes.com/2013/06/24 /big-law-firm-to-cut-lawyers-and-some-partner-pay/; Joseph Ax, *Major law firms Weil, Patton Boggs face layoffs, defections*, Reuters.com (June 24, 2013), *available at* http:// www.reuters.com/article/2013/06/24/us-weil-layoffs-idUSBRE95N1DJ20130624; *The Layoff List*, AmericanLawyer.com http://www.americanlawyer.com/PubArticleTAL .jsp?id=1202425647706&THE_LAYOFF_LIST (last visited Aug. 1, 2013).
14. Press Release, National Association for Law Placement, *Law School Class of 2012 Finds More Jobs, Starting Salaries Rise — But Larger Class Size Hurts Overall Employment Rate* (June 20, 2013).

15. *Id.*
16. *Id.*
17. *See, e.g.,* Lincoln Caplan, *An Existential Crisis for Law Schools,* N.Y. Times, July 14, 2012, *available at* http://www.nytimes.com/2012/07/15/opinion/sunday /an-existential-crisis-for-law-schools.html?_r=1&pagewanted=print.
18. *See, e.g.,* Amanda Royal, *Reed Smith the Latest Big Firm to Drop Associate Lockstep,* Recorder (Oct. 28, 2009), *available at* http://www.law.com/jsp ./article.jsp?id=1202434987961&src=EMC-Email&et=editorial&bu=Law. com&pt=LAWCOM%20Newswire&cn=NW_20091028&kw=Reed%20Smith%20the%20 Latest%20Big%20Firm%20to%20Drop%20Associate%20Lockstep.
19. Stephen Gillers, *A Profession, If You Can Keep It: How Information Technology and Fading Borders Are Reshaping the Law Marketplace and What We Should Do About It,* 63 Hastings L.J. 953, 959–60 (2012) (citations omitted).
20. Robert A. Stein, *Lecture: The Future of the Legal Profession,* 91 Minn. L. Rev. 1, 7-8 (2006) (footnotes omitted).
21. American Bar Association, *supra* note 8.
22. National Law Journal, *The NLJ 350: 2013 Annual Survey of the Nation's Largest Law Firms* (2013), *available at* http://www.law.com/jsp/nlj/PubArticleNLJ .jsp?id=1202603325795.
23. *Id.*
24. Jeff Blumenthal, *Drinker Biddle Law Firm Starts Up E-Discovery Subsidiary,* Philadelphia Bus. J. (Oct. 12, 2012), *available at* http://www.bizjournals.com/philadelphia /print-edition/2012/10/12/drinker-biddle-law-firm-starts-up.html?page=all.
25. *The Andersen Trial at-a-Glance,* BBC News (June 15, 2002), http://news.bbc. co.uk/1/hi/business/1970463.stm.
26. Lynne Marek, *Law Firms Backing Away from Affiliate Businesses,* Nat'l L.J. (Nov. 2, 2007), *available at* http://www.law.com/jsp/llf/PubArticleLLF .jsp?id=1193907830345.
27. Cal. St. Bar. Comm. Prof. Resp., Eth. Op. 2012-184 (2012) (citation omitted).
28. *Id.*
29. Vanessa S. Browne-Barbour, *A Fork in the Road: The Intersection of Virtual Law Practice and Social Media,* 52 Washburn L.J. 267, 284 (Spring 2013).
30. *See also* Rachel M. Zahorsky, *New-Model Firm Plans Hiring Spree, 50 to 100 Lawyers a Year,* A.B.A. J. (Jan. 17, 2013), *available at* http://www.abajournal.com/lawscribbler /article/firm_seeks_to_liberate_lawyers_50_to_100_each_year/.
31. Westchester County Department of Law, http://www.westchestergov.com/law/ (last updated Aug. 16, 2012).
32. *Ill. Disciplinary Rule* 2-105(a)(3) (1988).
33. ABA Standing Committee on Specialization, *A Concise Guide to Lawyer Specialty Certification, available at* http://apps.americanbar.org/legalservices/specialization /downloads/June2007_Concise_Guide_Final.pdf (last visited Mar. 23, 2011).
34. ABA 2012 National Roundtable on Lawyer Specialty Certification, *Lawyer Specialty Certification by the Numbers, 1994–2011,* at 2, *available at* http://www.americanbar .org/.
35. ABA 2010 National Roundtable on Lawyer Specialty Certification, *Lawyer Specialty Certification by the Numbers, 1994–2009,* at 2, *available at* http://www.americanbar .org/content/dam/aba/migrated/2011_build/specialization/2010census. authcheckdam.pdf.
36. Jeffrey P. Miller, *Ethical Dilemmas by Use of Captive Law Firms,* 7 Haw B J. 34 (Mar. 2003).

37. *See, e.g.*, ALI-ABA Course of Study Materials, Litigating Employment Discrimination and Employment-Related Claims and Defenses in Federal and State Courts, Selected Ethics and Professionalism Issues in Labor and Employment Law Cases, Course No. SM097, n.p., May 2007.

38. Robert W. Hamilton, *Closely-Held Business Symposium: The Uniform Limited Partnership Act: Entity Proliferation*, 37 Suffolk U. L. Rev. 859, 863 (2004).

39. Susan Saab Fortney, *Professional Responsibility and Liability Issues Related to Limited Liability Law Partnerships*, 39 S. Tex. L. Rev. 399, 401 (1998).

40. Susan Saab Fortney, *Symposium: Why Do Lawyers Need a General Counsel? The Changing Structure of American Law Firms: Law Firm General Counsel as Sherpa: Challenges Facing the In-Firm Lawyer's Lawyer*, 53 Kan. L. Rev. 835, 840 (2005) (citations omitted).

41. *Clifford Chance LLP v. Indian Harbor Ins. Co.*, 2006 NY slip op. 52460U at *2 (N.Y. Sup. Ct. Dec. 27, 2006), *aff'd*, 41 A.D.3d 214 (N.Y. App. Div. 2007).

42. *In re Coudert Brothers LLP*, No. 0612226 (Bankr. S.D.N.Y. chap. 11 petition filed Sept. 22, 2006).

43. Anthony Lin, *Coudert Breakup Voted After Merger Talks Fail*, N.Y. L.J., Aug. 19, 2005, *available at* http://www.law.com/jsp/law/LawArticleFriendly.jsp?id=1124355911064.

44. *Firm Files Chapter 11*, BCD News & Comment, Oct. 3, 2006, n.p.

45. *See, e.g.*, David Lat, *Howrey LLP, RIP: Partnership Votes to Dissolve*, AbovetheLaw.com (Mar. 9, 2011), http://abovethelaw.com/dissolution/.

46. Ashby Jones, *Wolf Block Partnership Votes to Dissolve the Firm*, WSJ Law Blog (Mar. 23, 2009), *available at* http://blogs.wsj.com/law/2009/03/23/wolf-block-partnership-votes-to-dissolve-the-firm/.

47. Joseph Ax & Sakthi Prasad, *Dewey Files for Chapter 11 in Record Law Firm Collapse*, Reuters (May 29, 2012), *available at* http://www.reuters.com/article/2012/05/29/us-deweyandlebouef-bankruptcy-idUSBRE84S01R20120529; *Entegra Power Group LLC v. Dewey & LeBoeuf LLP* (In re Dewey & LeBoeuf, LLP), 2013 WL 3327755 (Bankr. S.D.N.Y. July 2, 2013).

48. L. Harold Levinson, *Independent Law Firms That Practice Law Only: Society's Need, the Legal Profession's Responsibility*, 51 Ohio St. L.J. 229, 229 (1990).

3

Clients

Chapter Outcomes

By the end of this chapter, a student will be able to:

- Evaluate ethical quandaries arising in attorney-client relationships
- Formulate processes and approaches to manage the attorney-client relationship
- Identify client types
- Develop proposals for obtaining legal work appropriately
- Explain the significance of a firm's client base to its overall success in the marketplace

Law students and others in the legal field sometimes make judgments about clients and their suitability. Some say, "Oh, I would never represent a rapist" or "I could never work for the tobacco industry." Others maintain that someone accused of rape is the one who most needs a good lawyer so that he can be assured a fair trial. A lawyer who refuses to work for the tobacco industry might have a hard time determining where the tobacco industry ends. If a tobacco company has merged with a food company, can she represent the food company?

Some people like to put "good client" and "bad client" hats on an entire industry or set of clients without realizing that not all "good" clients are always good and not all "bad" clients are completely bad. As in every other area of the law, there tend to be shades of gray. Upstanding clients sometimes make inappropriate choices. Clients who have scuffled with the law in the past might have been subject to government overreaching or to police brutality. It all depends.

The attorney-client, or even law-firm–client relationship, is hardly a passive one. Lawyers and those supporting them must help gain and then retain clients. Providing good service and a satisfying outcome are only a part of the equation. How do you manage the negative outcome? How do you determine whether the client might need assistance from the firm in other areas? How can you make sure the client speaks positively about the firm to others?

Just as lawyers, paralegals, law office managers, and the entire legal team must be proactive in managing their relationships with clients, clients, too, are not necessarily passive in their approach to the lawyers who are helping them with the problem. Clients tend to want the maximum amount of value for the money they are paying. They want results, they want to be informed, and they don't want to feel like an inefficient operation is padding their legal bills.

Learning how to keep clients satisfied, and learning how to identify opportunities to gain more clients or more work—and then how to actually bring new clients and work aboard—are vital skills for those working in today's legal industry.

A. The Attorney-Client Relationship

A lawyer or a law firm will not be in business very long without clients. Great attention must be paid to client relationships by everyone in a firm, from the managing partner down through the receptionist. It should go without saying that all clients ought to be treated with courtesy and respect. Some lawyers go to great lengths to foster good client relations. Firms might buy their clients season tickets to sports events, or they might sponsor "spa days" for female lawyers and female clients to bond.

Naturally, the attorney-client relationship ultimately depends on the quality of the work performed by the lawyer for the client. Lawyers are ethically bound to provide competent service to their clients. Consider *Model Rules of Professional Conduct* Rule 1.1, available on the American Bar Association's Web site. Lawyers also must act with diligence and promptness in representing clients. Consider Model Rule 1.3.

Beyond being a moral obligation, providing this level of client service simply makes good business sense. After all, a lawyer wants nothing more than to generate recommendations and referrals and future business from the client.

Lawyers must keep their clients informed! Model Rule 1.4 requires prompt communication between lawyers and their clients.

As straightforward as these ethical requirements seem to be, lawyers still sometimes have difficulty meeting their obligations. The following disciplinary actions were taken by the Attorney Grievance Commission in Maryland:

- An attorney was disbarred "for failing to communicate with his clients, failing to comply with his clients' requests for information, failing to provide the legal services, and failing to return any portion of the unearned fee."[1]
- Another lawyer was disbarred "for failing to act with reasonable diligence and competence, failing to communicate with his clients, failing to return the clients' files upon request, failing to expedite litigation, and misrepresenting to his clients the status of their cases."[2]

- One lawyer was suspended for 60 days "for failing to appear at trial and failing to adequately communicate with his client. Upon termination of representation, Respondent entered into a settlement and release of claims agreement with the client without advising the client to seek independent counsel."[3]

B.   Types of Clients

Some law practices are highly dependent on having individuals as clients. Family law practices, for instance, are geared toward the individual client (typically, a person seeking a divorce). Other law practices have a mix of clients, both individuals and businesses. In developing their business, lawyers need to think about their mix of clients. Do they prefer to work for just a few steady corporate clients? Or is their business dependent on many one-time clients seeking their help? Lawyers should also give some consideration to the effect the loss of a client might have on their practice. The loss of a single client to a divorce lawyer with thousands of them might not have much of an impact; the loss of a corporate client who provides one-third of the firm's income every year could, however, be devastating.

As law firms grow, the level of service they provide to big clients as opposed to small clients needs to be considered. Lawyers tend to like clients with **deep pockets**—those that can easily afford steep legal fees. Lawyers are also drawn to **bread-and-butter clients**—those whose legal work might not be the most exciting but who generate a steady stream of business for the firm.

In running a business, lawyers must decide how they want to service their clients. Are all clients treated equally? Should they be? If a Fortune 500 corporate client is throwing $10 million worth of legal fees to the firm every year, shouldn't it command better service than a one-time client who is paying the firm $10,000 to handle her divorce? It is said that each client likes to think that it is the only client of the firm. That, no doubt, is probably true. But the reality is that a firm typically depends on a number of clients to survive. Shouldn't clients be tiered? Should some receive platinum-quality service, some receive gold service, and others receive silver service? Should a client who is paying a lawyer $100 per hour expect the same quality of service as one paying $600 per hour?

While depending on clients to generate fees, lawyers must nevertheless resist the temptation to "churn" client cases. **Churning** is the inappropriate practice of running up hourly legal fees with excessive discovery requests and other matters to create additional legal work, thus generating more fees.

In addition to **external clients** (outside entities that hire the firm to perform legal work), associates, paralegals, and others in a firm have **internal clients**—partners and other workers in the firm who give them assignments so that they can meet their billable-hour requirements. A lawyer in a firm may typically assign work to any number of associates or paralegals. A good associate or paralegal will make sure that she or he is at the top of the list of a lawyer who is doling out plum assignments.

deep pockets:
Abundant financial resources.

bread-and-butter client:
A steady client that generates a consistent stream of business for a firm.

churning:
The inappropriate practice of running up hourly legal fees with excessive discovery requests and other matters to create additional legal work, thus generating more fees.

external client:
Outside entities that hire the firm to perform legal work.

internal client:
Partners and others in a law firm who dole out assignments to lawyers, paralegals, and others in the law firm's staff.

1.   Corporate

A corporation is an artificial being created by law—in essence, a fictional person with legal rights and responsibilities. Lawyers working for corporations must remember that the corporation is the client, not the people who represent the corporation, such as the chief executive officer, the general counsel, or other actors. Some in-house lawyers resent efforts by their outside law firms to drum up business by pressuring the corporation's executives to hire them. These lawyers prefer that all legal matters be managed through the corporation's legal department.[4]

The *Model Rules of Professional Conduct,* in recognition of the difficulties associated with representing an organization, address some of the problems that might arise in the course of representing a business. Consider Model Rule 1.13, available on the American Bar Association's Web site.

Corporations vary in the ways they handle their relationships with outside counsel. Some companies have quite large in-house legal staffs and farm out only more mundane legal work. Others maintain a fairly small in-house team and outsource the bulk of the legal work. Either way, outside law firms tend to be subject to a fair amount of oversight by the in-house client, who is likely to negotiate fees, scrutinize bills, and question overall strategy.[5]

In addition to overseeing work done by outside counsel more closely, some corporate clients control legal budgets by, for instance, making law firms submit competitive bids for new work or consolidating the number of outside law firms they use, a practice referred to as **convergence.**

convergence:
A corporation's practice of consolidating the number of outside law firms it uses.

Many companies work with relatively few law firms—between two and ten.[6] Culling the number of outside firms used can be cost-effective for the corporation, as its outside lawyers become very familiar with the workings of the business and can be persuaded to offer discounts for a high volume of legal work and to hold seminars and other training for in-house counsel.

secondment:
The practice of lending associates to a corporate client so the associates gain an improved understanding of that client's business.

One way that law firms can strengthen their ties to their corporate clients is through **secondment,** the practice of lending associates to a corporate client so the associates can gain an improved understanding of that client's business. Typically, the law firm continues to pay the associates' salaries, although the client might pay for some expenses.[7]

2.   Association

Associations, like any other business, have legal needs that must be met. Contracts, employment, tax, real estate, insurance, litigation, and intellectual property are some areas in which associations might require legal advice. Some law firms have specific trade and professional associations practices dedicated to serving associations and nonprofit organizations.

3.   Individual

Individuals can need a lawyer's help for any number of reasons. They need wills prepared, they might need a prenuptial agreement to be drafted, they may be involved in a personal injury lawsuit. **Private clients** are individuals with a high net worth. Some law firms have private-client departments that focus on the special needs of these extremely wealthy individuals. This type of practice tends to involve tax and commercial work and other measures taken to protect assets. As wealthy individuals diversify their holdings, their legal needs tend to cross jurisdictions. Private-client practices are becoming increasingly global in nature.

private client:
An individual client who has a high net worth.

4.   Government

In 2010, government employment accounted for 18 percent of all attorney jobs.[8] "At the Federal level, attorneys investigate cases for the U.S. Department of Justice and other agencies. Government lawyers also help develop programs, draft and interpret laws and legislation, establish enforcement procedures, and argue civil and criminal cases on behalf of the government."[9] State and local governments hire lawyers as well. Many work in the criminal justice system.

The government also sometimes hires outside lawyers to help on cases. For instance, famed litigator David Boies, who went on to represent Vice President Al Gore in the controversy over which presidential candidate won the year 2000 election (*Bush v. Gore*, 531 U.S. 98 (2000)), was special trial counsel for the U.S. Department of Justice in its antitrust litigation against Microsoft. Boies had successfully defended IBM in an earlier antitrust matter pursued by the federal government.[10] The federal government saw how well a lawyer in the private sector could do; the next time around, the government had him on its side—at a bargain rate of $33.33 per hour.[11]

C.   Choosing Clients Well

A law firm is a business. Lawyers have services to sell, and lawyers need buyers, or clients. The question is, Does the client choose the lawyer, or does the lawyer choose the client?

Clients find out about prospective lawyers in any number of ways: by hearing word-of-mouth referrals, by doing research online or elsewhere, by seeing lawyers give speeches at industry conferences (referred to by many lawyers as "dog-and-pony shows"), and by inviting the lawyer to make a presentation to the client. Lawyers put on these presentations, referred to in the industry as "beauty pageants," for prospective corporate clients. A company might invite several law firms to make presentations on different days and then select the single firm it found most desirable.

A wise lawyer does not leave client selection to chance. A lawyer has to make a decision: Will just any client do? Can the client pay its bills? Is the client difficult? Is the client likely to generate more work for the lawyer or for the firm? If a lawyer had a choice between two clients, one who always paid his bills on time, had plenty of legal work to throw to the firm, and was pleasant to deal with, and another client whose account had to be in collection before he would pay a bill, who constantly harangued and lied to his lawyer, and who needed help on only a single matter, which client do you think the lawyer would rather accept?

Just as a client does not need to hire the first lawyer she interviews, a lawyer does not need to accept business from the first prospective client who walks through the firm's front door.

Client intelligence is the practice of gathering and analyzing information about clients or prospective clients:

> CI [competitive intelligence] can help a law firm figure out which other law firms have been representing a company that it is interested in targeting as a client. . . . If the company has worked with only one counsel for a number of years, the law firm may decide not to go after that company as a potential client. If the law firm discovers that the target corporation has worked with one law firm in the past but recently brought on another one, it might conclude that the company is looking for new counsel and that there is an opportunity that it should pursue. Another possibility is that the company "churns through law firms" and is therefore not a good prospective client at all.[12]

Today, law firms are aggressive in seeking business from good clients. Corporate clients aren't blindly loyal; they, like any other business or individual, are looking for a good deal. A law firm that is aware that a corporation might be shopping its legal work around will make an effort to win that business. Some large law firms even bring along project managers when pitching a prospective corporate client for more business.[13] Through **legal project management**, the work to be done can be clearly defined, the appropriate team selected, and the work to be done clearly planned and budgeted, undertaken, and supervised.

Of course, drumming up business must be done within the constraints of pertinent ethical rules. Soliciting clients inappropriately, such as by "chasing ambulances," is not acceptable. In 1978, the U.S. Supreme Court held that states or state bar associations "constitutionally may discipline a lawyer for soliciting clients in person, for pecuniary gain, under circumstances likely to pose dangers that the State has a right to prevent."[14] In short, lawyers are not permitted to "chase ambulances" or to hire **runners** to solicit clients.

legal project management:
The application of project management principles to legal matters to enhance value for clients while maintaining profitability for the law firm providing service to the client.

runner:
Someone hired to solicit personal injury cases on behalf of a lawyer.

Florida Bar v. Barrett
897 So.2d 1269 (Fla. 2005)

DISPOSITION: DAVID A. BARRETT IS HEREBY DISBARRED FROM THE PRACTICE OF LAW IN THE STATE OF FLORIDA.

JUDGES: PARIENTE, C.J., AND WELLS, ANSTEAD, LEWIS, QUINCE, CANTERO, AND BELL, J.J., CONCUR.
OPINION

Per curiam.

We have for review a referee's report regarding alleged ethical breaches by attorney David A. Barrett. We have jurisdiction. *See* Fla. Const. art. V, §15. We approve the referee's findings of fact and recommendations as to guilt. For the reasons explained below, we decline to approve the recommended sanction of a one-year suspension and instead disbar Barrett.

I. FACTS

The Florida Bar filed a complaint against respondent David A. Barrett, alleging numerous counts of misconduct involving two unethical schemes to solicit clients. After a multiple-day hearing, the referee issued a report making the following findings and recommendations.

Barrett was the senior partner and managing partner in the Tallahassee law firm of Barrett, Hoffman, and Hall, P.A. In approximately January 1993, Barrett hired Chad Everett Cooper, an ordained minister, as a "paralegal." Although Cooper had previously worked for a law firm in Quincy, Florida, Cooper's primary duty at Barrett's law firm was to bring in new clients. As Cooper testified, Barrett told him to "do whatever you need to do to bring in some business" and "go out and . . . get some clients." Cooper was paid a salary averaging $20,000 and, in addition to his salary, yearly "bonuses" which generally exceeded his yearly salary. In fact, Cooper testified that Barrett offered him $100,000 if he brought in a large case.

To help Cooper bring in more personal injury clients to the law firm, Barrett devised a plan so that Cooper could access the emergency areas of a hospital and thus be able to solicit patients and their families. In order to gain such access, Barrett paid for Cooper to attend a hospital chaplain's course offered by Tallahassee Memorial Hospital.

In approximately March of 1994, Molly Glass's son was critically injured when he was struck by an automobile while on his bicycle. While her son was being treated in the intensive care unit at Tallahassee Memorial Hospital, Cooper met the Glass family. Cooper, who dressed in "clothing that resembled a pastor," identified himself to the family as a chaplain and offered to pray with them. Thereafter, Cooper gave a family member of Molly Glass the business card of attorney Eric Hoffman, one of the partners in Barrett's law firm, and suggested that the family call the firm. Neither Barrett nor Cooper knew Molly Glass prior to Cooper's solicitation at the hospital. After her son died, Molly Glass retained Barrett's law firm in a wrongful death action. A settlement was negotiated, and she was pleased with the result until May of 1999, when she read a newspaper article about improper solicitation of clients and realized that Cooper's actions in the hospital constituted inappropriate solicitation. The referee specifically found that Cooper was Barrett's agent at the time that Cooper solicited Molly Glass and that Barrett ordered the conduct and ratified it by paying Cooper a salary and bonuses.

In April 1994, Cooper referred his friend, Terry Charleston, to Barrett's law firm. Charleston was an automobile accident victim whose injuries left him a quadriplegic. After the case was settled for over $3 million, Cooper was paid a bonus that year of $47,500.[1] Barrett attempted to justify the extremely large bonus,

---

[1] Since Cooper knew Charleston before referring him to the law firm, the only issue raised to the referee was whether Barrett had engaged in an improper fee-splitting plan with a nonlawyer.

contending that the bonus was based on personal services, pastoral services, and companionship that Cooper provided to Charleston. The referee rejected this explanation, finding that Barrett lied about the reason for the bonus. Instead, the referee found that Barrett gave Cooper the bonus for bringing in the case, and thus Barrett engaged in an illegal fee-splitting plan.

On September 19, 1997, Barrett, who had the ultimate authority for hiring and firing in his law firm, fired Cooper. . . . However, even after Cooper was fired, his relationship with Barrett did not end.

While Cooper obtained accident reports and solicited patients for a chiropractor, he also continued to solicit clients for Barrett. After the patients were seen by the chiropractor, the accident reports were forwarded to Barrett's law partner, Hoffman. Cooper was paid $200 for each client who was brought into the law firm. The referee specifically found that Barrett knew about this scheme and that he ratified the conduct of Hoffman and Cooper. Barrett micromanaged the office, especially the finances, and personally signed the checks to Cooper in the amount of $200 per client for soliciting eight clients. Moreover, Barrett inquired as to whether there was insurance coverage before authorizing the firm's checks written to Cooper for soliciting clients. In addition to Molly Glass, the referee found that Barrett improperly solicited twenty-one other clients in violation of the *Rules of Professional Conduct.*

Finally, in May 1996, Barrett sent Cooper to Miami and Chicago in order to solicit clients as a result of the Value Jet airplane crash in the Everglades. Although Barrett denied any knowledge about this, his own business records show that $974.24 was paid for Cooper's travel expenses. The referee found that Barrett's testimony regarding this matter was not credible. While neither solicitation resulted in clients for Barrett's firm, the referee concluded these were inappropriate solicitation attempts directed by Barrett.

Based on the above factual findings, the referee found that Barrett was guilty of violating the following sections of the *Rules Regulating the Florida Bar:* 4–5.1(c)(1) (responsibilities of a partner); 4–5.3(b)(3)(A) (responsibilities regarding nonlawyer assistants); 4–5.4(a)(4) (sharing fees with nonlawyers); 4–7.4(a) (solicitation); 4–8.4(a) (violating or attempting to violate the rules of professional conduct); 4–8.4(c) (engaging in conduct involving deceit); and 4–8.4(d) (engaging in conduct in connection with the practice of law that is prejudicial to the administration of justice). In turning to the recommended discipline, the referee found the following aggravating circumstances applied in this case: (1) Barrett had a dishonest or selfish motive; (2) he exhibited a pattern of misconduct; (3) he was guilty of multiple offenses; (4) he submitted false statements during the disciplinary process by lying to the referee; (5) the victim was in a vulnerable condition; and (6) Barrett had substantial experience in the practice of law. As to mitigation, the referee found that four mitigating circumstances applied here: (1) Barrett did not have a prior disciplinary record; (2) he made full and free disclosure to the disciplinary board or had a cooperative attitude toward the proceedings; (3) character witnesses testified to Barrett's good character and reputation; and (4) Barrett exhibited remorse as to the effect of his conduct upon his family, friends, and clients. After considering the foregoing aggravating and mitigating factors, the referee recommended that Barrett be suspended from the practice of law for one year and be ordered to pay the Bar's costs.

The Florida Bar appeals to this Court, contending that we should increase the discipline to disbarment. Respondent cross-appeals and challenges whether (1) the referee made independent findings of fact; (2) the referee improperly denied several preliminary motions; (3) there is sufficient proof to support the referee's findings of fact; and (4) the sentence is excessive in light of our previous Bar discipline decisions.

II. ANALYSIS

Discipline

Both parties appeal the recommended discipline of a one-year suspension. Barrett argues that a twenty-day suspension is appropriate based on previous solicitation cases. The Bar argues that the appropriate discipline for such egregious ethical misconduct is disbarment. We agree with the Bar.

Barrett used deception to gain access to hospital patients by paying for Cooper to complete a hospital chaplain's course and sending him under the guise of providing spiritual comfort to people in their most needy time, when at the time Cooper was an attorney's employee being paid to obtain clients. Barrett then changed his scheme when "it was getting pretty hot," instead relying on Cooper to obtain clients while he worked for a chiropractor. His schemes resulted in twenty-two improperly solicited clients. Additionally, Barrett also engaged in an illegal fee-splitting plan with Cooper. Moreover, this is not a situation where Barrett failed to realize his actions were wrong; he engaged in the conduct intentionally and then fired Cooper when he became concerned about the possibility of being caught. As this Court has held, when an attorney "affirmatively engages in conduct he or she knows to be improper, more severe discipline is warranted." *Florida Bar v. Wolfe,* 759 So.2d 639, 645 (Fla. 2000). Finally, the instant case had substantial aggravating circumstances, including that (1) Barrett engaged in this type of improper solicitations based on a selfish motive to obtain clients; (2) the improper solicitations were a part of organized schemes that lasted for years; (3) multiple offenses occurred, including two different schemes which led to at least twenty-two improper solicitations; (4) Barrett lied to the referee during the proceedings; (5) one of the victims was especially vulnerable and in fact retained Barrett's law firm only because she was angry that somebody else had tried to take advantage of her during a time in which she was clearly preoccupied with her son's critical injuries; and (6) Barrett had substantial experience in the practice of law. While the referee did find that mitigating circumstances applied, these pale by comparison to the aggravating circumstances in this case. Any discipline less than disbarment is far too lenient based on the amount and type of misconduct which occurred here and would not fulfill the three purposes of lawyer discipline.

In sum, members of The Florida Bar are ethically prohibited from the solicitation of clients in the manner engaged in by Barrett. The Court expects that its rules will be respected and followed. This type of violation brings dishonor and disgrace not only upon the attorney who has broken the rules but upon the entire legal profession, a burden that all attorneys must bear since it affects all of our reputations. Moreover, such violations harm people who are already in a vulnerable condition, which is one of the very reasons these types of solicitations are barred. Therefore, this Court will strictly enforce the rules that prohibit these improper solicitations and impose severe sanctions on those who commit violations of them.

III. CONCLUSION

We approve the referee's findings of fact and recommendations as to guilt, but we decline to approve the recommended discipline of a one-year suspension and instead disbar respondent. Accordingly, David A. Barrett is hereby disbarred from the practice of law in the State of Florida. The disbarment will be effective thirty days from the date this opinion is filed so that Barrett can close out his practice and protect the interests of existing clients. If Barrett notifies this Court in writing that he is no longer practicing and does not need the thirty days to protect existing clients, this Court will enter an order making the disbarment effective immediately. Barrett shall accept no new business after this opinion is filed.

It is so ordered.

The *Model Rules of Professional Conduct* limit the circumstances under which a lawyer may solicit prospective clients. Consider Model Rule 7.3.

D. Managing Client Relationships

Law is a service industry. Law firms emphasize client service and business development far more than they once did. Law firms might even form **client teams,** groups of lawyers, paralegals, and others within a firm who work for a given client. A group meets regularly to assess a client's needs.

Lawyers within a firm often seek **cross-selling** opportunities so that the client may retain the firm for other legal needs the firm might be able to service. For instance, a practice group doing environmental work for a corporate client might also try to market the firm's real estate practice to the client.

Client relationship management software can track client contacts and document a lawyer's contact with prospective clients. Such software can also track lawyer expertise, so if a client is looking for someone who happens to understand the pesticide registration process at the U.S. Environmental Protection Agency, a lawyer can do a search on the firm's **intranet** and find out who that lawyer is. Client relationship management software can also specify whether the firm represents a given company, and, if so, who the external contact is, who the internal contact is, and what types of legal matters are handled.

Some examples of client relationship management software are:

- ContactEase from Cole Valley Software (http://www.colevalley.com)
- InterAction by LexisNexis (http://www.interaction.com)

client team:
A group of lawyers, paralegals, and others within a firm who work together for a given client.

cross-selling:
Marketing other practice groups within a firm to a client.

intranet:
A computer network that allows users within the firm to access information and to communicate with one another internally.

- Office Accelerator from Baseline Data Systems (http://www.baselineconnect.com)
- ProLaw by Thomson Reuters (http://www.elite.com)

Such software can only document the real-world relationship that is occurring. Having good relationships with clients involves doing good work for them, being responsive to them, and anticipating their needs and responding appropriately to those needs. Personality, of course, is involved, too: a lawyer needs to get along well with clients. As the practice of law becomes more global, lawyers also need to understand cultural differences—and even alert their clients to them:

> These practices extend well beyond table manners. They extend deep into the work-place and can affect everything from where individuals are or should be seated, to how business will function after a deal is concluded. "There are tremendous cultural differences in the way people negotiate that are critical," . . . "Frenchmen and Englishmen will want to sit at different distances from other parties at a negotiating table" . . . . [15]

E. Retaining Clients

Clients will be wooed by others, so lawyers, as well as secretaries, paralegals, and other staff, must pay attention to client retention and to client service:

> Getting and keeping clients within the exceedingly competitive legal industry mandates a self-motivated and highly dedicated effort. Clients want to be solicited, courted, accommodated, and satisfied. To be successful, lawyers must go to the client, not wait for the client to come to them. Creating a sense of urgency and a passion for finding clients will result in new clients; waiting for the telephone to ring will not.[16]

Client retention also is an issue when a lawyer moves to another firm or when two firms merge. Optimally, a firm wants to keep all of its clients when it merges with another firm. Model Rule 1.6, which addresses the confidentiality of a client's information, now allows a lawyer to reveal certain information if a law firm merger or change of employment is contemplated so long as attorney-client privilege would not be compromised and the client would not be harmed. Clients should be informed as soon as possible of a firm's merger.

Ruby v. Abington Memorial Hospital
50 A.3d 128 (Pa. Super. Ct. 2012)

BEFORE: GANTMAN, SHOGAN AND LAZARUS, JJ.

OPINION BY SHOGAN, J.:

Appellant, Young, Ricchiuti, Caldwell & Heller, LLC ("YRCH"), appeals from the trial court's May 26, 2011 order denying YRCH's Petition for Determination of Attorneys' Fees and ordering that an earlier attorneys' fee award be apportioned such that Appellee, The Beasley Firm, LLC ("Beasley"), receives 75% of the fees and YRCH receives the remaining 25%. We affirm.

The trial court set forth the factual and procedural history of this matter as follows:

> Mr. Keith Erbstein, Esquire worked at the Beasley Firm, LLC., a Philadelphia-based personal injury law firm, for approximately 35 years. During the course of his employment with the Beasley Firm (hereinafter: Beasley or the Beasley Firm), Mr. Erbstein signed two separate employment contracts. The Undersigned ultimately found the two aforementioned contracts controlled the determination of the Petition for Determination of Attorneys' Fees.
>
> This Court is convinced that Mr. Erbstein was a highly intelligent, skilled and knowledgeable attorney at the time that he signed the employment contracts material hereto. The record reveals that in 1996 Mr. Erbstein signed an "Employment Agreement" with Beasley, wherein Mr. Erbstein specifically agreed to immediately reimburse the Beasley Firm any outstanding case costs and pay 75% of any fees recovered thereon should he leave the firm for any reason. (*See,* 1996 Employment Agreement, ¶ 8.) Thereafter, in 2004, Mr. Erbstein signed the "Operating Agreement," a second employment contract, with Beasley, wherein Mr. Erbstein once again confirmed his willingness to comport with the Firm's employment terms.
>
> To elucidate matters for the Appellate Court, the record confirms that Mr. Erbstein committed himself to the terms of the 2004 Operating Agreement in August 2004.[1] The Undersigned found that Mr. Erbstein agreed to the following material terms. First, "Withdrawal Require[d] by Firm" in § 9.2 of the 2004 Operating Agreement holds:
>
>> Subject to the provisions of Section 9.4 ['Obligations to Withdrawn Member'] below, **the Management Committee may at any time require a Member to withdraw from the Firm at any specified date by giving not less than three (3) months' prior written notice to such Member** [. . .]
>
> Second, the record reflects that Mr. Erbstein also agreed to § 9.5 governing the future handling of 'Client Files' and holds:
>
>> (i) **As to all client files which a withdrawing Member may take, pursuant to the written direction to the Firm by the respective Client,** the withdrawing Member shall, prior to withdrawal from the Firm, bill each such file; accurately account for time dedicated to a client file; provide an accounting to the Firm for all files, fees owed thereon and unreimbursed expenditures due and owing, up through the date of withdrawal; and all such fees and unreimbursed expenditures shall be payable to and **remain the sole property** of the Firm. (emphasis added).
>> [. . .]
>> (iii) Other provisions of this Agreement notwithstanding, **with reference to all 'contingency fee' cases succeeded to by the withdrawing Member pursuant to the terms of this Agreement, unless otherwise established by the Managing Member, the withdrawing Member shall account to the Firm for all fee arrangements on all such files in accordance with the provisions**

---

[1] The exact date on the copy of the contract provided to the court is not clear. Arguably it could be interpreted as either August 21, 2004 or August 31, 2004; therefore, the Undersigned was not more specific for fear of being incorrect as to the precise date.

of Exhibit 'C' [which is 'Form–Employment Agreement' confirming the afore-mentioned split fee agreement] hereto[2] (emphasis added).

Thereafter, in October 2004, Mr. Erbstein brought the above-captioned negligence case into the Beasley Firm. The Plaintiffs in the Ruby matter signed a contingency fee agreement with the Beasley Firm and Mr. Erbstein. The record indicates that the action was instituted shortly thereafter. The case continued through the normal uneventful litigation course while Mr. Erbstein was at Beasley.

Unfortunately, for reasons not disclosed to this Court, on November 17, 2005, Mr. Erbstein was notified in writing that he was going to be released from the Beasley Firm on February 17, 2006, three (3) months notice, in accordance with § 9.2 of the 2004 Operating Agreement. Thereafter, Mr. Erbstein obtained employment with the law firm of Young, Ricchiuti, Caldwell & Heller, LLC (hereinafter: YRCH). Mr. Erbstein worked his last day at Beasley on January 26, 2006.

On January 28, 2006, Mr. Erbstein notified the Rubys about his change in employment. In line with the terms of the employment agreements, Mr. Erbstein gave the Rubys the choice to continue their relationship with Beasley or to follow him to his new practice. The Rubys opted to have their case litigated by Mr. Erbstein as opposed to the Beasley Firm. As such, at the direction of Mr. Erbstein, the Rubys severed their relationship with the Beasley Firm and signed an almost identical contingency fee agreement with YRCH. Importantly, the record reveals that Mr. Erbstein maintained control of the file until sometime in the summer of 2008, when he contracted a severe illness. (*See,* YRCH Memorandum of Law in Support of Petition for Attorneys' Fees filed 3.11.11). Thereafter, other members of the YRCH Firm handled the case and brought it to its ultimate resolution in January 2011. (*See,* YRCH Memorandum of Law in Support of Petition for Attorneys' Fees filed 3.11.11). Subsequent to the settlement, a dispute arose regarding the distribution of the $643,333.32 in attorneys' fees between YRCH and Beasley. The matter was transferred from Montgomery County Orphans Court to the Undersigned for resolution. The Undersigned entertained several memorandums of law and oral argument on the dispute. Thereafter, this Court entered its May 20, 2011 Order determining that the Appellant, the law firm YRCH is only entitled to 25% of the attorneys' fees and the Appellee, the Beasley Firm, shall receive 75% of the fee, pursuant to the contract(s) which Mr. Erbstein signed while working at the Beasley Firm.

Trial Court Opinion, 10/13/11, at 1–4 (emphasis in original).

YRCH presents the following issues for this Court's consideration:

1. Can a law firm enforce an agreement with its members against another law firm not party to that agreement?
2. Can a law firm that discharges one of its members successfully assert a claim for work performed on his contingency fee cases so far in excess of

---

[2] Section 6 of the Employment Agreement (Exhibit "C") states "[i]n the event that you leave this office for any reason and a client or clients choose(s) to continue with your representation, you will receive 25% of the net fee on any case you take with you regardless of its age, or the time spent on the file before or after you leave the office. You will immediately reimburse the office for all costs then expended on the file before the file(s) leave(s) this office." (emphasis added)

quantum meruit that both his ability to practice law and his clients' rights to choose counsel are compromised?

YRCH's Brief at 2.

The trial court's determination in this case is based on its interpretation of the 1996 Employment Agreement and 2004 Operating Agreement. . . . .

In support of its first issue on appeal, YRCH argues that because it was not a party to the contracts establishing Beasley's claim, specifically the Operating Agreement and the Employment Agreement providing for Beasley's 75% share of fees recovered on Erbstein's cases, it is not legally bound by that contract. YRCH's Brief at 9–10. In support of the proposition that "a contract cannot legally bind persons not party thereto," YRCH relies on this Court's opinion in *In the Matter of the Estate of Barilla,* 369 Pa.Super. 213, 535 A.2d 125 (1987).

In *In the Matter of the Estate of Barilla,* this Court was asked to determine whether third parties to an antenuptial agreement could breach the terms of the agreement by acts which prevented the appellant's performance. *In the Matter of the Estate of Barilla,* 535 A.2d at 128–129. Such is not the case before us presently. Indeed, YRCH would have us ignore the reality of the circumstances giving rise to Beasley's claim. YRCH claims that Beasley is not entitled to the attorneys' fees contemplated in its agreement with Erbstein on the belief that YRCH may not be bound to a contract to which it is not a party. While this presents an interesting issue, it does not accurately characterize the relative importance of the employment contract or the parties' relationship to the same. The question is not whether YRCH is **bound** by the employment agreement, but whether, and to what degree, may YRCH take a share of the attorneys' fees subject to the employment agreement.

We observe, and discuss more fully below, that the trial court properly employed rules concerning contract interpretation to conclude that Beasley was entitled to its contractual share of the attorneys' fees. However, in order to reach the next analytical step to conclude that YRCH take its share of those fees subject to the terms of the employment contract, we must refer to concepts and ramifications contemplated in the Uniform Partnership Act. 15 Pa.C.S.A. §§ 8301–8365. Moreover, while the courts of this Commonwealth have had no occasion to address the precise issue presently before us, we do find significant similarity, in fact and legal analysis, in cases emanating from California's appellate courts. We agree with the sound reasoning of the California Court of Appeals and adopt the same, insofar as it applied identical statutory provisions of the Uniform Partnership Act to facts similar or identical to our own.

The California Court of Appeals in *Rosenfeld, Meyer & Susman v. Cohen,* 146 Cal.App.3d 200, 194 Cal.Rptr. 180 (1983), *overruled on other ground, Applied Equipment Corp. v. Litton Saudi Arabia Ltd.,* 7 Cal.4th 503, 28 Cal.Rptr.2d 475, 869 P.2d 454 (1994), was asked to determine whether departing partners breached their fiduciary duty to their former law firm when they continued representation of the firm's client following departure. *Cohen,* 146 Cal.App.3d at 216, 194 Cal.Rptr. 180. Importantly, the Court was also asked whether the firm was entitled to a share of the fees from the "unfinished business" performed by departing partners. *Id.* As in the case before us, the departing partners left the firm and contacted the firm's client, which in turn discharged the firm and retained the departing partners to continue representation of the client until the subsequent resolution of the lawsuit. The Court began its analysis by noting the following:

> The concept of unfinished business arises from the rule of law that upon the dissolution of a partnership, the partnership is not terminated but continues to exist for the limited purpose of winding up its affairs and completing all unfinished business.[4] Thus, on May 1, 1974, the day following the dissolution of RM & S, there existed three entities: C & R (comprised of [departing partners]), a new RM & S (comprised of the partners of [the former partnership] remaining on Apr. 30, 1974), and the dissolved RM & S which had not yet been wound up. Until the dissolved partnership was wound up, the partners of the dissolved RM & S continued to owe fiduciary duties to each other, especially with respect to unfinished business.

Id. (emphasis added). The Court then moved on to opine as to the consequences attending the client's discharge of the old firm and retention of the departing partners:

> Given the facts of this case, though [the client] had a right to terminate the contract with RM & S and hire C & R, C & R could not avoid what was tantamount to a conflict of interest—i.e., the fiduciary duty it owed to RM & S.
>
> > [The client's] purported discharge of RM & S is irrelevant to the issue of C & R's breach of their fiduciary duty to the remaining partners of RM & S. [ ]A partner's fiduciary duty to complete unfinished business on behalf of the dissolved partnership arises on the date of dissolution and governs each partner's future conduct regarding this business. [ ]Since the [client's] action remained exactly the same case before and after RM & S's dissolution, C & R's liability for failing to complete the [client's] case for the dissolved RM & S and for entering into a contract personally to profit from the unfinished business of the dissolved RM & S survived execution of the C & R [client] agreement and [client's] discharge of RM & S.

Id. at 219, 194 Cal.Rptr. 180 (internal headnotes omitted).

In *Jewel v. Boxer,* 156 Cal.App.3d 171, 203 Cal.Rptr. 13 (1984), as in the case at bar, departing law partners contacted clients whose cases had been handled by the old firm. *Jewel,* 156 Cal.App.3d at 175, 203 Cal.Rptr. 13. At issue before the Court of Appeals was the proper allocation of attorneys' fees received from those cases originating with the old firm but transferred to and resolved by the new partnership. *Id.* The appellants argued that "the substitutions of attorneys

---

[4] The Uniform Partnership Act provides: "**The dissolution of a partnership is the change in the relation of the partners caused by any partner ceasing to be associated in the carrying on as distinguished from the winding up of the business.**" (Corp. Code, § 15029.) "On dissolution the partnership is not terminated, but continues until the winding up of partnership affairs is completed." (Corp.Code, § 15030.) "Except so far as may be necessary to wind up partnership affairs or to complete transactions begun but not then finished, dissolution terminates all authority of any partner to act for the partnership, [¶] (1) With respect to the partners, [¶] (a) When the dissolution is not by the act, bankruptcy or death of a partner . . . ." (Corp.Code, § 15033.)

transformed the old firm's unfinished business into new firm business and removed that business from the purview of the Uniform Partnership Act," thereby limiting the old firm's recovery to *quantum meruit* damages based on services rendered by the old firm. *Id.* at 176, 203 Cal.Rptr. 13. The Court of Appeals disagreed and concluded that recovery should be based on the partners' respective interest in the old firm. Of particular relevance to the matter before us, the Court of Appeals offered the following discussion:

> [W]e must look to the circumstances existing on the date of dissolution of a partnership, not events occurring thereafter, to determine whether business is unfinished business of the dissolved partnership. Thus, in *Rosenfeld* a client's retention of a new firm consisting of two former partners of the dissolved firm that previously handled the client's case did not transform the case into new partnership business: **'It is clear that a partner completing unfinished business cannot cut off the rights of the other partners in the dissolved partnership by the tactic of entering into a 'new' contract to complete such business.'** Accordingly, the substitutions of attorneys here did not alter the character of the cases as unfinished business of the old firm. To hold otherwise would permit a former partner of a dissolved partnership to breach the fiduciary duty not to take any action with respect to unfinished partnership business for personal gain.

Id. at 177–179, 203 Cal.Rptr. 13 (internal citations omitted and emphasis added).

It is critical to note that *Jewel*, unlike the present case, did not involve a written agreement with respect to the allocation of attorneys' fees. Therefore, the Court of Appeals analyzed the Uniform Partnership Act as the default rule to be applied in the absence of a written agreement between the parties. Notwithstanding that distinction, the Court of Appeals acknowledged the role the Uniform Partnership Act played in the absence of a written agreement between the parties:

> [F]ormer partners are obligated to ensure that a disproportionate burden of completing unfinished business does not fall on one former partner or one group of former partners, unless the former partners agree otherwise. It is unlikely that the partners, in discharging their mutual fiduciary duties, will be able to achieve a distribution of the burdens of completing unfinished business that corresponds precisely to their respective interests in the partnership. **But partners are free to include in a written partnership agreement provisions for completion of unfinished business that ensure a degree of exactness and certainty unattainable by rules of general application.** If there is any disproportionate burden of completing unfinished business here, it results from the parties' failure to have entered into a partnership agreement which could have assured such a result would not occur. The former partners must bear the consequences of their failure to provide for dissolution in a partnership agreement.

Jewel, 156 Cal.App.3d at 179–180, 203 Cal.Rptr. 13 (emphasis added). Therefore, the rules promulgated in the Uniform Partnership Act provide the foundation on which parties, by way of a written partnership agreement, may expand the parameters of their relationship.

Unlike the parties in *Jewel*, Beasley and Erbstein did enter into an agreement that accounted for the distribution of attorney fees following Erbstein's departure which were attributable to cases originating with Beasley. Specifically, Erbstein agreed that, "[i]n the event [Erbstein] leave [s] this office for any reason and a client or clients choose(s) to continue with your representation, you will receive 25% of the net fee on any case you take with you regardless of its age or time spent on the file before or after you leave the office." Beasley's Response in Opposition to the Petition for Determination of Attorney's Fees of Young Ricchiuti Caldwell & Heller, LLC, 2/11/11, at Exhibit A ¶ 8. This distinction notwithstanding, we must look to the circumstances at the time Erbstein left Beasley to determine whether the Rubys' case constituted unfinished business. As there is no dispute that the Rubys' case was in the midst of litigation at the time of Erbstein's departure, there can be no doubt that it indeed constituted unfinished business. Consequently, Erbstein, and in turn YRCH, "cannot cut off the rights of the other partners in the dissolved partnership by the tactic of entering into a 'new' contract to complete such business." *Jewel,* 156 Cal.App.3d at 178, 203 Cal.Rptr. 13 (quoting *Cohen,* 146 Cal.App.3d at 219, 194 Cal.Rptr. 180). Accordingly, while YRCH is not bound by the contract between Erbstein and Beasley, it may only take its share of attorneys' fees subject to the terms of the employment agreement. Having determined that YRCH may take Erbstein's share of the attorneys' fees subject to the terms of the employment agreement, we turn to YRCH's claim regarding the enforceability of those terms.

In support of its second issue, YRCH claims and devotes considerable analysis to the notion that Beasley's claim for attorneys' fees, as provided for in the employment contract with Erbstein, is tantamount to a restrictive covenant designed to eliminate competition *vis-á-vis* Erbstein. YRCH's Brief at 10–14. YRCH concludes that insofar as the agreement contains a restrictive covenant on Erbstein's legal practice, it is unenforceable. Further, it makes a passing remark that the elimination of competition had the "added bonus of a financial gain far beyond the *quantum meruit* value of its services." *Id.* at 11. YRCH also claims that the fee-splitting arrangement between Erbstein and Beasley somehow impacts a client's right to choose his or her counsel. *Id.* at 10. All of YRCH's claims are without merit.

At the outset, we observe that YRCH does little more than make the bald proposition that the provision in the employment agreement splitting attorneys' fees is a restrictive covenant. Relying on case law inapplicable to the facts before us, YRCH then analyzes whether this provision is enforceable, concluding that it is not enforceable. YRCH's Brief at 11–14. However, YRCH fails to direct this Court to any authority suggesting that fee-splitting arrangements constitute a restrictive covenant.

Ordinarily, a restrictive covenant forbids or curtails a party's ability to work. *See Hess v. Gebhard & Co. Inc.,* 570 Pa. 148, 808 A.2d 912 (2002) ("Restrictive covenants, of which non-disclosure and non-competition covenants are the most frequently utilized, are commonly relied upon by employers to shield their protectible [sic] business interests."). By its terms, a restrictive covenant is simply a promise not to engage in some conduct otherwise permitted but for the presence of the covenant. YRCH proffers no evidence suggesting that either YRCH or Erbstein could not obtain its own clientele, successfully engage in the practice of law, or was either geographically or temporally limited in their practice because Beasley receives a share of a recovery in the cases it formerly held. YRCH purports that somehow Erbstein was restricted because he could not continue representation of the Rubys without compensating Beasley. We are not persuaded by YRCH's argument that one's ability to procure clients is constrained by some ancillary obligation having no bearing on clients retained after the dismissal of the obliged attorney.

YRCH also cursorily argues that Beasley's share of attorneys' fees eliminated competition and had the "added bonus of a financial gain far beyond the *quantum meruit* value of its services." YRCH's Brief at 11. To the extent that YRCH claims Beasley's award exceeded the amount it would have under a *quantum meruit* theory, we agree with the trial court wherein it states:

> This was not a *quantum meruit* type of situation. Beasley never attempted to say it was entitled to a portion of the over $600,000 fee because of work its attorneys did. Rather, Beasley has always only asserted that it was entitled to the fees in accordance with the Erbstein–Beasley employment contracts.

. . .

Trial Court Opinion, 10/13/11, at 9, 10–11.

In Pennsylvania, the quasi-contractual doctrine of unjust enrichment (*quantum meruit*) does not apply when a written agreement or express contract exists between the parties. *Lackner v. Glosser*, 892 A.2d 21, 34 (Pa.Super.2006) (citing *Mitchell v. Moore*, 729 A.2d 1200, 1203 (Pa.Super.1999)). As the trial court noted, there is a written agreement in controversy in this matter, namely the employment agreements between Beasley and Erbstein. Accordingly, a *quantum meruit* theory has no place in determining the rights of the parties in this action. Therefore, YRCH's arguments with respect to this theory of recovery fail.

Finally, to the extent that YRCH argues that the employment agreement somehow negatively impacts a client's right to choose his or her attorney, we disagree. Again, we look to the sound reasoning articulated by the California Court of Appeals in *Jewel*, where the appellant proffered a similar argument:

> [T]he right of a client to the attorney of one's choice and the rights and duties as between partners with respect to income from unfinished business are distinct and do not offend one another. Once the client's fee is paid to an attorney, it is of no concern to the client how that fee is allocated among the attorney and his or her former partners.

Jewel, 156 Cal.App.3d at 178, 203 Cal.Rptr. 13. We agree.

After review of the record, we glean nothing which would suggest that the change in representation had any impact whatsoever on the Rubys' choice of counsel or their recovery following settlement. Once their claim was resolved and attorneys' fees calculated, it was of no concern to the Rubys how that fee was allocated between Beasley and YRCH. Therefore, we are not persuaded that consideration of a client's right to choose counsel has any bearing on the facts and issues in this matter. Accordingly, we conclude YRCH's argument is without merit.

Order affirmed.

F. Client Satisfaction

In an effort to retain clients, some firms solicit feedback. This can be done informally in a face-to-face communication simply by having a servicing partner take a client out to lunch.

Some firms have begun conducting formal client satisfaction surveys in an effort to measure client satisfaction. Getting people to tell the truth in such surveys can be challenging, especially if the lawyer who worked on a matter is the same one who is conducting the survey. Even dissatisfied clients are sometimes reticent to tell their lawyers to their faces about unhappiness with the service received. A survey returned simply with superlatives doesn't add much value. As a result, some firms have hired outside third parties to conduct client satisfaction surveys.

One way to increase the return rate of written surveys is to include them with a client's bill. Because some people are disinclined to put criticism in writing, however, a client satisfaction interview may be more productive. Before the interview or the survey is conducted, careful thought should be put into how questions are worded. To get people talking, pose open-ended questions rather than ones that are likely to generate a yes or no answer.

Large corporate clients may have more formal measures in place to assess their own satisfaction with their outside counsel. Thanks to technological advances, they can compare and contrast the rates that their outside firms charge. They can dive deeper into those charges by assessing how much is paid per hour for associate work at outside law firms, how much time and money is spent on attorney travel, and how much money is spent paying law firms by the hour as opposed to by the project or according to some other means. Clients might use this data to drive down their legal fees through negotiations with firms that are exceeding certain performance metrics.[17]

Even as some clients might be looking more toward data-driven cost decisions, their lawyers, and the clients themselves, might wonder whether all aspects of a legal team's performance can be measured. A large corporate client faced with a daunting legal problem might opt for the big-name, expensive, high-profile attorney. Yes, another firm might have been able to handle the matter less expensively. But if the company loses the case, isn't its own general counsel going to be under fire for going with the cheaper lawyer?

G. Terminating Representation

Lawyers are obligated to maintain client confidentiality. A relationship of trust needs to develop between lawyer and client, and a certain measure of candor is necessary for the lawyer to fully represent a client. The law of evidence recognizes this need for confidential communications between lawyers and clients; typically, such confidences are said to be privileged communications not subject to disclosure. This is referred to as the attorney-client privilege.

Suppose, though, that a client charged with battering his wife tells his lawyer that he is going to kill her. Is the lawyer obligated to keep that information a secret?

Tarasoff v. Regents of the University of California, 551 P.2d 334 (Cal. 1976), held that therapists have a duty to warn if a client presents a serious danger. In 1969, Prosenjit Poddar killed Tatiana Tarasoff. Her parents, who brought a lawsuit against Poddar's therapists, maintained that Poddar had told his psychologist of his intent to kill Tarasoff. Poddar was briefly detained by campus police, but was released. The defendants asserted that they owed no duty of reasonable care to Tatiana Tarasoff. The Supreme Court of California held:

> that defendant therapists cannot escape liability merely because Tatiana herself was not their patient. When a therapist determines, or pursuant to the standards of his profession should determine, that his patient presents a serious danger of violence to another, he incurs an obligation to use reasonable care to protect the intended victim against such danger. The discharge of this duty may require the therapist to take one or more of various steps, depending upon the nature of the case. Thus it may call for him to warn the intended victim or others likely to apprise the victim of the danger, to notify the police, or to take whatever other steps are reasonably necessary under the circumstances.[18]

Should the duty to warn extend to lawyers as well? "Prior to 2002, the Rules allowed, but did not require, disclosure of confidential information regarding the representation of a client when the lawyer reasonably believed such a disclosure would prevent the client from committing a crime resulting in death or substantial bodily injury."[19]

In 2002, the *Model Rules of Professional Conduct* were modified to specify that a lawyer may reveal information to prevent death or significant harm. Consider Model Rule 1.6.

Ethically, lawyers are not permitted to help clients break the law, but they are allowed to discuss with clients the consequences of violating the law pursuant to Model Rule 1.2(d). If a client insists on breaking the law, a lawyer is obligated to stop representing that client, according to Model Rule 1.16.

There are plenty of other reasons to fire a client. Some see it as a good business measure to get rid of the three lowest-paying clients every year and to replace them with higher-paying clients. Clients who aren't paying their bills are ripe for termination. Clients who are difficult are good candidates as well.[20]

disengagement letter:
A letter from a lawyer terminating her representation of a client.

When terminating representation, a lawyer is obligated, under Model Rule 1.16, to return the client's file to the client or forward it to the client's new counsel. A lawyer should send the client a **disengagement letter** explaining that the lawyer is terminating the case. A lawyer cannot ethically drop a client in the middle of litigation without exigent circumstances; in that case, a lawyer might be required to seek a court's permission to withdraw from the case and could be ordered to continue serving that client.

Even after ending a relationship with a client, the lawyer still has an obligation not to take on a new client in the same or a similar matter whose interests are adverse to those of the original client under Model Rule 1.9.

Checklist

- Law firms depend on successful client relationships.
- Lawyers are obligated to provide competent service and to act with diligence in representing clients.
- Ethically, lawyers are required to communicate promptly with clients.
- There are four main types of clients: corporations, associations, individuals, and governments.
- A lawyer representing a corporation represents a business entity, not the individuals who make up that corporation.
- Lawyers should be proactive in seeking new clients. They can use client intelligence to target ideal clients.
- To be more efficient and to aid their clients, some law firms are implementing legal project management principles to plan, budget, and oversee the work that they will undertake for a client.
- Client solicitation must occur within the bounds of ethical rules. Ambulance chasing is impermissible.
- Client relationships should be closely managed so that a client's needs can be identified and met.
- Client satisfaction can be assessed with surveys, interviews, or informal client contacts.
- Although lawyers are obligated to keep client confidences, lawyers may reveal information to prevent reasonably certain death or substantial bodily harm.
- Lawyers may not help clients violate the law.
- A lawyer is obligated to withdraw from a case if a client insists on breaking the law.
- A lawyer may also fire a client for other reasons.
- A lawyer cannot drop a client in the middle of a lawsuit except in exceptional circumstances; a court's permission may be required.
- Even after ending a relationship with a client, a lawyer still has ethical obligations to that client.
- When a law firm is merging with another firm, clients should be informed as soon as possible of the change.

Vocabulary

bread-and-butter client (p. 59)

churning (p. 59)

client team (p. 66)

convergence (p. 60)

cross-selling (p. 66)

deep pockets (p. 59)

disengagement letter (p. 76)

external client (p. 59)

internal client (p. 59)

intranet (p. 66)

legal project management (p. 62)

private client (p. 61)

runner (p. 62)

secondment (p. 60)

Career Preparation Tips

As you contemplate your own future role in the legal industry, think about how you may help your firm—or yourself—obtain clients. Even if your formal entrance into the legal field is years away, what steps might you take now to develop the ability to get and retain clients? Are there fields that you might volunteer in to learn how a business works or to gain contacts already working in the area? For instance, if you plan to work for the real estate practice of a law firm, might you volunteer at a housing organization now? If you tend toward social reticence, are there social groups that you could join to develop speaking skills and the ability to make idle chitchat that could further your career? How might you improve your people skills?

If You Want to Learn More

The American Bar Association's Center for Professional Responsibility offers a lot of material on ethical issues. The *Model Rules of Professional Conduct* and commentary are accessible at this site. http://www.americanbar.org/groups/professional_responsibility.html

The Association of Corporate Counsel is a bar association for in-house counsel with 30,000 members in more than 75 countries. http://www.acc.com/

Bloomberg, the company founded by New York City Mayor Michael Bloomberg, chronicles business news. http://www.bloomberg.com

Fast Company covers business practices and trends and reports on innovative practices by companies. http://www.fastcompany.com

Forbes covers financial markets, business, technology, corporate governance, and other areas. http://www.forbes.com

Martindale offers a searchable directory of lawyers. Searches can be conducted by name, by state, and by other search terms. In-house counsel, government lawyers, and corporate legal departments can also be located. www.martindale.com

---

Reading Comprehension

1. What ethical obligations does a lawyer have to his or her current clients?
2. What are some of the reasons lawyers can face discipline for providing poor client service?
3. How does legal representation of a corporation differ from representation of an individual?
4. Why should a lawyer research prospective clients?
5. What are permissible ways for a lawyer to pursue prospective clients?
6. How does legal project management aid clients?
7. In what circumstances may a lawyer disclose confidential information provided by a client?
8. What are some examples of inappropriate solicitations of potential clients?
9. When should a lawyer fire a client?
10. Can a lawyer represent a fired client's opponent in a lawsuit?

Discussion Starters

1. Running up a client's legal bill by doing excessive work on the case can be very tempting to lawyers who must generate income to pay their own bills. Consider the following:

   Virtually all the economics of law practice—including those of the large firms who charge $250–600 per hour for their services—cut against ethical behavior. If a client has a deep pocket and is able to pay the lawyers' fees many lawyers **churn** the case in order to enhance earnings. If the clients can not afford the fees as the case progresses they risk receiving only "partial" representation in which lawyers may do just enough work to justify having used up the available money. When funds are depleted the lawyers then figure out how to dispose of the problem or claim, or provide bargain basement service in the sense of "you get what you pay for."[21]

What ethical rules are violated by the practice of churning? How can churning be proven? How can lawyers avoid the temptation to churn cases?

2. In 2013, e-mails about cost overruns from lawyers within a major law firm became part of the court record in a billing-dispute lawsuit. One of the e-mails read that a lawyer within the firm "had random people working full time on random research projects in standard . . . 'churn that bill, baby!' mode. That bill shall know no limits." Another lawyer wrote in regarding the matter, "I hear we are already 200k over our estimate—that's Team DLA Piper!" Exhibit 5 to Supporting Affidavit of Larry Hutcher, *DLA Piper LLP (US) v. Victor*, No. 650374/2012 (N.Y. Sup. Ct. filed Mar. 21, 2013). Much negative publicity followed, and the firm issued a statement maintaining that the e-mails simply represented "an unfortunate attempt at humor" and that the client was not overbilled. *DLA Piper Calls E-Mails Cited in Lawsuit an 'Offensive' Attempt at Humor*, N.Y. Times DealBook (Mar. 26, 2013), http://dealbook.nytimes.com/2013/03/26/dla-piper-warns-employees-against-offensive-humor-in-e-mails/

If you worked at the firm where this happened, how might you have addressed the negative publicity? Given the existence of these e-mails, did the firm's leadership make a cost-effective decision to pursue litigation seeking legal fees from the particular client at issue in this matter? If you became aware that a law firm's lawyers had written e-mails such as this, would you still retain the firm? What precautions might you take to ensure bills were not inappropriately padded?

3. Read *Florida Bar v. Barrett*. Were Barrett's clients dissatisfied with the service they received? Was Barrett effective at representing his clients? Was the punishment Barrett received too harsh? Look up your state's rules on solicitation of clients.

4. Research legal project management. Are there any negative impacts of implementing legal project management at a law firm? Why might anyone be opposed to legal project management at his or her firm? Might a client be opposed to legal project management? How can any resistance, by a law firm or by a client, be overcome?

5. Read *Ruby v. Abington Memorial Hospital*. What did you learn about partnership agreements from this case? Why was the lawyer at the center of this case dismissed from his previous firm? What impact do you think this litigation had on the client that was involved? Would this litigation impact client opinions about either law firm involved?

6. Draft a sample letter to a client informing her that your law firm is merging with another. What information should be included in such a letter? Of what rights should the client be informed? Should a letter be written in a way intended to keep the client as a client?

7. Draft a sample letter to a client informing her that the lawyer working on her case is moving to another law firm. What information should

be included in such a letter? How should this letter differ from the one involving a law firm merger?

8. Look up some sample client satisfaction surveys, and research recent law review articles on these surveys. What questions should be asked on such a survey? How might those questions be posed to generate a highly informative answer?

9. Suppose you work for a nonprofit organization dedicated to providing food to poor people in your state. The nonprofit is seeking outside counsel. What qualifications would you look for in a law firm? What size firm might be an ideal match for the nonprofit?

Case Studies

1. Select one large corporation in your area and conduct some competitive intelligence on it. What types of legal problems might the company face? Who is the company's general counsel? What law school did that general counsel attend? Who currently represents the corporation?

2. Your law firm is considering pitching both Walmart and Sears for legal work. What sort of legal representation might these two companies need? Who are their current counsel? What might be the advantage of working for one corporation rather than the other?

3. Look up a case where a lawyer sued a client for nonpayment of the client's bill. Were there any early indicators that the lawyer-client relationship would sour? Why didn't the client pay the bill? What was the outcome of the case?

4. Your client tells your firm that she will call the firm from her car while she is driving to her next appointment. Suppose that talking on a cell phone without a separate headset while driving is illegal in your state. Is your firm obligated to terminate its representation of the client?

5. Look up your state's rules on returning client files to the client when representation is terminated. You might also need to research case law and ethical opinions to determine the answers to the following questions: Must a lawyer's notes be provided to the client? Must copies of all e-mails be provided to the client? Should managerial documents (for instance, giving an assignment related to the file to an associate and specifying the number of hours to be spent on the task) be included?

Endnotes

1. Attorney Grievance Commission of Maryland, *37th Ann. Rep.*, *July 1, 2011 thru June 30, 2012*, at 2, *available at* http://www.courts.state.md.us/attygrievance/annualreport .html.
2. *Id.*
3. *Id.* at 4.
4. *See, e.g.,* Debra Cassens Weiss, *How Law Firms End Up on IBM GC's Do-Not-Hire-List*, A.B.A. J. (Apr. 4, 2013), *available at* http://www.abajournal.com/news/article/ibms_ general_counsel_explains_how_law_firms_get_on_his_do-not-hire_list.
5. *See, e.g.,* Ashley Post, 61% of GCs Unsatisfied with Law Firm Rates, Inside Counsel (July 16, 2013), available at http://www.insidecounsel.com/2013/07/16/61-of-gcs- unsatisfied-with-law-firm-rates?goback=.gde_117520_member_258523640.
6. *See, e.g.,* Megan Leonhardt, *Companies Use More Law Firms to Lower Costs*, Law360 (Oct. 17, 2012), *available at* http://www.law360.com/articles/387326/companies- use-more-law-firms-to-lower-costs.
7. Leigh Jones, *Firms Lend Associates to Clients*, Nat'l L.J. (Dec. 4, 2007), *available at* http://www.law.com/jsp/ihc/PubArticleIHC.jsp?id=1196676275514.
8. Bureau of Labor Statistics, U.S. Department of Labor, *Occupational Outlook Handbook, 2012-13 Edition, Lawyers, available at* http://www.bls.gov/ooh/legal/lawyers.htm (last updated Aug. 4, 2013).
9. U.S. Department of Labor, Bureau of Labor Statistics, *Occupational Outlook Handbook, 2010–11 Edition: Lawyers, available at* http://www.bls.gov/oco/ocos053.htm (last updated Dec. 17, 2009).
10. Jared Sandberg, *Microsoft's Tormentor*, Newsweek (Mar. 1, 1999, n.p.), *available at* http://libsys.uah.edu:3206/ehost/detail?vid=14&hid=103&sid=7c4f83bc-2bf3-4d66- 899c-d996aaedb652%40sessionmgr102.
11. *Id.*
12. Steven A. Meyerowitz, *Features: Eye on the Competition: What Are Rival Firms Doing? Are Clients Turning to Other Counsel? It's Not So Hard to Find Out—and It May Be Crucial to Your Professional Future to Do So*, 26 Pa. Law. 30, 30 (Jan./Feb. 2004).
13. For more information on legal project management, see, e.g., Alan Cohen, *The Eureka Moment—The Implementation of Legal Project Management*, LegalWeek.com (Sept. 14, 2012), *available at* http://www.legalweek.com/legal-week/feature/2204722 /the-eureka-moment-the-implementation-of-legal-project-management; Association of Corporate Counsel, *ACC Value Challenge: Guide to Project Management* (2011), *available at* http://www.acc.com/valuechallenge.
14. *Ohralik v. Ohio State Bar Assn.*, 436 U.S. 447, 449 (1978).
15. Lori Tripoli, *Disney-Style Debacles Prove Need for Client Sensitivity Training*, Of Counsel, Jan. 5, 1998, at 7, 8.
16. Julie A. Eichorn, *Feature: Looking Behind the Glass: 10 Critical Strategies to Developing New Client Business*, 69 Tex. B.J. 1064, 1065 (2006).
17. *See, e.g.,* Sharon D. Nelson & John W. Simek, *Big Data: Big Pain or Big Gain for Lawyers?*, 39 Law Practice Magazine n.p. (July/Aug. 2013), *available at* http://www .americanbar.org/publications/law_practice_magazine/2013/july-august/hot-buttons .html.
18. *Tarasoff v. Regents of the University of California*, 551 P.2d 334, 339 (Cal. 1976).

19. Joshua James Sears, *The 2003 Symposium Edition: Modern Methods in Legal Ethics: Theoretical and Practical Approaches: Comment: Blood on Our Hands: The Failure of Rule 1.6 to Protect Third Parties from Violent Clients, and the Movement Toward a Common-Law Solution*, 39 Idaho L. Rev. 451, 452–53 (2003).

20. *See, e.g.*, Mary L. C. Daniel, *Fire Your Clients. Or Your Staff. Or Yourself*, GPSolo, July/Aug. 2006, at 44, 45.

21. David Barnhizer, *Profession Deleted: Using Market and Liability Forces to Regulate the Very Ordinary Business of Law Practice for Profit*, 17 Geo. J. Legal Ethics 203, 223 (2004).

4

Ethics

Chapter Outcomes

By the end of this chapter, a student will be able to:

- Discuss ethical standards applicable to attorneys and to others working in the legal field
- Identify ethical quandaries present in factual scenarios
- Apply rules of professional conduct
- Take measures to prevent violations of ethical rules

Legal ethics are defined as the "*minimum* standards of appropriate conduct within the legal profession, involving the duties that its members owe one another, their clients, and the courts."[1] Of course, there is a difference between knowing what's right and actually doing what is right, so there is a set of rules, applicable to attorneys, the violation of which results in various degrees of punishment.

Students sometimes express surprise that lawyers get into ethical troubles. After all, who doesn't know that we shouldn't lie, shouldn't cheat, shouldn't steal? Lawyers, by virtue of their profession, are highly knowledgeable about the intricacies of the law—so one would think that, of anyone, a lawyer would not violate ethics codes. As with any law, however, there are the requirements and then there is reality. Lawyers, like everyone else, can be tempted to break the law in some way every single day. Even the *Model Rules of Professional Conduct* acknowledge that tensions among a lawyer's obligations to clients, to courts, and to himself will arise.[2]

Consider other types of laws, such as those prohibiting speeding or texting while driving. Those prohibited activities nevertheless occur quite often. Similarly, in a law office, an attorney can be tempted to violate ethical rules. One lawyer explained:

I know what I'm supposed to do, but from the business end, so many of those rules just lose context. . . . I know that every notary is supposed to be taken in front of the person on a completely filled out form. I also know that there's not a lawyer in [the] universe when his client comes in and needs a half a dozen medical authorizations, doesn't after six, after eight, . . . [have the client] sign them blank and [the lawyer will then] fill them out later because you can't have somebody sit in your office for an hour. And I know that if they sign them in front of me, the secretary notarizes them because I tell her to, but she didn't see the signature.[3]

As with any other law, legal ethics codes are violated. Some lawyers are caught, some are disciplined, and, surely, some get away with it.

Lawyers sometimes talk about "gray areas of the law," meaning vague or unclear aspects of the law. Some say, where ethics are concerned, there are no gray areas — merely bright lines:

> As members of a profession in which public reliance and trust is so essential and whose members' integrity must be assured to maintain vital public respect, we as attorneys must recognize the importance of a high standard by which our conduct is measured. Even where there is no thought of or intent to do wrong, if our conduct *appears* to be unethical, we weaken that respect and trust just as surely as if we had purposefully violated a specific rule.
>
> Countless situations arise in the day-to-day practice of law which raise questions of what course the attorney should take to resolve a problem whose solution is unclear. A difficult weighing and balancing of the interests of the client, the attorney, and the legal profession as a whole is required where that problem concerns a matter of professional conduct. But the bottom line should always be this: where it is a question of ethics, the answer is "no." There is no room for "close" **questions of professional propriety,** particularly at a time when public trust in and respect for the legal profession is not at its highest level.

> *G.A.C. Commercial Corp. v. Mahoney Typographers, Inc.*,
> 238 N.W.2d 575, 577-78 (Mich. Ct. App. 1975)

fiduciary duty:
A duty of good faith and trust owed to a beneficiary by a fiduciary.

Lawyers have a **fiduciary duty** to their clients. A fiduciary duty is a "duty of utmost good faith, trust, confidence, and candor owed by a fiduciary (such as a lawyer . . .) to the beneficiary (such as a lawyer's client . . .); a duty to act with the highest degree of honesty and loyalty toward another person and in the best interests of the other person."[4] If lawyers violate, or breach, that duty they owe, the client can, in turn, file a lawsuit against the lawyer and the firm.[5]

A.　Rules of Professional Conduct

To be able to practice law, a lawyer first must be admitted to the bar. Each state has its own requirements for admission to the bar, but, typically, a candidate must have graduated from an accredited law school, pass the bar exam, and demonstrate a character fit for the practice of law. When applying to the bar, a candidate must complete a detailed questionnaire. The character-related subjects a candidate for admission to the bar might have to disclose and explain include legal proceedings he has been involved in, his driving record, delinquent credit accounts, employment details (including any firings), and substance abuse problems.[6]

Once admitted to practice law in a state, the lawyer is subject to that state's code of conduct and can be disciplined by the state's highest court for violations of that code. The lawyer, not his or her law firm, is subject to **disciplinary action,** since lawyers, not law firms, are admitted to the bar. (Of course, a disgruntled client not only can make a disciplinary complaint against a lawyer but also can file a civil suit, such as a malpractice action, against both the lawyer and the firm.) A lawyer may be privately reprimanded, publicly reprimanded, suspended from practicing law for a period of time, or disbarred. A lawyer can be admitted to practice law in more than one state. There is no national bar admission that allows a lawyer to practice in every state.

disciplinary action:
Punishment taken against a lawyer for violating ethics codes.

As of this writing, all states except California[7] have enacted ethical rules based on the American Bar Association's *Model Rules of Professional Conduct,* which were approved by the ABA in 1983. The first rules on legal ethics issued by the ABA were the 1908 *Canons of Professional Ethics.* They were followed by the *Model Code of Professional Responsibility* in 1969.

Enforcement of the ethical rules rests with the highest court of a state. Typically, the court has an office dedicated to the professional responsibilities of lawyers. Each judicial district may have its own grievance committee. The investigative process is usually initiated when a client files a **grievance** with the relevant committee.

grievance:
A complaint filed by a client against a lawyer asserting violation of a state's ethical rules.

After a grievance is filed, the committee will investigate the complaint. More serious charges might be heard by select members of the committee during a hearing. This panel will then determine whether a lawyer breached the ethics rules and, if so, what disciplinary action is appropriate. This recommendation might then be directed to a disciplinary review board made up of lawyers. For serious violations, the board might hold an oral argument on the matter. The highest court of a state may determine whether **disbarment,** or revoking a lawyer's permission to practice law, is warranted.

disbarment:
Revocation of a lawyer's permission to practice law.

Lawyers who, while representing clients before courts, behave inappropriately can be subjected to sanctions. A lawyer's law firm can also be held responsible for the actions of its partners, associates, or employees. Lawyers are considered to be officers of the court and are expected to conduct themselves responsibly. The U.S. Supreme Court explained, "The license granted by the court requires members of the bar to conduct themselves in a manner compatible with the role of courts in the administration of justice."[8]

Some courts take a stern approach to rude behavior exhibited by some litigators. For instance, in *Laddcap Value Partners, LP v. Lowenstein Sandler, PC,* No. 600973-2007 (N.Y. Sup. Ct. Dec. 5, 2007), a lawyer involved in litigation asked a court to appoint a referee to supervise future depositions because the opposing counsel had been so rude. During a deposition, opposing counsel made a number of "inappropriate, insulting, and derogatory remarks" against the lawyer "concerning her gender, marital status, and competence."[9] Opposing counsel argued that "while he 'aspires to be civil' to other counsel, he is 'not aware of any rule or law which requires civility between counsel.'"[10] Opposing counsel had said, among other things, "You better get somebody else here to try this case, otherwise you're gonna be one sorry girl."[11]

The court, appointing a special referee to oversee future depositions in the case, wrote:

> Offensive and abusive language by attorneys in the guise of zealous advocacy is plainly improper, unprofessional, and unacceptable. An attorney who demonstrates a lack of civility, good manners and common courtesy taints the image of the legal profession and, consequently, the legal system, which was created and designed to resolve differences and disputes in a civil manner and an attorney's "conduct . . . that projects offensive and invidious discriminatory distinctions . . . based on race . . . [or] gender . . . is especially offensive[.]"[12]

How a lawyer responds to an accusation of ethical impropriety today can be influenced by technology. As one lawyer focusing on legal malpractice cases noted, a lawyer subjected to even minor professional discipline today is likely to see her name appear in an online search as having been disciplined. Because lawyers today must preserve their reputations on the Internet, some are disinclined to accept reprimands because these minor disciplinary actions are likely to be reported and accessible online. Instead, such lawyers may be inspired to defend more vigorously any accusation of inappropriate behavior.[13]

B.   Ethical Considerations for Law Office Managers

A law office manager, in conjunction with appropriate lawyers, should develop written policies for reporting ethical concerns within the law firm and for addressing those concerns promptly. Model Rule 5.1 requires partners in a firm to take efforts to make sure that others within the firm conform to the rules. A lawyer can actually be held responsible for another's violation of the rules if that lawyer approved the misconduct or if a supervising lawyer knew of a junior lawyer's inappropriate actions and could have taken action to minimize their consequences but failed to.

A lawyer accused of ethical misconduct and the staff with whom he or she works can be pitted against each other. The misbehaving attorney may be disinclined to accept responsibility for the misbehavior, or a disgruntled staffer may be prompted to exaggerate a claim of misconduct on the part of the attorney.

James v. Shapiro
No. B179194, 2006 Cal. App. Unpub. LEXIS 5666
(Cal. Ct. App. June 28, 2006)

NOTICE: NOT TO BE PUBLISHED IN OFFICIAL REPORTS. CALIFORNIA RULES OF COURT, RULE 977(A), PROHIBIT COURTS AND PARTIES FROM CITING OR RELYING ON OPINIONS NOT CERTIFIED FOR PUBLICATION OR ORDERED PUBLISHED, EXCEPT AS SPECIFIED BY RULE 977(B). THIS OPINION HAS NOT BEEN CERTIFIED FOR PUBLICATION OR ORDERED PUBLISHED FOR THE PURPOSES OF RULE 977.

OPINION

At issue in this appeal is whether a legal secretary may sue her former law firm for wrongful termination in violation of public policy after she reported that a partner was defrauding clients by submitting inflated legal bills. Because obtaining money through fraudulent legal bills violates Penal Code section 484, and because that statute inures to the benefit of the public and represents a substantial and fundamental public policy, we hold that she may sue.

Pauletta James (James) appeals the summary judgment entered in favor of respondents Christensen, Miller, Fink, Jacobs, Glaser, Weil & Shapiro (Christensen) and Robert Shapiro (Shapiro) on her causes of action for wrongful termination in violation of public policy and intentional infliction of emotional distress. We conclude that the trial court erred when it ruled that (1) James could not identify a public policy sufficient to support her cause of action for wrongful termination in violation of public policy, and (2) the intentional infliction of emotional distress cause of action is barred by the exclusivity provision of the workers' compensation scheme. However, James failed to show that the trial court erred when it ruled that Shapiro was not her employer.

We affirm the summary judgment entered in favor of Shapiro. We reverse the summary judgment entered in favor of Christensen and remand for further proceedings. On remand, the trial court shall consider Christensen's motion for summary adjudication regarding punitive damages.

James alleged: Christensen and Shapiro's "actions . . . in terminating [James's] employment in retaliation for her refusal to send fraudulent billing statements to clients violates California's whistle-blower statute which prohibits employers from terminating employees who threaten to expose a violation of the law." Their egregious and malicious conduct constituted wrongful termination in violation of public policy and intentional infliction of emotional distress.

The evidence in support of the motion portrayed James as a problem employee who was dismissed because no one wanted to work with her.

Shapiro declared that James worked as a legal secretary for Sara Caplan (Caplan) and him from March 2002 until January 2003. He explained that there were periods during which he was displeased with James's performance because she "continued to be away from her desk and to spend too much time talking to other employees[,] [which caused] many telephone calls to unnecessarily go to voice mail." In January 2003, he averred, their "ability to communicate effectively in person had deteriorated." After he assigned James the task of updating information in his personal directory and left her a voicemail to keep track of her time and work on nothing else until she completed her task, she told him: "I got your message. I will do one but not the other. I will complete the work but I will not keep track of time. I'm not on a plantation." Following that incident, Shapiro communicated with James only via e-mail. During the last week of her employment, it became impossible to work with her under such difficult circumstances. He was informed by Caplan that James gave incorrect information to a court clerk that could have jeopardized a case for one of his clients.

Caplan declared that she did not utilize James much because she "appeared to be too busy working on Shapiro's assignments and when Caplan did utilize James, she was generally rude and abrupt." By August 2002, Caplan expressed her dissatisfaction with James's performance to Meisler, noting that James ignored phone calls while she was speaking to friends at her desk, and she created conflict by constantly screaming at the paralegal. In January 2003, James had a trial preparation assignment for over a month and did not complete it. Then, according to Caplan: "I overhead James speaking on the telephone with a client of mine and Shapiro's. During this conversation I heard James indicating to our client how our client could report us to the State Bar of California for [m]alpractice. I relayed this conversation to both Shapiro and Meisler." When Caplan asked James to telephone a court and put a client's case on calendar, as previously arranged with a prosecutor, James failed to do so. . . .

In her declaration, Meisler explained that in August 2002 she learned of Shapiro's and Caplan's dissatisfaction. By the end of January 2003, Meisler spoke with James and Shapiro to determine if they could continue working together. Shapiro said he did not want to work with James. Meisler inquired as to whether other attorneys at Christensen would accept James as their legal secretary, but they declined. Because no other placement could be found, Meisler and Getz informed James that her employment was terminated effective January 28, 2003.

Beyond echoing some of the same details provided by Shapiro, Caplan and Meisler, Getz declared that he received numerous complaints from James about her work relationship with Shapiro, including that Shapiro was discriminating against her because of her race.

To identify a fundamental and substantial public policy to support her first cause of action, James relied on Penal Code sections 484 and 532, both of which make it a crime to obtain money by false pretenses.

The opposition points and authorities argued that there were triable issues because: James witnessed Shapiro and Caplan fabricating fictitious legal bills which were forwarded to clients. James also witnessed other improper activity. After she brought the improper activity to the attention of management on January 28, 2003, she was immediately terminated. Because she performed personal tasks for Shapiro, and because some of the clients belonged to him and not Christensen, Shapiro was James's employer.

James declared that not only did she work for Shapiro and Caplan as their legal secretary, she assisted Shapiro with billing clients. He frequently hired outside attorneys, such as Robert J. Waters (Waters), to do work on files, and then those attorneys would submit bills consisting of their hours and work. James maintained "a written ledger reflecting the amount Shapiro's clients were billed and paid on their matters" and "assisted Shapiro in drafting and processing bills and past due statements for clients." Prior to blowing the whistle on Shapiro, she received "excellent performance reviews by both Shapiro and Caplan in mid May 2002." Because Shapiro was so high on her work, he frequently sent her to expensive lunches.

It was in August 2002, James explained, that she first became aware of Shapiro's illegal billing practices. Shapiro called her into his office to discuss the bills for a client named Mogens Amdi Petersen (Petersen). Waters was doing some work on Petersen's case. "On that day," James declares, "Shapiro specifically instructed me not to show [Waters's] actual submitted hours to the accounting department at Christensen. In addition, Shapiro told me to white out the actual hours worked by Waters which appeared on [Waters's] invoices. [Shapiro] also specifically told me to not let [Getz] . . . see the actual bill from Waters or the actual hours worked by Waters." Later, James heard Shapiro "tell Getz to make up a certain number of hours for [Waters's] work and to include that on the bill which was to be sent to . . . Petersen. The hours for attorney Waters that Shapiro wanted included on [Petersen's] bill was not the number of hours that Waters submitted. Subsequently a draft bill for Petersen came across my desk. The hours in that bill being charged for [Waters's] time were dramatically inflated from the time entries on the original bill from [Waters] to us. [Shapiro] then approved the bill with the fraudulently inflated hours. I also saw the final bill to [Petersen] which contained these fraudulent and inflated hours. I saw this occur on 3-5 occasions . . . ."

Continuing on, James declared that when Shapiro was in a fee dispute with Dr. Ahmed but had no timesheets to back up his claimed fees, Shapiro and Caplan instructed James "to make up and create times sheets for Shapiro based on Caplan's work and time sheets." James explained: "As ordered, I took Caplan's time sheets, and based on those, created out of whole cloth time sheets for Shapiro. I provided these fictional time records to Shapiro for his review and approval. Shapiro then added additional hours to the time sheet and gave them back to me for revision. I sent the fraudulent bills to the attorney" who represented Shapiro in the fee dispute. James was instructed to do the same thing regarding a fee dispute with Gordan Jones (Jones).

In James's version of events, Shapiro became critical of her work after January 14, 2003. She complained to Getz on January 23, 2003 via e-mail. That same day, she overheard Shapiro tell Amanda Bossingham (Bossingham) to lie to the Federal Court in Arizona about the amount of money she previously paid to Shapiro in legal fees. James met with Getz on January 28, 2003, to discuss why her relationship with Shapiro had deteriorated. When she revealed his illegal billing practices, and that he told Bossingham to lie, Getz said that he would talk to Shapiro. After doing so, Getz said that Shapiro did not think that the relationship could be salvaged. James asked to be reassigned but was told that there were no other available positions and was asked to leave. By James's account, the criticisms of her work were all a pretext because she did not spend too much time away from her desk or too much time talking to people. She claimed that she always dealt with office personnel in a courteous and professional manner. Finally, she denied ever telling a client to sue Christensen for malpractice, and she denied failing to calendar a hearing. . . .

The first argument in James's appeal is that there are triable issues as to whether Shapiro was her employer. Indeed, this is a pivotal battle for her regarding her wrongful termination claim against Shapiro because "only an employer can be liable for the tort of wrongful discharge in violation of public policy." Similarly, if he was not her employer, then she cannot sue him for intentional infliction of emotional distress based on her alleged retaliatory termination.

The entirety of her opening brief argument is the following:

Regarding her employment, all we know is that James did not dispute in her opposing separate statement that she was hired by Christensen to work for Shapiro and Caplan. James did not offer conflicting evidence suggesting that she was hired by both Christensen and Shapiro. Moreover, James neglected to cite evidence establishing how Christensen was organized during the relevant time, i.e., whether it was a partnership, a limited liability company, or a corporation. We have been given no information regarding the legal relationship between Shapiro and Christensen. Beyond these deficiencies, James did not cite any law explaining how Shapiro can be legally categorized as her employer if she was hired by Christensen.

An at-will employee can be terminated from employment without good cause, but if the reason for the termination violates public policy, then the employee can sue her employer in tort. "To recover in tort for wrongful discharge in violation of public policy, the plaintiff must show the employer violated a public policy affecting 'society at large rather than a purely personal or proprietary interest of the plaintiff or employer.' In addition, the policy at issue must be substantial, fundamental, and grounded in a statutory or constitutional provision. Consistent with these principles, courts have recognized tortious wrongful discharge claims where an employee establishes he was 'terminated in retaliation for reporting to his or her employer reasonably suspected illegal conduct . . . that harms the public as well as the employer.'"

If an employee at a law firm reports that a partner is defrauding clients out of money by issuing inflated legal bills, then that report inures to the benefit of the public as well as to the law firm. Such a report deters crime and serves the interests of innocent clients who stand to be victimized by fraudulent legal bills when they overpay for legal services. Undeniably, such a report is a protected disclosure of illegal or unethical practices.

Based on a slate of favorable precedents, James argues that the trial court erred when it ruled that her second cause of action is barred by the exclusivity provisions in the workers' compensation scheme. We agree.

A cause of action for intentional infliction of emotional distress premised on wrongful termination in violation of public policy has been widely recognized.

The summary judgment entered in favor of Shapiro is affirmed. As to Christensen, summary judgment is reversed and remanded. On remand, the trial court shall consider Christensen's motion for summary adjudication regarding James's prayer for punitive damages. James is entitled to costs on appeal.

A procedures manual, with which all attorneys and nonlegal staff are familiar, can establish a system for addressing ethical concerns as they arise in a firm if someone within the firm—a lawyer or nonlegal personnel—violates an ethical rule. The manual can also address what to do if a client asks a lawyer to violate an ethical rule.

Having a series of procedures established for checking conflicts of interests, handling clients' money, and maintaining confidentiality can also help lawyers in a firm engage in appropriate behavior so that they'll avoid any misconduct in the first place.

C.   Unauthorized Practice of Law

Both lawyers and nonlawyers in a firm need to take care not to engage in the unauthorized practice of law. Lawyers, while admitted to practice in their own jurisdiction, must take care not to practice law inappropriately in other states. To do so would violate Model Rule 5.5.

Even if a lawyer is not admitted to practice in a state, the lawyer can still provide legal services on a temporary basis in that state if he hires local counsel to assist him. A lawyer can also seek to be **admitted pro hac vice,** or temporarily, to a different jurisdiction for the purpose of working on a specific case.

admittance pro hac vice: Admittance to the bar of another jurisdiction on a temporary basis for the purpose of working on a specific case.

Nonlawyers must also be concerned about engaging in the unauthorized practice of law. Because paralegals deal with legal subjects on such a regular basis, they can be very tempted to interpret the law for a client. This would be the unauthorized practice of law, however. States usually have statutes prohibiting the unauthorized practice of law (see Figure 4-1 for a sample state statute).

Requirements governing the unauthorized practice of law vary significantly from state to state.[14]

D.   A Lawyer's Supervisory Responsibility

A lawyer cannot avoid her ethical responsibilities by delegating inappropriate tasks to underlings, whether they're junior lawyers or nonlegal staff. Under *Model Rules of Professional Conduct* Rule 5.2, a junior lawyer is still obligated to follow the rules of professional conduct. That lawyer, however, can rely on the reasonable judgment of a supervising lawyer and avoid an ethics breach. Even so, junior lawyers cannot overlook inappropriate behavior by their superiors. Model Rule 8.3 obligates lawyers who see other lawyers violating the rules to report that violation to a professional authority in certain circumstances.

Model Rule 5.3 requires lawyers who are managers at law firms to make sure that the firm has measures in place to make sure that nonlawyer employees conform to the lawyers' professional conduct rules.

In 1991, the American Bar Association developed the *ABA Model Guidelines for the Utilization of Paralegal Services.* The guidelines, updated in 2003, focus on attorneys' responsibilities for overseeing paralegals. The guidelines can be accessed via the ABA Standing Committee on Paralegals Web site at http://www.americanbar.org/content/dam/aba/migrated/legalservices/paralegals/downloads/modelguidelines.pdf.

Paralegals, because they are not members of the bar, are not subject to disciplinary action in the way that lawyers are. Nevertheless, a paralegal who takes inappropriate steps could risk termination by her law firm, a civil suit by a disgruntled client, and sanctions, in certain instances, by courts. Some associations of legal assistants have adopted their own ethical codes.

E.   Duty to Prospective Clients

Even if a lawyer does not accept a case, that lawyer has certain responsibilities with respect to the potential client that she turns away. Under Model Rule 1.18,

FIGURE 4-1
Connecticut's Unauthorized Practice of Law Statute

Conn. Gen. Stat. §51-88 (2013)

§51-88. Practice of law by persons not attorneys.

(a) A person who has not been admitted as an attorney under the provisions of section 51-80 shall not: (1) Practice law or appear as an attorney-at-law for another, in any court of record in this state, (2) make it a business to practice law, or appear as an attorney-at-law for another in any such court, (3) make it a business to solicit employment for an attorney-at-law, (4) hold himself out to the public as being entitled to practice law, (5) assume to be an attorney-at-law, (6) assume, use or advertise the title of lawyer, attorney and counselor-at-law, attorney-at-law, counselor-at-law, attorney, counselor, attorney and counselor, or an equivalent term, in such manner as to convey the impression that he is a legal practitioner of law, or (7) advertise that he, either alone or with others, owns, conducts or maintains a law office, or office or place of business of any kind for the practice of law.

(b) Any person who violates any provision of this section shall be fined not more than two hundred and fifty dollars or imprisoned not more than two months or both. The provisions of this subsection shall not apply to any employee in this state of a stock or nonstock corporation, partnership, limited liability company or other business entity who, within the scope of his employment, renders legal advice to his employer or its corporate affiliate and who is admitted to practice law before the highest court of original jurisdiction in any state, the District of Columbia, the Commonwealth of Puerto Rico or a territory of the United States or in a district court of the United States and is a member in good standing of such bar. For the purposes of this subsection, "employee" means any person engaged in service to an employer in the business of his employer, but does not include an independent contractor.

(c) Any person who violates any provision of this section shall be deemed in contempt of court, and the Superior Court shall have jurisdiction in equity upon the petition of any member of the bar of this state in good standing or upon its own motion to restrain such violation.

(d) The provisions of this section shall not be construed as prohibiting: (1) A town clerk from preparing or drawing deeds, mortgages, releases, certificates of change of name and trade name certificates which are to be recorded or filed in the town clerk's office in the town in which the town clerk holds office; (2) any person from practicing law or pleading at the bar of any court of this state in his own cause; (3) any person from acting as an agent or representative for a party in an international arbitration, as defined in subsection (3) of section 50a-101; or (4) any attorney admitted to practice law in any other state or the District of Columbia from practicing law in relation to an impeachment proceeding pursuant to Article Ninth of the Connecticut Constitution, including an impeachment inquiry or investigation, if the attorney is retained by (A) the General Assembly, the House of Representatives, the Senate, a committee of the House of Representatives or the Senate, or the presiding officer at a Senate trial, or (B) an officer subject to impeachment pursuant to said Article Ninth.

---

a lawyer must maintain confidentiality with respect to the matters discussed. A lawyer also cannot go on to represent another client in the same case if the client's interests are adverse to a prospective client's interests. Indeed, if a lawyer has a conflict of interest with a client, no one in the lawyer's entire firm can represent that client under Model Rule 1.10 unless certain requirements are met.

Determining when an attorney-client relationship comes into existence is not always clear-cut. As the following case shows, the absence of a formal agreement between lawyer and client does not determine whether a relationship existed.

Shattles v. Bioprogress PLC
No. 1:05-CV-3179-MHS, 2006 U.S. Dist. LEXIS 48083
(N.D. Ga. July 14, 2006)

OPINION

There are several matters pending before the Court. The Court's rulings and conclusions are set forth below.

BACKGROUND

Plaintiff Larry Shattles is one of the original founders of Bioprogress Technology International, Inc., ("BTII") and has been with the company for over twelve years.

In late 2002, BTII retained the law firm of Dechert LLP ("Dechert") to represent BTII with respect to a corporate reorganization and admission to trading on the Alternative Investment Market of the London Stock Exchange in the United Kingdom ("U.K."). The transaction involved the incorporation of a new U.K. company, Bioprogress plc ("Bioprogress"). Bioprogress became the parent company to BTII.

Mr. Shattles and certain members of his family held U.S. BTII common stock, or "Founder's Stock." Mr. Shattles had received this special stock for his long time service with the company and its predecessors, and he and his family were the only shareholders of this special class of stock.

From November of 2002 through April 2003, attorneys at Dechert spoke with Mr. Shattles regarding the conversion of his personal stock shares. Dechert attorneys informed Mr. Shattles of the new stock structure and the impact it would have on his family's shares. These Founder's Stock shares were converted into 595,906 shares of C Series Preferred Stock before the merger of BTII.

On November 17, 2005, Mr. Shattles filed suit in Fulton County Superior Court against defendants Bioprogress and one of its subsidiaries, BioTec Films, LLC. Defendants removed the case to this Court on December 16, 2005, based on diversity jurisdiction. On February 24, 2006, Mr. Shattles filed an amended complaint adding his spouse, Loretta Shattles, as a plaintiff and adding defendants' alleged benefit plans as additional defendants.

In their amended complaint, plaintiffs allege several claims against defendants: breach of contract, breach of trust, deprivation of personal property, breach of fiduciary duty, interference with benefits and failure to pay benefits pursuant to the Employee Retirement Income Security Act ("ERISA"), and failure to produce plan documents pursuant to ERISA. Specifically, plaintiffs state that Mr. Shattles has already exchanged 341,373 shares of his BTII Series C Preferred Stock into ordinary shares of Bioprogress stock. Plaintiffs allege that Bioprogress has consistently refused to convert the remaining 245,533 shares of Series C Preferred Stock.

On March 10, 2006, defendants answered the amended complaint and defendant Bioprogress filed a counterclaim against plaintiff Larry Shattles for breach of fiduciary duty, breach of the duty of loyalty, conversion and misappropriation, and breach of contract.

Defendants are represented in this action by Smith Moore LLP and Dechert. Plaintiffs have filed a motion to disqualify Dechert as attorneys for defendants.

. . .

DISCUSSION

Plaintiffs argue that Dechert should be disqualified from the present action because of their prior attorney-client relationship with plaintiff and because the matter embraced within the pending suit is substantially related to the matter involved in the previous representation. Plaintiffs contend that Mr. Shattles sought the advice of Dechert attorneys regarding the conversion of the Founders Stock and that Dechert attorneys advised Mr. Shattles on this conversion. In addition, plaintiffs argue that Dechert's former representation of Mr. Shattles consisted of guidance and advice regarding his decision to convert his shares of Founders Stock to Series C Preferred Stock and that the present suit focuses primarily on Bioprogress's refusal to convert those same shares of Series C Preferred Stock. Finally, plaintiffs aver that the law presumes the firm received confidential information relevant to the present action during its prior representation of plaintiff.

Defendants argue in response that Dechert never had an attorney-client relationship with plaintiff. Defendants contend that plaintiffs have failed to meet their burden or offer sufficient proof of the existence of an attorney-client relationship, and instead defendants have put forth compelling evidence that no relationship existed. Defendants assert that the Court should not allow plaintiffs to deprive defendants of their choice of counsel in this case.

The Eleventh Circuit has developed a two part test for disqualification of counsel: "first, the party seeking disqualification must prove it once enjoyed an attorney-client relationship with the opposing lawyer; and second, the movant must show that the matters embraced within the pending suit are *substantially related* to the matters or cause of action wherein the attorney previously represented it.'" In addition, Local Rule 83.1(c) states that all lawyers practicing before this Court shall be governed by the Georgia Rules of Professional Conduct. Rule 1.9(a) of the *Georgia Rules of Professional Conduct* states that "[a] lawyer who has formerly represented a client in a matter shall not thereafter represent another person in the same or a substantially related matter in which that person's interests are materially adverse to the interests of the former client unless the former client consents after consultation." When an attorney actually represents a party, the attorney is charged with a virtually unrebuttable presumption that he/she has received confidential information from the company. Moreover, one attorney's knowledge may be imputed to his current partners or employees.

The first question for the Court is whether plaintiffs have met the threshold requirement of showing that an attorney-client relationship existed between Mr. Shattles and Dechert. The basic question with regard to the formation of an attorney-client relationship is whether plaintiffs have sufficiently established that advice or assistance of the attorney is both sought and received in matters pertinent to the profession. The attorney-client relationship cannot be created unilaterally in the mind of the client, and the state of mind of the alleged client is not sufficient to create a confidential relationship. Instead, a "reasonable belief" on the part of the would-be client that he/she was being represented by the attorney is all that is necessary. A reasonable belief is defined as one which is reasonably induced by representations or conduct by the attorney. The attorney-client relationship may be expressly created by written contract or may be inferred from the parties' conduct.

The parties agree that there was no attorney-client contract and that Mr. Shattles did not pay any fees to Dechert. Therefore, the Court must look to the conduct of Mr. Shattles and Dechert attorneys to determine whether an attorney-client relationship existed. After a review of the evidence, including several emails and telephone conversations that occurred between Mr. Shattles and Dechert attorneys, the Court finds that Mr. Shattles's belief that Dechert was representing him was reasonable.

According to the email correspondence, Dechert attorney Brian McCall contacted Mr. Shattles, told him that he might have some ways to help, and requested Mr. Shattles phone number so that they could discuss the matter. Mr. Shattles accepted his offer of help and gave attorney McCall his phone number. Next, Barry Muncaster, former Chief Executive Officer of BTII, emailed Mr. Shattles that he had a note from attorney McCall and Dechert attorney David Shapiro saying that the attorneys had worked out a way to handle Mr. Shattles stock. The next email from Dechert attorney Martin Rose to Mr. Shattles asks him to confirm which kind of stock he holds. Attorney McCall later sent Mr. Shattles an email confirming a conversation he had with attorney Rose and Mr. Shattles about how the restructuring of the stock would occur. Finally, Muncaster sent an email to attorney Rose explaining that he had forwarded attorney Rose's request directly to Mr. Shattles and suggesting that attorney Rose and Mr. Shattles work directly together. The representations and conduct of Dechert attorneys, namely contacting Mr. Shattles and offering ways to help him with the stock restructuring, created a reasonable belief that Dechert attorneys were working on behalf of Mr. Shattles. After Dechert attorneys contacted Mr. Shattles, he sought their help by providing answers to their questions and in turn he received their help with the restructuring.

Mr. Shattles states in his affidavit that it was his understanding that Dechert represented him in an individual capacity. However, Mr. Shattles's subjective belief is irrelevant. Attorney McCall contends that he told Mr. Shattles on more than one occasion that Dechert represented BTII and not him individually, and that Mr. Shattles might want to consider contacting an attorney to advise him personally. On the other hand, Mr. Shattles asserts that Dechert never informed him to retain other representation. Although the parties disagree about what was said regarding Mr. Shattles acquiring outside representation, the evidence submitted does not prove that any Dechert attorneys told Mr. Shattles to acquire outside counsel or informed Mr. Shattles that Dechert was not representing him individually. The emails submitted by attorney McCall only confirm McCall's version of the facts that he had told Mr. Shattles about acquiring outside counsel. Thus, the Court concludes that plaintiffs have sufficiently established that Mr. Shattles sought and received Dechert attorneys' legal advice or assistance about the stock conversion.

Having found that an attorney-client relationship existed, the Court now turns the second prong of the *Cox* inquiry to determine whether the matters in this suit are substantially related to the matters wherein Dechert attorneys previously represented Mr. Shattles. Dechert attorneys advised Mr. Shattles on the conversion of Mr. Shattles's Founder's Stock into Series C Preferred Stock before BTII was acquired by Bioprogress. Mr. Shattles alleges in his amended complaint a breach of contract claim against defendant Bioprogress for refusing to exchange his Class C Stock in BTII into Bioprogress Stock. Mr. Shattles further alleges that defendants created a constructive trust for him when it placed his Founder's Stock into Class C Stock. Mr. Shattles contends that defendants' refusal to turnover the corpus of the trust constitutes breach of trust, and defendants' refusal to return all of the Class C Stock constitutes a theft of personal property. The Court finds that the matters wherein Dechert attorneys previously rendered advice to Mr. Shattles are substantially related to the matters now pending in this case. Dechert attorneys advised Mr. Shattles on the conversion of his Series C Preferred Stock and this stock is now the subject of this suit.

Accordingly, the Court grants plaintiffs' motion to disqualify Dechert LLP as counsel for defendants in this case. The Court is cognizant of defendants' right to freely choose its own counsel. However, the Court does not believe that the disqualification of Dechert limits this right or places an undue burden on defendants because they are also represented by Smith Moore LLP. . . .

F. Checks on Conflicts of Interest

Under Model Rule 1.7, lawyers cannot represent a new client if the representation would cause a concurrent conflict of interest with another current client *unless* both clients consent to the representation in writing and the two clients are not pitted in litigation against each other.

Similarly, a lawyer must take care not to take on cases that would cause a conflict of interest for former clients. Under Model Rule 1.9, a lawyer cannot represent a client if that client's interests are materially adverse to those of a former client unless the former client consents to the representation in writing.

Whenever a client or prospective client approaches a firm for representation, a conflict of interest check should be conducted to ascertain that the firm would not be barred from representing the client due to a conflict. Some states actually require that a formal system be established within a firm for checking conflicts. For instance, New York's *Code of Professional Responsibility* specifies the following:

(e) A law firm shall make a written record of its engagements, at or near the time of each new engagement, and shall implement and maintain a system by which proposed engagements are checked against current and previous engagements when: (1) the firm agrees to represent a new client; (2) the firm agrees to represent an existing client in a new matter; (3) the firm hires or associates with another lawyer; or (4) an additional party is named or appears in a pending matter.

(f) Substantial failure to keep records or to implement or maintain a conflict-checking system that complies with paragraph (e) shall be a violation thereof regardless or whether there is another violation of these Rules.

(g) Where a violation of paragraph (e) by a law firm is a substantial factor in causing a violation of paragraph (a) by a lawyer, the law firm, as well as the individual lawyer, shall be responsible for the violation of paragraph (a).[15]

A law office manager should develop forms to be filled out during the initial client interview so that a conflicts check can be conducted. The client's business affiliation, spouse, former spouses, and other associations should be specified on the forms and circulated within the firm so that potential conflicts of interest can be identified.

Even if there is an apparent conflict of interest, lawyers within a firm are not necessarily barred from representing a client. A firm should establish a process for obtaining conflict waivers that would allow the firm to proceed with a representation.

Traditionally, when there is a conflict, an entire firm is disqualified from representing a client with whom there's a conflict unless the client consents to the representation despite the conflict. Some states also allow lawyers to create a "Chinese wall" or **ethical wall**.[16] Model Rule 1.11 allows such a screen to be created if a government lawyer goes to work for a law firm.

ethical wall:
Also called a Chinese wall or a firewall, an unbreachable wall built around a lawyer who has a conflict of interest so that others in the firm can still work on the matter.

These screens or walls are also referred to as firewalls. Calling an ethical wall a Chinese wall is not pejorative; the reference is to the Great Wall of China's impenetrability. The idea is that, if there is a conflict of interest, an unbreachable wall will be built around the lawyer who has the conflict so that others in the firm can still work on the matter. The lawyer with the conflict will have no access to the legal materials in the case and will not discuss the matter with anyone in the firm.

For instance, suppose a former lawyer for the U.S. Department of Justice prosecuted polluters who discharged chemicals and created hazardous waste sites. If that lawyer then moves to a law firm in the private sector that represents clients who pollute hazardous waste sites and are responsible for cleaning them up, the lawyer, when he moved to the law firm, would have a firewall around him for those hazardous waste sites that he worked on while he was at the Department of Justice. The law firm could continue to represent clients at those sites. The lawyers would not discuss the case with the former government lawyer or show him any documents.

Firewalls are also used in other situations if a nongovernment lawyer has a conflict of interest. It might occur with a law firm merger, or if a prospective client interviewed with a lawyer and, for whatever reason, the two decided not to work together. The law firm (but not that particular lawyer) would then be able to go on and represent someone else in the case.

The rules on ethical walls vary by state. This matter has been very controversial. Firewalls really depend on the integrity of lawyers. It's a matter of faith and trust that the lawyer with the conflict will not secretly help out the other lawyers in the firm who are working on the case.

Lawyers should also take into account the potential for conflicts of interest stemming from the activities or prior histories of their nonlegal staff, such as paralegals.

1.   *Available Software*

Some firms use simple index cards to track all contacts. Every time a lawyer meets with a prospective client, the lawyer fills out an index card and puts the prospective client's name on it. The names of other people or businesses associated with that prospective client (such as spouse's name, the names of businesses the client owns, the names of entities the client is interested in pursuing, etc.) are included on the card. Separate cards for each name on the original card are also created and filed alphabetically.

The lawyer then checks all the names on the cards against the cards already in the firm's conflict checking file. If there's a match, the lawyer can do further research to determine whether a conflict exists. Even if no conflict is found, the lawyer should record the fact that she conducted the conflict search and the date on which the search was conducted. This can be done simply by noting this fact in a notebook kept near the files of index cards. A memorandum can also be circulated to all staff members describing, briefly, the matter and asking anyone to identify any potential conflicts of interest. Although this method is now a bit obsolete, it is still used as a backup system for software programs that can check far more potential conflicts very quickly.

A number of software programs that include conflicts checking are commercially available—for example:

- AbacusLaw by Abacus Data Systems, Inc. (http://www.abacuslaw.com)
- Amicus Attorney from Gavel & Gown Software Inc. (http://www.amicusattorney.com)
- LSS Conflict of Interest software by Legal Software Systems, Inc. (http://www.legalsoftwaresystems.com)
- Time Matters owned by Lexis-Nexis (http://pm.lexisnexis.com/store/category/?cid=66)
- Thomson Reuters's Elite Conflicts Manager (http://www.elite.com/enterprise/conflicts-manager/)

These programs tend to allow very quick searching of a vast database of names.

2.   *Software Limitations*

Any software system, or even a paper backup system, is only as good as the people who use it. These systems need to be updated constantly and checked frequently. Failure to check for conflicts of interest can prove very embarrassing for a law firm.

When one firm accidentally served a subpoena on a client that a branch office of the firm was representing, an attorney from the firm's branch office sought to quash the subpoena. Although a court pondering the situation opted not to disqualify the firm, Pepper Hamilton, for a conflict of interest, the judge on the case did scold the firm for its sloppy conflict checking. In *Beilowitz v. General Motors*, 225 F. Supp. 2d 565, 567 n.1 (D.N.J. 2002), a federal judge wrote, "I strongly urge Pepper Hamilton to improve the manner in which it conducts 'conflicts of interest' checks between its regional offices. Serving a subpoena on an existing firm client is, to say the least, a professional embarrassment to be avoided at all costs."

G. Privacy Considerations

Lawyers must be very protective of their clients. Model Rule 1.6 specifies that lawyers generally are not to even acknowledge that they represent a given client unless the client consents to the disclosure of that information.

Clients reveal confidences to their lawyers so that the lawyers can provide the best possible representation. Lawyers are also obligated to keep communications from their clients confidential unless a lawyer reasonably believes that death or substantial bodily harm to someone would result if information were not revealed. Similarly, a lawyer may reveal information if she believes it will prevent the client from committing a crime. Generally, though, a client's confidences are confidential. The **attorney-client privilege** allows a client to prevent the release of information she gave to her attorney:

> The [attorney-client] privilege applies only if (1) the asserted holder of the privilege is or sought to become a client; (2) the person to whom the communication was made (a) is a member of the bar of a court, or his subordinate and (b) in connection with this communication is acting as a lawyer; (3) the communication relates to a fact of which the attorney was informed (a) by his client (b) without the presence of strangers (c) for the purpose of securing primarily either (i) an opinion on law or (ii) legal services or (iii) assistance in some legal proceeding, and not (d) for the purpose of committing a crime or tort; and (4) the privilege has been (a) claimed and (b) not waived by the client.[17]

attorney-client privilege:
An evidentiary privilege that allows a client to prevent the release of information given by a client to her attorney.

The client has the right to waive the privilege and allow otherwise privileged materials to be disclosed.

The **work product doctrine** is similar to attorney-client privilege in that it prevents certain documents prepared by a lawyer for a client from being disclosed during the discovery process in litigation.

work product doctrine:
An evidentiary doctrine that prevents certain documents prepared by a lawyer for a client from being disclosed during the discovery process in litigation.

H. Malpractice

Disgruntled clients can file not only a grievance against an attorney but also a legal malpractice claim in an effort to recover damages. For a malpractice claim to succeed, the client must show that an attorney-relationship existed, that the attorney owed a duty to the client that the attorney breached, and that the client suffered damages as a result.[18]

If a client does file suit against her lawyer, confidential information provided by the client can generally be used by the lawyer to defend himself against the suit, but the lawyer must take care not to disclose too much information that would go beyond that necessary to defend such a lawsuit.[19] Model Rule 1.6(b)(5) does allow lawyers to reveal information about the representation of a client in controversies between the client and the lawyer.

I.   Special Problems

As you learn about the Model Rules of Professional Conduct and about the specific rules applicable to lawyers in your area, consider whether these rules have kept abreast with technological advances and changing times, or whether they are outdated. Would you alter applicable rules in any way? If so, why do you suppose greater change has not already been implemented? Keep these questions in mind as you learn about some special problems arising in the area of legal ethics.

1.   Megafirms and Conflicts

As law firms grow larger and larger, conflicts become harder and harder to avoid as megafirms pick up practice groups, or even entire law firms through mergers. With fewer law firms to choose from, major corporate clients are likely to have used many major law firms, or many of their now-dispersed lawyers, at points in the not-too-distant past. Lawyers and those who work with them at these megafirms must take great care not to indulge in impermissible conflicts of interest.

Often that great care means that clients are more likely to be asked to sign waivers. Major clients may well be disinclined to sign such a waiver. Consider the impact that such a refusal may have on the relationship between the refusing client and the law firm. Now the law firm is prevented from making additional money from another client. Is it possible the relationship with the refusing client might now sour? Might the refusing client very much feel pressured to agree to a waiver that it really does not want to sign?

As law firms grow ever larger, lawyers must also be strategic in how they sign clients. Signing on a midsize client now might mean that the firm will need to forego representation of a very large competitor at some point in the future. Some believe that "a bird in the hand is worth two in the bush" — or that a paying client right now is better than the prospect of a better client in the future. Others might want the firm to pursue a business plan that seeks to land the larger clients and could be willing to disregard smaller clients that do not fit into that plan. Whether and to what extent conflicts may arise and whether either client will be willing to waive certain conflicts is a matter that should be contemplated before new clients are accepted.

2.   Virtual Law Offices

In the age of the Internet, where everyone can work from home, ethical rules pertaining to lawyers have posed particular problems. In the minds of some, ethical rules have not kept pace with technological advances. Others, however, think that those longtime rules provide protections to clients and to the legal profession at a moment of dramatic change. Concerns about supervision of attorneys and support staff, requirements for disclosing location, bar admission, and advertising the address of the legal practice can arise. For instance, if everyone in a law firm is working remotely, can a lawyer properly supervise a paralegal? If a lawyer is working from home, must she disclose her address in advertising? She might be concerned about the general public, and even clients, having her home address. If a lawyer is working from home, must that "home" be in the same state where she is admitted to practice? If not, could the attorney brush up against unauthorized-practice-of-law statutes in her home state?

The advantage of virtual law offices, aside from convenience for the attorney, is that overhead costs will be lower than those associated with brick-and-mortar law firms, and those savings could be passed along to clients. In addition, there's greater convenience for clients who interact with their lawyers via the Internet rather than having to set up in-person appointments at a law office.

Rules of professional responsibility must still be met, no matter where an attorney works. Acknowledging that clients are interested in obtaining legal services online, the eLawyering Task Force of the Law Practice Management Section of the American Bar Association formulated suggested minimum requirements for virtual law offices that identify some of the problems that can arise with such a practice and proposed means to thwart those problems.[20] In 2010, the Pennsylvania Bar Association Committee on Ethics and Professional Responsibility, in an advisory opinion that is not binding on the courts of the commonwealth, explicitly approved virtual law offices for lawyers practicing law in Pennsylvania.[21]

3. Temptations in the Digital Age

As much as technological innovations and ease of access to computers has helped lawyers provide legal services to clients more efficiently and cost-effectively, the ease of communication and mass broadcasting over the Internet, combined with security threats about confidential information being hacked or accidentally disclosed to a broad audience, have also given rise to some unique ethical and business quandaries.

Cloud computing has allowed lawyers and those who work for them, as well as clients, much greater access to data. A lawyer with a computer tablet, or even a smartphone, can access documents from a courthouse or from any remote location, as can a client. Massive amounts of documents can be stored "in the cloud" and searched more easily. Cloud-based storage providers include Dropbox (https://www.dropbox.com), Total Attorneys (http://www.totalattorneys.com), and Uptime Systems (http://www.uptimesystems.net). Even e-mail services such as Gmail and Hotmail are examples of cloud-based storage.

Working in the cloud, lawyers, clients, and others can collaborate more quickly and easily by marking up documents online via a secure site. The danger with such advances, however, is that security could possibly be breached and confidential information could be disseminated more widely than in the days when all documents were stored electronically in personal computers or internal computer

cloud computing: Use of remote servers for data and management allowing users to access data from any computer with an Internet connection (rather than programs and other materials being stored directly in one's personal computer or internal network).

networks. In this context, then, a lawyer's ethical obligation to protect a client's confidential information becomes even more important.

Recognizing that lawyers increasingly use cloud-based services, Model Rule 1.6(c), added in 2012, now requires lawyers to make reasonable efforts to prevent the disclosure of or unauthorized access to a client's information.[22] To help protect information stored in the cloud, lawyers should thoroughly research the credentials of vendors, develop an understanding of how information will be secured, and have a secure agreement in place that addresses confidentiality of information, payment, and notice regarding data in the case of nonpayment, and other matters of special concern to lawyers.[23]

Social media sites such as Facebook, LinkedIn, and Twitter have provided venues for lawyers and others to foster their reputations, to communicate quickly and easily with a vast audience, and to demonstrate their expertise. They also can be hazardous for lawyers who must comply with ethical rules. What contacts are inappropriate? Should a lawyer "Facebook friend" a judge? Is communication via social networking sites deemed to be advertising? Could a simple LinkedIn endorsement somehow be problematic? Consider the following:

> A somewhat thornier question is presented by the "recommendations" section of LinkedIn but fortunately not in Texas, because while some states prohibit the use of testimonials, Texas does not. But users should still prescreen recommendations before they are posted for public view. Be sure that the recommendation content complies with the disciplinary rules—Rule 7.02(4) prohibits comparisons to other lawyers' services, unless substantiated by verifiable objective data. Therefore, your client cannot say that you are "the best trial lawyer in town"—that would be a prohibited comparison. Also, be sure to avoid making reciprocal recommendations where the lawyer agrees to post a recommendation in exchange for receiving one. Rule 7.03(b) prohibits giving anything of value to a non-lawyer for soliciting prospective clients.[24]

Social networking sites, in addition to being great places to network, can also be fantastic sources of information about people. A lawyer who is following a judge, or an opponent, on such a site might glean information about that person's interests, sense of humor, work ethic, or whereabouts at a particular point in time. A lawyer posting offensive or inappropriate comments—about clients, cases, or other matters—could find himself subject to disciplinary action.[25] For instance, a lawyer who posts a status update like "Another great victory in court today! My client is delighted. Who wants to be next?" violates rules against client testimonials and requiring advertisements to be labeled, according to the State Bar of California Standing Committee on Professional Responsibility and Conduct.[26]

Checklist

- Legal ethics are minimum standards of behavior that lawyers must observe.
- Lawyers have a fiduciary duty to their clients.
- To be admitted to the bar, lawyers must demonstrate that they have a character fit for the practice of law.
- The *Model Rules of Professional Conduct* are ethical rules developed by the American Bar Association. Most states have enacted some version of the rules or of the older *Model Code of Professional Responsibility*.
- Both lawyers and paralegals must take care not to engage in the unauthorized practice of law. Lawyers cannot practice law in states in which they are not admitted to the bar.
- A lawyer cannot avoid her ethical responsibilities by delegating inappropriate tasks to staff members.
- The *Model Rules of Professional Conduct* require lawyers who are managers at law firms to make sure that the firm has measures in place to ensure that nonlawyer employees conform to lawyers' professional conduct rules (Model Rule 5.3).
- The *ABA Model Guidelines for the Utilization of Paralegal Services* address lawyers' responsibilities for supervising paralegals.
- A paralegal who violates ethical rules risks being fired, being subject to a civil suit by a disgruntled client, and being sanctioned by courts.
- Lawyers have a duty of confidentiality even to prospective clients who ultimately do not hire the lawyers.
- Lawyers cannot represent a new client if the representation would cause a concurrent conflict of interest with another current client *unless* both clients consent to the representation in writing (Model Rule 1.7).
- Lawyers cannot represent a client if that client's interests are materially adverse to those of a former client unless the former client consents to the representation in writing (Model Rule 1.9).
- Law firms should have a system for checking conflicts of interest.
- If a lawyer has an apparent conflict of interest, the lawyer might still be able to represent a client if a waiver is obtained from both the client and from the client with whom there is a conflict.
- Traditionally, when there is a conflict, an entire firm is disqualified from representing a client with whom there's a conflict unless the client consents to the representation despite the conflict.
- Some states allow lawyers to create a "Chinese wall" or "ethical wall," a firewall around lawyers who have conflicts of interest. The lawyer with the conflict will have no access to the legal materials in the case for which there is a conflict, and the lawyer will not discuss the matter with anyone in the firm.
- Software programs can check for conflicts of interest.
- Lawyers should protect a client's privacy. Lawyers generally are not to even acknowledge that they represent a given client unless the client consents to the disclosure of that information (Model Rule 1.6).

- A dissatisfied client can bring an attorney malpractice suit to recover damages.
- As law firms evolve into megafirms, lawyers may be faced with more conflicts. A strategy for signing on clients should be developed so that the firm can make a rational decision about taking on work from a client if it anticipates a conflict with other prospective clients in the future.
- Rules of professional responsibility must still be adhered to by lawyers working in virtual law offices.
- Measures to protect client confidentiality when using cloud computing should be undertaken.
- Social networking sites provide opportunities to those working in the legal field, but inappropriate postings or activities via such sites can conflict with ethical obligations.

Vocabulary

admittance pro hac vice (p. 93)
attorney-client privilege (p. 101)
cloud computing (p. 103)
disbarment (p. 87)
disciplinary action (p. 87)

ethical wall (p. 99)
fiduciary duty (p. 86)
grievance (p. 87)
work product doctrine (p. 101)

Career Preparation Tips

As you have learned throughout this chapter, ethical quandaries can arise in many elements of a law business, even when a lawyer is not representing someone. Consider where in a law firm you might want to work and contemplate the ethical obligations associated with working in that department. How might ethical problems be prevented? What procedural mechanisms can be put into place to minimize the risk that an ethical problem will arise? How might you demonstrate your knowledge of these ethical concerns and the means to address them during a job interview or in a cover letter seeking an interview?

You might open a career file and start a subfolder on points to raise in an interview or in correspondence. Remember to keep writing samples and to categorize those samples so that you submit appropriate ones to prospective employers.

If You Want to Learn More

ABA *Model Rules of Professional Conduct*. http://www.americanbar
.org/groups/professional_responsibility/publications/model_rules_of_
professional_conduct/model_rules_of_professional_conduct_table_of_
contents.html

ABA Model Guidelines for the Utilization of Paralegal Services
. http://apps.americanbar.org/legalservices/paralegals/downloads
/modelguidelines.pdf

ABA Commission on Ethics 20/20. http://apps.americanbar.org/dch
/committee.cfm?com=SC105020&new

ABA Standing Committee on Client Protection. http://www.americanbar
.org/groups/professional_responsibility/committees_commissions
/standingcommitteeonclientprotection.html

ABA Standing Committee on Lawyers' Professional Liability. http://www
.americanbar.org/groups/lawyers_professional_liability.htmlDirectory of
Lawyer Disciplinary Agencies. http://www.americanbar.org/content
/dam/aba/administrative/professional_responsibility/current_
disciplinary_agency_directory_online.authcheckdam.pdf-15k-2013-04-09

National Association of Legal Assistants, Inc. http://www.nala.org

National Client Protection Organization, Inc. http://www.ncpo.org

National Organization of Bar Counsel. http://www.nobc.org

National Federation of Paralegal Associations. http://www.paralegals.org

Michigan State Bar Association's *Guidelines for the Utilization of Legal
Assistant Services*. http://www.michbar.org/opinions/ethics/utilization
.cfm

Reading Comprehension

1. What must someone who wants to be lawyer do to be admitted to the bar?
2. What types of disciplinary actions can be taken against lawyers who violate ethical rules?
3. Who disciplines attorneys?
4. Are paralegals subject to the Model Rules of Professional Conduct?
5. How can a lawyer engage in the unauthorized practice of law?

6. When can an ethical wall be used?
7. What is a check on conflicts of interest?
8. In what circumstances can a lawyer reveal confidential information?
9. What are the elements of a malpractice claim?
10. What ethical issues are common to virtual law offices, cloud computing, and social networking sites?

Discussion Starters

1. Research statistics on disciplinary actions in your state. What are the most frequent types of violations that lawyers in your state commit? What types of punishments are meted out most frequently?
2. Look up and compare the application for bar admissions of two states. Does one ask more invasive questions than the other? Would a person with bipolar disorder be admitted? Would a person who has declared bankruptcy be admitted? May people with bipolar disorder or who have declared bankruptcy remain members of the bar if they are diagnosed or seek bankruptcy protection after admission? How do the number of disciplinary actions against attorneys in the two states compare?
3. Look up one recent legal decision in which an attorney was disbarred. What infraction was involved? How might the lawyer have avoided such a severe disciplinary action?
4. Read *James v. Shapiro*. How did the law firm characterize the legal secretary who brought the action? Did the legal secretary agree with the law firm's explanation of her work history at the firm?
5. Look up the unauthorized practice of law statute in your state. Does the statute really bar nonlawyers from engaging in any form of law practice? May a nonlawyer represent herself pro se in court? Is the "practice of law" defined? May a nonlawyer draft a will for himself? Is that practicing law? May a nonlawyer find a sample contract online and give it to a friend to use to draft a contract? Would that be the unauthorized practice of law?
6. Review *Shattles v. Bioprogress PLC*. How did the dispute addressed in the case arise? Did the plaintiff seeking to have the law firm disqualified from representing the defendant have a written contract with the law firm? Why did the court determine that an attorney-client relationship existed between the firm and the plaintiff?
7. Look up and read *Owens v. First Family Financial Services*, 379 F. Supp. 2d 840 (S.D. Miss. 2005). Who was determined to have a conflict of interest in the case? Why wasn't an ethical wall sufficient to shield the person who had the conflict of interest?
8. Select three commercially available conflict-of-interest programs. Which would be ideal for a large firm? Which would be optimal for a sole practitioner?

9. Consider the following excerpt from *City & County of San Francisco v. Cobra Solutions, Inc.*, 38 Cal. 4th 839, 847–48, 43 Cal. Rptr. 3d 771, 135 P.3d 20 (2006) (internal citations and quotation marks omitted), *quoted in J2 Global Communications, Inc. v. Easylink Services International Corp.*, No. CV 09–04189 DDP (AJWx), 2012 WL 6618609 at *4 (C.D. Cal. Dec. 19, 2012):

   > That enduring duty to preserve client confidences precludes an attorney from later agreeing to represent an adversary of the attorney's former client unless the former client provides an informed written consent waiving the conflict. If the attorney fails to obtain such consent and undertakes to represent the adversary, the former client may disqualify the attorney by showing a substantial relationship between the subjects of the prior and the current representations. To determine whether there is a substantial relationship between successive representations, a court must first determine whether the attorney had a direct professional relationship with the former client in which the attorney personally provided legal advice and services on a legal issue that is closely related to the legal issue in the present representation. If the former representation involved such a direct relationship with the client, the former client need not prove that the attorney possesses actual confidential information. Instead, the attorney is presumed to possess confidential information if the subject of the prior representation put the attorney in a position in which confidences material to the current representation would normally have been imparted to counsel. . . . When a substantial relationship between the two representations is established, the attorney is automatically disqualified from representing the second client. . . . Vicarious disqualification rules are a product of decisional law. Normally, an attorney's conflict is imputed to the law firm as a whole on the rationale that attorneys, working together and practicing law in a professional association, share each other's, and their clients', confidential information.

   Is the concept of "vicarious disqualification" fair to attorneys who have no actual knowledge of confidential information about one of their colleagues' clients? Should attorneys be vicariously qualified? Consider the decision by the court in *J2 Global Communications* (cited above), in which the above excerpt was quoted. Did the court in that case disqualify a law firm from a representation that had not done anything wrong or hired an attorney with a conflict of interest? Was the outcome in that case fair?

10. Look up the *Code of Ethics and Professional Responsibility* issued by the National Association of Legal Assistants, Inc., at http://www.nala.org/code.aspx. Is the code fair to legal assistants? What portions of the code would be most difficult to adhere to? What would you do if, as a legal assistant, your supervisor asked you to do something that would require you to violate the code?

11. Research letters that waive conflicts of interest. For instance, take a look at one available on the Milwaukee Bar Association's Professionalism Committee Web site, at http://www.milwbar.org/pdf/formletter_4.pdf. Compare and contrast several letters. What elements should such a letter include?

Case Studies

1. A trucking company wants to retain your law firm to represent it in litigation over the cleanup of a hazardous waste site in New Jersey. Many years ago, the company hauled waste to the site and dumped it there. Now the federal government is suing polluters of the site to recover its cleanup costs. Your firm also represents a chemical company that sent its trash to the site. Can your firm represent the trucking company as well?

2. Your law firm has its only office in California. One of the firm's clients is sued in Nevada. How can a lawyer from the firm represent the client in the Nevada litigation?

3. Suppose you are a paralegal in a law firm. A friend of yours is having trouble with her landlord. The apartment has leaking pipes, and the heat isn't working properly. Your friends asks you to do her a favor and send a threatening letter to the landlord on law firm letterhead so the landlord will be intimidated and fix up the property. You do. Have you violated any ethical rules? Has an attorney-client relationship been established?

4. A paralegal in a law firm is calculating the amount of time she worked on a client's case. Her supervising attorney tells her to "round up" when determining the hours worked on the matter. Have any ethical rules been broken? What should the paralegal do?

5. A law firm's nonlawyer marketing coordinator, charged with updating and maintaining the firm's Web site, revised it to specify that one practice group at the firm specializes in sustainability and helps businesses report their sustainability progress to their stockholders and customers. The firm's practice group has, in fact, done this. Have any rules of professional responsibility been broken? Could a supervising attorney be held responsible for the breaking of any of these rules?

6. A lawyer tweets that her opposing counsel in a civil trial looks "fresh-faced and inexperienced." What rules of professional responsibility may have been violated?

7. A hacker breached a cloud computing service and gained access to drafts of a client's contract for sale of his company to a larger company. What actions should the client's lawyer and law firm take?

Endnotes

1. *Black's Law Dictionary* 913 (8th ed. 2004) (emphasis supplied).
2. *See* American Bar Association, Model Rules of Prof'l Conduct Preamble ¶9, http://www.americanbar.org/groups/professional_responsibility/publications/model_rules_of_professional_conduct/model_rules_of_professional_conduct_preamble_scope.html.
3. Leslie C. Levin, *The Ethical World of Solo and Small Law Firm Practitioners*, 41 Hous. L. Rev. 309, 370 (2004).

4. *Black's Law Dictionary* 545 (8th ed. 2004).

5. *See, e.g., Gorski v. Smith,* 2002 Pa. Super. 334 ¶71 ("In *Maritrans GP Inc. v. Pepper, Hamilton & Scheetz,* 529 Pa. 241, 602 A.2d 1277 (Pa. 1992) our Supreme Court specifically recognized that an attorney owes a fiduciary duty to his or her client and is bound to execute that fiduciary duty properly. The Supreme Court held that part of the fiduciary duty which arises out of the attorney client relationship is that of undivided loyalty. This duty, the Court emphasized, prohibits an attorney from engaging in activity which constitutes a conflict of interest, and the Court held that a breach of that duty by the attorney is actionable.").

6. For interesting commentary on whether bar admission questionnaires are effective or too invasive, see, e.g., Melody Moezzi, *Lawyers of Sound Mind,* N.Y. Times (Aug. 5, 2013), http://www.nytimes.com/2013/08/06/opinion/lawyers-of-sound-mind.html.

7. American Bar Association, *Model Rules of Prof'l Conduct,* http://www.americanbar.org/groups/professional_responsibility/publications/model_rules_of_professional_conduct.html (last updated Aug. 8, 2013).

8. *In re Snyder,* 472 U.S. 634, 644-45 (1985).

9. *Laddcap Value Partners, LP v. Lowenstein Sandler, PC,* No. 600973-2007, slip op. at 2 (N.Y. Sup. Ct. Dec. 5, 2007).

10. *Id.*

11. *Id.* at 5.

12. *Id.* at 8 (quoting *Matter of Vincenti,* 554 A.2d 479, 474 (N.J. 1989)).

13. Carol Ann Martinelli, interviewer, *Career Paths: Donald D. Campbell,* Law Practice Today (June 2013), *available at* http://www.americanbar.org/content/newsletter/publications/law_practice_today_home/lpt-archives/june13/career-paths0613.html.

14. *See, e.g.,* Restatement (Third) of the Law Governing Lawyers §4 (2000).

15. N.Y. Rules of Professional Conduct 1.10(e)–(f), 22 N.Y. Comp. Codes R. & Regs. §1200.0 (2013).

16. 32 Am. Jur. 2d Federal Courts § 158 (2013).

17. *United States v. United Shoe Machinery Corp.,* 89 F. Supp. 357, 358-59 (D. Mass. 1950).

18. Richard H.W. Maloy, *Proximate Cause: The Final Defense in Legal Malpractice Cases,* 36 U. Mem. L. Rev. 655, 658-59 (2006).

19. *See, e.g.,* Carole J. Buckner & Robert K. Sall, *Ethically Speaking: The Self-Defense Exception to the Ethical Duty of Confidentiality,* 48 Orange County Law. 59, 61 (July 2006).

20. A.B.A. Law Practice Management Section eLawyering Task Force, *Suggested Minimum Requirements for Law Firms Delivering Legal Services Online* (Oct. 15, 2009).

21. Pa. Bar Ass'n Comm. on Legal Ethics & Prof'l Responsibility, Formal Op. 2010-200.

22. Ashley Hallene, *Clearing Up the Cloud,* 20 GP Solo 1 (Jan./Feb. 2013), *available at* http://www.americanbar.org/publications/gp_solo/2013/january_february/clearing_cloud.html.

23. J. Walter Sinclair, *Litigating in the Cloud — Security Issues for the Trial Practice* (presented at International Association of Defense Counsel 2013 Annual Meeting July 2013), *available at* http://www.iadcmeetings.mobi/meeting-materials/. *See also* State Bar of Cal. Standing Comm. on Prof'l Responsibility & Conduct, Formal Op. 2012-184.

24. Michael C. Smith, *Social Media Update,* 62 The Advoc. (Tex.) 197 (Spring 2013).

25. *See, e.g.,* John G. Browning, *Facebook, Twitter, and LinkedIn — Oh My! The ABA Ethics 20/20 Commission and Evolving Ethical Issues in the Use of Social Media,* 40 N. Ky. L. Rev. 255 (2013); *Lawyers and LinkedIn Endorsements: Proceed with Caution,* 101 Ill. B.J. 14 (Jan. 2013); Anna P. Hemingway, *Keeping It Real: Using Facebook Posts to Teach Professional Responsibility and Professionalism,* 43 N.M. L. Rev. 43 (Spring 2013).

26. State Bar of Cal. Standing Comm. on Prof'l Responsibility & Conduct, Formal Op. 2012-186.

5

Human Resources

Chapter Outcomes

By the end of this chapter, a student will be able to:

- Explain the importance of a law firm's mission statement
- Prepare a law firm history
- Contrast different types of employment within a firm
- Discuss applicable employment statutes within the context of the legal workplace
- Identify appropriate recruiting, hiring, and termination practices
- Assemble an employee handbook

To function effectively as a business, a law firm needs to be staffed by lawyers and nonlegal personnel who, in turn, need to be paid regularly and promptly. Benefits packages must be developed and maintained, schedules coordinating holiday and summertime absences must be developed, and applicable state and federal laws regulating the workplace must be followed.

The responsibilities for these tasks fall to someone charged with human resources management. In large law firms, an entire department might have these duties. In a small one, a law office manager might do these jobs as part of his day-to-day responsibilities. Details about recruiting and hiring staff fall to the human resources group, as do responsibilities for training personnel. A forward-thinking human resources staff is also concerned with employee retention and workplace morale.

At the very least, a successful human resources team must stay abreast of developments in employment law. As this chapter will demonstrate, failure to follow appropriate employment statutes can be very expensive.

A. Firm Mission Statement and History

mission statement:
A short description of the law firm explaining the type of work it undertakes and perhaps describing the firm's overall philosophy.

Leaders at law firms typically agree on a **mission statement**, a short description of the law firm explaining the type of work it undertakes and perhaps describing the firm's overall philosophy. A mission statement might be drafted by a law office manager and then tweaked by upper-level lawyers at the firm. The mission statement should identify the core values of the firm. The mission statement educates people about the firm's capabilities as well as its perspective and approach to the law. By reviewing a mission statement, both clients and prospective hires can learn where the law firm stands on certain issues—whether they are quality-of-life matters, particulars about billable hours and client service, the types of cases the firm focuses on, or the firm's understanding of a lawyer's role.

In drafting—and agreeing on—a mission statement, lawyers, unfortunately, sometimes end up writing a series of platitudes that could essentially describe any number of firms. For instance, a firm might describe itself in a mission statement as a "full-service firm where client service is paramount." Many firms, even ones that do not have enough staff to be truly full service and able to handle any legal problem, describe themselves in such a general way.

Ideally, a mission statement should be a straightforward explanation of who the law firm is, why it exists, and what it can do for clients. Distinguishing characteristics—key elements that separate the firm from its competition—should be included in the statement. Specific practice areas might be identified along with general categories of clients, such as businesses, Fortune 500 corporations, individuals, insurance companies, or criminal defendants.

The mission statement helps lawyers, staff, and clients understand the purpose and the approach of the law firm. The statement can be very useful to the firm itself as a basic guideline for making important business decisions. For instance, if the firm brands itself as a full-service one, then its long-range hiring plans might include expansion to points around the globe. The mission statement can be useful to prospective hires in educating them about the firm. By reviewing the mission statement, a job candidate can inform herself about the prospective law firm and decide whether the firm's approach and outlook are appealing.

In addition to crafting mission statements, some firms commission book-length histories. Some law firms in the United States have now been in existence for more than a century. A **firm history** can provide insight into how the firm, as an institution, has made its decisions and tell what has worked in the past and, possibly, what has not worked so well. Recitations of big wins and successful strategies create a bit of an institutional memory, which may fade with time and turnover. Lawyers who are aware of their firm's historical perspective have a better understanding of the organization they work for, why it functions as it does, and how and why it has historically succeeded.

firm history:
An explanation of a firm's purpose.

A firm history might discuss the founders of the firm, why the firm was originally formed, and how and why the firm expanded into different areas of law over the years. Both a mission statement and a firm history can be helpful recruiting and retention tools, giving prospective and current employees some understanding of what a firm is about, why it came into being, and how they are part of a team and of a tradition.

B.   Employment Law

Both federal and state laws govern employment conditions in workplaces. To function well, a law firm's human resources staff should be familiar with the intricacies of these laws and with their applicability to a given firm. Some laws apply only to businesses that have a threshold number of employees.

1.   *Types of Employment*

a)   EMPLOYMENT AT WILL

Typically, law firm staff, as well as associates, are **employees at will.** In other words, they do not have a contract with the firm specifying a period of employment. Rather, they work "at will." This means that either the employer or the employee can end the arrangement at any time.

employment at will:
A work relationship that has no contract and can be terminated at any time by either the employer or the employee.

b)   CONTRACT EMPLOYEES

To avoid the costs associated with recruiting new associates and grooming them for eventual partnership positions, law firms are increasingly turning to contract attorneys to help them with mundane, routine work. **Contract employees** might be hired to perform a certain job or to work for the firm for a certain period of time. When the job is finished or the time period ends, so does the contract attorney's employment with the firm. These positions typically offer no promotion potential. They can be attractive to lawyers who are unwilling to work the number of billable hours required of associates who are on the partnership track. The downside is that these positions are less prestigious and typically the work is not especially intellectually stimulating.

contract employee:
Someone hired on a temporary basis and typically with no benefits.

Some law firms are also hiring paralegals as contract employees to do work on a provisional basis, either for a certain time period or until a specified project is concluded. Again, the advantage to law firms is that they do not need to maintain a high level of staffing during slower periods.

2.   *Federal Statutes*

Although employment at a firm may be on an at-will basis (meaning, essentially, that employment can end at any time), employers are nevertheless bound to follow laws that are applicable to them. A discussion of some pertinent federal employment laws follows.

a)   EQUAL EMPLOYMENT OPPORTUNITY ACT

Title VII of the Civil Rights Act of 1964 prohibits employment discrimination based on race, color, religion, sex, or national origin. The law, which applies to employers with 15 or more employees, makes it unlawful to "fail or refuse to hire or to discharge any individual, or otherwise to discriminate against any individual with respect to his compensation, terms, conditions, or privileges of employment, because of such individual's race, color, religion, sex, or national origin."[1]

The law was amended in 1978 to bar discrimination on the basis of pregnancy.

Court decisions have interpreted Title VII to bar sexual harassment in the workplace. **Sexual harassment** is defined as follows:

sexual harassment:
Inappropriate advances, requests for sexual favors, or verbal or physical conduct of a sexual nature.

> Unwelcome sexual advances, requests for sexual favors, and other verbal or physical conduct of a sexual nature constitute sexual harassment when (1) submission to such conduct is made either explicitly or implicitly a term or condition of an individual's employment, (2) submission to or rejection of such conduct by an individual is used as the basis for employment decisions affecting such individual, or (3) such conduct has the purpose or effect of unreasonably interfering with an individual's work performance or creating an intimidating, hostile, or offensive working environment.[2]

Title VII also created the Equal Employment Opportunity Commission, a five-member commission charged with implementing and enforcing the statute and investigating complaints against employers. The commission is empowered to pursue violators in court.

The law has been strengthened by providing for compensatory and punitive damages for victims of intentional discrimination. Discrimination lawsuits may now be presented to juries rather than simply heard by judges.

Hishon v. King & Spalding
467 U.S. 69 (1984)

PRIOR HISTORY: **CERTIORARI TO THE UNITED STATES COURT OF APPEALS FOR THE ELEVENTH CIRCUIT.**

JUDGES: BURGER, C.J., DELIVERED THE OPINION FOR A UNANIMOUS COURT. POWELL, J., FILED A CONCURRING OPINION.

OPINION

Chief Justice BURGER delivered the opinion of the Court.

[1A] We granted certiorari to determine whether the District Court properly dismissed a Title VII complaint alleging that a law partnership discriminated against petitioner, a woman lawyer employed as an associate, when it failed to invite her to become a partner.

I

A

In 1972 petitioner Elizabeth Anderson Hishon accepted a position as an associate with respondent, a large Atlanta law firm established as a general partnership. When this suit was filed in 1980, the firm had more than 50 partners and employed approximately 50 attorneys as associates. Up to that time, no woman had ever served as a partner at the firm.

Petitioner alleges that the prospect of partnership was an important factor in her initial decision to accept employment with respondent. She alleges that respondent used the possibility of ultimate partnership as a recruiting device to induce petitioner and other young lawyers to become associates at the firm. According to the complaint, respondent represented that advancement to partnership after five or six years was "a matter of course" for associates "who [received] satisfactory evaluations" and that associates were promoted to partnership "on a fair and equal basis." Petitioner alleges that she relied on these representations when she accepted employment with respondent. The complaint further alleges that respondent's promise to consider her on a "fair and equal basis" created a binding employment contract.

In May 1978 the partnership considered and rejected Hishon for admission to the partnership; one year later, the partners again declined to invite her to become a partner. Once an associate is passed over for partnership at respondent's firm, the associate is notified to begin seeking employment elsewhere. Petitioner's employment as an associate terminated on December 31, 1979.

B

Hishon filed a charge with the Equal Employment Opportunity Commission on November 19, 1979, claiming that respondent had discriminated against her on the basis of her sex in violation of Title VII of the Civil Rights Act of 1964, . . . 42 U.S.C. §2000e *et seq.* Ten days later the Commission issued a notice of right to sue, and on February 27, 1980, Hishon brought this action in the United States District Court for the Northern District of Georgia. She sought declaratory and injunctive relief, backpay, and compensatory damages "in lieu of reinstatement and promotion to partnership." This, of course, negates any claim for specific performance of the contract alleged.

The District Court dismissed the complaint on the ground that Title VII was inapplicable to the selection of partners by a partnership. . . . A divided panel of the United States Court of Appeals for the Eleventh Circuit affirmed. We granted certiorari, . . . and we reverse.

II

At this stage of the litigation, we must accept petitioner's allegations as true. A court may dismiss a complaint only if it is clear that no relief could be granted under any set of facts that could be proved consistent with the allegations. . . . The issue before us is whether petitioner's allegations state a claim under Title VII, the relevant portion of which provides as follows:

"(a) *It shall be an unlawful employment practice for an employer —*
"(1) to fail or refuse to hire or to discharge any individual, or otherwise to *discriminate against any individual with respect to his* compensation, *terms, conditions, or privileges of employment, because of such individual's* race, color, religion, *sex,* or national origin." 42 U.S.C. §2000e-2(a) (emphasis added).

Petitioner alleges that respondent is an "employer" to whom Title VII is addressed.[3] She then asserts that consideration for partnership was one of the "terms, conditions, or privileges of employment" as an associate with respondent. . . . If this is correct, respondent could not base an adverse partnership decision on "race, color, religion, sex, or national origin."

Once a contractual relationship of employment is established, the provisions of Title VII attach and govern certain aspects of that relationship. In the context of Title VII, the contract of employment may be written or oral, formal or informal; an informal contract of employment may arise by the simple act of handing a job applicant a shovel and providing a workplace. The contractual relationship of employment triggers the provision of Title VII governing "terms, conditions, or privileges of employment." Title VII in turn forbids discrimination on the basis of "race, color, religion, sex, or national origin."

Because the underlying employment relationship is contractual, it follows that the "terms, conditions, or privileges of employment" clearly include benefits that are part of an employment contract. Here, petitioner in essence alleges that respondent made a contract to consider her for partnership. Indeed, this promise was allegedly a key contractual provision which induced her to accept employment. If the evidence at trial establishes that the parties contracted to have petitioner considered for partnership, that promise clearly was a term, condition, or privilege of her employment. Title VII would then bind respondent to consider petitioner for partnership as the statute provides, *i.e.*, without regard to petitioner's sex. The contract she alleges would lead to the same result.

. . .

B

Respondent contends that advancement to partnership may never qualify as a term, condition, or privilege of employment for purposes of Title VII. First, respondent asserts that elevation to partnership entails a change in status from an "employee" to an "employer." However, even if respondent is correct that a partnership invitation is not itself an offer of employment, Title VII would nonetheless apply and preclude discrimination on the basis of sex. The benefit a plaintiff is denied need not *be* employment to fall within Title VII's protection; it need only be a term, condition, or privilege *of* employment. It is also of no consequence that employment as an associate necessarily ends when an associate becomes a partner. A benefit need not accrue before a person's employment is completed to be a term, condition, or privilege of that employment relationship. Pension

---

[3] The statute defines an "employer" as a "person engaged in an industry affecting commerce who has fifteen or more employees for each working day in each of twenty or more calendar weeks in the current or preceding calendar year," §2000e(b), and a "person" is explicitly defined to include "partnerships," §2000e(a). The complaint alleges that respondent's partnership satisfies these requirements. App. 6.

benefits, for example, qualify as terms, conditions, or privileges of employment even though they are received only after employment terminates. . . . Accordingly, nothing in the change in status that advancement to partnership might entail means that partnership consideration falls outside the terms of the statute. . . .

We conclude that petitioner's complaint states a claim cognizable under Title VII. Petitioner therefore is entitled to her day in court to prove her allegations. The judgment of the Court of Appeals is reversed, and the case is remanded for further proceedings consistent with this opinion.

It is so ordered.

b) FAIR LABOR STANDARDS ACT

Overtime pay requirements, as well as minimum wage requirements, are governed by the Fair Labor Standards Act.[3] Periodically, the minimum wage is raised. "Time and a half," or 1.5 times an employee's regular pay rate, must be paid for overtime work, which is hours worked in excess of 40 per week. Some exemptions from these requirements are provided for administrative, professional, executive, outside sales, and certain computer employees.

The U.S. Department of Labor is empowered to pursue backpay from employers who have underpaid employees in violation of the statute. Both civil and criminal actions might be brought. Employees may also bring suit. Employers can be liable for backpay and for an equal amount as liquidated damages. Violators of the statute are subject to fines as well as imprisonment.

c) AMERICANS WITH DISABILITIES ACT

The Americans with Disabilities Act of 1990[4] bars discrimination against people with disabilities who are otherwise qualified to perform a job. Employers are required to make reasonable accommodation for employees so long as that accommodation does not cause undue hardship.

The statute, as amended, now applies to employers with 15 or more employees (Originally, only employers with 25 or more employees were subject to its requirements.)

The law also prohibits discrimination against people with disabilities by people or businesses who run a place of "public accommodation."

"Disabilities" are not defined very specifically in the statute. A disability is deemed to be "(A) a physical or mental impairment that substantially limits one or more of the major life activities of such individual; (B) a record of such an impairment; or (C) being regarded as having such an impairment . . . ."[5]

Both individuals as well as the federal government may bring suit against employers for violations of the statute.

Settlement Agreement Between The United States of America and Joseph David Camacho, Esquire, Albuquerque, New Mexico Under the Americans with Disabilities
Act DJ #202-49-37

BACKGROUND

1. This matter was initiated by a complaint filed under title III of the Americans with Disabilities Act ("ADA"), 42 U.S.C. §§12181 *et seq.*, with the United States Department of Justice ("Department") against Joseph David Camacho, Attorney At Law, Albuquerque, New Mexico.

2. The complaint was filed by the National Association of the Deaf Law and Advocacy Center on behalf of Carolyn Tanaka, alleging that Mr. Camacho refused to secure a qualified sign language interpreter when necessary to ensure effective communication with her.

3. The NAD Law and Advocacy Center made the following allegations: Ms. Tanaka is deaf and uses sign language for communication. Ms. Tanaka retained Mr. Camacho as legal counsel in *Tanaka v. University of New Mexico Hospital, et al.*, C. No: 04cv00645 in the United States District Court for the District of New Mexico. In that lawsuit, Ms. Tanaka alleged that the University of New Mexico Hospital failed to provide a qualified interpreter on numerous occasions during the admission of her son, K.T., then age six, to the hospital from April 30, 2002, through May 3, 2002. During the course of his representation of Ms. Tanaka, Mr. Camacho also failed to provide qualified interpreter services despite Ms. Tanaka's repeated requests. Instead, Mr. Camacho asked that Ms. Tanaka's then-nine-year-old son, K.T., "interpret" at appointments between Ms. Tanaka and Mr. Camacho. Ms. Tanaka refused to have her son act as an "interpreter" in these complicated legal matters. On or around September 2004, Mr. Camacho sent Ms. Tanaka Interrogatories and Request for Production of Documents for her to answer in connection with her complaint against the University of New Mexico Hospital. Ms. Tanaka had great difficulty understanding the Interrogatories and Request for Production of Documents. Ms. Tanaka again requested a qualified interpreter so that she could effectively communicate with Mr. Camacho regarding how to answer the discovery requests. Mr. Camacho again refused to provide a qualified interpreter in order to communicate effectively with and assist Ms. Tanaka in answering the Interrogatories and Request for Production of Documents. On October 28, 2004, Mr. Camacho sent Ms. Tanaka a letter stating in part, "It is my understanding that you refuse to cooperate unless I provide you with an interpreter, which will cost me approximately eighty dollars an hour. I have never had to pay to converse with my own client. It would be different if you did not have anyone to translate for you. However, you have a very intelligent son who can do it for you. It appears that we are not able to work together. I believe that you should find another attorney as I am going to withdraw from this case." First, he contends that he represented her

effectively and competently, and gave her the same quality of service that he provides to any other non-disabled client. On November 9, 2004, Mr. Camacho made a motion to withdraw as Ms. Tanaka's attorney, stating an "irreconcilable conflict." On December 20, 2004, Mr. Camacho's motion to withdraw was granted. The case against the Hospital was dismissed "due to her failure to respond to discovery."

4. Mr. Camacho disputes portions of Ms. Tanaka's allegations. He has submitted a statement to the Department contending that he was able to communicate effectively with Ms. Tanaka by means of written notes, e-mail, telephone relays and through the interpretation of Ms. Tanaka's nine-year-old son. He also points out that he hired an interpreter for the hearing on his withdrawal from Ms. Tanaka's case. To demonstrate that he communicated effectively with Ms. Tanaka, Mr. Camacho has submitted to the Department a list of pleadings that he prepared on Ms. Tanaka's behalf. He contends that he represented her effectively and competently, and gave her the same quality of service that he provides to any non-disabled client. Mr. Camacho maintains that he withdrew from the case because Ms. Tanaka stopped returning his phone calls and e-mail messages in connection with the discovery requests referred to above.

5. The Attorney General is authorized to enforce title III of the ADA. 42 U.S.C. §12188(a)(2). In addition, the Attorney General may commence a civil action to enforce title III in any situation where the Attorney General believes a pattern or practice of discrimination exists or a matter of general public importance is raised. 42 U.S.C. §12188(b)(1)(B).

6. Title III specifically defines discrimination as, among other things:

> the failure to take such steps as may be necessary to ensure that no individual with a disability is excluded, denied services, segregated or otherwise treated differently than other individuals *because of the absence of auxiliary aids or services,* unless the entity can demonstrate that taking such steps would fundamentally alter the nature of the good, service, facility, privilege, advantage, or accommodation being offered or would result in an undue burden.

> 42 U.S.C. §12182(b)(2)(A) (emphasis added); see 28 C.F.R. §36.303. The ADA defines "auxiliary aids" to include, among other things, "qualified interpreters or other effective methods of making aurally delivered materials available to individuals with hearing impairments . . . ." 42 U.S.C. §12102(1). A public accommodation is required to furnish appropriate auxiliary aids and services where necessary to ensure effective communication with individuals with hearing impairments. 28 C.F.R. §36.303. The preamble to the regulation lists communications involving legal matters as an example of a type of communication that can be "sufficiently lengthy or complex to require an interpreter for effective communication." 28 C.F.R. pt. 36, App. B at 703 (2005).

7. The title III regulation defines "qualified interpreter" as "an interpreter who is able to interpret effectively, accurately and impartially both receptively and expressively, using any necessary specialized vocabulary." 28 C.F.R. §36.104. The preamble to the definition of "qualified interpreter" explains:

Public comment also revealed that public accommodations have at times asked persons who are deaf to provide family members or friends to interpret. In certain circumstances, notwithstanding that the family member or friend is able to interpret or is a certified interpreter, the family member or friend may not be qualified to render the necessary interpretation because of factors such as emotional or personal involvement or considerations of confidentiality that may adversely affect the ability to interpret "effectively, accurately, and impartially."

28 C.F.R. pt. 36, App. B at 684-685 (2005) (internal quotes in original).

PARTIES

8. The Parties to this Settlement Agreement ("Agreement") are the United States of America ("United States") and Joseph David Camacho, Esq.
9. Joseph David Camacho is an attorney in private practice, providing legal services, and therefore, a public accommodation under Title III of the ADA. 42 U.S.C. §12181(7)(F); 28 C.F.R. §36.104.

FINDINGS

10. The United States has investigated the allegations that Mr. Camacho failed to provide Ms. Tanaka with effective communication and finds the allegations meritorious.
11. To resolve this matter without further litigation, Mr. Camacho is willing to agree to the terms of this settlement agreement. In exchange, the United States agrees to terminate its investigation of this matter, without resorting to litigation, except as provided in paragraph 18.
12. In order to avoid litigation of the issues discussed herein, and in consideration of the mutual promises and covenants contained in this Agreement, the Parties hereby agree to the following:

REMEDIAL ACTION

13. Consistent with the ADA, Mr. Camacho will not discriminate against any individual on the basis of disability in the full and equal enjoyment of the goods, services, facilities, privileges, advantages, or accommodations of his private practice by refusing or failing to secure qualified interpreters when necessary to ensure effective communication with clients who are deaf and use sign language.
14. Mr. Camacho will adopt, maintain, and enforce the policy attached hereto, and by reference incorporated herein, as Exhibit 1 to this Agreement on effective communication with individuals with disabilities. Within ten (10) days of the effective date of this Agreement, Mr. Camacho will post of the policy in a conspicuous area of his law office where members of the public can readily read the policy. . . .

MONETARY RELIEF FOR COMPLAINANT

15. The ADA authorizes the United States Attorney General to seek a court award of compensatory damages on behalf of individuals aggrieved as the result of violations of the ADA. 42 U.S.C. §12188(b)(2)(B); 28 C.F.R. §36.504(a)(2). Within thirty (30) days of the effective date of this Agreement, Mr. Camacho agrees to pay Carolyn Tanaka $1,000.00 in damages. . . .

EXHIBIT 1
POLICY ON EFFECTIVE COMMUNICATION
WITH INDIVIDUALS WITH DISABILITIES

To ensure effective communication with clients and companions who are deaf or hard of hearing, we provide appropriate auxiliary aids and services free of charge, such as: sign language and oral interpreters, note takers, written materials, assistive listening devices and systems, and real-time transcription services.

d) FAMILY AND MEDICAL LEAVE ACT

Under the Family and Medical Leave Act,[6] employees are allowed 12 weeks of unpaid leave due to health conditions, birth, adoption of a child, or care for a family member who is ill. The statute applies to employers with 50 or more employees. Eligible employees are those who worked 1,250 hours during the preceding year and who have been employed by the employer from whom leave is requested for at least one year. The employee, upon returning to work, must be given her prior job or an equivalent one. The employer must maintain group health plan benefits for the employee during the absence period on the same terms as if the employee had been in the office.

Employees may file suit against their employers for violations of the statute. They can receive both monetary damages and equitable relief (such as reinstatement to their previous jobs). The Department of Labor may also pursue employers for violations of the law.

e) AGE DISCRIMINATION IN EMPLOYMENT ACT

The Age Discrimination in Employment Act of 1967, as amended,[7] bans discrimination against people age 40 and older. It is unlawful for employers

(1) to fail or refuse to hire or to discharge any individual or otherwise discriminate against any individual with respect to his compensation, terms, conditions, or privileges of employment, because of such individual's age;

(2) to limit, segregate, or classify his employees in any way which would deprive or tend to deprive any individual of employment opportunities or otherwise adversely affect his status as an employee, because of such individual's age; or

(3) to reduce the wage rate of any employee in order to comply with this chapter.[8]

Although voluntary early retirement plans are permissible under the law, employee benefit plans may not "require or permit the involuntary retirement"[9] of employees because of their age. Mandatory retirement for employees who are executives or in high policy-making positions are permissible so long as these employees are entitled to retirement benefits.[10] Law firms sometimes have compulsory retirement ages for partners. These firms typically argue that the partners are not "employees" subject to age discrimination in employment laws.

Still, law firms can run into trouble when, in an effort to increase per-partner profits, they start getting rid of long-time practitioners who might be underperforming. Consider the following experience:

> It wasn't Mrs. O'Leary's cow who set things off in Chicago this time.
>
> Rather, it seems that the leadership of a local institution called Sidley & Austin [now known as Sidley Austin] has been kicking over the lanterns lately, presumably infusing much-needed new energy into the 134-year-old law firm. Guided by executive committee chairman Thomas Cole and management committee chairman Charles Douglas, the firm has big plans—for expanding abroad, for pushing its technology and e-commerce practice at home, and, most jarring for this collegial old organization, for pruning a few dead branches in the partnership.
>
> . . .
>
> Sidley's demotion . . . of some two dozen partners to senior counsel or counsel positions caused something of a gossip firestorm.
>
> Sidley "was always very genteel," observes one local lawyer. "No one ever got fired. That was just the Sidley way. Culturally, this just turns everything on its head."
>
> "The decision was driven by greed," maintains one consultant familiar with the doings. "At an October [1999] partnership meeting, the *AmLaw 100* was circulated. It showed that Sidley has good revenues, but profits per partner are much lower than at other firms."
>
> . . .
>
> So even the Sidleys of the world must nudge some people toward the door in any kind of economic weather. Some partners know they're not going to make it; they've been given the subtle hints, but they're going to hang on until the guards come and put their pens and folders into a box for them. They know what's expected, but they also know the minimum they need to do or pretend to do in order to survive—for awhile.
>
> . . .
>
> Sidley & Austin was founded five years before Chicago burned. It's seen a lot worse than the current brushfire and will likely be standing strong after a few of its more ruthless competitors have torn themselves in half.[11]

The U.S. Equal Employment Opportunity Commission filed suit "alleging that Sidley Austin Brown & Wood, the giant Chicago-based international law firm, violated the Age Discrimination in Employment Act (ADEA) when it selected 'partners' for expulsion from the firm on account of their age or forced them to retire."[12]

A lengthy inquiry took place. The commission informed Sidley of its investigation in July 2000 and filed suit against the firm in 2005:

> The EEOC case is a "class" age discrimination case brought, first, with respect to 31 former Sidley & Austin partners who were involuntarily downgraded and expelled from the partnership in October of 1999 on account of their age, and, second, with respect to other partners who were involuntarily retired from Sidley & Austin since

1978 on account of their age pursuant to a mandatory retirement policy. The ADEA prohibits employers with 20 or more employees from making employment decisions, including decisions regarding the termination of employment, on the basis of age (over 40). The ADEA also prohibits such employers from utilizing policies or rules which require employees to retire when they reach a particular age (over 40).[13]

Two years later, the firm settled the suit for $27.5 million (see Figure 5-1).

f) EQUAL PAY ACT

The Equal Pay Act of 1963, as amended, bars pay discrimination based on sex:

No employer having employees subject to any provisions of this section shall discriminate, within any establishment in which such employees are employed, between employees on the basis of sex by paying wages to employees in such establishment at a rate less than the rate at which he pays wages to employees of the opposite sex in such establishment for equal work on jobs the performance of which requires equal skill, effort, and responsibility, and which are performed under similar working conditions, except where such payment is made pursuant to (i) a seniority system; (ii) a merit system; (iii) a system which measures earnings by quantity or quality of production; or (iv) a differential based on any other factor other than sex: *Provided*, That an employer who is paying a wage rate differential in violation of this subsection shall not, in order to comply with the provisions of this subsection, reduce the wage rate of any employee.[14]

g) CONSOLIDATED OMNIBUS BUDGET RECONCILIATION ACT OF 1985

The Consolidated Omnibus Budget Reconciliation Act of 1985, or COBRA, allows employees who leave their jobs to continue their health insurance coverage for themselves, their spouses, and their children for 18 months (and, in some cases, longer if the employee became disabled) through the employer's group health plan by paying for it. The spouse and children have the right to elect to continue coverage on their own. In certain situations (such as divorce), the spouse and dependent children can keep the coverage for periods up to 36 months. New employees and their covered beneficiaries must be notified of their right to continuation benefits under COBRA.[15]

The law applies to employers with 20 or more employees.[16]

h) PATIENT PROTECTION AND AFFORDABLE CARE ACT (OBAMACARE)

In 2010, President Barack Obama signed into law the Patient Protection and Affordable Care Act,[17] which requires employers to provide health insurance coverage and requires individuals to maintain minimum levels of health insurance coverage or be subject to a penalty. Assessments of $2,000 per full-time employee will be made against employers with more than 50 employees if they do not offer health care coverage. Individuals must maintain health insurance, and, if they do not, will be required to pay a yearly financial penalty or 2.5 percent of household income (with some exceptions).[18] Small businesses and individuals can seek coverage through health insurance exchanges the new law created. The effective dates for various elements of the law are staggered over several years.

FIGURE 5-1
Press Release 10-5-07

$27.5 Million Consent Decree Resolves EEOC Age Bias Suit Against Sidley Austin

Law Firm Partners Brought Within Protection of Federal Law Against Employment Discrimination

CHICAGO—The international law firm of Sidley Austin LLP will pay $27.5 million to 32 former partners who the U.S. Equal Employment Opportunity Commission alleged were forced out of the partnership because of their age, under a consent decree approved by a federal judge. (EEOC v. Sidley Austin LLP, N.D. Illinois No. 05 C 0208.)

The EEOC brought the suit in 2005 under the federal Age Discrimination in Employment Act (ADEA). A major issue in the case was whether partners in the law firm were protected as employees under the ADEA. The decree was signed by Federal District Judge James B. Zagel of the Northern District of Illinois yesterday afternoon, October 4, 2007, and entered on the court's docket this morning. The decree provides that "Sidley agrees that each person for whom EEOC has sought relief in this matter was an employee with the meaning of the ADEA."

The consent decree also includes an injunction that bars the law firm from "terminating, expelling, retiring, reducing the compensation of or otherwise adversely changing the partnership status of a partner because of age" or "maintaining any formal or informal policy or practice requiring retirement as a partner or requiring permission to continue as a partner once the partner has reached a certain age."

Ronald S. Cooper, General Counsel of the EEOC, said, "This case has been closely followed by the legal community as well as by professional services providers generally. It shows that EEOC will not shrink from pursuing meritorious claims of employment discrimination wherever they are found. Neither the relative status of the protected group members nor the resources and sophistication of the employer were dispositive here."

Cooper added, "The demographic changes in America assure that we will see more opportunities for age discrimination to occur. Therefore, it is increasingly important that all employers understand the impact of the Age Discrimination in Employment Act on their operations and that we re-emphasize its important protections for older workers."

The $27.5 million will be paid by Sidley Austin to 32 former partners of the firm for whom the EEOC sought relief because they either were expelled from the partnership in connection with an October 1999 reorganization or retired under the firm's age-based retirement policy.

The amounts of the individual payments to the former partners were submitted under seal and approved by the court. The average of all the payments to partners under the decree will be $859,375. The highest payment to any former partner will be $1,835,510, and the lowest payment $122,169. The median payment (the value in the middle of all payments) is $875,572.

(continued)

During the term of the decree, which expires Dec. 31, 2009, Abner Mikva, retired Federal Court of Appeals Judge and former Member of Congress and White House Counsel, will deal with any complaints received from Sidley partners and report to the EEOC.

The EEOC litigation team has been headed by John Hendrickson, Regional Attorney for the Chicago District, and includes Supervisory Trial Attorney Gregory Gochanour and Trial Attorneys Deborah Hamilton, Laurie Elkin, and Justin Mulaire. Proceedings in the U.S. Court of Appeals for the Seventh Circuit were handled by Carolyn Wheeler and Jennifer Goldstein of the EEOC Office of General Counsel's Appellate Services.

Hendrickson said, "The EEOC v. Sidley Austin litigation has always been a high priority for both our agency and the law firm, and the litigation has reflected that—tough, determined, professional. The litigation has yielded a number of important legal decisions, ensuring the protection of professionals from discriminatory employment actions and ratifying the authority of EEOC to investigate and obtain relief for victims of age discrimination on its own initiative."

Hendrickson added, "The public has benefited because the EEOC and Sidley were able to sit down and talk with each other and craft a workable resolution in a complex lawsuit. That doesn't always happen. Not all employers are resolved to deal with tough issues and to get on with business. Sidley was so resolved, and today's decree reflects its determination to get this case behind it and to address a situation which the EEOC believed required its attention."

George Galland, Jr. of the Chicago law firm of Miner Barnhill & Galland acted as a mediator in the case and facilitated the parties' negotiations.

The EEOC enforces federal laws prohibiting discrimination in employment. Further information about the Commission is available on its web site at www.eeoc.gov.

Source: Press Release, U.S. Equal Employment Opportunity Commission (Oct. 5, 2007), http://www.eeoc.gov /press/10-5-07.html

After the Supreme Court upheld the constitutionality of the individual mandate requiring individuals to obtain health insurance coverage as a tax within the taxation powers of Congress,[19] the Obama administration announced that it was postponing until 2015 the requirement that employers offer health insurance to their employees or face fines.[20]

3.   *State Law*

States sometimes have more stringent versions of employee-protection statutes. Both federal laws and applicable state laws should be taken into consideration when developing a law office's procedures.

C.   Recruiting and Hiring Process

Typically, recruiting and hiring at law firms occur on two separate tracks: one for attorneys and a different one for support personnel. Although law office management staff may assist in hiring attorneys, most of these recruiting efforts fall to attorneys at a firm, who typically visit law schools in the fall of each year to interview prospective hires for summer associate or first-year associate positions. Lawyers within the firm also recruit more senior attorneys. Large law firms have a lawyer hiring committee or a lawyer recruiting committee. Law office management personnel likely assist in organizing the process, scheduling interviews, and coordinating the necessary paperwork. Some firms have dedicated recruitment coordinators to handle this function.

Law office management staff is likely to have a more direct role in the hiring of support staff, although, again, the supervising attorney typically has approval authority for any potential hire.

Some firms are using innovative ways to recruit—for example, by developing podcasts or by posting Web videos featuring interviews with associates about working at the firm. Others use traditional recruiting tools and might rely on advertising available positions and using outside recruiting firms, or **headhunters**, to assist in finding potential hires. After all, not only is a firm considering a candidate; the candidate is also assessing the firm. Potential hires often have numerous job offers; a law firm, as in other areas, must compete for the best candidates.

headhunter:
A recruiter.

1. Interviewing Candidates

During an interview, a law office manager or appropriate human resources staff person should provide the interviewee with information about the firm, about the job, and about the firm's expectations of the candidate chosen to do that job. A job candidate should be a good match for the firm. Ideally, a candidate's goals, work ethics, capabilities, experience, and accomplishments will mesh with the law firm's objectives in hiring for a given position.

An interview can sometimes seem like a casual conversation between two people new to each other, but the interviewer must take care not to pose inappropriate or illegal questions. Asking whether a candidate is a U.S. citizen, or if the candidate is pregnant or married, is not permissible. Prior to conducting an interview, the interviewer should consider the questions to be posed and draft them in ways that remain within the confines of the law. A manual on current employment law might be consulted.

Likewise, job candidates must prepare for the possibility that an inappropriate or illegal question will be asked during a job interview. The candidate should practice ahead of time how he will deal with such a question. Certainly, declining to answer is one option, as is exclaiming, "That's illegal and I could sue!" The likelihood that an interview would proceed well after such an utterance, is, however, not very high. That's not to say that a candidate should answer illegal questions; rather, the candidate might respond somewhat evasively. For example, in response to "Are you pregnant?" a candidate might answer, "Let's hope not!"

That does not really tell the interviewer whether the candidate is or is not pregnant and, at the same time, is responsive to the question.

2. Reference and Background Checks

Firms typically ask prospective hires for references. For fear of litigation, though, some references, and even some former employers, may be reluctant to give out more than very basic information. Law firms sometimes ask prospective hires to sign a waiver or release authorizing a reference or former employer to speak freely about the candidate without fear of reprisal in the form of a lawsuit.

Firms should confirm prior employment and verify educational background and degrees obtained. Doing so is especially important given that, on at least one occasion, someone posing as a lawyer has misled a law firm:

> Manhattan District Attorney Robert M. Morgenthau announced today the indictment of a 32-year-old man for pretending to be a lawyer and stealing at least $284,350.50 from the law firm where he had been employed.
>
> The defendant, Brian Valery, began working as a paralegal at the law firm of Anderson Kill & Olick, P.C. . . . in their New York office . . . on December 2, 1996. He earned a salary of $21,000 per year at that time. Within a five-year period, he was promoted to the position of Law Clerk, earning $70,000 per year.
>
> The investigation revealed that in the fall of 1998, Valery told his employers that he was enrolled at Fordham University School of Law in the evening division and they adjusted his work schedule to accommodate night classes for the next four years. In May 2002, Valery told the firm that he had graduated from Fordham Law School and he was promoted to the legal staff at Anderson Kill & Olick and started practicing as an attorney in the areas of General Litigation, Insurance Recovery, and Corporate and Commercial Litigation. His salary was increased to $115,000 per year.
>
> Soon after his purported graduation from law school, Valery took time off from work for the purpose of studying for the New York State bar examination. Subsequently, the defendant told his employers that he had failed the bar in both July 2002 and February 2003, but that he had passed the July 2003 exam and was admitted to the New York State bar in October 2004. Valery continued to practice as an attorney at Anderson Kill & Olick until October 2006. At that time, the firm discovered that Valery had not attended Fordham Law School, had never taken the New York State bar examination, and was not admitted to practice law. As a result, Anderson Kill & Olick fired him. His annual salary at that time was $155,000.
>
> Valery is charged with Grand Larceny for stealing the differential between the salaries he received while working in the position of attorney and the top paralegal salaries during that same period, plus $74,500 in bonuses.
>
> . . .
>
> Valery is being charged with Grand Larceny in the Second Degree, a class C felony, which is punishable by up to 15 years in prison, and Practicing and Appearing as an Attorney-at-Law Without Being Admitted and Registered, a class A misdemeanor, which is punishable by up to one year in prison. . . . The defendant was arraigned today in New York State Supreme Court, Part 60.[21]

Failure to verify education attained and to confirm that the candidate passed the bar exam was a costly mistake for this firm. The firm ended up offering to reimburse its clients for the lawyer fees they paid for the employee's services.[22]

The employee who posed as a lawyer eventually pleaded guilty to second-degree larceny and admitted to stealing more than $200,000 from his firm by "claiming" a lawyer's salary.[23] He was sentenced to five years' probation and had to perform 100 hours of community service and pay restitution of $225,000.[24]

D.   Workplace Policies and Procedures

A law firm should develop policies and procedures for dealing with all aspects of law firm operations, from scheduling vacation time to covering phones while the receptionist is at lunch to closing the office due to inclement weather, and so on.

Such policies and procedures rarely need to be developed from scratch. Many resources are available offering sample policies, which law firms can then modify to suit their own particular needs.

E.   Employee Handbook

Ideally, a law firm should have an employee manual, or handbook, that serves as an introduction to a law firm and addresses standard operating procedures for office conduct. These handbooks can be provided to all new hires. All employees should have them so that they can be easily referred to. The handbook might address the firm's operations, basic office procedures, standards of decorum (such as a dress code), and firm programs and benefits offered.

1.   Elements of a Handbook

The depth, breadth, and length of a handbook will vary depending on the size of the firm and on the level of interest from firm managers in crafting uniform procedures across all of the firm's offices. Although managing attorneys at a very large firm might be tempted to create a phone book–length directory covering many possible workplace functions and scenarios, the reader should be kept in mind. The more burdensome an employee manual becomes to a user, the less likely an employee is actually to use it.

To make the use of an employee handbook easier, firms develop electronic versions of handbooks. Employees can search for key terms electronically to find pertinent information quickly.

A handbook can contain any amount of information. Essentially, the material in a handbook covers the responsibilities an employee owes to the firm. The handbook might include the firm's mission statement and a short history of the firm, an explanation of how the firm is organized, a discussion of the types of clients the firm represents, and an overview of how the firm operates. Sometimes this material is referred to as a firm résumé.

The firm's organization should be covered in some detail in a handbook. Key people at the firm should be identified, as should departments, department chairs, committees (such as management committee, associates committee, etc.), committee chairs, and so forth. The handbook might include the entire roster of the firm, organized by practice group, department, and support function, such as human resources.

The handbook should provide contact information for managers as well as for other services, such as the mail room, whom to contact if an employee is sick, whom to call about getting a new client number, whom to call for computer problems, how to handle snow days, how to make vacation requests, and so forth. Other elements of a handbook may include the following:

- policy statements on e-mail and appropriate office use of the Internet
- policies and procedures for recruitment and promotion
- job descriptions for support personnel (e.g., legal secretaries, reception-ists, paralegals)
- rules of conduct
- a policy statement on lawyers or others serving on corporate boards of directors and on investing in clients' businesses
- a description of official office hours
- procedures for handling clients and others who visit the firm (for instance, some firms do not allow clients into lawyers' offices but limit them to conference rooms)
- procedures for reserving conference rooms
- a policy statement on protecting confidentiality
- telephone procedures and a script for answering phone calls, the proce-dure for delivering telephones messages, and so forth
- procedures for reporting and addressing sexual harassment
- policies on various matters, such as dress code, holidays, use of office equipment, and timekeeping
- legal notices on equal opportunity employment
- an explanation of disciplinary procedures
- a description of health and retirement plans
- an explanation of training opportunities
- information about facilities, where conference rooms are located, how to book them, where the library is, where administrative offices are, where reception is, etc.
- a discussion of security and emergency procedures
- reimbursement procedures (petty cash, travel, etc.)

Of course, a law firm's manual should also include certain legal niceties such as an explanation that the handbook can be modified. It's probably a good idea to include a disclaimer indicating that the handbook does not create an employment contract. Some courts have held that an employee manual can be considered a contract unless the manual includes a disclaimer clearly indicating that no contract is created.

Employees should be required to sign an acknowledgment that they have received and read the handbook. The contents of the handbook might be reviewed during a new employee's inaugural activities.

2.   *Orientation and Training*

Orientation can ease a new hire's stress. Entering a new environment, meet-ing new colleagues, and adapting to a new office's way of business can be anxiety-producing. Providing a welcome introduction to a particular firm not only puts the new employee at ease but also helps others in the firm accept the new hire.

Lawyers, in particular, are known for not engaging in a lot of on-the-job "hand holding." In other words, historically, they've tended to throw work to a new staff person and expect him or her to pitch in and learn the job by doing it. Nowadays many firms have made great strides in providing more formal orientation and training both for their new lawyers and for new staff people.

Ideally, a new hire should be provided with a job description enumerating his duties and should have a sit-down meeting both with his supervisor and with appropriate human resources staff people, who can make sure that all appropriate paperwork is completed and workplace notices and handbooks are provided to the new employee.

It should be remembered that new staff at a firm may have only limited knowledge about the firm and its functions or even about the job they are to perform. Assigning someone to show the new person around—to introduce her to the appropriate people at the firm, to show her where to park, to explain when she can go to lunch, to explain where the library is, and how the firm kitchen operates (does the person who takes the last cup of coffee make the next pot?), and so forth—can really make a new hire feel welcome.

Training should not be a one-time, introductory event but should reoccur at various times during an employee's tenure at the firm, such as when new technology is introduced or as part of career- or performance-enhancing initiatives. Some law firms have periodic seminars for associates as well as for the support staff who work with them so that everyone will have a better understanding about how a type of case or work will ideally be conducted and what the role of each individual assigned to the matter is.

F. Performance Evaluation

Some firms hire new employees on a trial basis for, say, an initial three-month period. At the end of the trial, the performance of the employee will be assessed, and a decision will be made about hiring the employee on a permanent basis. If, at the end of the three-month period, the employee's performance is deemed to be unsatisfactory, the individual and the firm will part ways. Such an arrangement helps a law firm rid itself of poor performers without undue hassle.

Even after initial trial periods, staff performances should be reviewed annually, as should the performance of lawyers at the firm. A firm might have a very formal process in which every lawyer a staffer works with completes a questionnaire assessing the employee's performance on a given project. These assessments are then compiled and presented to the employee by a human resources person and a supervising attorney. If the employee's performance requires improvement, an action plan may be developed and certain milestones identified.

G. Compensation and Benefits

An employee's salary and a description of benefits typically are included in an offer letter from the firm. Such a letter usually specifies that employment is at will. In other words, an employee can be fired without cause at any time. The letter might also indicate that a new hire is being hired initially for a trial period of, say, 90 days. During the probationary period, the new hire's performance will be assessed, and a decision whether to extend employment will be made.

When an applicant accepts the offer, additional details about benefits, payment schedules, and the like are provided to the new employee.

H. Employee Relations

At law firms of all sizes, some effort should be made to foster good relations between lawyers and nonlegal staff. Traditionally, there has been some tension between legal and nonlegal personnel, as lawyers tend to accrue greater benefits, both financial and otherwise, than nonlegal staff do. This difference can be very evident in some firms on simmering Friday afternoons when the lawyers gather in a conference room for cocktails, but secretaries and administrative support are excluded from the party.

Some friction occurs at all levels of the firm's hierarchy, from management committee members to partners to associates to paralegals to everyone else. After all, why shouldn't the managing partner of a major law firm command the best parking space in the lot? Every workplace has a pecking order. One group may believe that another group unfairly receives certain **perquisites,** but the group that receives them typically believes it is entitled to them and others are not. For example, lawyers at some law firms have become very contentious in dividing up of office space. Who should have the large corner offices with the best views? The firm's best rainmakers? Department chairs? Should space be assigned according to the number of years a lawyer has been in the profession? According to the number of years a lawyer has been with the firm? In some other way?

Wise law firm management will be focused on fostering teamwork rather than letting perceived slights fester.

perquisite, or "perk":
A benefit or special privilege bestowed on an employee in addition to salary.

I. Supervisory Techniques

Law firms can take measures to foster better relations among team members at a firm. Giving nonlegal staff a say in some policy decisions can make those staffers feel more affiliated with, and more loyal to, a firm.

When training new lawyers, some firms also include the support staff those new lawyers will be working with. Everyone is made to feel a part of the team. Other firms encourage "low-level" staff members to expand their list of duties. For instance, a receptionist who is going to school at night to earn her accounting degree might be given some number-crunching assignments to handle between answering phone calls. Similarly, a legal secretary might be consulted for input on a firm's new filing system, since she is likely to use it frequently. Firm activities that include lawyers as well as staff people also help build a team.

J.   Disciplinary Action

Unfortunately, some employees might turn out to be "bad actors"—people who are not dedicated to their jobs, who do not respect the clients or their coworkers, or who engage in inappropriate behavior.

Performance problems should be raised during annual, semiannual, or even periodic reviews. It's possible that an employee is experiencing a difficulty that, when known, could be resolved with some modifications to the employee's workload or with the addition of some training.

During a review, a plan of action might be discussed for improving the employee's performance, and a schedule might be worked out, with the implications of failure to improve made clear to the employee.

If performance problems stem from other sorts of behaviors, such as apparent abuse of sick leave, or inappropriate conduct, such as sexual harassment, a higher level of supervisory and human resources personnel might become involved in the matter. Disciplinary action, such as a warning placed in an employee's file or a reassignment, might be discussed. In certain instances, a firm might also consult an outside employment law lawyer to be certain it is conforming with the most recent legal requirements in dealing with problem employees or complaints by other employees about a problem employee.

K.   Termination

1.   Voluntary

It is customary for employees who are leaving a firm voluntarily to provide two weeks' notice of their departure. The procedure for giving notice might be mentioned in the employee handbook. Employees who are retiring may provide even more advance notice about their plans to retire.

Although an employee might be tempted to be less than cordial when leaving a firm, he or she should remember that potential future employers might be calling the firm to confirm employment and to seek references. If at all possible, an employee who leaves the firm voluntarily should maintain good relations with the firm.

2.   Involuntary

Unfortunately, sometimes circumstances require that a firm and an employee who is not measuring up part ways. Depending on the situation, a staff person's employment may be terminated immediately, or he or she may be given notice that her position is ending and that after a certain date she will no longer be employed by the firm.

L.   Employee Retention

Turnover at law firms can be strikingly high. Some estimates are that law firms lose 20 percent of associates in a year.[25] Replacing those lawyers is an expensive endeavor.

 Much attrition is attributable to billable-hours requirements for lawyers. In the early 1960s, if a lawyer billed 1,300 hours annually, he was considered to be working a full-time job.[26] Nowadays, billable hours exceed 2,000 hours. Over the past few decades, loyalty to one's firm has diminished, a situation not helped by the tendency of law firms to lay off lawyers as well as staff people during economic downturns. Leaders at firms are realizing that, in addition to high salaries, lawyers are interested in benefits, and some firms are boosting their benefits packages in an effort to retain lawyers. For example, one firm increased its parental leave policy, allowing 18 weeks, rather than 12 weeks, for birth mothers who are primary caregivers and for adoptive parents. Biological fathers and other primary caregivers can take 10 weeks off, up from 8. Associates can also work a reduced number of hours for six months upon their return and will not have the same billable-hours requirements as a full-time lawyer.[27]

attrition:
A reduction in the number of people in a group, such as law firm employees.

 Some firms are considering alternatives to billable hours and are designing alternative work schedules. Lawyers may be required to work in the office during certain core hours but then may telecommute for the remainder of the time. Other firms are focusing on perquisites such as on-site cafeterias and child care. Paid sabbaticals are another way to allow someone to take time away from the firm to explore other alternatives without severing the relationship entirely.

 Retention rates have also suffered as law firms have consolidated. Partners and associates may leap to other firms several times within a career. Compensation schemes for partners can also be detrimental to attorney retention. If partners become dissatisfied with the money that they are earning, they may be inclined to look for more profitable places to work.[28]

 In times of economic downturn, layoffs[29]—of both lawyers and staff can occur. For those who remain, the workplace can become more tense—which, in turn, may yield even more staff turnover.

M.   Diversity in Law Firms

Often criticized as white-male bastions,[30] law firms today are more diverse than they once were, though not yet ideal. In some measure, the shift toward law firms being more reflective of society as a whole is attributable to clients—some are assessing a law firm's diversity as well as the firm's level of expertise, depth, and cost. This shift is attributable to "A Call to Action," an initiative begun in 2005 by one general counsel of a corporation to encourage other corporations to look for diversity in the law firms those corporations retained. Signatories to A Call to Action pledged to consider diversity of lawyers at the law firms their corporations might hire.[31]

1. *Minorities*

The percentage of minority lawyers at large law firms has increased slowly, moving from 9.7 percent in 2000 and peaking at 13.9 percent in 2008. That percentage then dipped during the recession, only reaching 13.9 percent again in 2013.[32] Despite increased percentages of both women and minorities in law school classes, progress in the private sector has been slow in coming.

Although 33.3 percent of lawyers are female, as of 2012, only 19.9 percent are partners, and only 15 percent are equity partners. Just 4 percent of large law firm managing partners were women. Interestingly, 45 percent of associates in private practice in 2012 were women, and 46.3 percent of summer associates were female.[33]

The presence of minority lawyers in law firms is not reflective of enrollment of minorities in law schools. Minorities have made up some 20 percent of students at law schools since the 1998–1999 academic year. In the 2012–2013 school year, minorities made up 25.8 percent of enrollment. Back in 1971–1972, they accounted for just 6.1 percent of enrollment.[34]

2. *Women*

Gender diversity at law firms could also be improved. Women are sometimes challenged to continue working at top law firms given the time commitment required. Typically, women graduate from law school and, theoretically, work their way up the associate ranks toward partnership during their peak childbearing years. After a few years of putting in long hours at a law firm, many women opt out:

> There are two conflicting challenges to a female attorney's work-life balance. The first is the idea that successful attorneys with high numbers of billable hours cannot raise children if they are never home with them. The second is the perception that a good mother cannot rise to partnership if her priority is her home. In either case, she will lose. For some women, these roles demand a large amount of time, spreading them too thin to feel successful at either. The life of a professional woman is demanding; she must deal with the extreme pressures of work, only to come home to a "second shift" of caring for children and doing housework—activities in which most men fail to take their proportionate share.[35]

Law firms have made increasing efforts to accommodate the needs of their family-oriented attorneys. Some have offered part-time schedules and telecommuting options. At large law firms, a little over 6 percent of attorneys worked on a part-time basis in 2012. Of those, though, 70 percent were female.[36] These figures are low even though 98 percent of the law firms allowed part-time work in 2012.[37]

Although making up about 50 percent of law school classes for decades,[38] women are far from making up 50 percent of the leadership at law firms. Women at law firms hit what some describe as a "maternal wall," a barrier to success:

> In the legal workplace, the effect of the maternal wall becomes readily apparent when female attorneys become pregnant: it is the change in assignments once the

pregnancy is announced; it is the constant questions, rumors, and innuendos about whether she will return after her maternity leave; it is the receipt of a nominal or non-existent bonus during the year she has her baby. When she returns from maternity leave, the maternal wall is the non-challenging assignments she gets because everyone assumes her heart and head will be with her baby and not at work; it is the bonuses or promotions she does not get because she does not bill the same hours as her male colleagues, who also may be new fathers but who have wives to stay at home; it is the opportunities she does not get because they involve travel, and it is assumed she will not travel; it is being treated like half of an attorney if she tries to work a reduced-hour schedule. Sometimes, it is the decision to put off motherhood until her career is well-established; and finally, it is the heartbreak when she realizes that she may have waited too long.[39]

N. Workplace Morale

Lawyer retention continues to be a problem for law firms, particularly large firms that have hired associates from top law schools. The practice of law at a top law firm can be repetitive and unexciting—not at all as television shows or films depict the workday of an attorney:

> One cluster of problems involves the substance of legal practice and the gap between expectations and realities. Individuals often choose law as a career with little knowledge of what lawyers actually do. Law in prime time media offers some combination of wealth, power, drama, or heroic opportunities. Law in real time is something else, particularly for those at the bottom of the pecking order. The sheer drudgery of many legal matters, particularly in large firms, exacts a heavy price. It is not surprising that recent graduates from the most prestigious schools, although working in the most prestigious firms, express the greatest dissatisfaction with their careers; they expected more from their credentials.
>
> Commentators identify further problems with the substance of legal work. Delgado and Stefancic fault formalism, the law's excessive focus on precedent and authority. Critics also emphasize the adversarial, zero-sum, and uncivil aspects of practice, as well as the pressure without control that characterizes much of associate life. When lawyers function largely as scriveners, or as scapegoats for acrimony not of their own making, they are bound to feel disaffected.[40]

Law firms can make efforts to increase lawyer satisfaction. They might make efforts to provide more challenging assignments and try to improve the firm's culture.

1. Law Firm Stresses

Putting in a lot of hours, working as an adversary, and constantly picking apart an opponent's arguments all take their toll. Lawyers might turn to drugs or alcohol as a way to alleviate workplace stress. Some suffer silently. By some estimates, 19 percent of lawyers experience depression at some point, while only 6.7 percent of the general population does. An estimated 20 percent of lawyers—twice that of the general population—abuse alcohol.[41]

Some states have created lawyer assistance programs to help lawyers who have substance abuse problems. Indicators of substance abuse by attorneys include the following:

Early Stage

- **Professional:** client neglect, unreturned phone calls, late for depositions, cancelled appointments, numerous "sick" days.
- **Legal:** 1st DUI, open container, disorderly conduct.
- **Ethical:** late for hearings, "technical" trust violations (reconciliations, ledger cards), "last minute" filings, failure to diligently prosecute/defend.

Late Stage

- **Professional:** failure to come to the office and/or appear for hearings, intoxicated in court, unprofessional appearance/hygiene, inappropriate mood (depressed, angry, withdrawn), abandonment of practice.
- **Legal:** 2nd DUI, controlled substance charge, domestic violence.
- **Ethical:** substantive trust violations (misappropriation), statute of limitations violations, dishonesty to tribunal.[42]

2. Balancing Work and Personal Time

Ultimately, the individual lawyer is responsible for achieving a balance between work and personal time that satisfies, or at least is tolerable to, him or her. Law firms have made efforts to ease lawyers' pain, but the reality of big-firm practice still demands dedication and a concomitant time commitment. Lawyers who do not want to dedicate 80 hours a week to their careers have sought out alternative paths—moving to smaller law firms, going on part-time status, working in-house, telecommuting. Some lawyers actually do put their careers on hold for a while as they pursue other interests, and then they return to the profession, or even to their original law firm, years later.

Checklist

- The human resources management team at a law firm is charged with handling all phases of employment at a firm, from hiring to performance appraisal through termination and retirement.
- A law firm's mission statement specifies the type of work a firm does, explains the firm's philosophy and core values, and educates prospective clients about the firm's capabilities and its approach to the law.
- Associates as well as staff at law firms are typically hired as employees at will. Some firms hire temporary, or contract, employees to work for the firm for specified periods of time or to handle specific projects.
- The Equal Employment Opportunity Act prohibits employment discrimination based on race, color, religion, sex, or national origin.

- The Fair Labor Standards Act establishes a minimum wage and overtime pay requirements.
- The Americans with Disabilities Act bars discrimination against people with disabilities who are capable of performing a job. Employers are required to make reasonable accommodation for employees so long as that accommodation does not cause undue hardship.
- The Family and Medical Leave Act provides that employees may take 12 weeks of unpaid leave due to health conditions, birth, adoption of a child, or care for a family member who is ill.
- The Age Discrimination in Employment Act of 1967 bans discrimination against people aged 40 and older.
- The Equal Pay Act bars discrimination based on sex.
- The Consolidated Omnibus Budget Reconciliation Act of 1985, or COBRA, allows employees who leave their jobs to continue their health insurance coverage for themselves, their spouses, and their children for 18 months (and, in some cases, longer if the employee became disabled) through the employer's group health plan by paying for it.
- The Patient Protection and Affordable Care Act, known as Obamacare, requires employers to provide health insurance coverage and individuals to maintain minimum levels of insurance or they face a penalty.
- Typically, recruiting and hiring at law firms occur on two separate tracks: one for attorneys and a different one for support personnel.
- A law firm should have an employee manual, or handbook, that serves as an introduction to a law firm and addresses standard operating procedures for office conduct.
- Turnover at law firms is expensive for the firms. Firms are taking steps to reduce their attrition rates and to improve workplace morale.
- Firms are paying greater attention to diversity and are making efforts to hire more women and minorities.
- Many states have created lawyer assistance programs to help lawyers who have substance abuse problems.

Vocabulary

attrition (p. 135)
contract employee (p. 115)
employment at will (p. 115)
firm history (p. 114)

headhunter (p. 128)
mission statement (p. 114)
perquisite, or "perk" (p. 133)
sexual harassment (p. 116)

Career Preparation Tips

Remember when undertaking a job hunt that you are selecting an employer as much as an employer is selecting you. Research law firm mission statements and firm histories, search for any case law or record of employment violations, and look at the media coverage of firms or other organizations for which you would like to work. Consider how you might modify mission statements or otherwise add value to a firm with respect to its human resources obligations. Assess whether you might be interested in being involved with human resources and talent management. How might you enhance a firm's culture?

If You Want to Learn More

The Center for WorkLife Law is a nonprofit organization focusing on research and advocacy in the area of worklife law. The PAR Research Institute, formerly known as the Project for Attorney Retention, studies retention and develops best practices and is now part of the Center for WorkLife Law. http://www.worklifelaw.org

Information about equal employment opportunity law is available from the Equal Employment Opportunity Commission. http://www.eeoc.gov

Information on the Americans with Disabilities Act, proposed regulations, enforcement actions, legal briefs, settlement agreements, and the like is Act home page. http://www.ADA.gov

The Fair Labor Standards Act is addressed on the site of the U.S. Department of Labor. http://www.dol.gov/compliance/laws/comp-flsa.htm

The Web site Lawyers with Depression, started by a practicing lawyer who suffered from depression, is dedicated to lawyers who are similarly afflicted. http://www.lawyerswithdepression.com/

Materials helpful for human resources management and other aspects of law office management are available from the Legal Management Resource Center, which is hosted by the Association of Legal Administrators. Some materials are accessible by nonmembers. http://www.alanet.org/research/

Minority Corporate Counsel Association. http://mcca.com/

Information about the Family and Medical Leave Act is available from the U.S. Department of Labor. http://www.dol.gov/whd/fmla/

Reading Comprehension

1. How does a firm's mission statement differ from a firm's history?
2. What are the negative aspects to working for a law firm as a contract employee?
3. How have law firms tried to evade liability for workplace discrimination?
4. Can a lawyer decline to represent a prospective client because the prospective client has a disability?
5. Must a firm hold a job open for an employee who takes time off pursuant to the Family and Medical Leave Act?
6. Why is it important to conduct a background check of a prospective employee?
7. For what purposes is an employee handbook used?
8. What steps are some law firms taking to encourage employee retention?
9. What challenges do women and minorities still face at law firms?

Discussion Starters

1. Read *Hishon v. King & Spalding*. How did the defendant law firm attempt to evade its responsibilities under the Equal Employment Opportunity Act? Consider the circumstances in which an individual associate was pursuing a high-powered law firm. Do you think that was an intimidating situation to be in? Do you think the outcome of the case was fair?
2. Review the settlement agreement between Joseph David Camacho and the United States. How did Camacho violate the Americans with Disabilities Act? Do you think the punishment was fair or overly broad? What impact to you think this matter had on Camacho's law practice?
3. Read the U.S. Equal Employment Opportunity Commission's announcement concerning its settlement of an age discrimination suit with the law firm Sidley Austin. What misbehavior was the law firm accused of? How did the firm attempt to evade its responsibilities under the Age Discrimination in Employment Act? Do you think the settlement was fair?
4. Consider the information presented in the chapter on the percentages of women and minorities in law firms. Given the increasing numbers of women and minorities attending law school, why aren't more of them becoming partners and associates in law firms? What do you suppose women and minority law school graduates do if they are unable to obtain a job at a major law firm?
5. Suppose you are a young lawyer at a major law firm. Would you be willing to accept a lower salary in exchange for a reduction in billable-hours requirements? Would the amount of your education loans have an impact on your decision?

Case Studies

1. Locate a law firm's mission statement online and review and critique it. What message does the statement convey? What are the statement's weak points? How might the message be strengthened? Is the statement too general?

2. Choose one element of a law firm staff manual to study. Research variations for drafting the element, and compare and contrast them. For instance, one element in a law firm manual might address casual Fridays.

3. Look at several law firm histories and compare and contrast them. You might consider accessing these sites:

   - http://www.drinkerbiddle.com/about-us
   - http://www.saul.com/about-history.html
   - http://www.cgsh.com/about/firmtimeline/
   - http://www.arnoldporter.com/about_the_firm_who_we_are_history.cfm
   - http://www.youtube.com/watch?v=QFEWV64RISU

   In undertaking your analysis, address each of the following. What common elements does each firm history have? Which history is more compelling? How do you think the firms want the reader to respond to the history? What does the history tell prospective employees and prospective clients about the firm's character and track record? What might have been omitted from the firm's history? Research negative episodes in the firm's past. Were those covered in the firm history? How long is the firm's history? Is the length appropriate, or should it be shorter or longer? Why?

4. Suppose you are a candidate in a job interview, and the interviewer asks an inappropriate question, such as "How will you handle child care?" How might you respond? Would your response differ depending on the amount of interest you have in being offered the job for which you are interviewing?

5. How would you react to receiving a poor performance evaluation?

6. Suppose you are a human resources manager at a law firm who has been asked to deal with a mail-room clerk who is chronically late and frequently absent from work. How would you address the problem?

Endnotes

1. 42 U.S.C. §2000e-2(a)(1).
2. 29 C.F.R. §1604.11(a) (2013).
3. 29 U.S.C. §§201–219.
4. 42 U.S.C. §§12101 *et seq.*
5. 42 U.S.C. §12102(2).

6. 29 U.S.C. §§2601 *et seq.*

7. 29 U.S.C. §§621 *et seq.*

8. 29 U.S.C. §623(a).

9. 29 U.S.C. §623(f)(2)(A).

10. 29 U.S.C. §631(c)(1).

11. Lori Tripoli, *New Leaders at Sidley Pursue New Profits, but Not at Any Cost*, Of Counsel, Jan. 3, 2000, at 1, 9-12.

12. Press Release, U.S. EEOC, EEOC Charges Sidley & Austin with Age Discrimination (Jan. 13, 2005), *available at* http://www.eeoc.gov/press/1-13-05.html.

13. *Id.*

14. 29 U.S.C §206(d)(1).

15. §§ 1 *et seq.*, 100 Stat. 82; 29 C.F.R. pt. 2590.

16. U.S. Department of Labor, Employee Benefits Security Administration, *Fact Sheet: Consolidated Omnibus Budget Reconciliation Act (COBRA)*, http://www.dol.gov/ebsa /newsroom/fscobra.html (last visited Aug. 16, 2013).

17. Pub. L. No. 111–148, 124 Stat. 119 (2010), amended by Health Care and Education Reconciliation Act of 2010, Pub.L. No. 111–152, 124 Stat. 1029 (2010).

18. Henry J. Kaiser Family Foundation, *Focus on Health Reform: Summary of Coverage Provisions in the Affordable Care Act*, *available at* http://www.kff.org (last updated July 17, 2012).

19. *National Federation of Independent Business v. Sebelius*, 132 S.Ct. 2566 (2012).

20. Peter Grier, *Obamacare 101: Why Major Part of Health Law Is Delayed, and Who's Affected*, CSMonitor.com (July 3, 2013), *available at* http://www.csmonitor.com /USA/DC-Decoder/2013/0703/Obamacare-101-Why-major-part-of-health-law-is-delayed-and-who-s-affected-video. For more information about the Patient Protection and Affordable Care Act and its implementation, see U.S. Department of Labor Employee Benefits Security Administration, Affordable Care Act, *available at* http:// www.dol.gov/ebsa/healthreform/ (last visited Aug. 16, 2013).

21. News Release, New York County District Attorney's Office (June 5, 2007), on *file with author*.

22. Alison Leigh Cowan, *Case of the Paralegal Who Played a Lawyer Raises Many Questions*, N.Y. Times (Jan. 22, 2007), *available at* http://www.nytimes.com/2007/01/22 /nyregion/22lawyer.html?pagewanted=1&_r=1.

23. Associated Press, *Manhattan: Fake Lawyer Pleads Guilty*, N.Y. Times (Oct. 11, 2007), http://www.nytimes.com/2007/10/11/nyregion/11mbrfs-lfake.html?scp=1&sq=%22 Brian+Valery%22&st=nyt.

24. Laura Italiano, *Bogus Att'y Takes a Trip*, N.Y. Post (Jan. 31, 2008), http://www.nypost .com/p/news/regional/item_amUYyNTZ5jHRRQBAyBeH3M.

25. Deena Shanker, *Why Are Lawyers Such Terrible Managers?*, CNN Money (Jan. 11, 2013), *available at* http://management.fortune.cnn.com/tag/turnover/.

26. *See* Denise Howell, *On Life Support: Was the Formula for a Good Work/Life Balance Figured Out in the 1970s?*, Am. Law., Apr. 1, 2008, *available at* http://www.law.com /jsp/tal/PubArticleTAL.jsp?hubtype=Inside&id=1207065967602.

27. Kellie Schmitt, *Latham Ramps Up Parental Benefits; Will Other Firms Follow?*, Recorder (San Francisco), Dec. 14, 2007, *available at* http://www.law.com/jsp/article .jsp?id=1197597876583.

28. *See* Noam Scheiber, The Last Days of Big Law, 244(12) New Republic 24–33 (Aug. 5, 2013).

29. *See, e.g.*, Peter Lattman, Mass Layoffs at a Top-Flight Law Firm, DealBook (June 24, 2013), *available at* http://dealbook.nytimes.com/2013/06/24/big-law-firm-to-cut-lawyers-and-some-partner-pay/?_r=0; Andrew Strickler, *Jones Day Lays Off 65 IT Workers*, Law360 (June 21, 2013), *available at* http://www.law360 .com/articles/452281/jones-day-lays-off-65-it-workers; Andrew Ramonas & Matthew

Huisman, *As Profits Sink, Patton Boggs Lays Off 65,* AmLaw Daily (Mar. 3, 2013), *available at* http://www.americanlawyer.com/PubArticleFriendlyALD .jsp?id=1202590750045.

30. *E.g.,* Don J. DeBenedictis, *Survey: New Grads Changing Bar: Minority, Female Lawyers Increasing, but Their Pay Is Below That of White Males,* 77 A.B.A. J. 34 (Nov. 1991); Martha Craig Daughtrey, *Commentary: Going Against the Grain: Personal Reflections on the Emergence of Women in the Legal Profession,* 67 Mont. L. Rev. 159, 160 (2006); Alex M. Johnson, Jr., *Why I Am Not a Lawyer: A Contextual Reply,* 8 Nexus 13 (2003).

31. *Call to Action: Diversity in the Legal Profession, Commitment Statement, available at* http://apps.americanbar.org/women/leadershipacademy/2010/handouts/calltoaction .pdf (last visited Aug. 16, 2013).

32. Brian Zabcik, *2013 Diversity Scorecard: Firms Regain Lost Ground,* American Lawyer (June 6, 2013), *available at* http://www.americanlawyer.com/PubArticleTAL .jsp?id=1202600856240&2013_Diversity_Scorecard_Firms_Regain_Lost_ Ground&slreturn=20130503092008.

33. A.B.A. Commission on Women in the Profession, *A Current Glance at Women in the Law* (Feb. 2013), *available at* http://www.americanbar.org/content/dam/aba /marketing/women/current_glance_statistics_feb2013.authcheckdam.pdf.

34. American Bar Association Section of Legal Education & Admissions to the Bar, *First Year J.D. and Total J.D. Minority Enrollment for 1971-2012,* http://www.americanbar .org/content/dam/aba/administrative/legal_education_and_admissions_to_the_bar /statistics/jd_enrollment_1yr_total_minority.authcheckdam.pdf (last visited Aug. 16, 2013).

35. Lea E. Delossantos, *COMMENT: A Tangled Situation of Gender Discrimination: In the Face of an Ineffective Antidiscrimination Rule and Challenges for Women in Law Firms—What Is the Next Step to Promote Gender Diversity in the Legal Profession?* 44 Cal. W. L. Rev. 295, 303-304 (2007).

36. Press Release, NALP, *Rate of Part-Time Work Among Lawyers Unchanged in 2012 — Most Working Part-time Continue to Be Women* (Feb. 21, 2013), *available at* http:// www.nalp.org/part-time_feb2013?s=part%2Dtime%20lawyers.

37. *Id.*

38. *See, e.g.,* American Bar Association Section of Legal Education & Admissions to the Bar, *Legal Education Statistics, First Year and Total J.D. Enrollment by Gender 1947-2011,* http://www.americanbar.org/content/dam/aba/administrative/legal_education_and_ admissions_to_the_bar/statistics/jd_enrollment_1yr_total_gender.authcheckdam.pdf (last visited Aug. 16, 2013).

39. Nicole Buonocore Porter, *Re-Defining Superwoman: An Essay on Overcoming the "Maternal Wall" in the Legal Workplac*e, 13 Duke J. Gender L. & Pol'y 55, 56 (2006).

40. Deborah L. Rhode, *Symposium: Perspectives on Lawyer Happiness: Foreword: Personal Satisfaction in Professional Practice,* 58 Syracuse L. Rev. 217, 223–24 (2008).

41. *See, e.g.,* Cassens Weiss, *Lawyer Depression Comes Out of the Closet,* A.B.A. J. L. News Now (Dec. 13, 2007), http://www.abajournal.com/news/lawyer_depression_comes_ out_of_the_closet; Tyger Latham, *The Depressed Lawyer,* Psychology Today (May 2, 2011), http://www.in.gov/judiciary/ijlap/substance-abuse/signs-symptoms.html.

42. Indiana Judges and Lawyers Assistance Program, *Signs and Symptoms in Attorneys,* *available at* http://www.in.gov/judiciary/ijlap/2357.htm (last visited on Aug. 16, 2013).

6

The Physical Law Office

Chapter Outcomes

By the end of this chapter, a student will be able to:

- Recognize facility management issues that arise with respect to law firms and propose solutions
- Develop workplace safety hazards for law offices and devise means to minimize those hazards
- Discuss how law firms are incorporating principles of sustainability in facility operations
- Evaluate a firm's selections of equipment and supplies and office design and decor
- Plan a law office's move

As bland as some law offices appear to be, a fair amount of thought may actually have gone into the presentation of the space. Walk into the reception area of a large law firm, and you might be met with a decor that signals cold, clean efficiency. Walk into a street-level firm that focuses on immigration law in a poor area, and you might see what looks like a storefront, with big windows and welcoming signs in English and in other languages—making a foreigner's experience of asking for legal help in a non-native land a bit less intimidating. A law office, with its space alone, conveys an image. Is this a luxurious, high-end firm where every client's whim will be accommodated? Is this a family law practice, with a lot of clients traipsing in to see their lawyers and bringing their kids along? The right planning can enhance a client's experience—and satisfaction—as well as make a lawyer's workday more pleasant.

Signals about firm culture can be gleaned from a firm's space. Is the managing partner in an office on the top floor, or can the firm's leaders be found "in the trenches" near lower-level partners and associates? Are paralegals relegated to dark, cramped spaces in lower floors, or are their offices or workstations near the lawyers they interact with frequently? Is the art on the walls staid and old, or is it contemporary and brightly colored? Are the walls white or paneled? Many elements of a firm's appearance can signal information about a firm's approach to the law, to its clients, and to its personnel. And, of course, a well-planned workspace can boost efficiency.

A.   Facility Management

A law firm might be a tenant in a building, own its own building, or even own a portion of a building. No matter what the arrangement, someone needs to assume the responsibility for **facility management.** If the space is leased, a landlord or its management company typically makes sure that the windows are cleaned periodically, that the boiler in the building is functioning, and that public hallways and the lobby are maintained. Responsibility for general cleaning of the firm's offices may vary—again, the landlord's cleaning team might dust, vacuum, and empty trash cans. Alternatively, the firm might be responsible for hiring its own cleaning crew. If that is the case, someone needs to make those arrangements, schedule cleaning, and be sure that the cleaning crew is paid. These tasks might fall to a law office manager.

facility management:
Coordination of a business's workspace, involving oversight of buildings as well as services.

The responsibilities for different sorts of facility management tasks might be given to various people. An overhead light bulb might blow out, a pipe might burst, carpeting might have become stained and need to be cleaned. How is each of these scenarios handled both within the firm itself and with respect to the landlord or managing agent? If an associate spills a cup of coffee on the carpeting in her office, whom should she contact to get it cleaned? A point person within the firm may be designated to handle facilities issues. That person, in turn, might carry on any necessary correspondence with building management or with the firm's hired cleaning crews or other vendors servicing the firm, such as plumbers, fish-tank maintenance crews, or florists. If the refrigerator in the firm kitchen breaks, who fixes it? Who is responsible for making the call to get someone to fix it? Who is responsible for paying the repairperson? All of these matters must be addressed.

Environmental concerns are also addressed in facility management and elsewhere within law firms. Law firms might decrease the impact of their businesses on the environment by taking measures to reduce the amount of energy used in their offices, by recycling paper and other materials, and by taking other steps to preserve and protect resources. In so doing, law firms may realize significant financial savings while being better "corporate citizens." The U.S. Environmental Protection Agency explains that **sustainability** is "the conditions under which humans and nature can exist in productive harmony, that permit fulfilling the social, economic and other requirements of present and future generations."[1]

sustainability:
The conditions in which humans and nature can exist in harmony so that social, economic, and environmental needs of current and future generations can be met.

The Council of American Bar Association Section of Environment, Energy and Resources has approved a Sustainability Framework for Law Organizations that demonstrates how sustainability relates to the legal industry. The framework includes a model policy and implementation guidelines. Efforts to become more sustainable typically begin by conducting a benchmark survey indicating how many resources are used and where. Then a plan for reducing the amount of resources used can be developed and implemented.[2] Some firms are also developing sustainability policies, reporting on their efforts, creating committees on sustainability, and hiring chief sustainability officers or other staff to manage sustainability efforts.[3]

Law firms undertake sustainable efforts for many reasons. They can demonstrate that they are concerned about the planet, improve workplace morale, and save money.[4] Corporate clients increasingly are inquiring about their lawyers' sustainability efforts. Becoming more sustainable can be a way for law firms to be more competitive.

B. Workplace Safety

Despite being staffed with fine legal minds, law firms are, unfortunately, not crime-free zones. An employee might still be involved in an ugly divorce and an embittered, about-to-be-former spouse might stalk the person, an office worker could commit a petty theft and lift wallets from lawyers' purses, a disgruntled former client might hack into the firm's Web site, or a random act of violence might occur. Crime can happen anywhere, at firms of all shapes and sizes, in high-end buildings and low-rent ones.

Consider these events that have happened in law firms:

- In July 2013, a former client of the Upton Law Firm, a small firm in Covington, Louisiana, began shooting a gun in the firm's parking lot, then broke through its security system while its law firm manager was inside, and fired more shots in the office before killing himself there.[5]
- A temporary worker in the Atlanta, Georgia, office of Paul Hastings shot and killed a secretary at the firm before killing himself outside the building. Apparently, the two had been romantically involved at one point.[6]
- A partner at Boggs, Boggs & Bates in Clayton, Missouri, was shot and killed and found by the office cleaning people. Another lawyer in the building told a reporter that security was nonexistent in the building.[7]
- A 26-year-old Florida lawyer who had recently been elected to the board of governors of his state bar association's young lawyers division and who was expecting his first child with his wife, was shot and killed in his office by his father-in-law.[8]
- In July 1993, an unhappy former client of Pettit & Martin in San Francisco went on a rampage at the firm's offices and shot 14 people, killing eight of them, before killing himself.[9]

Although no office is really impenetrable, law firms can take measures to better insulate themselves from the likelihood of violence and other crimes. They can engage in better employee screening and "harden" their office building to make it more secure from attacks on power lines, on the Internet, or from human outsiders. Security measures can be developed, implemented, and enforced. For instance, a firm might require all visitors, even deliverypersons, to sign in. Those who have business with someone at the firm might be escorted to the appropriate meeting place so that they cannot wander freely around the offices. Staff may be taught about workplace violence issues. For example, a firm might train employees how to recognize the warning signs of violence and what to do if violence erupts at the law firm.[10]

The possibility of someone engaging in inappropriate behavior in an office can be decreased if visiting clients are required to be escorted by a firm employee. A firm should establish whether messengers may deliver documents to someone personally in the office or whether they must leave their material with the firm's receptionist. A firm might also install a "panic button" that would alert either the police or senior firm officials to an immediate problem. A code phrase might be established for the firm's receptionist to use in case of trouble that would not be apparent to an evildoer. Procedures for locking office doors should be established. Will the doors be locked at 5:00 P.M. every day? Who will be responsible for locking them? Who is entitled to have a key to the office for weekend access? Those keys should be tracked. If an employee leaves the firm, the key must be turned in.

Procedures should be developed for handling emergencies. Important telephone numbers should be posted at several places in an office, along with the firm's address and location. People typically know to dial 911 in an emergency. But must a 9 be dialed first to get to an outside line? If an office building has guards at the front desk, is their number posted so that security could be summoned before police arrive? Knowing one's own workplace address might seem obvious, but workers under duress typically are not able to focus on details such as addresses. They might come to work via subway and never really notice the exact street name or number. If an office building is in an office park, a worker might not be able to accurately describe which building the firm is in.

The procedures manual should address various scenarios, such as what to do if someone has a heart attack in the office or suffers an injury on the job. Where are first-aid materials located? Who is responsible for notifying the person's family or significant others? Where can that information be found? A firm should also develop fire evacuation plans as well as plans for responding to natural calamities such as floods, earthquakes, or hurricanes. Procedures for something as seemingly minor as a power failure should also be established. Who is responsible for calling in the problem to the appropriate utility? Must an account number be accessed? Where is that information stored? Should all computers be turned off if a power failure occurs? Should other precautionary steps be taken? These sorts of matters should be thought about ahead of time—procedures should be developed and distributed, and everyone at the firm should be educated about them.

C.   Disaster Preparedness

Responses to large-scale catastrophes should also factor into a law firm's planning. As unlikely as these sorts of events are, they do happen—and their consequences can be far-reaching for businesses. The 9/11 terrorist attacks on the World Trade Center in New York City in 2001 dislocated some law firms and inspired leadership at others to take **disaster preparedness plans** seriously.[11]

All sorts of calamities—floods, fires, terrorist attacks—may occur. Think of the bombing of the Alfred P. Murrah Federal Building in Oklahoma City in 1995, the delivery of anthrax-contaminated letters to government and private offices in 2001, the blackout on much of the East Coast of the United States in 2003, the impact of Hurricane Katrina on New Orleans and Mississippi in 2005, and the damage brought by Hurricane Sandy to the East Coast of the United States in 2012. In such cases, landline phone systems might not work, cell phones may be jammed, e-mail messages may not be delivered through servers, and employees might not know where or to whom they are supposed to report. While it is impossible to envision every sort of worst-case scenario, a plan should be developed for employees to follow in emergency situations. Should they all be required to report within a certain time? To whom should they report if the office is no longer accessible? How will employees who do not report be contacted? Via phone? Via their own personal e-mail accounts? Who will be responsible for contacting these people? Where are updated contact lists kept and maintained?

Technological aids can help law firms in times of crisis. Electronic alert systems can be set up in advance and instant notifications sent out.[12]

In addition, a disaster preparedness plan should include data backup, procurement and maintenance of appropriate insurance, and a means for keeping employee contact information up to date. People must be able to contact one another. Along those lines, more than one person at a firm should know where its assets are and should maintain account numbers, inventories, and records of service providers and service contracts. Perhaps most important, the firm should not merely draft a disaster response plan—it should also actually conduct disaster exercises in which employees practice implementing that plan.

A **business continuity plan** should establish a hierarchy of people responsible for handling the firm's business in the event of a disaster. Who will phone key clients to reassure them? Where are their names and contact information? Who is responsible for contacting insurers? Where are copies of appropriate policies? Files should be backed up and stored in remote locations or in the cloud. After 9/11, some New York City law firms had to call their adversaries to try to re-create their files.[13] Although a spirit of cooperation tends to exist after a terrorist attack, better preparation can prevent the scampering that some firms had to do when disaster did indeed strike. A business continuity plan will help a firm determine damage to its personnel, building, and technology, and will provide a roadmap of steps to take to get the business operational again following a disaster.[14]

It should also be remembered that disasters have a psychological impact on people. Employees, stunned by events and, perhaps, by grief at the loss of coworkers and friends, probably will not be functioning as well as they normally do. Disasters are life-changing. It's only to be expected that the trauma of such an occurrence will trickle down to the workplace. A firm might consider bringing in grief counselors or providing employees with other options should the stress of events have too great an impact on their work.

disaster preparedness plan:
A set of procedures devised for responding to emergency situations.

business continuity plan:
A set of procedures and information for continuing to provide services in the face of a disruptive event.

D. Equipment and Supplies

Lawyers need certain basic materials to work with: paper, pens, computers, printers, copiers. They also need access to a law library and to online databases of the law, such as Lexis or Westlaw. Someone needs to order those supplies, arrange for access to fee-based databases, and purchase and maintain the equipment. A law office manager might be responsible for reordering supplies, planning for future needs, making sure that equipment is maintained, overseeing service contracts and warranties, and making sure that new hires get the machines they need, such as a desktop computer, a laptop, an iPhone, or other smartphone that has Internet access and e-mail capability, and a tablet computer.

Large law firms may have information technology (IT) departments to handle technological issues for the entire firm. These firms are in positions to develop their own software when it is needed or to have it specially developed by someone else. IT specialists within a firm might vet products and make recommendations to a law firm committee that has purchasing authority. Because a large firm makes significant purchases, vendors might bid for the firm's business. Other firms might look to outside consultants when making IT decisions. It is important to let the people who will actually be using an application give it a try to make sure they like it. Firms might try to obtain an evaluation copy of a software program prior to making a major purchase:

> There's usually a big difference between what people say things can do and what they actually can do. . . . It's not that those software vendors are used car salesmen trying to unload lemons. "They just don't necessarily know the intricacies of your environment and how you've customized other applications[.]"[15]

No matter the size of the firm, data storage, accessibility, and backup must be addressed. Decision makers also must be sure that lawyers and staff know how to use office equipment and software. Lawyers tend to resist taking time out for training sessions, while administrative staff tend to be better trained on applications. If the lawyers at a firm are not going to take the time to learn how to use all of the fancy add-ons in a computer program, why pay to procure them?

Lawyers must be able to communicate with their clients. A client who cannot open attachments because her lawyer is using an older version of a software program is quickly going to become an unhappy client. A firm's aptitude with technology can actually affect firm retention and recruiting. Lawyers want and need the support of technology to do their jobs well; a law office lagging in this area will not be so attractive to them. Moreover, the comments to Model Rule 1.1 addressing competence specify that a lawyer should keep current about applicable technology used in law practice along with its benefits and risks.[16]

In the past, law firms largely drove the decision about which technology to use. Would the firm use computers or Mac-based applications? Would the word processing program be WordPerfect or Microsoft Word? Now, more and more, clients are driving that decision.

Lawyers must remember to plan for the future and anticipate their upcoming technological needs. At this point, typewriters are essentially obsolete, and, with the improvement in scanning capability from document to computer, fax machines are not often needed anymore either.

With advances in technology, there is always talk about shifting to a paper-free office. Despite advances in digital storage and scanning abilities, law offices still require significant amounts of paper, although they may use less paper than in earlier decades as lawyers rely less on printouts and review more documents and correspondence on-screen. Client files may be more accessible—and more portable—on a computer than in a thick accordion file. Lawyers rely less on paper products such as books and magazines, as they have moved to a digital medium.[17]

Even so, hard copies of many documents must still be kept and maintained. Among its supplies, a law firm needs a fair number of filing cabinets as well as a means of tracking files and providing long-term storage for them.

E. Telecommunication Systems

Much of a lawyer's business is conducted via telephone, whether land-based or wireless. Similarly, lawyers do a lot of work via the Internet, transmitting documents and sending e-mail messages to clients, courts, opposing counsel, and others. Clients might expect a response to an e-mail message within hours, not days. A lawyer's need for e-mail access can be nearly constant. Security of these **telecommunication systems** must be maintained so that data transmitted or accessed from a remote location are safe. Telecommunication systems may need to be expanded as the firm and its needs grow.

telecommunication system:
Means of transmitting signals for the purpose of communicating via telephone, computer, radio, television, and other devices.

Very basic questions about a firm's telephone service must be addressed. How are calls handled that are received at the firm's main telephone number? How easily are those phone calls forwarded to appropriate extensions or to lawyers in remote offices? What happens during busy times? Are calls automatically directed to voice mail? If a call is placed on hold, does music play? If so, what is the source of that music? Are radio stations clients of the firm? Should their stations be played? What arrangements must be made for a conference call to be conducted, recorded, and transcribed? Does caller ID work even if a call is first received at the firm's main phone number and then forwarded to a lawyer? Does each phone time calls to help lawyers track their billable hours? How quickly can employees learn the phone system?

Lawyers and appropriate personnel at firms must keep up with technological advances, such as the use of **Voice over Internet Protocol** (VoIP), which can reduce costs. Advances in telephone capabilities allow each lawyer to have a single phone number that forwards calls seamlessly and makes communications from clients easier. Wireless capacity, both for cell phone calls and for transmission of data, must also be considered, budgeted for, and securely protected.

Voice over Internet Protocol (VoIP):
A means of transmitting voice communications over the Internet.

When a firm procures a new telecommunication system, a strategy for converting to the new system must be developed. For instance, a firm might roll out its new telecommunication system in one office at a time, starting with smaller ones, to see how it goes and work out glitches before the large home office makes the transition. Sometimes, despite a firm's best intentions and significant investment, major malfunctions occur.[18]

F.   Parking Spaces

Parking would seem to be a simple matter. If there's a lot, park in it; if not, park wherever you can. Yet all sorts of issues can arise if a law firm has a designated parking area. Who will get the best spots? Will they be reserved for senior partners? For an "employee of the year"? Or should parking simply be first come, first served? Should spaces closest to the office be designated for clients?

Will free parking be provided for lawyers only, or for lawyers and staff? Will clients be reimbursed for their parking costs or have their parking tickets stamped? All clients or only major clients? And who will decide?

A firm might choose to use parking as a sustainability incentive for its personnel. For instance, bike racks might be set up close to the firm's front doors, and the closest parking spaces might be reserved for people who carpool or for those who drive an environmentally friendly car, such as a Toyota Prius.

Parking can also be linked to security. If someone is leaving the firm after dark, should an escort to the parking lot be provided? If so, who is that escort? A security guard from the firm's building? Is escort service provided as part of the firm's lease? If not, will additional fees be charged for escort service? Will escort service be available to everyone, or only to clients or lawyers?

G.   Office Design and Decor

A law firm's physical appearance makes a statement about the firm's mission, its attitude, and even its level of success. Old, aristocratic, staid law firms might still choose dark, wood-paneled interiors and artwork featuring centuries-old paintings of forebears or ships. Firms doing business with a lot of dot-com, cutting-edge, new-generation companies might choose a bright interior with design elements conveying a message of high energy and creativity. A firm with battered wooden desks and dust bunnies in the corners or one with a decor not updated since the 1970s also sends a message about how it is performing—and the message might not be such a good one.

Ideally, a firm's space should be efficient as well as effective in both conveying the image the firm seeks and pleasing clients. Balancing all three with budgetary needs can be challenging. If a firm's decor appears too luxurious, it may actually be off-putting even to high-end clients who might believe their legal bills are going to fund the firm's interior designer. An interior that features contemporary, progressive art may offend big-business clients who have a more conservative view of the world.

Both a firm's exterior and public spaces must be considered, as should individual lawyer offices and staff work areas. A firm might develop basic or very detailed guidelines for lawyers and others about decorating their workspaces. The firm's lease might limit some of the changes that can be made, such as to window treatments and wall colors. Firms might have standard-issue furniture for everyone or allow partners to choose from a few different models—or grant them free rein entirely in selecting office furniture. Some lawyers choose to incorporate elements of the practice in decorating their spaces. For instance, one prominent divorce lawyer collects antique marriage certificates, which she has framed and mounted on her office walls. Whether clients are permitted to visit a lawyer's office may influence how it is decorated. Lawyers tend to spend a lot of time in their offices and may opt to create a workspace that is pleasing to them personally.

For staff, a firm should consider the extent to which decoration of personal workspace will be permitted. Again, whether clients ever view the space should be a consideration. Some offices hold "decorate your carrel" contests—with sometimes outrageous results. Guidelines, ideally, should be drafted and included in the firm's handbook.

1. *Firm Image*

Color, furniture style, wall coverings—all convey subtle messages about a law firm. Are the drapes clean or dusty? Is the firm's reception area bright and full of light, or does it darkly convey an air of solemnity? Is the overall effect of a firm's decor one of lavishness or of stark efficiency? Will clients be impressed, or will they think they are paying their lawyers too much money?

Not only are clients affected and influenced by a firm's appearance, but so are the people who work there. In making decorating decisions, a firm should consider its demographics. Older lawyers might prefer a more hierarchical approach to offices, with large ones designated for more senior partners. The younger generation might be satisfied with good electronics—up-to-the-minute computers with speakers and in-office wireless Internet access so they can use their laptops anywhere.

The appearance of the firm's offices can also affect recruiting. Do paralegals work in high-walled, gray cubicles in windowless interior space, or do they have a more open workspace or even an office? Must junior associates share an office? Are more senior support staff granted personal office space? The work environment may be a vital factor in a prospective hire's willingness to come on board.

2. *Firm Politics: Varying Office Size Based on Rank Versus Same-Size Offices*

Traditionally, large offices in law firms were designated for senior-ranking partners. Both office size and location (such as in the corner of a building and on a high floor) conveyed one's place in the firm's hierarchy. Windowless, interior offices were designated for paralegals or other firm staff; offices that have windows were reserved for lawyers, with office size increasing as the lawyer's status within the firm rose.

More recently, though, office space has been shrinking. When one Philadelphia- based boutique firm relocated, partner offices were downsized from 20 feet by 15 feet at the firm's former space to 15 feet by 15 feet in the new one. Everyone was issued a standard set of furniture, except for some partners who brought their own.[19]

Determining who gets the prime real estate in a law office can cause political intrigue. A firm might base such decisions on pecking order (with firm leadership getting the prime choices), on tenure with the firm, on the number of years since graduating from law school, or on any number of factors. Sometimes jockeying for a prime office can seem like playing musical chairs. Having a system in place for determining how office spaces are assigned, though, can minimize the amount of politics and grousing about who gets what and when.

As for the furnishings in the offices, the law firm itself might choose the furniture for associates and for staff. At one time, when a lawyer was elevated to partner, he or she was given a stipend of $12,000 or more to decorate the office. As budgets have tightened, some firms stopped doing that, and some even require that uniform furniture be used or that selections be made from several predetermined options.[20] Nowadays freshly minted partners might be a bit reticent to spend a lot of money on their new offices, since they know they'll be switching offices within their firm as their careers proceed, or they might even switch firms at some point in the future.

3. Ergonomics

ergonomics:
The study of the relationship between people and their working environment geared toward maximizing productivity while ensuring health and safety of workers by providing appropriately designed tools for work-related tasks.

The term *ergonomics* refers to how well people interact with the objects that they use. **Ergonomics** is defined as "an applied science concerned with the characteristics of people that need to be considered in designing things that they use in order that people and things will interact most effectively and safely—called also *human engineering, human factors engineering*[.]"[21]

Lawyering might seem like a relatively hazard-free position, but job-related injuries can still occur. If your computer screen is not set at a proper level, your neck might hurt at the end of the day, or your back might ache from sitting in an improperly positioned chair. Repetitive stress injuries, such as carpal tunnel syndrome, can occur in workers who use computer keyboards.

In addition to providing well-designed office furniture and equipment, law firms (and any other business, for that matter) should make sure that computers and related equipment are properly positioned. Workers should be trained to maintain appropriate posture. Ergonomics experts can be hired to assist in office design and setup and to teach personnel how to properly use equipment to minimize the risk of repetitive stress injury. Productivity can increase in an ergonomically designed office.

4. Efficiency

Workspaces and, indeed, entire law offices should be designed to maximize worker efficiency. To the extent a budget allows, sufficient electrical outlets, telephone extensions, Internet connections, printers, and other equipment should be provided so that workers, whether staff or attorneys, do not waste time on unbillable activities.

At the same time, a firm, both for economic reasons and to be economically responsible, may want to incorporate sustainable design elements into the workplace. Natural lighting might be used to reduce electricity bills, office lights might be turned off at night, and temperature levels might be lowered during nighttime hours in the winter and raised in the summer. Energy-efficient light bulbs might be procured and other efforts taken to reduce waste and to recycle otherwise discarded items.

5. *Professional Designers*

Architects, interior designers, and other consultants who focus on office space or even specialize in the design of law offices can be retained to provide advice on how a firm can develop the most impressive, yet functional, workspace given its budgetary constraints. It may seem that all that's needed are a few desks, chairs, phones, and computers, but to be in business, far more attention to workspace is needed to create an appealing environment that is attractive to both workers and clients. Getting advice from experts can prevent a firm from making costly mistakes. So, for example, a decorator might be able to inform an otherwise oblivious firm that gray is not the ideal color for carpeting. Yes, it's neutral, inoffensive, and likely to hide dirt, but it's also associated with boredom, sadness, and grief. Intense colors, though possibly unappealing to some, can improve workers' creativity, energy levels, and productivity.

Other consultants, such as feng shui experts, can also help law firms optimize their workspace. Practitioners of **feng shui** believe that the placement of objects affects the energy flow within a space.[22] Feng shui principles are incorporated into many buildings in Asian countries but are a more recent consideration in Western ones.

feng shui:
A Chinese term meaning "wind and water"—an ancient Chinese practice of harmonizing the environment and balancing its energy patterns to achieve health, happiness, and prosperity.

H. Office Space Planning When Making a Move

A law firm might need to move into new space for any number of reasons. A firm might have outgrown its current location, firm finances might have improved or worsened, or a lease might simply be terminating. A firm might relocate to a new building entirely, or it may be able to add space to its current location by, for example, leasing additional floors in a building. Depending on the flexibility of the firm's space, a firm experiencing growth might be able to renovate—move walls and rearrange other aspects of the office—to accommodate either more or fewer lawyers.

Should a firm opt to move, a checklist identifying all of the tasks that must be considered and undertaken should be developed and followed.

1. *Location*

Real estate agents like to say that location is everything, and in many ways it is. But a location that might be optimal for one law firm may be far less than ideal for another. Much depends on the size of the firm, the types of law it practices, and the residential and transportation needs of its lawyers and employees. Are lawyers in the firm in court a lot, or do they not really litigate but instead focus on transactions-based work? If the lawyers do make frequent court appearances, should the firm be near the county courthouse or a federal courthouse? Should the firm be near a government agency it frequently interacts with?

How to attract and keep clients should be considered as alternative locations are evaluated. What sorts of clients will be visiting the firm? Will they be primarily corporate clients who are used to certain amenities, such as nearby parking and guest space so that they can temporarily use desks, telephones, and computers to remain in contact with their own offices? Or are many of the firm's clients individuals involved in family law issues, such as divorce and custody agreements? These clients might be more interested in a law firm that has a children's play area or that is less intimidating than one catering to a corporate clientele.

Attracting and keeping employees are also important. Staff, too, might be keenly interested in the availability of public transportation, in nearby places to eat lunch or to grab a cappuccino, and in the overall atmosphere of the building and the firm's space.

2.   Cost

The cost of relocating the firm from an old space to a new one must be considered. Although the rent on a new space might be significantly lower than the rent at the firm's current location, once the costs of packing everything up, having it moved, preparing the new space for the firm, and changing the firm's stationery, signage, Web site, and advertising materials are factored in, staying put might actually be the better choice.

Typically, commercial space is rented by the square foot. Rates per square foot vary depending on the area in which a building is located, whether it's in an urban or more remote area, and on the quality of the building itself. Top-tier buildings (typically referred to as Class A buildings) with luxurious lobbies, doormen, security, and other amenities command the highest prices. Lower-tier buildings, with fewer amenities, rent at lower rates.

3.   Lease Options

When renting commercial office space, a law firm might be obligated to sign a lease committing it to the space for a number of years. Depending on the terms of the lease, the firm might be obligated to pay for all expenses associated with the space, such as maintenance and upkeep, utilities, and other costs.

Of course, a firm does not have to rent space at all. It could consider buying space on its own. It does not have to purchase an entire building; it might instead buy a commercial condominium or commercial cooperative.

Real estate costs can be a significant component of a firm's annual budget. Given client interest in reducing legal costs and advances in technology, firms tend to be using smaller spaces than they once did. Interior spaces once dedicated to administrative staff are increasingly being used for junior lawyers.[23]

4.   Growth Projections

Before committing to a particular space for a period of years, a law firm should consider its plans for expansion or, in a worst-case scenario, for contraction if, for instance, a practice group should leave. Will the firm be obligated to pay rent for empty office space? If the firm is unable to recruit more lawyers immediately, can it sublet the space? If the firm is interested in expanding, can it get an option to rent the floor immediately above or below it when leases for those spaces expire?

The physical space a firm is interested in obtaining should be assessed for its flexibility in being modified. Would adding additional lawyers, or even entire practice groups, be relatively easy? Space that can be easily modified might be preferable if a firm is anticipating significant growth. Can interior walls be easily modified, or adjacent office space easily rented?

Consideration should also be given to a firm's additional equipment needs as it expands. A space's electrical wiring should be inspected to determine whether it could handle anticipated spikes in energy needs. If the wiring is not adequate, can it be relatively easily and inexpensively upgraded?

Of course, a firm might be planning to add personnel but still might not need a whole lot of extra space if, for instance, those personnel might be telecommuting or spending significant chunks of time outside the office.

5. Accessibility

How, exactly, the space will be used by the people who work there should be assessed. Will conference rooms frequently be used for depositions and negotiations with opposing counsel and their clients? Are the people visiting the firm likely to be combatants (e.g., a divorcing husband and wife)? Should there be separate reception areas? Will conference rooms frequently be commandeered by litigators who need a "war room" to prepare for major trials? Who will be coming to the firm, and how often? Are high-profile people clients of the firm? If so, alternative entrances might be considered so that these clients can avoid recognition and limit press coverage.

Access for people with disabilities must also be addressed. Depending on the size of the firm and other factors, handicapped-accessible entrances might be required, and handicapped-accessible bathrooms may need to be installed.

6. Public and Work Areas

Some areas of the firm will be accessible to clients, messengers, delivery persons, and others doing business with the firm, while other portions of the firm, such as staff break rooms, are unlikely to be seen by anyone other than employees. Those staff-only areas may be decorated in a more functional, efficient way than public areas through which clients are likely to pass.

In addition, of course, if the firm is in a building that houses other businesses, public areas of the building itself—such as the entrance, lobby, elevators, and hallways—will make an impression. Moreover, there may be varying levels of security depending on the location of the building. Firm security might require all visitors to sign in upon entering the building. These public spaces can convey all sorts of messages to visitors. Is the lobby plush and spacious? Are people loitering outside the front of the building and smoking cigarettes? Are the elevators fast-moving, or are they old and rickety? Are hallways wide, clean, and well lit, or are they narrow and poorly maintained?

a)   RECEPTION

In its reception area, a firm makes an initial impression on everyone who walks through the firm's doors. A receptionist should greet every visitor immediately. Busy firms may have more than one receptionist stationed at the entrance. Depending on the firm, visitors might be offered coffee or other beverages.

Although firms sometimes like to have their receptionists answer telephones and handle mail as well as assist visitors to the firm, the receptionist's work area should be designed to maintain appropriate confidentiality of any materials the receptionist is working on.

Attention should be paid to security as well. The firm should develop a policy concerning when doors into the reception area will be locked and unlocked and should establish who will be responsible for locking the doors at appropriate times. At the very least, a receptionist should have a telephone with emergency numbers either programmed into it or easily accessible. Additional security measures might include a silent alarm that the receptionist can activate should he or she experience any difficulty with a visitor. Additionally, access to other firm areas might be barred until someone arrives to escort a visitor to an appropriate area. The receptionist, too, might have the ability to remotely lock or unlock doors to the interior of the law firm.

b)   ATTORNEY AREAS

Before designing its space, a law firm should determine who will have access to the lawyers' offices and the firm's conference rooms. Some firms require that all meetings take place in conference rooms, so those areas are carefully maintained and well decorated, while lawyer and staff offices might not be quite so sumptuous. If lawyers are likely to meet with clients in their offices, then more money may be allotted to fixing up those spaces to make a positive impression.

c)   STAFF AREAS

Paralegal workspaces, secretary stations, the firm's mail room, file rooms, copy and fax centers, and a staff lounge are areas that are unlikely to be visited by clients. Of these, secretary stations are probably the most visible, so they should be appealing and well maintained. If there's likely to be a lot of client traffic, the workspace should be designed to protect the privacy and security of client documents that might be worked on, and the secretary should take precautions to make sure that such materials are not unattended and open to view should she step away from her workspace.

A staff lounge or kitchen might contain cabinets, a sink, coffee makers and hot water heaters (for tea and other hot beverages), a microwave oven, a toaster, a refrigerator, table and chairs, and possibly a television. A dishwasher may also be included. Large law firms may feature a cafeteria.[24]

A delivery room for mail and privately delivered parcels might be set up in an area easily accessible to postal carriers and other delivery people but somewhat remote from lawyers and other personnel. Procedures for identifying and handling suspicious packages should be established. Lawyers often work on high-profile cases that can generate all sorts of responses from members of the general public. Similarly, clients or the opposing side in a case can sometimes take inappropriate actions. Precautions should be taken when handling materials delivered to the firm.

d)   CONFERENCE ROOMS

Large law firms might have a dozen or more conference rooms at each branch. These rooms might be of varying sizes and used for varying purposes. Some firms have reservation systems to book conference rooms. Small firms can often get by with a less formal approach. Litigators tend to take over conference rooms for months at a time as final preparations for trial are made. They tend to use these rooms on a round-the-clock basis and keep many vital documents in these rooms when they are in use.

Conference rooms are generally equipped with long, large tables and luxurious chairs. They typically have conference call capabilities and might feature screens for PowerPoint and video presentations. Conference rooms might also have a wet bar area, because drinks and food are often served during conferences. Small conference rooms may not have such amenities.

7.   Security

The firm's people and the documents the firm houses must be kept safe. Files should be kept in fireproof safes, and important documents, such as wills, should be kept in a firm safe. Access to files should be limited, and files should be tracked when they are removed from cabinets. Backup files should also be maintained, and digital versions should be backed up, too, so that they are recoverable in the case of a system crash of some sort.

8.   Amenities

Lawyers and staff members tend to spend a lot of time in the office. They often work late and on weekends. Given the amount of time people spend in the office, some firms provide amenities. A kitchen is a basic one, but a firm might also have a gym on the premises so that lawyers can exercise during work hours without having to leave the office. Lawyers have been known to pull all-nighters at the office, so bathrooms with showers might be provided as well.

Large firms may also offer on-site or nearby daycare and designate nursing rooms for new mothers.

Libraries are continually evolving as more material is placed in digital format and available on the Internet. Libraries have increasingly been scaled down as more and more resources are available digitally and can be accessed on computers, tablets, and smartphones.[25] Libraries, depending on the firm, might serve different functions. At large law firms, they might have several full-time librarians and staff people. Libraries at small firms might also be used as conference rooms, or they might house paralegal staff.

9. Image

From the quality of the building a firm is housed in to the quality of its interior decor, a firm is making an overall presentation. Some consideration should be given to the neighbors of the firm. Are nearby businesses other, similar firms that are likely to compete with the firm? Or might there be opportunity for referral of overflow work? Are businesses that the firm might like as clients situated nearby?

The firm's clientele should be similarly assessed before any decision about a new firm location is made. If, for instance, one of the firm's clients is Verizon, should the firm be in a high-rise building that is home to other telecommunication companies? If the firm represents conservative religious groups, should it share a building with quite liberal companies? Similar questions should be asked when the firm buys supplies. If Hewlett-Packard is a client, should the firm be buying Xerox printers? If Staples is a client, should the firm use legal pads and pens from OfficeMax?

10. Parking

Lawyers at a small firm might like nothing more than to practice in a converted old Victorian building that's in the center of the business district. But if clients visit the office frequently, they need a place to park unless the firm is in a city like New York, where many people take taxis or use public transportation to get from point to point. Other areas are more car-centric. Does that charming Victorian even have a driveway? Is there only 30-minute metered parking in front of the building, or are longer periods allowed? Where is the closest public parking lot? How much does parking there cost?

Such a charming Victorian space may still be perfect for a practice that doesn't see a lot of client traffic. Is most work with clients done over the phone or via e-mail? Do the lawyers typically visit clients at their businesses? Is public transportation easily accessible? If so, then lawyers might have more freedom in choosing an unconventional space for their office.

11. Mechanical Systems

Although lawyers don't need to become experts in building maintenance to become a tenant in one, they should nevertheless give some thought to a building's heating and cooling system and its ventilation. Some buildings have mold problems. Indoor air quality is important to workers. As energy prices rise, utility bills are increasingly important to everyone.

An office space with programmable thermostats and the ability to heat or cool specific zones at different times can save on energy bills. A firm seeking out a new space might inquire about the energy efficiency of a building. More buildings are incorporating environmentally friendly and energy-efficient features. Natural building materials might be used, solar panels may provide some energy for the building, and natural light might be more available than in older, less **green buildings**.

green building:
A structure that uses resources efficiently and is environmentally friendly.

Checklist

- A law office, with its space alone, conveys an image.
- Law firms increasingly are making their operations and facilities more sustainable.
- Signals about firm culture can be gleaned from a firm's space.
- A law firm might be a tenant in a building, own its own building, or even own a portion of a building. No matter what the arrangement, someone needs to take care of maintenance of the facility.
- Workplace safety is a topic of concern for law firms. Law firms can take measures to better insulate themselves from the likelihood of violence and other crimes. They can engage in better employee screening and "harden" their office building to make it more secure from attacks on power lines, on the Internet, or from human outsiders. Security measures can be developed, implemented, and enforced.
- Firms should develop a disaster preparedness plan and should practice evacuating the firm in case of a calamity. Such a plan should include arrangements for lawyers and staff to contact one another if there is an evacuation. In addition, the plan should address data backup, procurement and maintenance of appropriate insurance, and a means for keeping employee contact information up to date.
- A business continuity plan should establish a hierarchy of people responsible for handling firm business in the event of a disaster.
- No matter the size of the firm, data storage, accessibility, and backup must be addressed. Decision makers also must ascertain that lawyers and staff know how to use office equipment and software. Lawyers must remember to plan for the future and anticipate their upcoming technological needs.
- Not only are clients affected and influenced by a firm's appearance, but so are the people who work there. In making decorating decisions, a firm should consider its demographics.
- Recently, office space and firm libraries have been shrinking.
- In addition to providing well-designed office furniture and equipment, law firms (and any other business, for that matter) should make sure that computers and related equipment are properly positioned for employees.
- Law firms planning a move should create and follow a checklist.
- When a law firm is making a decision about a new space, location, cost, lease options, growth projections, accessibility, public and private work areas, security, amenities, firm image, parking, and mechanical systems should all be considered.

Vocabulary

business continuity plan (p. 149)
disaster preparedness plan
(p. 149)
ergonomics (p. 154)
facility management (p. 146)
feng shui (p. 155)

green building (p. 160)
sustainability (p. 146)
telecommunication system
(p. 151)
Voice over Internet Protocol
(VoIP) (p. 151)

Career Preparation Tips

In trying to assess the financial viability of prospective employers, you might research information about their office space and how much money they are spending on it. The physical locations of law firms, and the years they have committed to specific locations, can give an indication of the firm's long-range plans for the location and for its expansion plans. A viable place to begin researching information about law firms' physical locations is in real estate trade publications and in the real estate sections of newspapers.

In planning your own career, you might consider where you want to work. Do you want to work in the location where you currently reside, in another specific city, or wherever you get a desirable job? Research law firms in areas where you would like to work. If granted an interview at a firm, consider asking questions about physical space and sustainability. You might also ask for a tour of the firm and of your potential workspace.

If You Want to Learn More

American Red Cross. http://www.redcross.org

Centers for Disease Control and Prevention. http://www.bt.cdc.gov/planning/

Department of Homeland Security. http://www.dhs.gov

Federal Emergency Management Agency. http://www.fema.gov

Human Factors and Ergonomics Society. http://www.hfes.org

Law Technology News. http://www.lawtechnews.com

Disorders that can result from job environments and conditions and suggestions for ways to avoid work-related injuries are addressed at the Medline Plus Web site. http://www.nlm.nih.gov/medlineplus/ergonomics.html

Learn about the Occupational Safety and Health Administration's approach to preventing musculoskeletal disorders in the workplace. https://www.osha.gov/SLTC/ergonomics/

Access a checklist developed by the Alabama State Bar for setting up a new law office. http://www.alabar.org/pmap/articles/011110-Checklist.pdf

U.S. Green Building Council. http://www.usgbc.org

The ABA Section of Environment, Energy and Resources Law Firm Sustainability Framework provides a model policy and implementation guidelines to help law offices become more sustainable. http://www.americanbar.org/groups/environment_energy_resources/projects_awards/model_law.html

The Law Firm Sustainability Network promotes sustainability in the legal industry. http://www.lfsnetwork.org

Reading Comprehension

1. What information about a law firm's culture can be gleaned from an assessment of its physical interior?
2. What is sustainability, and why are some law firms taking measures to become more sustainable?
3. What sorts of security threats do law firms face, and how can firms minimize or prevent those threats?
4. What elements should be included in a disaster preparedness plan?
5. How can a firm's information technology capabilities affect firm retention?
6. How might a law firm's decor vary depending on the types of clients the firm services?
7. What are disadvantages to leasing office space rather than owning the space?
8. How can office space and other amenities be used to provide incentives to lawyers and staff?
9. Why might a firm be interested in being in an environmentally friendly building?

Discussion Starters

1. Research a recent disaster that affected a business in your area. What precautionary steps might the business have taken to minimize the damage? What could other businesses learn from this experience?
2. How might the business continuity plan of a small firm differ from that of a large firm?
3. Find a recent court decision in your state involving a repetitive stress injury in an office environment. Who brought the suit? Against whom? Who won? How could the employer in the case have created a better work environment?
4. Research commercial office space rental rates in your area. What is the cost of rental space? How do rates for high-end space compare with those at the low end? Which amenities would you be willing to forgo?
5. A real estate firm issued a press release indicating that a major law firm had renewed a lease for 26 floors of an office building for 20 years. The size of the space and the cost of its rental was included in the press release, which also included a quotation from the law firm's chief operating officer. Why would a law firm consent to such details about its business being publicized? Are there any negative repercussions to information about a firm's real estate transactions concerning its own business being reported in the media?
6. Consider the tasks involved in setting up a new law office. Which would best be handled by an attorney, which by a law office manager, which by a paralegal, and which by a secretary?

Case Studies

1. Suppose a partner in a two-lawyer firm dies unexpectedly. What actions need to be taken by the other lawyer at the firm and by the firm's paralegal and secretary?
2. A 60-lawyer office currently located in an urban area is considering relocating to the suburbs, where rents are considerably lower. How should the firm go about determining whether to undertake such a move?
3. Suppose you are a supervising attorney at a law firm where six paralegals sit in a central bay area in carrels. An older paralegal whose workstation was next to a window is retiring. Who should get the retiring paralegal's space, and how should the decision be made?
4. You are on your law firm's art committee. Your firm is a 50-lawyer firm in a major city that focuses on business litigation. Art needs to be placed in

the firm's reception areas on several floors and in three large conference rooms. What type of art, and by which artists, would you recommend that the firm purchase? How much do you recommend paying for the art?

5. You have just been elevated from associate to partner at the branch office of a 500-lawyer firm with offices in 12 cities. You have an $8,000 stipend to buy furniture and decorate your office. Provide an itemized list identifying the materials you would purchase and their prices.

6. Locate the sustainability policies of several law firms and compare and contrast them. What elements do these policies have in common? How do they differ? What aspects of the policies relate to the physical law office? What elements relate to procurement? Might any prospective clients be opposed to these policies? Do the policies seem sufficiently proactive given the number of attorneys and staff at the firm? What sorts of clients does the firm have? How might they have impacted the development of the firm's sustainability policy?

   Some sources to consider:

   http://www.pepperlaw.com/About_Sustainability_Policy.aspx
   http://www.porterwright.com/sustainability_policy/
   http://www.hogefenton.com/about-us/sustainability
   http://www.lowestein.com/?p=3524
   http://www.millermartin.com/our-firm/sustainability
   http://www.hatlawfirm.com/about/sustainability

   Also consider whether the firms that have posted their sustainability policies have also reported on the results of their sustainability efforts.

7. Locate the sustainability reports of several law firms and critique them. In what areas might law firms make more efforts to achieve sustainability? Are the firms proceeding quickly enough? Are the reports very specific, or are they somewhat vague and general? How might the reports be improved?

8. Review the ABA Special Committee on Disaster Response and Preparedness guide, *Surviving Disaster: A Lawyer's Guide to Disaster Planning* (available at http://www.americanbar.org) and compare the elements described in the guide to a law firm's response to a recent disaster. From what you have been able to learn, did the firm follow the measures in the guide? How might the firm have responded differently to the disaster?

Endnotes

1. U.S. Environmental Protection Agency, *Sustainability: Basic Information*, http://www.epa.gov/sustainability/basicinfo.htm (last visited Aug. 18, 2013).
2. For additional information on how a law firm can become more sustainable, *see, e.g.,* U.S. Environmental Protection Agency, *ABA/EPA Law Firm Climate Challenge*, http://www.epa.gov/greenpower/initiatives/aba_challenge.htm (last updated Oct. 16, 2012).
3. *See, e.g.,* Lori Tripoli, *Sustainability: What Law Firms Have at Stake*, Of Counsel 19–22 (May 2012); William R. Blackburn, *Sustainability: How Values-Driven Law Firms Are Surviving Tough Times and Prospering Over the Long Term,* Law Practice Today (Sept. 2010), *available at* http://apps.americanbar.org/lpm/lpt/articles/pdf/ftr09103.pdf; ABA, *The ABA-EPA Law Office Climate Challenge*, http://www.americanbar.org/groups/environment_energy_resources/projects_awards/aba_epa_law_office_climate_challenge.html (last visited Aug. 18, 2013).
4. *See, e.g.,* William R. Blackburn, *SEER Sustainability Framework for Law Organizations* (Dec. 10, 2010), *available at* http://www.americanbar.org.
5. Heather Nolan, *One Dead After Bizarre Shooting at Covington Law Firm,* Times-Picayune (July 30, 2013), *available at* http://www.nola.com/crime/index ssf/2013/07/police_investigating_bizarre_s.html; Martha Neil, *Ex-Client Committed Suicide After Breaking into Law Firm and Firing Dozens of Rounds, Say Police,* ABA J. (July 30, 2013), *available at* http://www.abajournal.com/news/article/ex-client_presumed_dead_after_breaking_into_la_law_firm_and_shooting_every/.
6. *Murder-Suicide at Paul Hastings in Atlanta,* Above the Law (blog), (Apr. 28, 2008).
7. Allison Retka, *'Prince of a Guy' Shot Dead in Clayton Law Office,* Daily Rec. (St. Louis), Dec. 21, 2006, n.p.
8. *Meador Murdered at Work: 30-Year-Old Lawyer Was Just Elected to YLD Board,* Fla. B. News, Feb. 2005, at 10.
9. *See, e.g.,* Benjamin Sells, *Our Fears Ignite When Tragedy Strikes So Close to Home,* Ill. Legal Times, July 1994, at 29; Jill Chanen, *After San Francisco, Law Firms Take Aim at Office Security,* Chi. Law., Aug. 1993, at 78.
10. *See, e.g.,* Jill E. Jachera & Joseph A. Piesco Jr., *Violence in the Workplace,* Metropolitan Corp. Couns., Northeast Ed., Nov. 2001, at 24.
11. Brenna G. Nava, *Comment, Hurricane Katrina: The Duties and Responsibilities of an Attorney in the Wake of a Natural Disaster,* 37 St. Mary's L.J. 1153, 1161–62 (2006) (citations omitted).
12. *See, e.g.,* Geoffrey N. Smith, *Thinking the Unthinkable,* Law Firm Inc., Nov. 2007 (quoting Steven Spiess, executive director, Cravath, Swaine & Moore).
13. *See, e.g.,* Constance L. Hays, *Trying to Reweave Threads of Tattered Offices,* N.Y. Times, Sept. 23, 2001, at Money and Business 7.
14. ABA Special Committee on Disaster Response and Preparedness, Surviving Disaster: A Lawyer's Guide to Disaster Planning (2011), available at http://www.americanbar.org/groups/committees/disaster.html.
15. Lori Tripoli, *Don't Get Caught with a 1.0 in a 5.0 World,* Of Counsel, May 2007, at 10, 12 (quoting Mark Wilson, senior manager of applications development and project management at Dickstein Shapiro in Washington, D.C.).
16. Model Rules of Prof'l Conduct R. 1.1 cmt (2013).
17. Paper cut, 26(37) Lawyer 30 (Sept. 24, 2012).
18. *See, e.g.,* Matt Hamblen, *Detroit Law Firm Fends off 'Nasty' VoIP Problems,* Computerworld (Aug. 9, 2006), http://www.computerworld.com/action/article.do?command=viewArticleBasic&articleId=9002298.
19. Lori Tripoli, *Trading Spaces,* Law Firm Inc., Jan./Feb. 2006.
20. *Id.*

21 Medline Plus Medical Dictionary, entry for ergonomics, http://www2.merriam-webster .com/cgi-bin/mwmednlm (last visited Aug. 18, 2013).

22. *See, e.g.*, David Leffler, *Going Solo: How to Feng Shui Your Law Office*, GP Solo (July/ Aug. 2012), *available at* https://www.americanbar.org/newsletter/publications/gp_ solo_magazine_home/gp_solo_magazine_index/solo_lawyer_office_feng_shui_clean_ organize.html.

23. Jennifer Smith, *Law Firms Say Good-Bye Office, Hello Cubicle*, Wall Street J. *(July 15, 2012), available at* http://online.wsj.com/article/SB10001424052702303612804577 528940291670100.html.

24. *See, e.g.*, Lydia DePillis, *Cafeteria Society*, Washington City Paper (Feb. 15, 2012), *available at* http://www.washingtoncitypaper.com/blogs /housingcomplex/2012/02/15/cafeteria-society/; Elie Mystal, *'Cravatheteria' Rebounds—And Other Firm Cafeterias Clean Up Their Acts as Well*, Above the Law (Aug. 20, 2012), *available at* http://abovethelaw.com/2012/08/cravatheteria-rebounds- and-other-firm-cafeterias-clean-up-their-acts-as-well/; Julie Triedman, *Dishing the Dirt on Where the Am Law 200 Dines*, Am Law Daily (Mar. 7, 2012), *available at* http:// amlawdaily.typepad.com/amlawdaily/2012/03/nyc-health-department-on-law-firm- cafeterias.html.

25. *See, e.g.*, Lucy Rieger, *The NEW Normal Library Space*, AALL Spectrum 24-27 (Dec. 2011).

7

Communications

Chapter Outcomes

By the end of this chapter, a student will be able to:

- Describe professionalism and appropriate law office decorum
- Develop and implement office protocols
- Assess dress codes and discuss their implications for the workplace
- Generate properly formatted written correspondence
- Understand and follow an acceptable use policy
- Develop best practices for dealing with difficult people
- Describe a communications strategy

Law is a service industry that depends on communications, both written and spoken. Lawyers, legal assistants, law office managers, tech support people—indeed, all of the actors in a law firm—need to be able to communicate effectively. Sometimes, communications are basic professional interactions. Other times, tough-minded negotiations are required. In some circumstances, a soothing approach may be needed to placate a disappointed client. In most exchanges, a basic, professional, yet friendly tone is all that is required.

Ultimately, someone in the legal industry needs to gauge the appropriateness of various means of communication. Communication skills, like other types of skills, must be learned and refined. A two-year-old faced with a frustrating situation is unlikely to react in the same way a teenager would. Similarly, someone who has been working in the legal business for 30 years is probably able to finesse an uncomfortable situation—and these inevitably arise—more capably than a recent hire would. Observing how more senior people at a firm handle challenging situations can be instructive.

A.   Professionalism

Even the most casual firm expects all its employees to display a certain measure of professionalism. A law firm, after all, is a place where business is conducted. Providing prompt, efficient service to clients is what keeps a law firm in business. A client's first line of contact is typically with the person answering the phone or greeting a visitor in the firm's reception area. There is a saying that first impressions are lasting impressions. Making a positive impact at that very first encounter is vital, not only to foster client-law firm relations but also to bolster the law firm employee's own career. There is both an external market at a law firm (in which outside clients seek out individual lawyers or even request the services of certain legal assistants or other service providers at the firm) and an internal market (in which lawyers and others mete out plum assignments to the most deserving). Maintaining a good personal image and good relations with people both within a firm and outside it can only help boost one's career. After all, the goal is not to just get an entry-level job at a law firm and remain there. Ultimately, greater responsibility—and greater financial remuneration—is the reward for moving up the career ladder. Moving up that first rung can happen only if one conducts oneself professionally.

1.   Decorum

protocol:
A procedure or set of rules.

decorum:
Behavior that is in good taste and propriety.

Every office has its **protocols** and ways of behaving, or **decorum**. A new employee should learn an office's routines and adopt them. There may be a very specific script for answering the telephone, for forwarding someone to voice mail, for receiving deliveries, and for announcing visitors and escorting them to appropriate areas within a firm. Often, these protocols are described in the firm's handbook. Other firms may have only a standard business routine that is transmitted orally to new employees when they are hired. If a new hire is not sure how to conduct herself in the office, she should ask. "How would you like me to answer the telephone?" is a perfectly legitimate inquiry.

Whether and to what extent a paralegal or other nonlawyer should respond to client inquiries should be established before the situation arises. Should a paralegal take a call from a client if the attorney is not at her desk? How responsive should that paralegal be to an inquiry? Should the paralegal respond to questions about whether a brief is finished, whether an answer to a complaint has been received, whether depositions have been scheduled? These sorts of matters should be clarified. If a lawyer or law office manager does not instruct a new hire about these likely tasks, the new employee should ask.

Procedures may be addressed in the firm's employee handbook. For example, a firm might have policies on whether staff may eat lunch at their desks, whether staff may consume drinks such as sodas or coffee at their workstations, when and how employees are to take breaks, how the telephone should be answered and messages taken, and what other duties are necessary for the day-to-day operation of the law firm. There may be a designated area for employees' coats but a separate coat closet for clients' coats. Whether and to what extent staff may decorate their workspaces might be addressed. If the firm has no written procedure, a new staff member should ask a manager how a given matter should be handled.

Doing the least that is expected is unlikely to meet with success in a law firm. If an employee's workload is too light, the employee should make superiors aware that she is available for additional assignments. Similarly, if someone is overwhelmed by her job responsibilities, she should request additional support. Ambition is likely to be rewarded.

Maintaining an appropriate tone at the office is important as well. All of us have inevitably dealt with someone on the telephone who has a bad attitude, conveys an air of laziness or uncaring, speaks inappropriately, or clearly has priorities other than her work. Do we admire such people and hope to deal with others like them soon? Or do these people frustrate us as we attempt to accomplish our own business goals? A law firm's employees should be aware that they represent the firm to the public; as a service business, the firm relies on the goodwill conveyed by its employees in servicing clients and others.

As such, personal matters should stay out of the office. Even if you are having a bad day, going through a lengthy divorce proceeding, or feeling stressed by family obligations, your task at work is to support the firm — a task, after all, that enables workers to have those personal lives that they sometimes complain about!

2.   Standards of Dress

Like it or not, people pay attention to appearances. Work is not the time to make a statement, to assert your individuality, to flaunt your difference. You are not working for yourself; you are representing a law firm.

How you dress can affect not just a paycheck but your entire career. As much as many of us might want to pretend otherwise, an employee's attire affects that person's job prospects. One workplace survey found that 82 percent of human resources professionals and 68 percent of workers believe that how an employee dresses directly affects that person's chance for a promotion.[1] Appearances really do count. Consider the following examples:

> Beauty indisputably plays a significant role in our society, and although beauty is subjectively "in the eye of the beholder," there is a common objective standard of what people generally find attractive. To illustrate, consider the presidential debates between John F. Kennedy and Richard Nixon in which radio listeners thought Nixon was triumphant, whereas TV viewers thought the more attractive John F. Kennedy was the victor. . . . To prove that looks do indeed matter, even in the employment context, [the television program] 20/20 conducted an experiment in which two women with virtually identical resumes and behaviors applied for the same job. Not surprisingly, the interviewer was friendlier to the more attractive applicant and extended the job offer to her; whereas, the less attractive applicant never even received a return phone call.[2]

If you are fortunate enough to work in a law office, look like you work in an office. Observe the people in your office who are more senior than you or more successful, and mimic their conduct. If they wear suits, you wear a suit.

Of course, there are legal protections for people who wear certain garments for religious reasons. But if you are wearing a certain type of clothing or a particular piece of jewelry simply to make a fashion statement, consider the impact that your individuality might ultimately have on your long-term success in a law firm.

Cloutier v. Costco Wholesale Corp.
390 F.3d 126 (1st Cir. 2004)

OPINION

Lipez, Circuit Judge. Kimberly Cloutier alleges that her employer, Costco Wholesale Corp. (Costco), failed to offer her a reasonable accommodation after she alerted it to a conflict between the "no facial jewelry" provision of its dress code and her religious practice as a member of the Church of Body Modification. She argues that this failure amounts to religious discrimination in violation of Title VII, 42 U.S.C. §2000e-2(a). The district court granted summary judgment for Costco, concluding that Costco reasonably accommodated Cloutier by offering to reinstate her if she either covered her facial piercing with a band-aid or replaced it with a clear retainer. We affirm the grant of summary judgment, but on a different basis. . . . We hold that Costco had no duty to accommodate Cloutier because it could not do so without undue hardship.

Kimberly Cloutier began working at Costco's West Springfield, Massachusetts store in July 1997. Before her first day of work, Cloutier received a copy of the Costco employment agreement, which included the employee dress code. When she was hired, Cloutier had multiple earrings and four tattoos, but no facial piercings.

Cloutier moved from her position as a front-end assistant to the deli department in September 1997. In 1998, Costco revised its dress code to prohibit food handlers, including deli employees, from wearing any jewelry. Cloutier's supervisor instructed her to remove her earrings pursuant to the revised code, but Cloutier refused. Instead, she requested to transfer to a front-end position where she would be permitted to continue wearing her jewelry. Cloutier did not indicate at the time that her insistence on wearing her earrings was based on a religious or spiritual belief.

Costco approved Cloutier's transfer back to a front-end position in June 1998, and promoted her to cashier soon thereafter. Over the ensuing two years, she engaged in various forms of body modification including facial piercing and cutting. Although these practices were meaningful to Cloutier, they were not motivated by a religious belief.

In March 2001, Costco further revised its dress code to prohibit all facial jewelry, aside from earrings, and disseminated the modified code to its employees. Cloutier did not challenge the dress code or seek an accommodation, but rather continued uneventfully to wear her eyebrow piercing for several months.

Costco began enforcing its no-facial-jewelry policy in June 2001. On June 25, 2001, front-end supervisors Todd Cunningham and Michele Callaghan informed Cloutier and another employee, Jennifer Theriaque, that they would have to remove their facial piercings. Cloutier and Theriaque did not comply, returning to work the following day still wearing their piercings. When Callaghan reiterated the no-facial-jewelry policy, Cloutier indicated for the first time that she was a member of the Church of Body Modification (CBM), and that her eyebrow piercing was part of her religion.

The CBM was established in 1999 and counts approximately 1000 members who participate in such practices as piercing, tattooing, branding, cutting, and body manipulation. Among the goals espoused in the CBM's mission statement are for its members to "grow as individuals through body modification and its teachings," to "promote growth in mind, body and spirit," and to be "confident role models in learning, teaching, and displaying body modification." The church's website, apparently its primary mode for reaching its adherents, did not state that members' body modifications had to be visible at all times or that temporarily removing body modifications would violate a religious tenet. Still, Cloutier interprets the call to be a confident role model as requiring that her piercings be visible at all times and precluding her from removing or covering her facial jewelry. She does not extend this reasoning to the tattoos on her upper arms, which were covered at work by her shirt.

After reviewing information that Cloutier provided from the CBM website, Callaghan's supervisor, Andrew Mulik, instructed Cloutier and Theriaque to remove their facial jewelry. They refused. The following day, Cloutier filed a religious discrimination complaint with the Equal Employment Opportunity Commission (EEOC), which is empowered to enforce Title VII. 42 U.S.C. §2000e-5.

When Cloutier returned to work for her next shift on June 29, 2001, she was still wearing her facial jewelry. She met with Mark Shevchuk, the store manager, about her membership in the CBM and the EEOC complaint. During the course of the meeting, Cloutier suggested that she be allowed to cover her eyebrow piercing with a flesh-colored band-aid. Shevchuk rejected the suggestion and told Cloutier that she had to remove the piercing or go home. She left.

Theriaque also returned to work wearing her facial jewelry on June 29, 2001 and was reminded of the dress code. She asked whether she could wear clear plastic retainers in place of her jewelry to prevent the piercings from closing. For purposes of our summary judgment analysis, we accept Cloutier's contention that Theriaque wore the retainers to work for several weeks unnoticed before Costco gave her permission to do so.

Although Cloutier learned during the week of July 2, 2001 that Theriaque had returned to work with retainers, she chose to wait for her EEOC complaint to be resolved rather than following suit. During the week of July 7, 2001, Cloutier inquired of her superiors whether she could use vacation time to cover her absences and was told that she had been suspended. The following week, on July 14, Cloutier received notice in the mail that she had been terminated for her unexcused absences resulting from noncompliance with the dress code. She claims that this was her first notice that Costco had decided not to grant her request for an accommodation that would reconcile the dress code with her religious requirement of displaying her facial jewelry at all times.

The parties remained in contact after Cloutier's termination through the EEOC mediation process. During a meeting on August 10, 2001, Costco offered to let Cloutier return to work wearing either plastic retainers or a band-aid over her jewelry (the same accommodation that Cloutier had suggested prior to her termination). . . .

. . . Cloutier . . . now maintains that neither of the proffered accommodations would be adequate because the CBM's tenets, as she interprets them, require her to display all of her facial piercings at all times. Replacing her eyebrow piercing with a plastic retainer or covering it with a band-aid would thus contradict her religious convictions. Cloutier asserts that the only reasonable accommodation would be to excuse her from Costco's dress code, allowing her to wear her facial jewelry to work. Costco responds that this accommodation would interfere with its ability to maintain a professional appearance and would thereby create an undue hardship for its business.

The EEOC determined in May 2002 that Costco's actions violated Title VII of the Civil Rights Act of 1964. It found that Cloutier's refusal to remove her facial jewelry was "religiously based as defined by the EEOC," that Costco did not allow her to wear her facial jewelry at work, and that there was no evidence that allowing her to wear the jewelry would have constituted an undue hardship. Based on this determination, Cloutier filed a suit against Costco in federal district court. . . .

The district court . . . allowed the federal and state discrimination claims to proceed. Costco then moved for summary judgment on the discrimination claims.

In ruling on that motion, the court applied the two-part framework set forth in *EEOC v. Union Independiente de la Autoridad de Acueductos y Alcantarillados de Puerto Rico*, 279 F.3d 49, 55 (1st Cir. 2002). First, the court evaluated Cloutier's *prima facie* case, which required her to show that (1) a bona fide religious practice conflicted with an employment requirement, (2) she brought the practice to Costco's attention, and (3) the religious practice was the basis for the termination. *Id.* The court expressed serious doubts as to whether Cloutier's claim was based on a "bona fide religious practice" for purposes of the first element, noting that even assuming arguendo that the CBM is a bona fide religion, it "in no way requires a *display* of facial piercings *at all times.* The requirement that she display her piercings, open and always, represents the plaintiff's personal interpretation of the stringency of her beliefs." The court also questioned the sincerity of Cloutier's personal interpretation, given that she initially offered to cover her piercing with a band-aid, an alternative that she now claims would violate her religion.

The court ultimately avoided ruling on whether the CBM is a religion or whether Cloutier's interpretation of the CBM tenets is protected by Title VII. Instead, the court concluded that even if Cloutier had met her *prima facie* case, Costco should prevail because it fulfilled its obligations under the second part of the Title VII framework. Specifically, the court found that Costco met its burden of showing that it had offered Cloutier a reasonable accommodation of her religious practice.

In granting summary judgment on the Title VII claim, the court stressed that "the search for a reasonable accommodation goes both ways. Although the employer is required under Title VII to accommodate an employee's religious beliefs, the employee has a duty to cooperate with the employer's good faith efforts to accommodate." *Id.* at 198. The court also noted that Title VII does not require Costco to grant Cloutier's preferred accommodation, but merely a reasonable one. While Costco's suggested accommodation balanced Cloutier's beliefs with its interest in presenting a professional appearance, Cloutier "offered no accommodation whatsoever." *Id.* at 200.

Cloutier now appeals, arguing that the court erred in finding no violation of Title VII . . . and that disputed material facts made summary judgment inappropriate.

On appeal, Cloutier vigorously asserts that her insistence on displaying all her facial jewelry at all times is the result of a sincerely held religious belief. Determining whether a belief is religious is "more often than not a difficult and delicate task," one to which the courts are ill-suited. *Thomas v. Review Bd. of*

Indiana Employment Sec. Div., 450 U.S. 707, 714, 67 L. Ed. 2d 624, 101 S. Ct. 1425 (1981). Fortunately, as the district court noted, there is no need for us to delve into this thorny question in the present case. Even assuming, *arguendo*, that Cloutier established her *prima facie* case, the facts here do not support a finding of impermissible religious discrimination.

Although the district court's decision rested on the conclusion that Costco had offered Cloutier a reasonable accommodation, "we may affirm . . . on any grounds supported by the record." *Estades-Negroni v. Associates Corp. of North America*, 377 F.3d 58, 62 (1st Cir. 2004). We find dispositive that the only accommodation Cloutier considers reasonable, a blanket exemption from the no-facial-jewelry policy, would impose an undue hardship on Costco.

Title VII of the Civil Rights Act of 1964 prohibits employers from discriminating against employees on the basis of, among other things, religion. 42 U.S.C. §2000e-2(a). Under Title VII, an employer must offer a reasonable accommodation to resolve a conflict between an employee's sincerely held religious belief and a condition of employment, unless such an accommodation would create an undue hardship for the employer's business. 42 U.S.C. §2000e(j).

. . .

Cloutier asserts that the CBM mandate to be a confident role model requires her to display all of her facial piercings at all times. In her view, the only reasonable accommodation would be exemption from the no-facial-jewelry policy. Costco maintains that such an exemption would cause it to suffer an undue hardship, and that as a result it had no obligation to accommodate Cloutier.

An accommodation constitutes an "undue hardship" if it would impose more than a *de minimis* cost on the employer. This calculus applies both to economic costs, such as lost business or having to hire additional employees to accommodate a Sabbath observer, and to non-economic costs, such as compromising the integrity of a seniority system.

. . .

The district court acknowledged that "Costco has a legitimate interest in presenting a workforce to its customers that is, at least in Costco's eyes, reasonably professional in appearance." Costco's dress code, included in the handbook distributed to all employees, furthers this interest. The preface to the code explains that, "Appearance and perception play a key role in member service. Our goal is to be dressed in professional attire that is appropriate to our business at all times. . . . All Costco employees must practice good grooming and personal hygiene to convey a neat, clean and professional image."

It is axiomatic that, for better or for worse, employees reflect on their employers. This is particularly true of employees who regularly interact with customers, as Cloutier did in her cashier position. Even if Cloutier did not personally receive any complaints about her appearance, her facial jewelry influenced Costco's public image and, in Costco's calculation, detracted from its professionalism.

. . .

Costco has made a determination that facial piercings, aside from earrings, detract from the "neat, clean and professional image" that it aims to cultivate. Such a business determination is within its discretion.

Cloutier argues that regardless of the reasons for the dress code, permitting her to display her facial jewelry would not be an undue hardship because Costco already overlooks other violations of its policy. In support of her position, she cites affidavits from two Costco employees identifying co-workers who "were allowed to wear facial piercings . . . and were not disciplined." Costco responds that any employees who displayed facial jewelry did so without its permission or knowledge, noting that constant monitoring is impossible in a facility with several hundred employees.

. . .

Cloutier appears to reason that because other employees have violated the no-facial-jewelry policy, it would not be an additional burden on Costco's effort to present a professional workforce for her to display her piercings as well. But there is an important distinction between an employee who displays facial jewelry unnoticed in violation of the dress code and one who does so under an exemption from the dress code. In the first scenario, Costco can instruct an employee to remove facial jewelry as soon as it becomes aware of a violation. In the second scenario, Costco forfeits its ability to mandate compliance and thus loses control over its public image. That loss, as we have discussed, would constitute an undue hardship.

Affirmed.

business casual attire:
Clothing that is less formal than standard workplace attire but not as casual as weekend wear.

Some law firms have casual Fridays or allow employees to wear **business casual attire** on other days of the week. Some are very precise in specifying the clothing to be worn on these "casual" days—khaki pants and button-down shirts might be specified, while certain items, such as tee shirts, denim, sleeveless shirts, and open-toed shoes might be banned.

Understanding the difference between casual attire and business casual clothing can be tricky. Some lawyers are reticent to turn into "clothing police," so they just establish a policy requiring that business attire be worn every day.

B. Telephone Etiquette

Many of us have probably had negative experiences with businesses when we telephoned them. We might get lost in never-ending computerized instructions or finally get a "live" person only to be greeted with an unhelpful attitude. The tone of voice you use when answering a call—and the degree of helpfulness you provide—reinforces the law firm's reputation.

> The person who first answers the phone becomes the greeter for the entire firm. One of the goals for that person is to make the caller feel welcome and appreciated.

Setting a friendly, warm tone is important because doing so sets the stage for the interaction that follows. When the person answering the phone is friendly, the caller is likely to reciprocate. If the caller hears an icy, too formal voice on the other end, she is likely to respond in kind.[3]

It is tempting to let voice mail pick up every call, but many people simply hang up without leaving a message if their call is not answered.[4] That could mean that a prospective client simply moves on to the next law firm name on her list. Answer a ringing telephone promptly—ideally, on the first or second ring—and be polite. Obtain the caller's name, his or her affiliation, and the reason for the call. If you are unable to respond to the caller's needs and it is your job to do so, inform the caller that you will need to conduct some additional research and get back to her. If possible, provide a time frame for responding. If you need to take a message for someone else, keep the following guidelines in mind when interacting with the caller:

- As appropriate, you might ask whether the caller would prefer to leave a message with you or be sent to voice mail.
- Clearly identify the recipient of the call. If there are two people named "Jim" in the office, be certain to identify which Jim the caller was seeking.
- Ask for the proper spelling of the person's name.
- Do not make fun of the person's name. For instance, the author of this book's surname is Tripoli, which is pronounced "Triple E." Many phone call answerers have said, "I thought you were from Triple-A" or "I thought you spelled your name E-e-e." That was clever the first five times someone said it; now it is just annoying. If a caller has an unusual name or one that reminds you of something else, keep that thought to yourself.
- Ask for the person's affiliation—and obtain the proper spelling, if necessary.
- Ask for the person's telephone number, and be certain to include the area code.
- Request any specific message the caller would like to convey.
- Record the date and time the person called.
- Identify yourself as the person taking the message.
- Be certain to deliver the message to the intended recipient.

A law firm might have a set procedure for delivering messages. Messages might be placed in carrels. Less formal offices might allow messages to be left on a lawyer's chair or in his or her inbox. Typically, a copy of the message is recorded in a log book.

When you are making a telephone call, identify yourself and your affiliation. For instance, you might say, "This is Mika Yatauro with Blocker & Jones calling for James Esson" rather than "Hello, may I please speak to Jim?"

Before placing the call, consider the intent of the communication. You might make notes prior to the call or even write out a script if you think the call will be difficult or challenging for some reason. What do you hope to accomplish with the call? What questions do you need to ask? What is the purpose of the telephone call? For billing purposes, be certain to note preparation time, phone call start time and end time, and follow-up period.

In this time of instant communication, with e-mail and text- and instant messaging, clients often expect calls to be returned the same day and e-mails, text messages (typically transmitted via smartphone in which messages are transmitted to a person whose name and phone number you know), and instant messages (transmitted over a data network via applications such as Google Chat) to be responded to within hours or even immediately. Keeping client service in mind, be certain to update your voice mail message frequently. You might indicate whether you are in the office on a particular day and provide numbers for emergency contacts if you happen to be out of the office. If you are on vacation, you do not necessarily need to say so—you can leave a voice mail message indicating that you will be out of the office for a specific time period and say when you will return. You can also leave an alternative contact for callers who need to reach someone right away.

C.   Written Correspondence

Much of a law firm's work is conducted via written communication, whether a formal courthouse filing, a letter, an internal memorandum of law, an e-mail, or a text or instant message. Many actors within a law firm might participate in preparing such communications. A legal secretary might type a first draft based on her notes from her supervising attorney, a paralegal might conduct some of the preliminary legal research, and, in large law firms, an in-house editor may even review the material before it is sent. With every communication, the danger that someone other than the intended recipient might receive the material should be considered, as should the requisite privacy of the communication.

1. *Letters*

Letters are communications sent to recipients outside the firm. They might be sent to opposing counsel in an effort to launch negotiations, to a client to lay out a legal case, or to a third party. Letters may be quite short and direct or long and elaborate. Printed on the firm's stationery, or letterhead, the letters should include the following elements:

- date the letter is being sent
- name and address of the recipient
- a line, typically labeled "Re," indicating the subject of the letter
- a salutation, such as "Dear Ms. Jones," "Dear John Roe," or "Dear Judge Smith"
- the body of the letter (the substantive information that is being conveyed)
- a closing, such as "Sincerely" or "Yours truly"
- the name and title of the sender
- identification of the typist
- a list of enclosed documents

- a list of recipients of copies of the letter, indicated by the initials **CC**, which stand for courtesy copy or carbon copy (prior to the existence of copying machines, letters were duplicated with the help of carbon paper)

A file copy should also include a list of recipients who are "blind carbon copied," or **BCC**'d. These are people who are being sent a copy of the letter but whose names are not disclosed to the letter's recipient. If a communication is being sent via certified mail, that should also be specified on the letter itself, ideally along with the tracking number for the correspondence.

A firm's style for letters may be prescribed in the firm manual. For example, the firm might prefer **block format**—in which every line of the letter (including the date and signature line) is flush with the left margin. For an example of a letter using block format, see Figure 7-1. Other firms use a modified block format in which the date might be flush right and the closing and author lines are placed about two-thirds across the page. The firm might also specify the salutations and closings that are to be used in every letter.

a) LETTERHEAD

Law firm letterhead provides the name, location, and contact information (telephone and fax numbers, e-mail addresses) of the firm. At one time, letterhead was fairly dull, printed with a single-color text (often black). The name of the firm was typically centered on the page, and a list of partners might appear on the left. Over time, letterhead style shifted somewhat as law firms grew larger and became more cognizant of the message-conveying potential of something as mundane as stationery.[5] As firms focus more on marketing and branding their organizations, some have added additional colors and logos to make their letterhead more eye-catching.

i) RULES ON LISTING LAWYERS

Ethics rules limit the material that can be included on the letterhead. Rule 7.1 of the ABA's *Model Rules of Professional Conduct* prohibits lawyers from making false or misleading communications about the lawyer or the lawyer's services. Model Rule 7.5 specifically addresses law firm names and letterhead. Law firms with offices in more than one jurisdiction may use the firm name in all of the jurisdictions, but if lawyers' names are listed, the areas where they are authorized to practice must be identified. This information is sometimes indicated with the use of asterisks (*) and other symbols. For instance, a law firm with offices in Maryland, Washington, D.C., and Virginia might include an asterisk after the names of lawyers who are admitted only in Virginia. An explanation of the meaning of the asterisk (*admitted in Virginia only*) should be placed prominently on the letterhead.

Some state ethics rules are even more detailed and specify whether the names of deceased partners and lawyers deemed to be "of counsel" might be listed on letterhead.[6]

ii) IMPRESSION

It is important that all letters sent out on firm letterhead be well crafted, accurate, and proofread. The quickest way to annoy a client is to misspell her

CC:
Courtesy copy or carbon copy, identifying a list of recipients other than the addressee.

BCC:
Blind courtesy copy or blind carbon copy, indicating a list of recipients who are not identified in a communication.

block format:
The layout of a letter in which each line is flush with the left margin and there is an extra space between paragraphs.

FIGURE 7-1
Sample Letter

[FIRM LETTERHEAD]

VIA CERTIFIED MAIL
1234 1111 2222 3333 4444

August 12, 2013

James Dean
Investor Services Coordinator
Widget Corporation
P.O. Box 32
New York, New York 10286

　　　　RE:　Estate of Joseph Edward Jones
　　　　　　　DOD: June 9, 2013
　　　　　　　ACCOUNT NUMBER: 0001234

Dear James Dean:

Enclosed please find the paperwork to transfer the Widget stock owned by Joseph E. Jones and Helen M. Jones jointly to Helen M. Jones individually. Also enclosed are sealed copies of Joseph Jones's death certificate and the certificate appointing Lori Smith the executrix of his estate. The law firm of Bentley, Poole represents the estate of Joseph Jones.

Please let me know when these shares have been transferred.

If you have any questions, or if you need any additional information, please contact me.

Sincerely,

J. Madison Poole
Attorney at Law

enc.　stock power form
　　　　affidavit of domicile form
　　　　death certificate
　　　　short certificate

cc:　　Lori Smith
　　　　Executrix, Estate of Joseph E. Jones

name. With each piece of correspondence sent from a firm, the firm is creating an impression about its own competence. Missives sent with partial addresses, material that was clearly cut and pasted from other documents and not modified to suit the current letter, and grammatical errors and typos are not likely to intimidate opposing counsel or reassure a wavering client. Take the extra time to review letters before they are sent out and, if possible, have someone else at the firm review the work for errors. If you are not a lawyer, never send a letter on firm stationery unless you have the approval of your supervising attorney. Do not use firm stationery for casual notes to friends or to try to intimidate someone in your personal life. That sort of inappropriate use of firm stationery could create negative repercussions if the recipient were to contact a senior person at the firm or if the recipient was led to believe that the firm was formally representing you.

In certain situations, letterhead used inappropriately may violate a statute.

Lesher v. Law Offices of Mitchell N. Kapy, PC
650 F.3d 993 (3d Cir. 2011)

COWEN, Circuit Judge.

Darwin Lesher filed a complaint in the United States District Court for the Middle District of Pennsylvania alleging that debt-collection letters he received from the Law Offices of Mitchell N. Kay (the "Kay Law Firm") were deceptive under the Fair Debt Collection Practices Act (the "FDCPA" or the "Act"). The District Court agreed and granted Lesher's motion for summary judgment. The Kay Law Firm now appeals from the District Court's order. For the reasons that follow, we will affirm.

I. BACKGROUND

The Kay Law Firm is a law firm that acts as a debt collector. On January 11, 2009, the Kay Law Firm sent a letter to Lesher seeking to recover a debt he owed to Washington Mutual on a home equity loan. The letter was presented on the Kay Law Firm's letterhead, which displays the words "Law Offices of Mitchell N. Kay, P.C." in large characters at the top of the page. . . . The letter, after referencing Lesher's account with Washington Mutual, states as follows:

> Please be advised that your account, as referenced above, is being handled by this office.
> We have been authorized to offer you the opportunity to settle this account with a lump sum payment, equal to 75% of the balance due—which is $9,080.52!
> Unless you notify this office within 30 days after receiving this notice that you dispute the validity of this debt or any portion thereof, this office will assume this debt is valid.
> If you notify this office in writing within 30 days from receiving this notice that you dispute the validity of this debt or any portion thereof, this office will: Obtain verification of the debt or obtain a copy of a judgment and mail you a copy of such judgment or verification.

If you request this office in writing within 30 days after receiving this notice, this office will provide you with the name and address of the original creditor, if different from the current creditor.

You are invited to visit our website **www.lawofmnk.com** to resolve this debt privately, or to write to us or to update your personal information.

. . . After a large blank space, the letter directs Lesher to "PLEASE ADDRESS ALL PAYMENTS TO" the "Law Offices of Mitchell N. Kay, P.C." at their New York address. (*Id.*) Immediately below the address, the letter states: "Notice: Please see reverse side for important information." (*Id.*) A box surrounds this notice, below which is a detachable payment stub.

On the back, the letter sets forth four "notices," including the following two:

This communication is from a debt collector and is an attempt to collect a debt. Any information obtained will be used for that purpose.

At this point in time, no attorney with this firm has personally reviewed the particular circumstances of your account.

. . .

On February 15, 2009, the Kay Law Firm sent a second letter to Lesher. This letter was not printed on the same letterhead, but instead stated in smaller characters at the top that it was from the "Law Offices of Mitchell N. Kay, P.C." . . . The letter offers the choice of a six-month repayment plan or a settlement, and again instructs the reader to "see reverse side for important information." . . . The back of the letter sets forth the same disclaimers as the first letter. . . .

In March 2009, shortly after receiving these letters, Lesher filed a complaint in the District Court against the Kay Law Firm. In the complaint, Lesher alleged that the letters violated, *inter alia,* section 1692e of the FDCPA, 15 U.S.C. § 1692e (1996), by misleading him to believe that an attorney was involved in collecting his debt, and that the attorney could, and would, take legal action against him.

. . . Upon review, the District Court found that the . . . letters plainly implied that an attorney was involved in the collection, and implicitly threatened legal action, in violation of § 1692e. Viewing the letters from the perspective of the "least sophisticated debtor," the District Court rejected the Kay Law Firm's contention that the disclaimers on the back of the letters mitigated the impression of potential legal action. The District Court awarded Lesher $1,000 in damages. *See* 15 U.S.C. § 1692k(a)(2)(A).

The Kay Law Firm now appeals from the District Court's order.

. . .

III. DISCUSSION

A. FDCPA Background

Congress enacted the FDCPA in 1977 in response to the "abundant evidence of the use of abusive, deceptive, and unfair debt collection practices by many debt collectors." 15 U.S.C. § 1692(a). At that time, Congress was concerned that "[a]busive debt collection practices contribute to the number of personal bankruptcies, to material instability, to the loss of jobs, and to invasions of individual privacy." *Id.* Congress explained that the purpose of the Act was not only to eliminate abusive debt collection practices, but also to "insure that those debt collectors who refrain from using abusive debt collection practices are not competitively disadvantaged." *Id.* § 1692(e). After determining that the existing consumer protection laws were inadequate, *id.* § 1692(b), Congress gave consumers a private cause of action against debt collectors who fail to comply with the Act. *Id.* § 1692k.

. . .

B. Section 1692e of the FDCPA

Lesher claims that the January 11 and February 15, 2009 letters that he received from the Kay Law Firm violate section 1692e of the FDCPA, which prohibits the use of "false, deceptive, or misleading representation or means in connection with the collection of any debt." 15 U.S.C. § 1692e. The sixteen subsections of section 1692e set forth a non-exhaustive list of practices that fall within this ban. These subsections include:

> (3) The false representation or implication that any individual is an attorney or that any communication is from an attorney.
>
> . . .
>
> (5) The threat to take any action that cannot legally be taken or that is not intended to be taken.

15 U.S.C. § 1692e. Because the list of the sixteen subsections is non-exhaustive, a debt collection practice can be a "false, deceptive, or misleading" practice in violation of section 1692e even if it does not fall within any of the subsections. . . .

D. Applying the Least Sophisticated Debtor Standard to the Kay Law Firm's Letters

. . . The District Court found that the least sophisticated debtor, upon receiving these letters, would believe that they had been sent by an attorney who might pursue legal action if he did not pay the debt. The District Court acknowledged that the letters included a disclaimer notifying Lesher that an attorney had not reviewed his account, but found that the disclaimer did not mitigate the impression of potential legal action. The Kay Law Firm now challenges the District Court's decision.

We agree with the District Court that the Kay Law Firm's letters violate section 1692e's general prohibition against "false, deceptive, or misleading" communications because they falsely imply that an attorney, acting as an attorney, is involved in collecting Lesher's debt. In our view, the least sophisticated debtor, upon receiving these letters, may reasonably believe that an attorney has reviewed his file and has determined that he is a candidate for legal action. . . .

Nor do we believe that the disclaimers included in the letters, which are printed on the backs, make clear to the least sophisticated debtor that the Kay Law Firm is acting solely as a debt collector and not in any legal capacity in sending the letters. . . .

[W]e believe that it was misleading and deceptive for the Kay Law Firm to raise the specter of potential legal action by using its law firm title to collect a debt when the firm was not acting in its legal capacity when it sent the letters. . . .

IV. CONCLUSION

We will affirm the District Court's order granting summary judgment in Lesher's favor with respect to his 15 U.S.C. § 1692e claim.

[Dissenting opinion and endnotes omitted].

b)   STANDARD FIRM FORMAT

Certain types of letters are sent repeatedly. A firm might have available a database of **templates,** or standard formats, for letters that, for instance, set up meetings or accompany certain documents for transactions the firm typically works on. These templates should be reviewed and tailored to individual circumstances.

Even if a law firm does not have a specified style for its letters, individual lawyers might. Ask them for a template and then mirror your own work accordingly.

template:
A model with a standard format.

2.   E-mail

A measure of informality has crept into communications that are instantaneously transmitted. Many people use e-mail and text and instant messages for their personal communications where a more casual tone is perfectly acceptable. When communicating via e-mail for a law firm employer, however, certain formalities should still be observed. Even information sent speedily over the Internet creates an impression on the recipient. Treating this means of communication too informally can create a negative impression of the firm on those who read these materials. Here are some suggestions for proper e-mail communication:

- When sending an e-mail message to more than one person, consider using the "bcc" option so that recipients' e-mail addresses are not visible to other recipients, particularly when a communication is being sent to many people. Some people object to their e-mail address being given to others.
- DO NOT SHOUT! Using all capital letters to communicate is akin to yelling.
- Correctly identify the subject of the communication.
- Greet the recipient.

- Include a sign-off, such as "Sincerely."
- Include your contact information, including your name, title, firm name, address, phone number, and e-mail address.

Lawyers must take precautions even when reading an e-mail message that they received from a prospective client who is unknown to them. Model Rule 1.18 generally bars lawyers from using information revealed in a consultation even when no lawyer-client relationship results from that consultation.[7] The extent to which a lawyer must refrain from using or revealing information received in an unsolicited e-mail message is an evolving area of the law. Some bars have indicated that unsolicited e-mails are not disqualifying e-mails, nor are e-mails sent from law firm Web sites that contained a warning not to transmit confidential information or a warning that an attorney-client relationship is not being created by the transmittal.[8]

a) APPROPRIATE TOPICS IN E-MAIL MESSAGES

Use common sense and some caution when communicating via e-mail. Maintain the confidentiality of client information and take precautions to make sure that information is not accidentally disclosed by, for instance, sending an e-mail message to someone whose name or e-mail address is similar to that of the intended recipient. When writing an e-mail message, keep in mind the very real hazard that the message will be transmitted to people whom you would prefer not to see the communication. E-mail messages are easily forwarded and sometimes misdirected if the address contains a typographical error.

b) PERSONAL USE OF FIRM ACCOUNTS FOR E-MAIL MESSAGES

A law firm might have an **acceptable use policy** specifying the purposes for which e-mail and computers may be used. Some policies forbid employees from sending and receiving personal e-mail messages or, more likely, may specify that such correspondence is to be kept to a minimum. Certain Web sites may actually be blocked. Sometimes information technology personnel at firms are charged with reviewing an employee's use of the Internet. A law firm policy may limit Web surfing and forbid access to sites that contain pornographic material. Violations of such firm policies may be met with a warning, a note placed in the employee's file, or even more serious sanctions.

> **acceptable use policy:** Guidelines for the appropriate use of technology.

Remember that employers have access to your work computer. If you would be embarrassed to have your supervisor read an e-mail message you send, then that message is not an appropriate one for your work account. Use your private e-mail account on your at-home computer. Do not use your work e-mail account for personal communications, and keep in mind that your employer will have access to your work. Do not risk the possibility that your colleagues will see personally embarrassing correspondence.

c) DISCLAIMERS FOR MISDIRECTED E-MAIL MESSAGES

E-mail messages are easily forwarded or could be accidentally misdirected to someone whose e-mail address is similar to that of the intended recipient. In

disclaimer:
A statement appended to an
e-mail or fax transmission
aimed at minimizing
liability, such as for breach
of confidentiality, when the
communication is delivered
to an unintended recipient.

an effort to protect the confidentiality of e-mail correspondence and to prevent its inappropriate distribution, many law firms include a **disclaimer** at the end of every e-mail message, such as this one:

> **Disclaimer**: The contents of this message and any attachments are intended solely for the addressee(s) named in this message. This communication is intended to be and to remain confidential and may be subject to applicable attorney/client and/or work product privileges. If you are not the intended recipient of this message, or if this message has been addressed to you in error, please immediately alert the sender and then destroy this message and its attachments. Do not deliver, distribute or copy this message and/or any attachments and if you are not the intended recipient, do not disclose the contents or take any action in reliance upon the information contained in this communication or any attachments.

E-mail disclaimers are holdovers from the days when transmissions by fax machine were prevalent—they were often added to fax cover sheets as well. Such disclaimers are intended to protect the attorney-client privilege, although some lawyers maintain that if disclaimers are automatically generated with each outgoing e-mail message, their protection is minimal.[9]

3. Texts and Instant Messages

In addition to e-mail, lawyers and other members of the legal team sometimes use text and instant messages to communicate with clients. Text messages, more formally known as Short Messaging Service (SMS), are transmitted via cell phone to another cell phone or other Voice over Internet Protocol (VOIP) phone number (such as Skype), or to an e-mail address.[10] These messages are limited in length to 160 characters or so. The first text message was sent in December 1992. By 2012, 2.2 trillion texts were sent a year in the United States, and 8.6 trillion were sent globally each year.[11]

Lawyers sometimes limit the types of communications they send via text because of their short length to very basic communications (e.g., "I've marked up the contract and e-mailed it for your review," or "Looking for parking. Will be in your office in 5 minutes"). Text messages can be very useful for certain purposes, like letting a member of the legal team know that she is needed immediately in a certain place ("the jury returned its verdict; get back to the courtroom now"). Text communications can be difficult to print if a lawyer wants to keep a record of them, and billing a client for time dedicated to texting can be challenging because texting tends to be done in very short spurts that, over a long period, can add up.[12] Short messages, especially with abbreviations, can be misconstrued easily. Lawyers might not want to be available on a 24/7 basis to respond to text messages, which can be received at any time of day. Nevertheless, clients might be very interested in engaging in this means of communication. A lawyer who disregarded text messages sent from a client was suspended from practice in *Iowa Supreme Court Attorney Disciplinary Board v. Humphrey*, 812 N.W.2d 659 (Iowa 2012). The lawyer's clients had sent 35 text messages in a period of slightly more than a year. The lawyer only responded via text three times, the first time almost a year after the first text message was sent by the clients. The lawyer also did not respond promptly to other forms of communication.

Lawyers also correspond with clients and others via instant messaging, often referred to as IMing. Instant messaging is an online chat in real time over the Internet. Instant messaging can be very useful for internal matters as it tends to be more instantaneous than the back-and-forth of e-mail. A lawyer can ask a paralegal a quick question and get a response right away. If too much detail would be necessary for an instant message, a call or e-mail can be placed. Although there are not character limits on the length of instant messaging, instant messages still tend to be very short.

D. Dealing with Challenging Clients

Clients in need of a lawyer may well be experiencing a very challenging time in their personal or professional lives. Unfortunately, people in those situations do not always behave as well as they would in calmer circumstances. The law business is really a service-oriented one, and that should be remembered. Ultimately, a firm needs to be accommodating to client needs and wants if the firm hopes to retain that client's business.

On occasion, a firm may actually fire a client, but that is not a decision for the paralegal or other staff person to make. While a client is a client, that client should be treated with courtesy and professionalism. On occasion, a paralegal or other staff person might have to interact with an irate client. Try to have some sympathy for the client's situation—someone going through a contested divorce, or whose company is filing for bankruptcy, is undoubtedly dealing with a lot of stressors. Remember, too, that law firms make mistakes sometimes, so it is possible that a client's anger is justified.

If you happen to answer the phone and are caught off guard by an irate client, try to remember to stay calm. That, of course, is easy advice to give and harder to put into practice. Some people have found that sticky notes posted near their telephone with suggestions like "Remain calm" or "Speak slowly" can be helpful reminders. Even when a client is expressing dissatisfaction with you, your firm, or your work, try to respond evenly. Of course, every situation is different, but you might ask the caller to explain exactly what is upsetting him or her and then offer to look into the matter and explain that either you or an attorney will get back to the caller. Sometimes people just need to vent, and you might be the unfortunate target.

Even the calmest person can be antagonized, though. If you find yourself at a point where you are beginning to lose your temper with a client, remember the hold button on your phone! A simple "Excuse me for just a minute, I have to put you on hold for a moment" can give you a bit of breathing space and an opportunity to calm down. Mute buttons can also be useful—so the caller cannot hear you, for instance, pounding your desk. Another way to avoid escalating a situation is to stand up while speaking to someone on the phone.

Try to prepare in advance for the moment when you might be the recipient of a client encounter that is less than pleasant. Sometimes clients are angry or scared, or they are having a bad day and cannot necessarily see how their legal problems will ever be satisfactorily resolved. Being involved in legal troubles can be frightening and disheartening for a client. That is easy to forget, of course, when the client is yelling at you over the telephone. Try to treat every client as if she is the only one the firm has. Make efforts to keep that client.

E.   Handling Difficult Employees

Dealing on occasion with a client who is upset can seem easy compared to dealing on a daily basis with a coworker who is unpleasant. Like the unhappy client, the difficult office worker might be dissatisfied for any number of reasons, none of which might have anything to do with you. A secretary might resent having to do work for nonpartners or might be angry that she was not promoted to a paralegal position. An information technology person, well versed in the language of computers, might not have highly developed people skills. A career paralegal without a college degree might be envious that a junior paralegal fresh out of a prestigious college is earning almost as much as she is. No matter what the circumstance, eventually you will run into someone in the office who simply is unpleasant to deal with.

Again, your response will depend on the unique facts of the situation. There are a number of different approaches you might try. One is to simply exhibit continuing kindness to the person, no matter how surly he is, in the hope that he will, eventually, experience an attitude adjustment. Do an unsolicited favor for the person, or invite him to lunch, or simply display a sunny disposition whenever you must interact with the person. Another option is to maintain a professional demeanor with someone who seems antagonistic toward you. You need not try to befriend the person; simply treat him or her as you would anyone else in the office and do not engage.

If a situation becomes intolerable, you might want to approach a mentor, or even a supervising attorney, for advice on how to handle it. Others in the office might be aware that a particular person is the organization's "grouch" and might have suggestions for how you can cope. Even in frustrating moments, try to think about what you can learn from this situation about conduct, professionalism, and basic human decency.

F.   Working with Lawyers

Law is a deadline-oriented, high-stress profession that requires a certain level of intensity on the part of its practitioners. Lawyers can be exceedingly smart, intellectually engaging, skilled interrogators, and fierce advocates. Many of them work hard, spend untold hours at the office, and are very committed both to their clients and to their practices. Lawyers can also experience a great deal of stress as they juggle multiple clients or prepare for trial.

Many lawyers do not engage in a lot of handholding. They expect their support staff to be go-getters. If you are sitting around with nothing to do, ask for more work. Take some initiative and organize materials on your own, or take a bit of time to gain expertise on some aspect of your computer work.

When you are given an assignment, take notes. Ask for the due date if one is not provided. Try to specify the **parameters** of an assignment to the extent that you can. Is the attorney expecting a two-page basic memorandum by the deadline, or a 20-page analysis of the law? If you have conflicting deadlines, ask him to help you prioritize. You might ask for pointers—such as any suggestions on where to begin your research. At the very least, the lawyer might be able to direct you to a specific case or statute, or suggest some search terms and Lexis files for you to try.

parameter:
Boundary; a factor that determines a range of variations.

G.   Crisis Management

At times, a law firm might be handling a high-profile matter that is making the nightly news, major newspapers, and the blogosphere. When a case is drawing a lot of attention, it can result in additional phone calls, media stakeouts, and possibly even protests. Lawyers and staff should be prepared to deal with these "in the spotlight" situations.

1.   A Client's Emergency

Lawyers must manage client expectations in high-stakes situations. There might be both a legal matter that needs resolution and a public relations issue that requires significant attention. The type of emergency that might arise could involve almost anything from soda pop to cigarettes:

> It could be crude oil floating in Prince William Sound. It might involve a little radio-active blip over Tokyo, or a widely prescribed diet-pill combination that seems to be causing catastrophic heart-valve problems, or a badly handled antitrust trial that causes a company—and its lawyers—to get socked by the press.[13]

Whether and to what extent the law firm will deal with publicity should be established with the client. " 'Lawyers and business people should be working with each other and not independently,' "[14] said a name partner at one law firm that has worked on high-visibility matters for clients. " 'The lawyers sometimes get caught up in just winning the case and don't pay attention to the grand strategy of the company. Conversely, the business people, including PR, have to be aware [that] seemingly innocuous statements can have negative [legal] consequences.' "[15]

Even if a law firm is not involved in dealing with the press, the firm should develop a **communications strategy** so that vital staff people are aware of how important callers and inquiries should be handled—because reporters and other key figures may well call anyway. Suppose the White House chief of staff calls? Or the mayor? Or a *New York Times* reporter on deadline? Should messages ever be taken for these people, or should the person they are attempting to contact be tracked down?

Staff people should be wary when dealing with the media and, ideally, should be provided with some additional training even if their contact with reporters is

communications strategy:
A plan for controlling the transmittal of information to the public, the press, clients, or the workforce.

likely to be minimal. Journalists are adept at ferreting out information from people, whether by having a seemingly casual conversation in an elevator, by sharing a smoke with someone in front of a building, or even by haranguing an unsuspecting secretary.

In time-sensitive crises, a law firm might hold an "all hands" meeting of a legal team to divvy up the work, establish a chain of command, and set up schedules. Extra support might be brought in from within the firm or through temporary hires. Employees might be expected to log in extra hours until the crisis has passed.

2.   *Media Glare*

A high-visibility incident becomes even more delicate when the law firm itself is the cause of it for some reason. Sometimes lawyers do things they should not. Bad behavior can occur at even the very best, most prestigious law firms in the country. Given the growth in major law firms, some legal industry observers "are now more convinced than ever that severe, often multiple or continuous missteps are virtually impossible for even well-regarded firms . . . to avoid. 'The best law firm in the world will from time to time have problems,'" said the managing partner of one major firm.[16] Should a catastrophic event occur at a law firm—a top rainmaker is arrested for embezzling, a managing partner is caught with a prostitute, a big-name partner is professionally disciplined for violating ethics rules—the firm might consider turning to outside professional services firms for their crisis management expertise.

Someone needs to deal with the press, but someone also needs to deal with clients who might be misinformed. Calls to clients, or even a mass mailing, may be necessary. Morale within the firm itself should also be addressed. "[F]irm managers . . . [should] invest time talking with partners, associates—and staff as well. 'The *esprit de corps* is as important as how people outside [the firm] feel,'"[17] said the head of one legal public relations firm. The information shared with staff as well as with outsiders should be carefully managed but truthful:

> The specific message conveyed in the firmwide outreach should be that the firm is, in fact, dealing with a difficult situation, but that it will survive and prevail because it does excellent work. It won't hurt either if firm leaders pointedly remind the troops that those who misbehaved are paying the price for their sins.[18]

Though seemingly never-ending while it is being endured, a crisis will eventually blow over—either it will be resolved or a more significant one will arise elsewhere that captures the attention of the media. Until that happens, though, a firm should be well prepared.

Checklist

- Communication skills are vitally important in a law office.
- Office protocols should be followed.
- Law offices observe certain formalities in how telephones are answered, letters are written, and other recurring duties are performed.
- A law firm's employees should be aware that they represent the firm to the public; as a service business, the firm relies on the goodwill generated by its employees in servicing clients and others.
- Dress professionally if you work in a law office.
- When receiving a telephone call, obtain the caller's name, affiliation, and reason for calling.
- When taking a message for someone else, be certain to clearly identify the person to whom the message is addressed, obtain the proper spelling of the caller's name and an accurate telephone number including area code, and note any message as well as the date and time the person called. Be certain to identify yourself as the person who wrote down the message.
- When placing a telephone call, identify yourself by first and last names, specify your affiliation, and identify the person you are calling.
- If you must place a call that is likely to be unpleasant or challenging, practice beforehand by writing down a potential script of the statements you want to make.
- Clients often expect calls and e-mail messages to be returned the same day. Responses to text messages and instant messages are expected even sooner and often immediately.
- Keep clients and other callers informed about your availability by frequently updating your voice mail message.
- Letters are formal communications printed on stationery that are sent to recipients outside the law firm.
- Rule 7.1 of the *Model Rules of Professional Conduct* prohibits lawyers from making false or misleading communications about a lawyer or the lawyer's services.
- When designing law firm letterhead, keep the *Model Rules of Professional Conduct* and state ethics rules in mind. These rules govern whether deceased partners can be listed on the letterhead and what information must be included for firms that have offices in more than one jurisdiction.
- All letters sent out on firm letterhead must be well crafted, accurate, and proofread.
- Do not misuse law firm stationery.
- Observe certain formalities even when sending an e-mail message.

- Lawyers must take precautions even when reading an e-mail message that they received from a prospective client who is unknown to them. Model Rule 1.18 generally bars lawyers from using information revealed in a consultation even when no lawyer-client relationship results from that consultation.
- The extent to which a lawyer must refrain from using or revealing information received in an unsolicited e-mail message is an evolving area of the law. Maintain confidentiality of client information and take precautions to make sure that it is not accidentally disclosed via e-mail.
- Do not use your work e-mail account for personal communications, and keep in mind that your employer will have access to your work. Do not risk the possibility that colleagues will see personally embarrassing correspondence.
- Clients in need of a lawyer may well be going through a very challenging time in their personal or professional lives. Unfortunately, people in those situations don't always behave as well as they would in other, more calm circumstances.
- Remain calm when dealing with a distressed client.
- Consider a variety of approaches when dealing with a difficult coworker.
- When receiving an assignment from an attorney, try to get her to specify the parameters of the assignment.
- A law firm involved in a high-profile case should develop a communications strategy for dealing with media inquiries.

Vocabulary

acceptable use policy (p. 185)

BCC (p. 179)

block format (p. 179)

business casual attire (p. 176)

CC (p. 179)

communications strategy (p. 189)

decorum (p. 170)

disclaimer (p. 186)

parameter (p. 189)

protocol (p. 170)

template (p. 184)

Career Preparation Tips

Don't wait until a job hunt to begin improving your speaking and writing skills. If you are fortunate enough to have access to professionals, observe and model their behavior. When in other situations, think about how you would handle them differently. For example, this author recently visited a stationery store and observed a salesperson eating a dinner salad at the ordering table where customers view and order custom invitations. This employee's act was very much a deterrent to customers. The store should provide a private space for employees to lounge, and it should create and enforce policies about eating on the store floor. You can think about policies that you would develop when you observe inappropriate behavior in a retail situation. Jot down some ideas and think about activities that members of the legal team undertake that might actually deter prospective clients.

Improve speaking skills by volunteering for organizations where you will get a chance to speak, or by joining a group that will provide speaking opportunities, such as Toastmasters International (http://www.toastmasters .org).

Develop and improve organizational skills by volunteering to take on projects for organizations with which you are already involved (e.g., churches, temples, scouting, community improvement centers)—or join some!

Improve writing skills by keeping a daily journal, and try to focus your writing on career hopes and goals. Writing really does improve with time and practice.

Enhance your knowledge of the legal industry by reading legal newspapers and blogs regularly. Create and maintain a folder with articles that have particular appeal for you.

If You Want to Learn More

ABA Commission on Lawyer Assistance Programs. http://www .americanbar.org/groups/lawyer_assistance.html

Lawyers with Depression. http://www.lawyerswithdepression.com

PRWeek provides news about public relations. http://www.prweekus.com

Public Relations Society of America. http://www.prsa.org

The full text of the *Model Rules of Professional Conduct* is available online. http://www.americanbar.org/groups/professional_responsibility /publications/model_rules_of_professional_conduct/model_rules_of_ professional_conduct_table_of_contents.html

Reading Comprehension

1. What is the difference between an external market and an internal market at a law firm?
2. Where are a law firm's written procedures likely to be collected?
3. What elements are likely to appear in a law firm's acceptable use policy specifying the purposes for which e-mail and computers may be used?
4. How does an e-mail disclaimer protect the sender of the communication?
5. What are some strategies for dealing with a disgruntled client on the telephone?
6. How should a terminally cranky coworker be treated?
7. Which are the advantages of communicating by e-mail, text, or instant message?
8. What dangers are associated with communication by e-mail, text, or instant message?
9. How can any hazards associated with communication by e-mail, text, or instant message be minimized?

Discussion Starters

1. Read the excerpt of *Cloutier v. Costco Wholesale Corp.* in this chapter.
    a. Why do you suppose plaintiff/appellant Kimberly Cloutier originally filed the lawsuit?
    b. How do you think her decision to file suit affected her career?
    c. Are you committed to a certain style of dress or an accessory such that you would be willing to risk being fired for continuing to wear it?
    d. What changes in attire, makeup, hairstyle, or accessories would you be willing to make in order to advance your career?
2. Find a recent case involving e-mailed correspondence and confidentiality, and briefly describe the decision by identifying the facts, the issue, the rule, the application of that rule to the facts in the case, and the holding. Who filed suit against whom, and why? Did an employee make an error in either e-mailing material or maintaining confidentiality? How many resources do you suppose were spent in litigating the case? Do you think there were any repercussions for the person whose misdeed was at the center of the litigation? What would you do if faced with a similar scenario in your own work life?
3. Find a disciplinary action involving law firm letterhead. What inappropriate action was the lawyer charged with? Were others in his or her office

involved? What triggered the complaint against the lawyer? How might the disciplinary problem have been avoided in the first instance?

4. Suppose a client whose case you have worked on as a paralegal calls you to complain about the bill received and begins to be verbally abusive to you, calling you an idiot, stupid, a dumb blonde, and other names. How would you react? Suppose that same client, in the same call, makes a racially or ethnically inappropriate remark. How would you respond? Suppose that, after getting off the phone with you, the client immediately calls the managing partner of the firm to complain about you. What would you do if the partner then asked you to call the client and apologize for your response in the telephone call?

5. Envision a scenario where a conservative client asks a female paralegal who is wearing a knee-length skirt to cover her bare legs. How should the paralegal respond? What if the client asked the paralegal to wear a head scarf? Suppose the client asked the paralegal to don a veil covering her face. Would that be acceptable?

6. Read *Lesher v. Law Offices of Mitchell N. Kapy, PC*. How might the correspondence at the center of the dispute been written appropriately so that a violation of law would not have occurred? What do you suppose the repercussions of the litigation were for the law firm that was the defendant in the action?

7. Suppose you are a paralegal working for a corporate client who is having difficulties with a regulatory agency. Your supervising attorney is aware that the agency has maintained records on the client's compliance with laws. The attorney wants copies of those records and has directed you to obtain them. When you call your contact at the agency to request the records, the immediate answer you are given is no. What would you do?

8. You have been e-mailing a client about her upcoming trial on fraud charges related to her work. By accident, you send an e-mail message about the firm's litigation strategy to a journalist who is covering the trial. What would you do?

9. The governor of your state has recently been arrested for visiting a prostitute. Your firm represents the governor in the criminal case brought against him. You are a paralegal working on the case. You answer the telephone one day and discover that a famous TV journalist is calling you and asking for information about the governor "off the record," meaning your name and firm will not be identified. The attention from such a famous person is highly flattering. He even offers to meet you over lunch. Would you go? Would you consult your supervising attorney first? Would you provide information to the reporter? Would your willingness to provide the information depend on the type of information sought? Would it depend on how much you disapproved of the governor's actions and thought that they were wrong?

10. Your first name is the same as the name of another paralegal at your large law firm. After submitting a legal memo you worked on at length, you receive a harsh critique from the associate to whom you submitted it.

As you scroll down the e-mail message, you see that the associate and another lawyer within the firm made fun of the work and made scathing comments about your personality—except you realize that the person whose work they are critiquing and whom they are making fun of is the other person at the firm who has the same first name as yours. How would you react? Should you alert the sender to the error? Would you tell the other paralegal about the harsh assessment of that paralegal's work?

11. Critique the letter in Figure 7-1. What are its strengths and weaknesses? How could it be improved?

Case Studies

1. You have been asked to develop a dress code for a 20-lawyer, intellectual property firm that has a single office in Silicon Valley, Calif. All of the firm's partners are aged 40 or younger, and the firm's clients are Internet start-ups.
   a. How would the dress code at this office differ from the dress code at a 1,000-lawyer firm with offices in ten countries around the world that provides full service for corporate clients?
   b. What factors should be considered as the dress code is developed?
   c. How should the code be enforced?
   d. What should be the penalty for violating the code?
   e. May head scarves be prohibited in the law firm? May hoodies? Why would law firm management seek to ban these items of clothing? Look up the latest case law on this subject and write a memo responding to these questions.

2. You have been asked to develop a template for setting up meetings with opposing counsel for your firm.
   a. What information should be included in the body of the letter?
   b. Who should sign the letter?
   c. How might this correspondence differ from an in-house memo announcing the location of the office holiday party?

3. You have been asked to draft the letterhead for a five-lawyer firm in your hometown. Research state rules on letterhead. If you are a paralegal at the firm, can your name and title be included on the letterhead?

4. Research recent news items involving public figures, major corporations, or famous people who broke the law. Is the coverage in the media positive or negative? From what you have read, how might the press have been dealt with differently? Were the lawyers representing the subject of the articles quoted at all? How substantive were their responses?

Endnotes

1. *HRF News Briefs*, HRfocus, Dec. 2007, n.p.
2. Heather R. James, *Note: If You Are Attractive and You Know It, Please Apply: Appearance Based Discrimination and Employers' Discretion*, 42 Val. U. L. Rev. 629, 636-37 (Winter 2008).
3. Linda L. Edwards, *Law Office Skills* 30 (2003).
4. *No Worries: Call Response Service Guarantees Answered Calls*, Leg. Mgmt., Nov./Dec. 2006, at 14.
5. *See, e.g.*, Burkey Belser, *100 Law Firm Letterheads Tell a Story of Cautious Change*, Brand Thinking (Mar. 1, 1997), http://www.greenfieldbelser.com/articles/100-law-firm-letterheads-tell-a-story-of-cautious-change.
6. *See, e.g.*, New York State Rules of Prof'l Conduct R. 7.5, *available at* http://www.nysba.org/Content/NavigationMenu/ForAttorneys/ProfessionalStandardsforAttorneys/Professional_Standar.htm (effective Apr. 1, 2009 as amended through Dec. 20, 2012).
7. American Bar Association, Model Rules of Prof'l Conduct R. 1.18, *available at* http://www.americanbar.org/groups/professional_responsibility/publications/model_rules_of_professional_conduct/rule_1_18_duties_of_prospective_client.html (last visited Aug. 22, 2013).
8. *See, e.g.*, Thomas E. Spahn, *The Ethics of Email and Social Media: A Top Ten List — Hypotheticals and Analyses* (presented at NSBA Council of School Attorneys, April 11-13, 2013, San Diego, Cal.), *available at* http://www.nsba.org.
9. *See, e.g.*, Dean R. Dietrich, *Swim at Your Own Risk: Email Disclaimers*, 86 Wis. Law. 41 (Feb. 2013); *compare Stengart v. Loving Care Agency, Inc.*, 201 N.J. 300 (2010).
10. *See, e.g.*, Ohio B. Comm'ners on Grievances & Discipline, Op. 2-13-2 (Apr. 5, 2013).
11. Heather Kelly, *OMG, the Text Message Turns 20. But Has SMS Peaked?* CNN.com (Dec. 3, 2012), *available at* http://www.cnn.com/2012/12/03/tech/mobile/sms-text-message-20.
12. *See, e.g.*, Josh Camson, *Lawyers Texting Clients, Srsly*, Lawyerist (June 3, 2011), *available at* http://lawyerist.com/lawyers-texting-clients-srsly/.
13. Lori Tripoli, *When Clients Get Caught in a Crucible, Where Do Their Counselors Turn?*, Of Counsel, Oct. 18, 1999, at 6.
14. *Id.* at 7.
15. *Id.*
16. Lori Tripoli, *Morgan Lewis' Turbulent Trip to Troublesome Gulch*, Of Counsel, Apr. 20, 1998, at 1.
17. Lori Tripoli, *A Partner's Been Arrested, the Press Is on the Line, Don't Panic!*, Of Counsel, Apr. 20, 1998, at 13.
18. *Id.*

8

Marketing

Chapter Outcomes

By the end of this chapter, a student will be able to:

- Draft a law firm mission statement
- Develop a law firm marketing plan
- Assess legal advertising for ethical appropriateness
- Compare and contrast different advertising venues for legal organizations

Law firms need to have clients, and they need to plan ways to get both more clients and more work from their existing clients. Getting new business "by word of mouth"—essentially, good references from others—is great, but, with increasing competition, lawyers have found they must be far more proactive in generating business. Sitting idly by while competing law firms snap up clients is not a means of ensuring a law firm's longevity.

Any effort to gain new clients must, of course, be conducted within ethical boundaries—and, typically, within budgetary constraints. Marketing efforts should be highly targeted, and their success should be measured.

A. Marketing the Law Firm

Marketing is the process by which firms promote and sell their services. A written law firm **marketing plan**, approved by the firm's leadership, can help guide the firm's marketing efforts. Such a plan should identify new clients and new matters that are sought; it should articulate objectives, establish a budget, assess

marketing:
The process by which firms promote and sell their services.

marketing plan:
A guide for promoting a firm's services that identifies business development goals, specifies target markets, and indicates means for achieving the firm's goals.

mission statement:
An explanation of a firm's purpose.

brand:
The associations and experiences that define an entity, person, or service.

the competition, and measure results. A law firm **mission statement** should be crafted that explains the law firm's purpose and distinguishes the firm from its competitors.

In a marketing plan and a mission statement, the firm's **brand** should be identified:

> Branding answers the question, What are we known for? A business is branded in the minds of customers if it is known for something which others are not (or cannot be), and its image is uniform among employees, clients, prospects, referral sources and the press. Volvo (safety), Marlboro cigarettes (machismo), Federal Express (overnight, guaranteed) and Audi (leading-edge design) are all branded and enjoy strong market share and/or high profitability.[1]

Law firms are sometimes criticized for crafting bland mission statements, such as "We provide client-oriented service." While, admittedly, some lawyers are better at satisfying clients than others, doesn't every lawyer really provide client-oriented service? Does that phrase have any special meaning? Often, a firm's statement is too generic. A well-crafted mission statement, on the other hand, can attract greater interest from prospective clients. Mission statements should be distinctive and inspiring. Ideally, they should inspire prospective clients to hire the firm.

The marketing plan itself can be relatively short and straightforward or, for a larger firm, rather lengthy. The most important aspect of a marketing plan is that it be implemented. Putting all sorts of grand strategies on paper or into a computer file won't land a firm more clients. Taking action will. A firm's marketing plan should help a firm achieve its business development goals and objectives. A goal is broad in scope and identifies a desired outcome (such as "become one of the top three family law firms in the city"), and objectives are more specific, and measurable, targets (such as "add 50 new clients this year" or "be the named attorney in 30 percent of the actions that are filed this year") that must be reached to attain the goal.

As the plan is developed, a budget for marketing should be created. The amount dedicated to marketing will vary from firm to firm, even at firms of comparable size. The type of firm and its location can all impact the amount it will need to spend on marketing. Firms based in areas where advertising or costs in general are expensive might need to spend more. Plaintiffs' attorneys might need to spend more than defense firms, as one client for a defense firm may bring a number of lawsuits or quite a bit of work, whereas a plaintiff's attorney may handle more work on a single-case basis.[2] One business development advisor recommends that firms spend at least 2.5 percent of their gross revenues on direct marketing activities plus fees and salaries for those who the firm hires to do the marketing.[3]

competitive intelligence:
Information about an industry and market served.

Competitive intelligence is an important element of any marketing plan. A firm should consider what its competitors are doing and whether those competitors are more successful than the firm is. The marketing plan should identify market trends in the legal field and in the business or type of client the law firm is seeking.

As best as possible, the plan should identify the market size and the firm's market share so the firm can set realistic goals and objectives. Various marketing efforts may be taken to yield different results. Some may be geared more toward the long-term building of name recognition, while others may be more directly focused on actually getting new business immediately.

The plan might include an analysis identifying strengths, weaknesses, opportunities, and threats (SWOT) in brief entries on a grid (see Figure 8-1). Based on the outcome of this analysis, the firm can more easily identify action items it will take with respect to marketing and to overall firm planning.

The marketing plan should not be developed in a vacuum. The marketing team should solicit input from and have conversations with all attorneys in the firm and with other members of the legal team as well. Specific initiatives to be undertaken should be identified. Elements of the plan should be specific and measurable. For instance, the plan might indicate that three partners will publish five articles in scholarly publications; that the firm will post on its blog four times each week; that partners will identify five prospective corporate clients and then take specific steps to woo them; that advertising will be undertaken in specific outlets; that free seminars and lunches will be provided to certain top current clients in an

FIGURE 8-1
Sample SWOT Analysis of a Hypothetical Boutique Environmental Law Firm

STRENGTHS	WEAKNESSES
Partner depth in areas of air, water, hazardous waste, hazardous substances	Not as much partner expertise in areas of sustainability, pesticides, toxic substances
Firm-negotiated major settlements favorable to firm clients in hazardous waste regulatory matters in last year are appealing to prospective clients	Insufficient number of midlevel associates
	Lateral partners, although highly knowledgeable, have resulted in firm being conflicted out of some high-profile cases in region
Litigated one-fifth of hazardous substance cleanup cases in region in last year; won 70 percent and settled favorably 10 percent	
OPPORTUNITIES	THREATS
Primary competitor is experiencing a lot of departures and financial challenges	One long-term corporate client is relocating its headquarters to the other coast in 18 months
Senior partner with expertise in water has a law book being published in the fall and is media savvy	Small startup firms spun off from disintegrating primary competitor will have lower overhead and rates
More and more clients are interested in sustainability and in impact of climate change on their business	Megafirm with strong environmental practice opened a branch office in region that is headed by an environmental partner

effort to obtain more work; and so on. Based on the overall firm marketing plan, individual lawyers should also develop their own personal marketing plans and implement those as well.

The results of any marketing effort should be tracked from year to year. The amount spent for various initiatives should be compared to the number of new clients gained. The most and least successful marketing venues should be identified.

Many law firms have marketing directors who oversee and guide the firm's marketing efforts. Large firms might have a marketing staff as well as a chief marketing officer who supervises marketing initiatives. Any marketing team should be the appropriate size for the firm given its needs, interests, and size. A full-time marketing person for every 20 to 30 lawyers is considered appropriate by some.[4]

B.   Advertising

1.   History

Today, lawyers advertise their services on television, on the Web, on billboards, in newspapers, and in just about any other vehicle imaginable. Yet, in the not-too-distant past, lawyer advertising was considered unseemly and even barred by ethics rules.[5] Advertising was viewed as having an adverse effect on an attorney's professionalism:

> The key to professionalism, it is argued, is the sense of pride that involvement in the discipline generates. It is claimed that price advertising will bring about commercialization, which will undermine the attorney's sense of dignity and self-worth. The hustle of the marketplace will adversely affect the profession's service orientation, and irreparably damage the delicate balance between the lawyer's need to earn and his obligation selflessly to serve. Advertising is also said to erode the client's trust in his attorney: Once the client perceives that the lawyer is motivated by profit, his confidence that the attorney is acting out of a commitment to the client's welfare is jeopardized. And advertising is said to tarnish the dignified public image of the profession.[6]

The ban on advertising has its roots in the British legal system. Lawyers in Great Britain saw their livelihood as a public service, not a mere "trade."[7] Moreover, consumers of legal services might be misled by lawyer advertising—and they might even be inspired to file fraudulent claims. Lawyers were left to rely on referrals to generate more work for themselves.

And yet—lawyers can generate even more business by advertising. Clients, in turn, can get better deals thanks to increased competition among lawyers:

> [A]t least four studies have been conducted—including two through grants from the National Science Foundation and one by the Federal Trade Commission—intended to measure the effect of advertising on the pricing of legal services. All came to the same conclusion. Competition among lawyers, in the form of commercial advertising, has resulted in lower prices to consumers.[8]

2.   Restrictions

Eventually, the long-time ban on lawyer advertising was challenged.

a)   COURT CASES

The Supreme Court of the United States, in a landmark decision in *Bates v. State Bar of Arizona*, 433 U.S. 350 (1977), held that advertising by lawyers is a form of commercial speech that is protected by the First Amendment. While deciding that "advertising by attorneys may not be subjected to blanket suppression,"[9] the high court nevertheless noted that there are some clearly permissible restrictions on lawyer advertising, such as ads that are false, deceptive, or misleading. The Court wrote, "[W]e recognize that many of the problems in defining the boundary between deceptive and nondeceptive advertising remain to be resolved, and we expect that the bar will have a special role to play in assuring that advertising by attorneys flows both freely and cleanly."[10] In the years since the *Bates* decision was issued, the limits of restrictions on attorney advertising have been litigated.[11]

b)   BAR RULES

As the Supreme Court's approach to lawyer advertising has evolved over time, so, too, have ethical requirements governing such ads. Today, several of the American Bar Association's *Model Rules of Professional Conduct* pertain to lawyer advertising—in particular, Rules 7.1, 7.2, and 7.3. Although lawyer advertising is allowed (Rule 7.2), it cannot be false or misleading (Rule 7.1). Direct solicitation of prospective clients is severely limited under Rule 7.3.

A law office manager should be aware of the model requirements specified by the ABA as well as the requirements of the local jurisdictions in which the firm practices because the ethical codes that apply may contain significant variations or additional requirements. The growth of national and international law firms poses a new set of challenges in advertising, as these firms must comply with the specific rules in various states and countries.

It is imperative that a law office manager stay current on requirements applicable to a given law firm's advertising venues.

c)   TRUTH IN ADVERTISING

In addition to Model Rule 7.1's proscription against false or misleading communications and to state ethical requirements barring similar conduct, lawyers may be subject to other statutes aimed at protecting consumers from false advertising. For instance, the Colorado Supreme Court has ruled that lawyers in Colorado can be sued under the state's consumer protection act.[12] Law office managers must also be cognizant of laws that are not necessarily associated with operating a law firm but that may nevertheless apply.

C.   Tombstone and Other Ads

tombstone ad:
A law firm announcement, typically published in black and white.

Initially, law firm advertising was on the dull side—largely consisting of new-partner notices in what the industry refers to as "**tombstone ads**"[13] typically announcing that a lawyer has joined a law firm or an associate has been promoted to partner.[14]

Just as the law has evolved over time, so, too, has lawyer advertising. Faced with increasing competition, the acceptance of advertising as a legitimate means to seek clients, and the need to differentiate themselves, law firms began using more creative advertisements and no longer limited themselves to the dull black-and-white announcements of personnel changes within the firm. Ads are no longer limited to placement in newspapers and Yellow Pages directories. Some law firms—even large, well-respected ones—advertise on television. In 2001, Brobeck, Phleger & Harrison (which later was liquidated in bankruptcy proceedings) reportedly spent $3.5 million on ads on cable news stations.[15] Today, lawyer ads can also be found on the Internet.

Even though lawyer ads may seem conventional to people nowadays, on occasion, a particularly provocative advertisement will garner a lot of attention. For example, a billboard in Chicago featured the slogan "Life's Short. Get a Divorce" along with a photo of an attractive woman in lingerie and a bare-chested, well-toned man with a scale of justice—and the law firm's Web address between the two. The billboard was removed because the law firm purportedly had not received an appropriate permit for the ad.[16]

One means of advertising that gained a lot of publicity was a special advertising section placed in mainstream publications featuring lawyers designated as "Super Lawyers" or as the "Best Lawyers." In 2006, the New Jersey Supreme Court Committee on Attorney Advertising banned such advertising in Opinion 39. The committee concluded that designations as Super Lawyers or Best Lawyers violated state rules against advertisements that are "inherently comparative in nature" or that create "an unjustified expectation about results."[17] The publishers of "Super Lawyers" and "Best Lawyers" challenged the validity of the ban on this type of advertising. The New Jersey Supreme Court, in *In re Opinion 39*, 197 N.J. 66 (2008) (citation omitted), determined that "'state bans on truthful, fact-based claims in lawful professional advertising could be ruled unconstitutional when the state fails to establish that the regulated claims are actually or inherently misleading and would thus be unprotected by the First Amendment commercial speech doctrine.'" The Court vacated the New Jersey Supreme Court Committee on Attorney Advertising's Opinion 39 and directed that the rule on advertising be revised. In 2009, N.J. Rules of Professional Conduct R. 7.1 was revised to specify that a communication is false or misleading if it compares the lawyer's services with other lawyers' services, unless (i) the name of the comparing organization is stated, (ii) the basis for the comparison can be substantiated, and (iii) the communication includes the following disclaimer in a readily discernable manner: "No aspect of this advertisement has been approved by the Supreme Court of New Jersey[.]"

Since the New Jersey Supreme Court addressed the legality of lawyers advertised as "Best Lawyers" or "Super Lawyers," other states have considered whether lawyer superlatives should be permissible in advertising. Some have specifically allowed comparisons to other lawyers to be advertised and assessments about the quality of a lawyer's services to be included in an advertisement.[18]

The extent to which a lawyer may boast about his or her designations as superior in his or her field continues to raise concerns about the ethical propriety of these communications.

N.J. Supreme Court Committee on Attorney Advertising
Op. 42 (2010)

The Committee on Attorney Advertising recently considered a grievance regarding an attorney's solicitation letter that touted his inclusion in a "Super Lawyers" attorney ranking list and membership in the "Million Dollar Advocates Forum." The grievance was resolved informally after the attorney revised his solicitation letter. Because the problem is likely to recur, the Committee decided to issue this opinion to provide guidance to the bar on permissible language when communicating inclusion in such lists or referring to membership in organizations such as the "Million Dollar Advocates Forum."

In 2006, the Committee on Attorney Advertising issued Opinion 39, concerning attorneys advertising inclusion in ranking lists published by organizations such as Best Lawyers of America ("Best Lawyers") and Key Professional Media ("Super Lawyers"). 185 *N.J.L.J.* 360, 15 *N.J.L.* 1549 (July 24, 2006). The New Jersey Supreme Court granted a petition for review of Opinion 39 and remanded the matter to a Special Master, who held a hearing and issued a comprehensive Report that was presented to the Court. *In re Opinion 39 of the Committee on Attorney Advertising*, 197 *N.J.* 66 (2008). In its decision, the Court acknowledged that the language of *Rule of Professional Conduct* 7.1(a)(3) prohibited statements comparing attorneys' services and held that it would revise the *Rule* to "take into account the policy concerns expressed by the *Rule* while, at the same time, respecting legitimate commercial speech activities." *Id.* at 79-80.

The Court issued amendments to *Rule of Professional Conduct* 7.1 effective November 2, 2009. Amended *Rule of Professional Conduct* 7.1(a)(3) provides that "a communication is false or misleading if it . . . compares the lawyer's services with other lawyers' services, unless (i) the name of the comparing organization is stated, (ii) the basis for the comparison can be substantiated, and (iii) the communication includes the following disclaimer in a readily discernable manner: 'No aspect of this advertisement has been approved by the Supreme Court of New Jersey' . . . ." The official comment to amended *Rule of Professional Conduct* 7.1 provides:

> A truthful communication that the lawyer has received an honor or accolade is not misleading or impermissibly comparative for purposes of this Rule if: (1) the conferrer has made inquiry into the attorney's fitness; (2) the conferrer does not issue such an honor or accolade for a price; and (3) a truthful, plain language description of the standard or methodology upon which the honor or accolade is based is available for inspection either as part of the communication itself or by reference to a convenient, publicly available source.

[Official Comment to *RPC* 7.1.]

Amended *Rule of Professional Conduct* 7.1(a)(3), therefore, requires that the factual basis for a comparison of attorneys' services must be verifiable. Further, the attorney must include the name of the comparing organization and must be satisfied that the conferrer has made appropriate inquiry into the attorney's fitness. The attorney must include a description of the standard or methodology on which the accolade is based. Lastly, the attorney must state that the advertisement has not been approved by the Supreme Court. This information is necessary to protect consumers from communications that are misleading and likely to raise unjustified expectations. When adequate information is available to consumers of legal services, they should be able to differentiate between accurate puffery and unsupportable exaggeration.

The solicitation letter recently reviewed by the Committee provided: "Because of my dedication to our clients and success in the courtroom, I have been named as a **Super Lawyer** by **New Jersey Monthly Magazine** for five (5) consecutive years (2006 through 2010), and I am a **Life Member** of the **Million Dollar Advocates Forum, which puts me in an elite group of less than one percent (1%) of all lawyers in the United States.**" This language grossly violates the rules governing attorney advertising.

The advertisement calls the attorney "a Super Lawyer" instead of saying that he was included in the "Super Lawyers" list published by Thomson Reuters. There is an obvious and crucial difference between stating that one is "a Super Lawyer" and stating that one received an accolade or honor by being included on a list called "Super Lawyers." This point was addressed by the Special Master in the Report submitted to the Court in *In re Opinion 39 of the Committee on Attorney Advertising, supra*:

> Where superlatives are contained in the title of the list itself, such as here, the advertising must state and emphasize only one's **inclusion** in the *Super Lawyers* or *The Best Lawyers in America* list, and **must not** describe the attorney as being a "Super Lawyer" or the "Best Lawyer."

[Special Master Report, June 18, 2008, page 303.]

The claim in the solicitation letter that the attorney is in "an elite group of less than one percent (1%) of all lawyers in the United States" also is improper. As the Special Master stated in the Report:

> Likewise, claims that the list contains "the best" lawyers or, *e.g.*, "the top 5% of attorneys in the state," or similar phrases are misleading, are usually factually inaccurate and should be prohibited.

[*Ibid.*]

The Committee agrees with these comments of the Special Master regarding permissible language and phrasing to be used by attorneys touting this type of honor or accolade. The claim that an attorney is "super," "best," "elite," or in a top percentile of attorneys, cannot be factually substantiated. Such hyperbolical words and phrases are utterly and inherently misleading and may not be used in attorneys' communications.

Attorneys must also refrain from making inaccurate or misleading statements about the reasons for inclusion in such lists or membership in organizations such as the "Million Dollar Advocates Forum." In the solicitation letter reviewed by the Committee, the attorney stated that he was included in the list called "Super Lawyers" and obtained membership in the "Million Dollar Advocates Forum" "because of [his] dedication to [his] clients and success in the courtroom."

An attorney obtains inclusion in the list generated by Thomson Reuters ("Super Lawyers"), Best Lawyers in America ("Best Lawyers"), and similar organizations by receiving a sufficient score or rating in accordance with the organization's standards and methodology. As required by amended *Rule of Professional Conduct* 7.1(a)(3), the advertisement must include a description of the standard or methodology used by the organization. An attorney obtains membership in the "Million Dollar Advocates Forum" because the attorney obtained a recovery of at least one million dollars in a case and then paid a substantial fee to the "Forum" for lifetime membership. Advertisements must include a description of the criteria to be met to obtain membership in organizations such as the "Forum." Attorneys may not casually state that a reason such as "dedication to clients" was the basis for their receipt of this type of honor or accolade.

It has also come to the Committee's attention through the hotline that some newspapers conduct contests to anoint attorneys, businesses, and pizza parlors as "top" in the region. Apparently, this type of accolade is conferred based on online voting by newspaper readers. There is no indication that the newspaper conducts an inquiry into the fitness of the attorneys who "win" such contests. These appear to be mere popularity contests and attorneys may not refer to such honors or accolades in any communications about the attorney's services.

Accordingly, attorneys may communicate that they are included in ranking lists only if the factual basis for the comparison of attorneys' services can be substantiated or verified, and the comparing organization has made appropriate inquiry into the attorney's fitness. The attorney must include in the communication the name of the comparing organization and a description of the standard or methodology on which the honor or accolade is based. The attorney must state that the advertisement has not been approved by the Supreme Court. The attorney must include the year the honor or accolade was conferred and the specialty, if any, for which the attorney was listed. When the title of the list contains a superlative such as "super," "best," "leading," "top," or "elite," the attorney must state and emphasize only the attorney's inclusion in the list and must not state that he or she *is* "super," "best," "leading," "top," or "elite." Similarly, an attorney may not state that the list in which he or she is included reflects "the best" attorneys or a "top percentage" of attorneys, or that he or she belongs to an organization comprising an "elite percentage" of attorneys. Such statements cannot be substantiated and are inherently misleading.

Law office managers as well as attorneys themselves should keep abreast of developments on legal advertising in the states in which they practice.

D.   Firm Brochure

brochure:
A marketing tool, frequently in print as well as online, describing the capabilities of a law firm or practice group.

As lawyers began to focus more on marketing after the Supreme Court's decision in *Bates,* some firms began to publish **brochures** identifying their practice areas. Initially, these efforts yielded fairly basic publications.[19] Over time, brochures evolved to become much more appealing documents featuring eye-catching graphics, photographs, and marketing-oriented copy. At large firms, individual practice groups may have their own brochures. Materials from various practice groups may be presented to prospective clients based on those clients' anticipated needs.

Today, firms often publish the materials in their firm brochure on their Web sites.

E.   Newsletters

newsletter:
A bulletin sent out periodically that provides updates about legal developments of interest to a firm's clientele and prospective clients.

One way to keep a law firm's name in front of current and prospective clients as well as to demonstrate a firm's expertise in a subject area is to develop and distribute a **newsletter** on a specific subject. Topics covered should, of course, be timely, and articles should be engagingly written. The newsletter's layout should be attractive.

Partners or associates might write articles for the newsletters. In-house editors or marketing people may finesse the content and heighten its interest for prospective readers. Ideally, newsletters should be published on an established, regular basis. Some might be published monthly, some quarterly, and even weekly. At the outset, lawyers within a firm might commit to meeting the deadlines for producing a newsletter, but as real-world commitments interfere, lawyers may sometimes have difficulty getting content ready on a regular schedule. Some law firms turn to outside marketing firms and even to ghost writers to develop content for their newsletters.

Initially sent by mail or by fax, newsletters nowadays are typically distributed via the Internet.

F.   Web Sites and Blogs

blog:
A shortened form of the term Web log—a frequently updated online diary or journal-type writing that chronicles recent developments; sometimes called a "blawg" in the legal field, a blend of the terms law and blog.

Lawyer advertising continues to evolve, having moved from traditional print sources to the Internet. One survey found that 24 percent of law firms spend more than 75 percent of their marketing budgets on Internet-related efforts.[20] Today, many law firms have Web sites, and more and more lawyers are writing **blogs** to keep clients and prospective clients informed about general developments in the law. One survey found that 27 percent of U.S. law firms had blogs in 2012, compared to 14 percent in 2010.[21] Some lawyers also offer podcasts—video recordings—that people can listen to.

Web sites have become an easily accessible form of advertising and are used by many prospective clients as they research potential lawyers. Some estimates are that upward of 75 percent of prospective clients research prospective lawyers via their Web sites.[22] The cost of a Web site can vary from very little to tens of thousands of dollars. Although it is possible to develop Web sites in house, a more professional look may be obtained by hiring a Web site design firm to develop or overhaul a law firm's Web site.

No matter who is designing the site, a firm's **domain name** must be registered and a Web site hosting service must be selected. The **Web site hosting service** may serve as a registrar that registers the domain name with the Internet Corporation for Assigned names and Numbers (ICANN). ICANN is a nonprofit organization that oversees identifiers, or names, used on the Internet.

domain name:
A unique name that identifies a Web site that concludes with a domain suffix, such as .com or .net. The domain name may begin with www followed by a period.

Web site hosting service:
An entity that stores Web pages and makes them accessible on the Internet.

If a Web site design firm is being used, a law firm should have a contract in place that addresses ownership of software, schedules, specifications regarding design, maintenance, and security. Custom-built Web sites can look more professional than those developed in-house by a firm. Ideally, a custom-built site can be easily updated by lawyers or firm employees.

Content of a law firm's Web site should include contact information as well as information about a firm's attorneys, its practice areas, its accomplishments, and updates about its activities. Images, video, and animations may also be included. News releases might be available, as might policies on diversity and sustainability. Firm blogs might also be accessed via its Web site along with other publications, such as newsletters, that the firm has issued. Buttons to social networking sites like LinkedIn, Twitter, and Facebook might also be included in a firm's Web site. A firm history can provide background about the firm and its longevity.

Most rules on advertising were developed prior to the increase in Internet usage. Bar associations have made efforts to adapt their rules and policies to the relatively new forms of advertising made possible by the Internet.[23] Even on the Web, ethical rules must still be complied with. A firm's Web site and blogs may need to include notice that it is an advertisement as well as a disclaimer that no attorney-client relationship is being established and no legal advice is being presented. A warning not to submit confidential information via the Web site should also be considered.

Hunter v. Virginia State Bar ex rel. Third District Committee
285 Va. 485 (2013)

OPINION BY JUSTICE CLEO E. POWELL.

In this appeal of right by an attorney from a Virginia State Bar ("VSB") disciplinary proceeding before a three judge panel appointed pursuant to Code §54.1–3935, we consider whether an attorney's blog posts are commercial speech, whether an attorney may discuss public information related to a client without the client's consent, and whether the panel ordered the attorney to post a disclaimer that is insufficient under Rule 7.2(a)(3) of the Virginia Rules of Professional Conduct.

I. FACTS AND PROCEEDINGS

Horace Frazier Hunter, an attorney with the law firm of Hunter & Lipton, PC, authors a trademarked blog titled "This Week in Richmond Criminal Defense," which is accessible from his law firm's website, www.hunterlipton.com. This blog, which is not interactive, contains posts discussing a myriad of legal issues and cases, although the overwhelming majority are posts about cases in which Hunter obtained favorable results for his clients. Nowhere in these posts or on his website did Hunter include disclaimers.

As a result of Hunter's blog posts on his website, the VSB launched an investigation. . . .

On March 24, 2011, the VSB charged Hunter with violating Rules 7.1, 7.2, 7.5, and 1.6 by his posts on this blog. Specifically, the VSB argued that he violated rules 7.1 and 7.2 because his blog posts discussing his criminal cases were inherently misleading as they lacked disclaimers. The VSB also asserted that Hunter violated Rule 1.6 by revealing information that could embarrass or likely be detrimental to his former clients by discussing their cases on his blog without their consent.

In a hearing on October 18, 2011, the VSB presented evidence of Hunter's alleged violations. . . .

At the hearing, Hunter testified that he has many reasons for writing his blog—including marketing, creation of a community presence for his firm, combatting any public perception that defendants charged with crimes are guilty until proven innocent, and showing commitment to criminal law. Hunter stated that he had offered to post a disclaimer on his blog, but the offered disclaimer was not satisfactory to the VSB. Hunter admitted that he only blogged about his cases that he won. He also told the VSB that he believed that using the client's name is important to give an accurate description of what happened. Hunter told the VSB that he did not obtain consent from his clients to discuss their cases on his blog because all the information that he posted was public information.

Following the hearing, the VSB held that Hunter violated Rule 1.6 by "disseminating client confidences" obtained in the course of representation without consent to post. . . . The VSB further held that Hunter violated Rule 7.1. The VSB's conclusion that Hunter's website contained legal advertising was based on its factual finding that "[t]he postings of [Hunter's] case wins on his webpage advertise[d] cumulative case results." Moreover, the VSB found that at least one purpose of the website was commercial. The VSB further held that he violated Rule 7.2 by "disseminating case results in advertising without the required disclaimer" because the one that he proposed to the VSB was insufficient. The VSB imposed a public admonition with terms including a requirement that he remove case specific content for which he has not received consent and post a disclaimer that complies with Rule 7.2(a)(3) on all case-related posts.

Hunter appealed to a three judge panel of the circuit court and the court heard argument. . . . The court . . . ruled that the VSB's interpretation of Rule 1.6 violated the First Amendment and dismissed that charge. The court held VSB's interpretation of Rules 7.1 and 7.2 do not violate the First Amendment and that the record contained substantial evidence to support the VSB's determination that Hunter had violated those rules. The court imposed a public admonition and required Hunter to post the following disclaimer: "Case results depend upon a variety of factors unique to each case. Case results do not guarantee or predict a similar result in any future case." This appeal followed.

II. ANALYSIS

A. Whether "[t]he Ruling of the Circuit Court finding a violation of Rules 7.1(a)(4) and 7.2(a)(3) conflicts with the First Amendment to the Constitution of the United States."

Rule 7.1(a)(4), which is the specific portion of the Rule that the VSB argued that Hunter violated, states:

(a) A lawyer shall not, on behalf of the lawyer or any other lawyer affiliated with the lawyer or the firm, use or participate in the use of any form of public communication if such communication contains a false, fraudulent, misleading, or deceptive statement or claim. For example, a communication violates this Rule if it:

. . . .

(4) is likely to create an unjustified expectation about results the lawyer can achieve, or states or implies that the lawyer can achieve results by means that violate the Rules of Professional Conduct or other law.

The VSB also argues that Hunter violated the following subsection of Rule 7.2(a)(3):

(a) Subject to the requirements of Rules 7.1 and 7.3, a lawyer may advertise services through written, recorded, or electronic communications, including public media. In the determination of whether an advertisement violates this Rule, the advertisement shall be considered in its entirety, including any qualifying statements or disclaimers contained therein. Notwithstanding the requirements of Rule 7.1, an advertisement violates this Rule if it:

. . .

(3) advertises specific or cumulative case results, without a disclaimer that (i) puts the case results in a context that is not misleading; (ii) states that case results depend upon a variety of factors unique to each case; and (iii) further states that case results do not guarantee or predict a similar result in any future case undertaken by the lawyer. The disclaimer shall precede the communication of the case results. When the communication is in writing, the disclaimer shall be in bold type face and uppercase letters in a font size that is at least as large as the largest text used to advertise the specific or cumulative case results and in the same color and against the same colored background as the text used to advertise the specific or cumulative case results.

In response to these allegations, Hunter contends that speech concerning the judicial system is "quintessentially 'political speech'" which is within the marketplace of ideas. . . .

The VSB responds that Hunter's blog posts are inherently misleading commercial speech.

. . .

While it is settled that attorney advertising is commercial speech, *Bates v. State Bar of Arizona*, 433 U.S. 350, 363–64, 97 S.Ct. 2691, 53 L.Ed.2d 810 (1977), *Bates* and its progeny were decided in the era of traditional media. In recent years, however, advertising has taken to new forms such as websites, blogs, and other social media forums, like Facebook and Twitter. . . .

Thus, we must examine Hunter's speech to determine whether it is commercial speech, specifically, lawyer advertising. . . . Simply because the speech is an advertisement, references a specific product, or is economically motivated does not necessarily mean that it is commercial speech. *Bolger v. Youngs Drug Products Corp.*, 463 U.S. 60, 67, 103 S.Ct. 2875, 77 L.Ed.2d 469 (1983). "The combination of *all* these characteristics, however, provides strong support for the . . . conclusion that [some blog posts] are properly characterized as commercial speech" even though they also discuss issues important to the public. *Id.* at 67–68, 103 S.Ct. 2875 (emphasis in original).

Certainly, not all advertising is necessarily commercial, e.g., public service announcements. *See id. at 66, 103 S.Ct. 2875* . . . . However, all commercial speech is necessarily advertising. . . .

Here, Hunter's blog posts, while containing some political commentary, are commercial speech. Hunter has admitted that his motivation for the blog is at least in part economic. The posts are an advertisement in that they predominately describe cases where he has received a favorable result for his client. He unquestionably references a specific product, i.e., his lawyering skills as twenty-two of his twenty-five case related posts describe cases that he has successfully handled. Indeed, in nineteen of these posts, he specifically named his law firm in addition to naming himself as counsel.

Moreover, the blog is on his law firm's commercial website rather than an independent site dedicated to the blog. *See* Howard J. Bashman, How Appealing Blog (Feb. 11, 2013, 9:40 AM), http://howappealing.law.com (an independent blog by a Pennsylvania appellate attorney that is accessible through Law.com at http://legalblogwatch.typepad.com/). The website uses the same frame for the pages openly soliciting clients as it does for the blog, including the firm name, a photograph of Hunter and his law partner, and a "contact us" form. The homepage of the website on which Hunter posted his blog states only:

> **Do you need Richmond attorneys?**
>   Hunter & Lipton, CP [sic] is a law practice in Richmond, Virginia specializing in litigation matters from administrative agency hearings to serious criminal cases. As experienced Richmond attorneys, we bring a genuine desire to help those who find themselves in difficult situations. Our partnership was founded on the idea that everyone, no matter what the circumstance, deserves a zealous advocate to fight on his or her behalf.
>   People make mistakes, and may even find themselves in situations not of their own making. And for these people, the system can be extraordinarily unforgiving and unjust—but you do not have to face this system alone.
>   **If you find yourself in a difficult legal situation, the Richmond attorneys of Hunter & Lipton, LLP would consider it a privilege to represent you. Please contact our office with any questions or to schedule a consultation.**

This non-interactive blog does not allow for discourse about the cases, as noncommercial commentary often would by allowing readers to post comments. . . .

Instead, in furtherance of his commercial pursuit, Hunter invites the reader to "contact us" the same way one seeking legal representation would contact the firm through the website.

Thus, the inclusion of five generalized, legal posts and three discussions about cases that he did not handle on his non-interactive blog, no more transform Hunter's otherwise self-promotional blog posts into political speech, "than opening sales presentations with a prayer or a Pledge of Allegiance would convert them into religious or political speech." *Fox,* 492 U.S. at 474–75, 109 S.Ct. 3028. . . . Advertisers should not be permitted to immunize false or misleading product information from government regulation simply by including references to public issues." *Bolger,* 463 U.S. at 68, 103 S.Ct. 2875. When considered as a whole, the economically motivated blog overtly proposes a commercial transaction that is an advertisement of a specific product.

Having determined that Hunter's blog posts discussing his cases are commercial speech,

> we must determine whether the expression is protected by the First Amendment. For commercial speech to come within that provision, it at least must concern lawful activity and not be misleading. Next, we ask whether the asserted governmental interest is substantial. If both inquiries yield positive answers, we must determine whether the regulation directly advances the governmental interest asserted, and whether it is not more extensive than is necessary to serve that interest.

Central Hudson Gas & Elec. Corp. v. Public Serv. Comm'n, 447 U.S. 557, 566, 100 S.Ct. 2343, 65 L.Ed.2d 341 (1980); *Adams Outdoor Advertising v. City of Newport News,* 236 Va. 370, 383, 373 S.E.2d 917, 923 (1988).

. . . Of the thirty posts that were on his blog at the time of the VSB hearing, twenty-two posts named himself as counsel and discussed cases that he handled. With one exception, in all of these posts, he described the successful results that he obtained for his clients. While the States may place an absolute prohibition on inherently misleading advertising, "the States may not place an absolute prohibition on certain types of potentially misleading information, . . . if the information also may be presented in a way that is not deceptive." *In re R.M.J.,* 455 U.S. 191, 203, 102 S.Ct. 929, 71 L.Ed.2d 64 (1982). Here, the VSB's own remedy of requiring Hunter to post disclaimers on his blog posts demonstrates that the information could be presented in a way that is not misleading or deceptive.

. . . [T]he VSB has a substantial governmental interest in protecting the public from an attorney's self-promoting representations that could lead the public to mistakenly believe that they are guaranteed to obtain the same positive results if they were to hire Hunter.

Because the VSB's governmental interest is substantial, we must now determine "whether the regulation directly advances the governmental interest asserted." *Central Hudson,* 447 U.S. at 566, 100 S.Ct. 2343. The VSB's regulations permit blog posts that discuss specific or cumulative case results but require a disclaimer to explain to the public that no results are guaranteed. Rules 7.1 and 7.2. This requirement directly advances the VSB's governmental interest.

Finally, we must determine whether the VSB's regulations are no more restrictive than necessary. . . . The disclaimers mandated by the VSB shall precede the communication of the case results. When the communication is in writing, the disclaimer shall be in bold type face and uppercase letters in a font size that is at least as large as the largest text used to advertise the specific or cumulative case results and in the same color and against the same colored background as the text used to advertise the specific or cumulative case results.

Rule 7.2(a)(3). This requirement ensures that the disclaimer is noticeable and would be connected to each post so that any member of the public who may use the website addresses to directly access Hunter's posts would be in a position to see the disclaimer. Therefore, we hold that the disclaimers required by the VSB are "not more extensive than is necessary to serve that interest." *Central Hudson*, 447 U.S. at 566, 100 S.Ct. 2343.

Hunter's blog posts discuss lawful activity and are not inherently misleading, but the VSB has asserted a substantial governmental interest to protect the public from potentially misleading lawyer advertising. *See Central Hudson, 447 U.S. at 566, 100 S.Ct. 2343.* These regulations directly advance this interest and are not more restrictive than necessary, unlike outright bans on advertising. *Id*. We thus conclude that the VSB's Rules 7.1 and 7.2 do not violate the First Amendment. As applied to Hunter's blog posts, they are constitutional and the panel did not err.

B. Whether the circuit court erred in holding that the VSB's application of Rule 1.6 to Hunter's blog violated his First Amendment rights.

Rule 1.6(a) states, that with limited exceptions,

[a] lawyer shall not reveal information protected by the attorney-client privilege under applicable law or other information gained in the professional relationship that the client has requested be held inviolate or the disclosure of which would be embarrassing or would be likely to be detrimental to the client unless the client consents after consultation, except for disclosures that are impliedly authorized in order to carry out the representation. . . .

The VSB argues that the circuit court erred in holding that its interpretation of Rule 1.6 violates the First Amendment and that Hunter violated that rule by disclosing potentially embarrassing information about his clients on his blog "in order to advance his personal economic interests." VSB argues that lawyers, as officers of the Court, are prohibited from engaging in speech that might otherwise be constitutionally protected. . . . In response to these allegations, Hunter argues that the VSB's interpretation of Rule 1.6 is unconstitutional because the matters discussed in his blogs had previously been revealed in public judicial proceedings and, therefore, as concluded matters, were protected by the First Amendment. Thus, we are called upon to answer whether the state may prohibit an attorney from discussing information about a client or former client that is not protected by attorney-client privilege without express consent from that client. We agree with Hunter that it may not.

The cases cited by VSB in support of its position differ from this case in a substantial way; the cases relied upon by VSB involve pending proceedings. It is settled that attorney speech about public information from cases is protected by the First Amendment, but it may be regulated if it poses a substantial likelihood of materially prejudicing a *pending* case. . . .

. . . All of Hunter's blog posts involved cases that had been concluded. Moreover, the VSB concedes that all of the information that was contained within Hunter's blog was public information and would have been protected speech had the news media or others disseminated it . . .

The VSB argues that it can prohibit an attorney from repeating truthful information made in a public judicial proceeding even though others can disseminate this information because an attorney repeating it could inhibit clients from freely communicating with their attorneys or because it would undermine public confidence in the legal profession. Such concerns, however, are unsupported by the evidence. To the extent that the information is aired in a public forum, privacy considerations must yield to First Amendment protections. In that respect, a lawyer is no more prohibited than any other citizen from reporting what transpired in the courtroom. Thus, the circuit court did not err in concluding that the VSB's interpretation of Rule 1.6 violated the First Amendment.

Whether the circuit court erred in requiring Hunter to post a disclaimer on his website that does not comply with the requirements of Rule 7.2(3) and therefore does not eliminate the misleading nature of his blog posts.

The VSB argues that the single disclaimer that the circuit court ordered Hunter to post on his blog was insufficient to comport with Rule 7.2(a)(3) because it did not eliminate the misleading nature of the posts.

As we have already concluded, Hunter's blogs are commercial speech and, thus, constitute lawyer advertising. When advertising cumulative or specific case results, Rule 7.2 requires that a disclaimer

> shall be in bold type face and uppercase letters in a font size that is at least as large as the largest text used to advertise the specific or cumulative case results and in the same color and against the same colored background as the text used to advertise the specific or cumulative case results.

Rule 7.2(a)(3).

Here, the VSB required Hunter to post a disclaimer that complies with Rule 7.2(a)(3) on *all* case-related posts. This means that Hunter's disclaimers "shall be in bold type face and uppercase letters in a font size that is at least as large as the largest text used to advertise the specific or cumulative case results and in the same color and against the same colored background as the text used to advertise the specific or cumulative case results." Rule 7.2(a)(3). The circuit court, however, imposed the following disclaimer to be posted once: "Case results depend upon a variety of factors unique to each case. Case results do not guarantee or predict a similar result in any future case."

While the substantive meaning of the imposed disclaimer may conform to the requirements stated in Rule 7.2(a)(3)(i) through (iii), it nevertheless is less than what the rule requires. In contrast to the committee's determination, there is no provision in the circuit court's order requiring that the disclaimer be formatted and presented in the manner required by Rule 7.2(a)(3), and the text of the disclaimer prescribed by the circuit court is not itself formatted and presented in that manner. Even so, Hunter does not argue that the disclaimer required by the circuit court is an appropriate, less restrictive means of regulating his speech and, therefore, we decline to so hold. Based on the arguments presented to it, the circuit court erred by imposing a disclaimer that conflicted with the rule. . . .

III. CONCLUSION

For the foregoing reasons, we hold that Hunter's blog posts are potentially misleading commercial speech that the VSB may regulate. We further hold that circuit court did not err in determining that the VSB's interpretation of Rule 1.6 violated the First Amendment. Finally, we hold that because the circuit court erred in imposing one disclaimer did not fully comply with Rule 7.2(a)(3), we reverse and remand for imposition of disclaimers that fully comply with that Rule.

Affirmed in part, reversed in part, and remanded.

[Dissent omitted]

A firm's Web site and any communications transmitted through it should be sufficiently secure so they are not vulnerable to hackers.

To increase its visibility, a firm's Web sites should be designed for search engine optimization (SEO) so the firm will appear higher in the list of results from online searches.

Some lawyers have even begun using **virtual worlds**, such as Second Life, to make their services known:

> A few innovative lawyers are recognizing a potential business opportunity in Second Life and a new way to recruit real-world clients. By chatting with fellow participants, advertising in virtual world classifieds, and participating in virtual world activities, lawyers are engaging potential clients they might not otherwise meet in the real world or reach through traditional advertising.[23]

The American Bar Association has even held a conference on virtual worlds in Second Life.[24]

Undoubtedly, other venues for online advertising will be developed in the future, and law firm managers must keep informed about potential advertising vehicles and the rules that apply to them.

G.   Social Media Strategy

In much the same way that lawyers can interact with prospective clients at a bar association meeting or at a seminar, they can do so online—where the audience is much larger and the interactions can be much quicker. **Social networking** sites like LinkedIn, Facebook, Twitter, YouTube, and others are now being used by

virtual world:
A computer-based simulated environment allowing a group of people to gather at an online location and interact primarily via the Internet rather than face-to-face.

social networking site:
An online community that permits its members to post information about themselves.

lawyers to promote themselves and their businesses—in a sometimes subtle way. Some lawyers express concern that they are mixing personal information with business information or that these sites seem too informal—but ignoring them as a venue for building their own books of business is a mistake. Social networking sites are a viable venue for legal business today:

> While the legal profession's embrace of social media was initially little more than the digital equivalent of a perfunctory handshake, it is certainly warming to the idea. According to one recent study by ALM Legal Intelligence, nearly 85% of U.S. law firms are employing social media for marketing purposes. Another study, the 2012 ABA Legal Technology survey, found 88% of the responding firms reported having a LinkedIn presence, while 58% use Facebook, and another 13% are on Twitter. Twenty-two percent of the firms surveyed indicated that they maintained a blog (an increase of 15% from the previous year).[25]

On social networking sites, lawyers can engage in conversations, post materials about themselves and about their work, such as links to published articles or court decisions, and begin to build more personal relationships with a vast group of prospective clients. Social networking sites allow lawyers and law firms to establish and maintain their brand—and to alert a very broad audience about its activities—at very little cost. These networking activities must be maintained, of course, and require fairly frequent participation. Merely posting information about oneself without adding more is unlikely to generate a lot of interest. Firms and lawyers must decide what sort of information will be posted, how often, and by whom. Should they tweet every hour? Every day? Several times a week? Lawyers and firms must also determine how often to engage with others on various social media platforms. Of course, they can also research what their competitors are doing on social media.

A firm should develop a social media strategy to plan and pursue social media activities. In such a strategy, the types of information to be conveyed, the frequency of posting, and engagement can all be planned, as can certain measurements. A firm might seek to expand the number of followers or "Likes" that it has, along with the number of "conversations" it has with others. It can also consider the quality of those conversations, of followers, and of "Likes" and tweak its social media strategy to pursue more of the intended market.

Lawyers and others who use social media must take care not to post unprofessional pictures or images that would be a deterrent to new business or to their progress on the career ladder. They must also take care not to have inappropriate contacts with judges, jurors, and others involved in cases they are actively litigating.

Social networking activities, like other forms of communication, are subject to the rules of professional conduct. Lawyers must take care not to violate rules on advertising, solicitations, endorsements, and so on.[26]

Undoubtedly, other social networking sites and other means of online advertising will develop in the future. Law office managers must remain current on new developments and help their firms maximize the opportunities as these new advertising venues become available.

H.   Annual Reports

Some law firms have begun preparing annual reports that they then post on their Web sites. As an internal document, these can be vital indicators of how the firm is doing and serve to inform lawyers at especially large firms about areas of the firm with which they might not be familiar. These documents can also inform lawyers at large firms about the future direction of the firm. When these reports are released publicly (typically in downloadable form on a firm's Web site), a firm is letting both prospective hires as well as current and prospective clients know about its activities and its solvency.

In comparison to firm brochures, annual reports might contain much more specific information about a firm's activities on behalf of clients. Significant wins and other successes might be chronicled. Permission should be obtained from clients to highlight information about work done for them. Some firms just produce annual reports in major practice areas. These, too, can provide some insight on a firm's priorities and on the depth of its expertise.

Because reporting efforts are voluntary and not required by any regulator (at least in the United States), their openness and depth leave much to be desired. Nevertheless, these are good ways for outsiders to gain some insight about a firm, and thus can be a viable marketing mechanism for the firm itself.

I.   Outreach

Keeping a lawyer's or a firm's name in front of a client is important so that when that client needs help with a legal matter, the client contacts the firm. Lawyers have tried many ways to maintain their visibility. The mechanisms for doing so have become increasingly sophisticated with the growth of the Internet. Lawyers and others within a law firm must spend time on client development to keep a continuing stream of business coming into the firm. They may use a number of means to both find prospective clients and foster relationships with them.

1.   Seminars

As the law has become highly specialized, seminars, often organized by third parties, such as organizations involved in the continuing education business, on special topics are frequently conducted by practitioners in the field. Attended by in-house counsel and other members of the affected industry, these seminars, often referred to as "dog-and-pony shows" in industry parlance, are effective platforms for establishing an attorney as an expert in a given subject. Opportunities to network at social functions at these seminars, such as lunches or dinners, provide an additional venue for a lawyer to gain some visibility for herself and for her firm. These seminars are sometimes covered by trade industry reporters, who might then write articles about the seminar's proceedings—again providing an opportunity for the savvy lawyer to make a connection with a journalist, to create a good working relationship with that journalist, to provide, possibly, a pithy quote to accompany the journalist's story, and to establish a future connection, so that when that journalist is writing another piece on the subject, he can call the lawyer for a "sound bite" or commentary.

Lawyers might also visit a corporate client on-site to hold a brown-bag lunch discussion of a particular legal topic of interest to the client. Webinars, or online seminars featuring audio, video, and slides, might also be held or sponsored to help solidify a firm's reputation.

2. Professional Associations

Both legal and other associations provide opportunities for lawyers to meet potential clients, to interact with colleagues and judges, and to promote their own expertise. In addition to the American Bar Association, numerous state and local bar associations (city bar associations or specialized ones such as women's bar associations, Italian-American bar associations, African-American bar associations, and so on) host activities, such as golf outings, luncheons, or charitable events. Getting to know people on a personal as well as a professional basis can bolster a lawyer's brand in a given community.

3. Publications

To establish and maintain credibility, and to keep their names in front of current and prospective clients, lawyers might write columns for **law journals**; long, well-researched pieces for **law reviews**; and articles for **trade publications** likely to be read by current or prospective clients. Lawyers might also serve on editorial boards of publications and participate as peer reviewers of the work of others. A firm's marketing team might help arrange for pieces to be placed. More junior lawyers might conduct some of the research on a piece, draft portions of it, and even be listed as co-authors. Paralegals may check citations and conduct research as well. It's possible that a law firm's marketing person might vet the piece to help ensure that a firm's message is getting across well to prospective readers. The marketing person might also oversee the formal submittal of an article for consideration by a publication.

Some law reviews have been criticized because of the long lag time between submission of an article for publication and actual publication. The review and editing process can be much longer than it might be for law journals or for trade publications. By the time a scholarly piece is ready to be published in a law review, it can sometimes be out of date. Nevertheless, law reviews can be desirable places to publish because they might advance a lawyer's reputation for scholarly thought on a particular subject.

In addition to writing for periodicals, lawyers might also write books or treatises on legal subjects for publishers. These might be textbooks, books written for practitioners, or broader books written for a lay audience. Books might be published by legal publishers, or a lawyer or a firm might choose to self-publish, possibly in ebook format. Although historically self-published books were not viewed as favorably as those published by established publishers, ebooks are gaining

law review:
A periodical edited by law students containing scholarly articles written by practitioners, law professors, and judges; essays, case notes, book reviews; and other topical information.

law journal:
A periodical (typically a newspaper or magazine) focused more on topics pertinent to actual law practice, often published by bar associations.

trade publication:
A periodical geared to a specific business or industry.

greater credibility. If a lawyer or firm plans to publish an ebook, a member of the marketing team might be involved in overseeing the process toward publication.

4. *Social and Charitable Events*

Not every sponsored event has to have a work theme. A firm might become part of a baseball league and have its team compete against teams whose members are current or prospective clients—or even other law firms. Sporting events, or spa days for current clients, or other social activities can help lawyers get to know people on an informal, relaxed basis. Similarly, a firm might sponsor charitable events. Some of those activities could be geared toward helping its lawyers or staff improve their skills (such as organizing or speaking publicly), or they could be focused on general areas in which the firm has expertise.

Checklist

- Firms must market their services to generate business.
- A marketing plan and a mission statement should be developed and followed as the firm pursues additional business.
- Competitive intelligence is an important element of any marketing plan.
- Actions a firm might take to improve its position in the legal market are easier to plan if a firm analyzes is strengths, weaknesses, opportunities, and threats.
- Results of marketing efforts should be measured.
- Historically, advertising by lawyers was considered unseemly and barred by ethics rules until a 1977 Supreme Court decision holding that advertising by lawyers is a form of commercial speech that is protected by the First Amendment.
- Rules of professional conduct govern lawyer advertising, as do statutes aimed at protecting consumers from false advertising.
- There has been some controversy about advertisements that compare lawyers to one another or that create expectations about results.
- New means of lawyer advertising via the Internet and social networking sites have developed in recent years.
- A firm might increase its visibility and enhance its reputation by advertising, issuing firm brochures, publishing newsletters, publishing and maintaining Web sites and blogs, and pursuing social media strategy. An annual report can appeal both to prospective clients and to prospective hires. By conducting outreach via seminars, professional associations, publishing, and sponsoring social and charitable events, a firm can also become better known in a community.

Vocabulary

blog (p. 208)
brand (p. 200)
brochure (p. 208)
competitive intelligence (p. 200)
domain name (p. 209)
law journal (p. 219)
law review (p. 219)
marketing (p. 199)

marketing plan (p. 199)
mission statement (p. 200)
newsletter (p. 208)
social networking site (p. 216)
tombstone ad (p. 204)
trade publication (p. 219)
virtual world (p. 216)
Web site hosting service (p. 209)

Career Preparation Tips

You need not wait until you are searching for a job in the legal field to begin networking. You might join Facebook and begin "liking" legal organizations, you might join LinkedIn and follow certain businesses, and you might joint Twitter and begin following and interacting with various people involved in the legal field. You can start building up your own following and interacting, as appropriate, with people active in the legal arena. Develop your own marketing plan and social media strategy.

At the same time, if you are already involved with social networking sites for personal reasons, you might begin researching privacy options and determine ways to limit dissemination about your personal life. For instance, you might only disclose information to contacts who appear on certain lists. You might also remove images or negative or inappropriate comments so that more professional contacts do not see them.

If You Want to Learn More

The American Bar Association's Model Rules of Professional Conduct are accessible online. http://www.americanbar.org/groups/professional_ responsibility/publications/model_rules_of_professional_conduct.html

ABA's Web site has links to state ethics rules on lawyer advertising, solicitation, marketing, and other matters. http://www.americanbar.org/ groups/professional_responsibility/resources/links_of_interest.html

Legal Marketing Association. http://www.legalmarketing.org

Second Life is an online virtual community. http://www.secondlife.com

Second Life Bar Association http://slbarassn.ning.com

ABA Section of Science & Technology Law: Virtual Worlds and Multi-user Online Games Committee. http://apps.americanbar.org/dch/committee .cfm?com=ST252000

Information about technology resources for lawyers. http://www.llrx.com

Internet Corporation for Assigned Names and Numbers. http://www .icann.org

National Conference of Law Reviews. http://www.nclrlaw.com/index.php

Reading Comprehension

1. What is the difference between a law firm's marketing plan and its mission statement?
2. Suppose you need to hire a real estate lawyer to conduct a house closing. You've located two prospective lawyers whose qualifications seem to be comparable, but one is listed in "Best Lawyers" and the other is not. Would this fact alone drive your decision on which lawyer to hire? What are some possible reasons to hire the lawyer who is not listed in Best Lawyers?
3. What is the difference between a firm's brochure and its newsletter?
4. Compare the information about users accessible on LinkedIn and on Facebook. Which site do you think is a better marketing tool?
5. Suppose your firm specializes in energy law. On what type of Web sites would you place a firm advertisement? Why?
6. What ethical problems could arise when a law firm uses social networking sites?
7. Why might a lawyer prefer to publish an article in a trade publication rather than in a law review?

Discussion Starters

1. Suppose you are the law office manager for a firm of 50 attorneys. You have been asked to hire a Web site developer to update your firm's site. The developer will also be drafting content for the site. What precautions about images and content will you provide to the developer?

2. A major corporation is laying off 10 percent of its workforce in your city. Your supervising attorney wants a paralegal to stand on the sidewalk outside the corporation's headquarters and hand out fliers proclaiming "Recession prices! Divorce, $500. Employer/employee severance packages and related claims, $1,000" along with the law firm's name, address, phone number, and Web site address. Is this permissible in your area?

3. Locate several legal blogs on bankruptcy law, and compare and contrast them. When was the last entry on the blog? Does the blog allow comments? How professional in appearance is the blog site? Does the author clearly identify himself? Which of the authors would you be most interested in contacting if you had a bankruptcy law problem that needed to be resolved?

4. Consider Model Rules 7.1, 7.2, and 7.3. Do you think they are too restrictive? Are they too permissive? Do you think the rules assume that consumers of legal services are uneducated and uninformed? Do consumers need to be protected from unscrupulous lawyers?

5. If you were drafting an advertisement for your law firm, which terms in Model Rules 7.1, 7.2, and 7.3 would you be concerned about? Which terms would you like to see be defined further?

6. Has your state developed a rule on lawyers' advertising that they have been designated "Super Lawyer" or "Best Lawyer"? Do you agree with the rule?

7. Assess the strengths, weaknesses, opportunities, and threats identified for an environmental law firm in Figure 8-1. Given the status of the firm, what would be your marketing strategy? What might be overall firm goals the firm should work toward? What objectives should be identified and acted upon?

Case Studies

1. Suppose you are a paralegal hired to work for a sole practitioner who handles personal injury cases. The lawyer asks you to go to your local hospital emergency room and hand out his business cards to people in the waiting area. He suggests that you introduce yourself and say, "If you think you need legal help with your problem, you might contact this

fellow," and then hand the person the business card. Is such a practice permissible under ABA's Model Rules of Professional Conduct? Is the practice permissible under the ethical requirements in your home state?

2. You have been asked by your supervising partner to develop a firm newsletter on patent law. The partner has asked you to research marketing services that the firm might be able to hire for assistance with this task. Research several such services, and compare and contrast their abilities. What factors should you consider before hiring such a service? What additional information would you want to obtain from the service? What questions would you ask of their references?

3. Locate recent announcements of disbarments in your state. Did any of the offending conduct relate to advertising or inappropriate solicitation of prospective clients? What did the disbarred attorney do? Do you think the attorney should have lost her ability to practice law for engaging in the conduct she was accused of?

4. You are a law office manager at a full-service firm with 500 attorneys in ten major cities. The firm's managing partner asks you to set up a fan page about the firm on Facebook. What information will you include? What sorts of updates will you post regularly? Is a fan page a permissible form of advertising in all of the jurisdictions in which the firm practices?

5. Look up the annual reports of three major law firms and compare and contrast them. Which firm would you prefer to work for, and why? What should prospective clients be concerned about? Are all offices of the firm equally stable, or can you tell? What additional information would you like to find out about the firm before going to work there? What additional information would you need if you were a prospective client and were thinking about hiring the firm?

6. Suppose that you work for a major international law firm in its environmental practice group where your team focuses on sustainability. What entities would you "like" on Facebook? What organizations would you follow on Twitter and on LinkedIin? Why?

Endnotes

1. Charles A. Maddock, *Law Firm Branding: Is It Working?* 1 (Altman Weil Report to Legal Management, Feb. 2000), *available at* http://www.altmanweil.com/dir_docs/resource/b55a03e9-08da-4018-8a00-33318727191a_document.pdf.

2. *See, e.g.,* Cepac, Marketing Budgets for Law Firms, http://www.cepac.com/Marketing-Budgets.html (last visited Aug. 26, 2013).

3. Larry Bodine, *The Ten Most Effective Law Firm Marketing Techniques,* LarryBodine.com, http://www.larrybodine.com/articles.asp?Action=GetOneArticle&ArticleID=70 (last visited Aug. 24, 2013).

4. Micah U. Buchdahl, *Proper Hiring and Staffing of Your Law Firm's Marketing Team,* 39(4) Law Practice n.p. (July/Aug. 2013), *available at* http://www.americanbar.org/publications/law_practice_magazine/2013/july-august/marketing.html.

5. *See, e.g.,* L. Thomas Lunsford II, *7305 Nights at the Bates Motel,* N.C. St. B.J., *available at* http://www.ncbar.com/ethics/eth_articles_bates.asp (last visited Sept. 2, 2013).

6. *Bates v. State Bar of Arizona,* 433 U.S. 350, 368 (1977).

7. *Id.* at 371.

8. Van O'Steen, *Bates v. State Bar of Arizona: The Personal Account of a Party and the Consumer Benefits of Lawyer Advertising,* 37 Ariz. St. L.J. 245, 250-51 (2005).

9. *Bates,* 433 U.S. 350, 383.

10. *Id.* at 384.

11. *See, e.g., Florida Bar v. Went For It, Inc.,* 515 U.S. 618 (1995); 7 C.J.S. Attorney & Client § 46 (2013).

12. *Crowe v. Tull,* 126 P.3d 196 (Colo. 2006) (holding that attorneys in Colorado can be sued under the state's consumer protection act for deceptive advertising), *distinguished by General Stell Domestic Sales, LLC v. Hogan & Hartson,* LLP, 230 P.3d 1375 (Colo. App. Mar. 18, 2010).

13. Leigh Jones, *Law Firm Ads No Longer Afraid to Name Names,* Nat'l L.J., May 4, 2005, *available at* http://www.law.com/jsp/article.jsp?id=1115111119049.

14. *See, e.g.,* Ross Fishman *"First, Let's Sell All The Lawyers": A Personal View of Legal Marketing's Long, Strange Journey,* Law Prac., Oct./Nov. 2005, at 30.

15. Leigh Jones, *After 30 Years, Law Firm Advertising Is Slow to Change,* Nat'l L.J., June 8, 2007, *available at* http://www.law.com/jsp/llf/PubArticleLLF.jsp?id=1181207138051.

16. *See, e.g.,* Dirk Johnson, *Look at This Ad, but Don't Get Any Ideas,* N.Y. Times, May 13, 2007, sec. 4, at 14.

17. *Opinion 39 of the Sup. Ct. Commn. on Attorney Adver.,* 185 N.J. L.J. 360, 15 N.J. Law. 1549 (July 24, 2006).

18. *See, e.g.,* N.Y. Rules of Prof'l Conduct R. 7.1 (22 N.Y. Comp. Codes R. & Regs. pt. 1200), *available at* http://www.nysba.org/Content/NavigationMenu/ForAttorneys/ProfessionalStandardsforAttorneys/Professional_Standar.htm (effective Apr. 1, 2009 as amended through Dec. 20, 2012).

19. Fishman, *supra* note 14.

20. Avvo & LexBlog, *2012 Legal Marketing Survey Report* at 3 (2012), *available at* http://kevin.lexblog.com.

21. Larry Bodine, *19% of Lawyers Got a New Client via Social Media,* Law Marketing Blog (Aug. 28, 2013), *available at* http://blog.larrybodine.com/2013/08/articles/social-media/19-of-lawyers-got-a-new-client-via-social-media/.

22. Janet Ellen Raasch, *Next Generation of Law Firm Websites Influenced by Social Media,* Law Marketing Blog (Nov. 2, 2012), *available at* http://blog.larrybodine.com/2012/11/articles/marketing/next-generation-of-law-firm-websites-influenced-by-social-media/.

23. Susan Corts Hill, *Current Development 2007–2008: Living in a Virtual World: Ethical Considerations for Attorneys Recruiting New Clients in Online Virtual Communities,* 21 Geo. J. Legal Ethics 753, 754 (2008).

24. Stephanie Kimbro, *ABA Hosts Virtual Reality Law Conference in Second Life,* Virtual Law Practice (June 24, 2008), http://virtuallawpractice.org/2008/06/aba-hosts-virtual-reality-law-conference-in-second-life/.

25. John G. Browning, *Facebook, Twitter, and LinkedIn—Oh My! The ABA 20/20 Commission and Evolving Ethical Issues in the Use of Social Media,* 40 N. Ky. L. Rev. 255, 256 (2013) (citations omitted).

26. For a discussion on the uses of social media for lawyers, see, e.g., Michael C. Smith, *Social Media Update,* 62 The Advoc. (Texas) 197 (Spring 2013); Michael J. Zussman & Glen R. McMurry, *44 Million Reasons Why You Should Use Social Media in Your Law Practice,* 60 (JUN) Fed Law. 16 (June 2013).

9

Money Management

Chapter Outcomes

By the end of this chapter, a student will be able to:

- Discuss money management needs of law firms
- Interpret different types of budgets
- Distinguish between billable and unbillable time
- Track time for recordkeeping and billing purposes
- Compare and contrast fee arrangements
- Explain fee collection
- Prepare a client bill
- Compare client trust accounts to law firm funds and escrow funds
- Propose safeguards to protect client and law firm funds

In good times and in bad, a law firm's finances must be well managed. Lawyers and other timekeepers in a firm must track their productivity, clients must be sent bills and then pay them, and someone within the firm needs to follow up if a client is remiss in making a payment. The firm's revenues must be managed, and operating expenses must be paid. After all, someone needs to make sure that the firm's own bills—for rent, utilities, supplies, and the like—are paid, and, of course, the firm needs to make payroll. To remain in business, a firm must remain profitable. Firms also must take precautions to prevent employees from embezzling money.

In 2012, DLA Piper generated $2.44 billion in revenue. In all, 20 large law firms grossed more than $1 billion each in revenue in 2012[1]—so there is a lot of money to be overseen.

A.   Financing a Law Practice

The primary way a law firm makes money is by providing legal services to clients who pay for them. While lawyers are happily representing clients, they're also incurring overhead costs associated with running their business. Rent on the law firm's office space must be paid, technology systems must be purchased, utility bills come due, insurance premiums must be paid, and the payroll for support staff and associates must be met.

Although every law firm's financial resources must be managed, lawyers aren't always adept at managing them. Historically, law school education focused on teaching students to "think like a lawyer"—not how to run their business once they become one. Firms might hire an in-house accountant or outsource some of this work to external accountants or to financial advisors. It's imperative that someone at the firm manage its resources well—otherwise, a firm risks disaster. Consider the example of Dewey & LeBoeuf, a major law firm that sought bankruptcy protection. Founded in 1909 in New York City, the firm that eventually became Dewey & LeBoeuf at one time had more than 1,400 lawyers,[2] in excess of 300 partners, and more than $600 million in annual gross revenue before collapsing in 2012 and filing for bankruptcy.[3] A law firm is a business that must be financially sound. When a law firm is experiencing a degree of difficulty that requires it to seek bankruptcy protection, employees, clients, and creditors may be shortchanged. Partners may be involved in litigation concerning the firm and may have to pay to settle these suits.[4]

B.   Budgets

budget:
An estimate of a firm's revenues and expenses.

A **budget**, which estimates the firm's revenues and expenses, is a helpful tool for attorneys in managing their business. For large firms, creating the upcoming year's budget can be a time-consuming process as they estimate the revenue each partner, associate, and billing staff (law clerks, paralegals, and so on) is likely to generate. These figures might be based on the results of prior years or on additional research and interviews of the income generators, or some mix of each. For instance, a changing economy or the loss—or addition—of a major client can have a significant impact on a firm's projected revenues.

The amount of income a firm is likely to generate is calculated by multiplying the number of hours each timekeeper will bill by the hourly rate charged. So, if Lawyer A charges $400 per hour and is expected to bill 2,000 hours, then the amount of income that lawyer will generate is $800,000.

Of course, in the real world, firms set billable-hour expectations, but lawyers and others don't always meet them. A lawyer might get sick, a paralegal might go on parental leave, a partner's primary client might leave the firm, or a billing partner might write off some hours of a junior associate because the inexperienced lawyer was inefficient in completing a project and billing the client for more would not really be fair. To anticipate such events in budget preparation, a firm might use a **time-to-billing percentage,** adjusting downward the amount that will actually be billed to clients. So, if the firm requirements for all

time-to-billing percentage:
The amount of time billed divided by the amount of time recorded.

timekeepers amount to 100,000 hours to be billed, the firm, to anticipate more realistic revenue, might use a time-to-billing percentage of 95 percent, anticipating that bills for only 95,000 hours will be sent to clients. In an income budget, the amount of revenue the firm projects will be further reduced by the firm's **realization rate**, the percentage a firm actually receives from clients as opposed to the amount billed. So, if a firm bills for 95,000 hours at a rate of $100 per hour, or $9,500,000, but receives only $8,500,000 from clients, the firm's realization rate is 89 percent.

Clients might not pay their bills, they might argue their bills down, or they might even declare bankruptcy. In these situations, the law firm itself will not receive 100 percent of the amount it billed. The firm, for instance, might realize only 80 percent of the amount it bills clients—meaning the firm has an 80 percent realization rate.

By putting together an **income budget** that projects all sources of income, a firm can estimate its gross income, or revenues received before the payment of any expenses. Of course, just as each source of income is an entry in a budget, so, too, must all expenses be identified. The **net profit** or loss of a firm is revenues minus expenses. Expenses include costs associated with the following items:

- salaries
- malpractice insurance
- rent
- utilities
- professional accounting services
- copying costs
- employee benefits, such as health insurance, paid by the firm
- taxes
- housekeeping
- travel that is not billed to clients
- legal books and periodicals
- access to legal databases such as Lexis and Westlaw
- bar association dues
- office supplies
- equipment, such as computers, office furniture, and copiers
- software
- marketing

One of the ways to manage a firm's finances is to establish an **operating budget**, which indicates projected revenues as well as projected expenses. Periodically, the projected figures in a budget should be compared to the actual ones so that the firm's leaders can assess how the firm is doing. **Variance reporting** is a comparison of the numbers actually achieved with the estimated amounts.

The actual results should be tallied so the firm can do a better job of predicting its operating budget entries and controlling its finances. If a firm is experiencing a shortfall in revenues during a given month, for example, it may then take efforts to either increase revenues or decrease expenses. Figure 9-1 displays a sample operating budget.

Firms must also manage their cash flow, which is cash receipts minus cash payments over a period of time. After bills are sent out, money does not start

realization rate: The percentage a firm actually receives from clients as opposed to the amount billed.

income budget: A projection of all sources of income.

net profit: Revenues minus expenses.

operating budget: A projection of both revenues and expenses.

variance reporting: A comparison of the projected expenses and income with the amounts actually achieved.

FIGURE 9-1
Sample Law Firm Budget

BUDGET

Year: 20xx

Income:	Budgeted	Actual
Fee income	$	$ . . . .
Other income	$	$ . . . .
Total Income:	**$ . . . .**	**$ . . . .**

Expenses:	Budgeted	Actual
Salaries	$	$ . . . .
Malpractice insurance	$	$ . . . .
Rent	$	$ . . . .
Utilities	$	$ . . . .
Professional accounting services	$	$ . . . .
Copying costs	$	$ . . . .
Employee benefits	$	$ . . . .
Taxes	$	$ . . . .
Housekeeping	$	$ . . . .
Travel that is not billed to clients	$	$ . . . .
Legal books and periodicals	$	$ . . . .
Access to legal databases such as Lexis	$	$ . . . .
Bar association dues	$	$ . . . .
Office supplies	$	$ . . . .
Equipment, such as computers, office furniture, copiers	$	$ . . . .
Software	$	$ . . . .
Marketing	$	$ . . . .
Total Expenses:	**$ . . . .**	**$ . . . .**
Profit (income – expenses)	**$ . . . .**	**$ . . . .**

---

trickling in right away. Clients might take two months or longer to actually pay their bills.[5]

Law firms must plan to have sufficient cash on hand to honor their own obligations. During a recession, clients tend to pay their bills less promptly. In response, a firm can bill more frequently (weekly rather than monthly) or specify on its bills that payment is due on receipt (rather than within 30 days).

C.   Timekeeping

timekeeping:
The practice of tracking and recording time.

The practice of tracking and recording time spent on various projects is called **timekeeping**. Clients typically are billed according to the number of hours lawyers, paralegals, and others within a firm worked on a project. If the time spent on various tasks for a client is not tracked, bills requesting payment for that time cannot reasonably be sent out.

1. Tracking Time

Time should be tracked on a daily basis on a time sheet, which is either manually written on paper or entered into a computer. Accuracy and thoroughness are vital in recording time spent on a legal matter. A law firm typically sets a date by which all time sheets for a given month must be submitted so that bills to clients can be promptly prepared.

Keeping track of every single thing done in a workday can be difficult to get used to. To the extent possible, a timekeeper should record time contemporaneously with the work being performed. Inevitably, though, a lawyer might have some rushed, high-pressure days and may not get around to recording her time. To help reconstruct the tasks performed, keep a handwritten personal calendar identifying work projects. Figure 9-2 shows a sample time sheet.

A law firm may require that time be recorded in 6-minute increments (a tenth of an hour, or .10) or in 15-minute increments (a quarter of an hour, or .25).

What is billable? Time spent researching, whether online or using actual books from a library, is billable, as is time spent reading and analyzing the materials found. Time dedicated to drafting and writing a document should be recorded, as should time spent updating research and checking citations. Time used for correspondence with the client, whether by telephone call, letter, fax, or other means, should be recorded, as should the preparation time for such calls and correspondence. Even time spent on e-mail exchanges should be recorded.

FIGURE 9-2
Sample Time Sheet

Attorney: _____

Date	Client No./Matter No.	Task	Time
08/01/2013	1743/633084	Prepare complaint	2.00
08/01/2013	1541/000004	Participate in conference call with client and opposing counsel	1.00
08/01/2013	1541/000004	Revise defense strategy	2.50
08/01/2013	1649/790123	Research caselaw on liability for formaldehyde releases	1.75

Though not directly billable to clients, time spent on marketing or working on pro bono projects should also be recorded. Firms might have separate requirements for time dedicated to business development or pro bono work. Whether or not the firm records the time, a timekeeper should keep track of the time spent in support of firm activities even when those activities cannot be directly billed to a client. If a timekeeper falls short in billable work, the timekeeper at least can point to other effort that will enhance experience (pro bono work) or eventually generate income for the firm (client development and marketing).

2.   *Billable-Hour Requirements*

Requirements at law firms vary. Attorneys might be required to bill between 1,600 and 2,200 hours per year.[6] Someone who does not meet the firm's requirements could be reprimanded or, in a worst-case scenario, fired. Both lawyers and other timekeepers should monitor their billable hours so that if they fall short in time, they can seek additional work.

3.   *Timekeeping Systems*

Today, many large law firms use integrated systems that manage information for many applications, such as billing and accounting, checking conflicts of interest, keeping records, and so forth. Some of these systems are "off the shelf," but some law firms hire consultants or use their own information technology personnel to develop custom-made systems. Law firm practice management software programs constantly evolve along with advances in technology, and new ones are always developed. Some law practice management systems are listed here:

- Abacus Law (http://www.abacuslaw.com)
- Aderant (http://www.aderant.com/products/)
- Amicus (http://amicusattorney.com)
- Elite (http://www.elite.com)
- HoudiniEsq (http://houdiniesq.com)
- Juris (http://www.lexisnexis.com/law-firm-practice-management/juris/)
- Time Matters (http://www.lexisnexis.com/law-firm-practice-management/time-matters/)
- PCLaw   (http://www.lexisnexis.com/law-firm-practice-management/pclaw/)
- Rocket Matter (www.rocketmatter.com)
- Tabs3 (http://www.tabs3.com)
- Sage Timeslips (http://na.sage.com/Sage-Timeslips/)

D.   Client Billing

If a bill is not sent to a client, that client likely is not going to just send in a payment. Rather, a bill is prepared, and the billing lawyer reviews it. The billing partner may make some changes to the bill. For instance, a billing partner who believes that a junior associate spent too much time on a task might write off some of the time spent, thus reducing the amount billed to the client.

A firm might establish a billing policy requiring client bills to be prepared as of the fifth of the following month. Time sheets and cost records indicating outlays made on behalf of clients must be submitted for processing by a law firm's accounting department or other designated person responsible for preparing bills, such as a billing clerk.

A **client activity report** for each active client is generated that specifies the activities performed by attorneys and other timekeepers at the firm, the hours spent on these activities, and the hourly rate of each timekeeper. The **hourly rate** is the amount each timekeeper charges for one hour of work. In setting hourly rates, firms consider a person's expertise, but they also must cover their expenses. So an hourly rate is designed to cover the timekeeper's salary as well as overhead and to generate profit for the firm. The billing partner reviews this report and may deduct any excessive hours before the information in the report is presented in a bill that will be sent to a client.

client activity report:
A description of the activities performed by attorneys and other timekeepers at the firm for a specified client, the hours spent on these activities, and the hourly rate of each timekeeper.

hourly rate:
The amount a timekeeper charges for one hour of work.

1. What Exactly Is a Client Charged For?

In addition to being obligated to pay for legal services provided, clients typically are billed for their costs, such as filing fees and process services. The services a law firm provides or uses while offering legal counsel are also billed to the client. Postage and FedEx charges, copying of documents, word processing, travel, and the like are all billed to the client.

2. Contents of a Bill

Bills contain a description of the services rendered and the amount owed (see Figure 9-3). Some clients require more details than others. While one client might be satisfied with an entry such as "conference call with client," another might specify that the topic of the conference call be indicated on the bill along with its outcome. (Did the client decide to pursue settlement options? Did the client direct the lawyer to prepare to file suit?) Other clients prefer that minimal information be on the bills themselves.

3. Billing Systems

A firm's billing system software may be able to generate bills as well as productivity reports that can flag poorly performing practice areas or timekeepers who are not meeting their billable-hour requirements. "Good billing software is very flexible and can cost anywhere from just over $100 to as much as $750 per license. Good applications include . . . the ability to undo and reprint billing statements, along with various formats for displaying and transmitting bills (e.g., PDF, HTML, or RTF)."[7] Clients might also be able to specify the precise format they require for billing.

FIGURE 9-3
Legal Bill

Jones, Kearns, Lewis & Barber
1963 Main Street
Third Floor
Bedford Hills, NY 10507
(914) 555-4321
Federal Tax ID: 06-1234567

January 5, 2013

Pinkmoondust Productions
 ATTN: Hadley Heuess
268 Babbitt Road
Bedford Hills, NY 10507

Our identifying code for this case PM-100467
Invoice number 023

Services Rendered

Atty services rendered		Hours	Amount
12/01/12 LNT	Preparation for conference call with client re strategy for cleaning up Baylis site and conference call with client	1.25	500.00
12/02/12 VLL	Research and identify other potentially responsible parties at Baylis site	2.00	390.00
12/03/12 LNT	Write letters to other potentially responsible parties at Baylis site informing them of cleanup obligations	1.75	700.00
12/10/12 LNT	Strategy session with client re measures to be taken against other responsible parties at Baylis site	.75	300.00

Summary	Hours	Rate	Amount
Lori N. Tripoli	3.75	400.00	1,500.00
Victor L. Laino	2.00	195.00	390.00

Costs advanced	Amount
12/01/12 Photo copy charge	37.25
12/03/12 Postage charge	43.95
Total advanced costs	$81.20
Total current fees and costs	$1,971.20
Prior balance	$0

TOTAL AMOUNT DUE AND PAYABLE	**$1,971.20**

Increasingly, lawyers are turning to electronic billing, or e-billing. E-billing cuts down on paper consumption and postage costs and sends the client's bills electronically. Bills might be e-mailed or uploaded via a client's or a third party's Web site.

Examples of e-billing systems are listed here:

- DataCert (http://www.datacert.com)
- e-BillingHub (http://www.elite.com/enterprise/ebillinghub/)
- Interbill (http://www.interbill.com)
- Serengeti (http://www.serengetilaw.com/Pages/default.aspx)

E.   Fee Agreements

Clients are charged in different ways, depending on the agreement the client reached with the lawyer. Some clients agree to legal fees charged on an hourly basis, others agree to pay based on completion of a given task, some agree to an incentives program in which fees are higher if the work is done more quickly or efficiently, and some pay on a contingency basis only if the lawsuit is victorious.

Rule 1.5 of the ABA's *Model Rules of Professional Conduct* specifies that "unreasonable" rates shall not be charged. Model Rule 1.5(b) indicates that fee agreements should be in writing.

The fees themselves generally may not be shared with nonlawyers, such as paralegals, pursuant to Model Rule 5.4. If someone other than the client is paying the client's legal bill, a lawyer may not allow that person to direct the lawyer in rendering legal services. These rules are designed to allow the lawyer independence in making professional judgments.

1.   Hourly Rates

Under an hourly rate agreement, clients agree to pay the firm for each hour spent on a case. Different lawyers bill their time at different rates. New associates' rates are lower than those of seasoned practitioners. The average hourly rate for partners was $369 in 2012, and $242 for associates.[8] Rates can be significantly higher for lawyers at large law firms.

Hourly billing has been heavily criticized as rewarding slowness. With an hourly billing arrangement, someone who performs a task quickly might bill less than someone who plods along.

Given this seemingly valid criticism of hourly rates, why are they still used? In some situations, the amount of time that will be needed isn't clear, such as when major litigation is involved.

Sometimes, a client will agree to pay a **blended rate,** which is a rate based on the legal talent that will be working on a matter. For example, a blended

blended rate:
An hourly rate established based on the legal team that will be working on a matter.

rate might be developed based on a matter to be worked on by a senior partner, several low-level associates, and one paralegal. In some states, the "blend" must apply only to lawyers, not to legal assistants.

2.   Task-Based Billing

Billing hourly can create inefficiencies. The longer a project takes, the more a lawyer can bill for it. If a lawyer proceeds quickly, she actually earns less for the firm than she would if she took her time. Clients interested in reducing the fees they pay sometimes pursue alternatives to billable-hour arrangements.

One option is to charge a specified amount to perform a given task: $500 to prepare a simple will, for example, or $1,000 for a residential real estate closing. Such a rate structure can encourage a firm to staff a matter efficiently. When alternative arrangements are selected, a very specific engagement letter with the client must be drafted that clearly identifies the agreed-upon billing scenario. A firm should closely track performance under alternative billing arrangements to ensure that it can meet its own income goals.

3.   Incentive Billing

Recognizing the inefficiencies inherent in billing based on billable hours, some law firms have moved toward alternative billing arrangements that emphasize performance. For instance, a firm might agree to a lower fixed fee on a trial but arrange to receive a bonus if the client wins the case or if a certain level of settlement is achieved. A client might agree to pay a flat rate for a certain task, but then agree to pay more if the task is completed early, or less if a task is submitted past a specified deadline.

4.   Contingent Fees

With a contingent fee arrangement, a fee is paid only if the lawyer wins a lawsuit. The amount is a percentage of the award for damages. If the lawyer loses the suit, no fee is due. Contingent fee arrangements are typically used in personal injury cases or in worker compensation claims. Arrangements are typically made, too, for a fee to be paid in the event that the case is settled before trial or before a verdict is reached. Even though a client will not have to pay attorney fees if the lawyer loses the lawsuit, the client is typically obligated to pay for costs associated with the litigation, such as filing fees.

Model Rules of Professional Conduct Rule 1.5 specifically allows contingent fees except in cases involving domestic relations or in criminal cases. Rule 1.5(c) directs that contingency fees be in writing.

What happens when lawyers who have a contingent fee agreement are fired by the client before a lawsuit is resolved? See the following case for one example.

Campbell v. Bozeman Investors of Duluth
964 P.2d 41 (Mont. 1998)

JUDGES: JUSTICE JAMES C. NELSON DELIVERED THE OPINION OF THE COURT. WE CONCUR: J. A. TURNAGE, CHIEF JUSTICE, KARLA M. GRAY, WILLIAM E. HUNT, SR., W. WILLIAM LEAPHART, JUSTICES.

OPINION

Justice JAMES C. NELSON delivered the Opinion of the Court.

Jeannie Rosseland Campbell (Campbell) brought an action in the District Court . . . to recover damages from Bozeman Investors of Duluth d/b/a Holiday Inn of Bozeman and Patrick Lund for personal injuries she sustained in a motor vehicle collision. Two of Campbell's attorneys in this action, Charming Hartelius (Hartelius) and Gregory Morgan (Morgan), filed a Notice of Lien claiming entitlement, from the proceeds of Campbell's claim, to payment of their costs and attorney fees as well as reimbursement for advances made to Campbell. The District Court found the lien to be valid and awarded judgment in favor of Hartelius and Morgan. From this judgment Campbell appeals; Hartelius and Morgan cross-appeal. We affirm.

The issues, as framed by this Court, are:

Whether the District Court erred in concluding that Hartelius and Morgan are entitled to attorney fees totaling $8800.

Whether the District Court erred in failing to require that Campbell reveal the amount she received as settlement of her claim.

FACTUAL AND PROCEDURAL BACKGROUND

On December 3, 1992, Campbell was seriously injured when her vehicle collided with a van operated by Patrick Lund (Lund). The van was owned by Lund's employer, Bozeman Investors of Duluth d/b/a the Holiday Inn of Bozeman (Bozeman Investors). Bozeman Investors' insurer paid Campbell for the damage to her vehicle as well as $4,000 to $5,000 of her medical bills.

In January 1994, Bozeman Investors' insurer made an unsolicited offer to settle Campbell's claim for the sum of $22,000, less the amounts already paid for medical care and for the damage to Campbell's vehicle. Campbell, who had not yet consulted a physician to determine the extent of the injuries to her back, rejected the offer. On April 29, 1994, Campbell filed a personal injury action against Lund and Bozeman Investors.

Campbell had retained Stephen Pohl (Pohl) to represent her in her personal injury action. However, when Campbell separated from her husband in November 1994, she perceived that there existed a possible conflict of interest with Pohl as Campbell had originally been referred to Pohl by Campbell's mother-in-law for whom Pohl had performed legal services.

Consequently, on December 8, 1994, Campbell entered into a contingent fee agreement with Hartelius and Morgan to render legal services in her suit against Bozeman Investors. The agreement provided that Campbell was to pay Hartelius and Morgan "33-1/3% of any settlement obtained in said case if same is settled at any time prior to instituting suit and 40% of any settlement obtained in said case if same is settled at any time after institution of suit." Pohl provided a complete copy of Campbell's file to Hartelius and Morgan and agreed to wait until the case was resolved to receive reimbursement for costs he expended on Campbell's behalf. Hence, on April 19, 1995, Hartelius and Morgan were substituted as counsel of record.

By this time, Campbell had quit her job and was attending physical therapy on a regular basis. She was also receiving treatment from a surgeon in Billings and was looking into going to a specialist in Minnesota to determine whether she required back surgery.

In April 1995, counsel for Bozeman Investors deposed Campbell. Although neither Hartelius nor Morgan met with Campbell in person before her deposition, Hartelius spoke with her on the phone and attended the deposition. It was determined at the deposition that Bozeman Investors had not been provided with copies of all of Campbell's medical records.

In June 1995, Campbell was examined by Dr. Michael Smith, an orthopedic surgeon in Minneapolis, Minnesota. Dr. Smith indicated that he would perform the necessary surgery on Campbell's back. However, in August 1995, Campbell learned that Medicaid would not pay for an operation performed out-of-state, thus she was forced to seek another surgeon. Campbell contacted Dr. Greg McDowell, a Billings orthopedist, who agreed to perform the surgery.

During this time, Campbell was experiencing financial difficulties since she was not working and had not received any further payments for her medical bills from Bozeman Investors. She had applied for Social Security disability benefits, but was turned down on December 1, 1995. Consequently, Hartelius obtained approval from this Court to loan money to Campbell for her living expenses. To that end, Hartelius loaned her $2,745.29.

On May 6, 1996, Campbell sent a letter to Hartelius and Morgan expressing dissatisfaction with their services and discharging them. Campbell later testified that she became dissatisfied with Hartelius and Morgan because they never wrote to Bozeman Investors' insurer requesting an advance payment for medical costs for surgery, did not request that a trial date be set, and did not adequately advise her about obtaining Social Security disability benefits. Hence, on June 6, 1996, Campbell filed a motion for substitution of counsel, requesting that Pohl be substituted as attorney of record in place of Hartelius and Morgan. The court granted her motion on June 25, 1996.

After they were dismissed by Campbell, Hartelius and Morgan . . . filed a Notice of Lien claiming entitlement from the proceeds of Campbell's claim against Bozeman Investors for payment of their costs and attorney fees and requesting reimbursement for the money they had advanced her.

On October 22, 1996, Campbell was examined at the request of Bozeman Investors' attorney by Dr. Peter Wendt, an orthopedic surgeon practicing in Anaconda. A settlement conference was held in December 1996, at the conclusion of which Campbell's personal injury claim against Bozeman Investors was settled. In accordance with the terms of the settlement, the amount of the settlement was kept confidential. On April 3, 1997, a Stipulation and Order of Dismissal was filed by Campbell and Bozeman Investors and the District Court entered its order dismissing with prejudice Campbell's claim against Bozeman Investors.

After the settlement of Campbell's claim, Hartelius and Morgan were reimbursed for the full amount of the costs and advances as itemized in their

Notice of Lien, but they did not receive any payment for attorney fees. Instead, Campbell filed a motion for determination of attorney fees and for the release of the lien. . . .

On March 5, 1997, the District Court entered its Findings of Fact and Conclusions of Law wherein the court determined that Hartelius was entitled to a fee of $6,600 and that Morgan was entitled to a fee of $2,200. The court entered judgment in accordance with these findings and conclusions on March 14, 1997.

Campbell appeals from the District Court's judgment regarding attorney fees and Hartelius and Morgan cross appeal.

Whether the District Court erred in concluding that Hartelius and Morgan are entitled to attorney fees totaling $8800

The District Court concluded that a client's right to discharge an attorney employed under a contingency fee contract is an implicit term of the contract and the client's discharge of the attorney, with or without cause, does not constitute a breach of that contract. The court further concluded that a client who discharges an attorney employed under a contingency fee contract for cause has no obligation to pay a fee to that attorney unless the attorney has substantially performed the services for which he was retained.

On that basis, the court determined that Campbell had not breached the contract by discharging Hartelius and Morgan. Moreover, the court determined that although Hartelius and Morgan were discharged for cause, they substantially performed the services for which they were retained prior to their discharge.

Therefore, they were entitled to a fee limited to the reasonable value of their services. Thus, the court awarded $6600 to Hartelius and $2200 to Morgan.

The standard of review of a district court's conclusions of law is whether the court's interpretation of the law is correct. . . .

First, we must determine whether, as Hartelius and Morgan contend, a client's discharge of his or her attorney is a breach of contract thus entitling the attorney to contract damages. We hold that it is not and does not.

In 1916, the New York Court of Appeals held that a contract under which an attorney is employed by a client has peculiar and distinctive features which differentiate it from ordinary contracts of employment, thus a client may, at any time for any reason or without any reason, discharge his or her attorney. *Martin v. Camp*, 219 N.Y. 170, 114 N.E. 46, 47-48 (N.Y. 1969), *modified*, 220 N.Y. 653, 115 N.E. 1044. Thus, the court reasoned that if the client has the right to terminate the relationship of attorney and client at any time without cause, the client cannot be compelled to pay damages for exercising a right which is an implied condition of the contract. *Martin*, 114 N.E. at 48. The court held that although the attorney may not recover damages for breach of contract, the attorney may recover the reasonable value of the services rendered. *Martin*, 114 N.E. at 48.

A majority of jurisdictions have since adopted the "client discharge rule" as set forth in *Martin*. . . .

Finding considerable merit in the "client discharge rule" as expressed in *Martin, Rosenberg,* and *Olsen,* we follow those jurisdictions in holding that the discharge of an attorney by a client is not a breach of contract and does not give rise to contract damages. Therefore, we affirm the District Court on this issue.

We next must determine whether Hartelius and Morgan are entitled to a fee and on what basis that fee, if any, should be determined. The District Court concluded that Hartelius and Morgan were discharged for cause, however, they substantially performed the services for which they were retained and are thus entitled to a fee based on the reasonable value of the services rendered. Campbell alleges error in the court's determination arguing instead that this Court should formally adopt a rule that an attorney discharged for cause is not entitled to any fee. She contends that we endorsed a similar rule in *Bink v. First Bank West*, 246 Mont. 414, 804 P.2d 384 (1991). However, Campbell's reliance on *Bink* is misplaced.

In *Bink*, we remanded the case to the district court for an evidentiary hearing to determine whether the client discharged his attorney for cause and to determine the amount of attorney fees and costs. We did not, as Campbell suggests, endorse any rule espousing the idea that an attorney discharged for cause is not entitled to a fee and we decline to adopt such a rule now.

Instead, we agree with those jurisdictions that hold that regardless of whether an attorney was discharged with or without cause, that attorney is entitled to a *quantum meruit* recovery for the reasonable value of his services rendered to the time of discharge. *Fracasse v. Brent*, 6 Cal. 3d 784, 494 P.2d 9, 14-15, 100 Cal. Rptr. 385 (Cal. 1972). We note one exception to this general rule, however—situations where the discharge occurs "on the courthouse steps," just prior to settlement and after much work by the attorney. In those cases some reviewing courts have, on appropriate facts, found that the entire fee was the reasonable value of the attorney's services. *Fracasse*, 494 P.2d at 14. Here, however, Hartelius and Morgan were not discharged "on the courthouse steps," and, accordingly, we need not address this exception. Rather, the general *quantum meruit* rule applies.

Moreover, in the case *sub judice*, because we have determined that the general rule applies, it is not necessary for us to entertain a discussion of the reasons *why* Campbell discharged Hartelius and Morgan or whether those reasons constituted "cause." Rather, we review whether the District Court was correct in concluding that the reasonable value of the services rendered by Hartelius and Morgan was $6600 and $2200, respectively.

Hartelius testified at the hearing that he does not normally record his time in contingency fee cases, so he had to reconstruct the time he spent on the case. Thus, he estimated that he spent at least 100 hours on the case, his paralegal spent an additional 50 hours on the case and Morgan spent 22 hours on the case. At the conclusion of the hearing, the parties stipulated that the attorney fees on an hourly basis for Hartelius and Morgan would be $110.

Campbell contends that there was no evidence presented at the hearing to demonstrate the value of the services Hartelius and Morgan performed, thus the evidence was insufficient to award them any fee. Moreover, she contends that the fee should be based on the reasonable value to her of their services. She argues that, because Hartelius and Morgan did not turn her file over to her after she discharged them, their services did not benefit her in the settlement of her case and that her case was settled mainly on the basis of a report from a doctor with whom Hartelius and Morgan had no involvement.

"The amount fixed as attorney fees is largely discretionary with the District Court, and we will not disturb its judgment in the absence of an abuse of that discretion." *Talmage v. Gruss,* 202 Mont. 410, 412, 658 P.2d 419, 420 (1983) (citing *Carkeek v. Ayer,* 188 Mont. 345, 347, 613 P.2d 1013, 1015 (1980)). . . . Moreover, in *First Security Bank of Bozeman v. Tholkes,* 169 Mont. 422, 429-30, 547 P.2d 1328, 1332 (1976), we set forth several guidelines for a trial court to consider in determining the amount to be awarded as reasonable attorney fees:

> the amount and character of the services rendered, the labor, time and trouble involved, the character and importance of the litigation in which the services were rendered, the amount of money or the value of property to be affected, the professional skill and experience called for, the character and standing in their profession of the attorneys. . . . The result secured by the services of the attorneys may be considered as an important element in determining their value.

We hold that, in the case before us, the District Court did not act arbitrarily, exceed the bounds of reason or ignore recognized principles in determining the amount of attorney fees to be awarded to Hartelius and Morgan. In its Findings of Fact Nos. 27 and 28, the District Court set forth ten specific instances in the record evidencing work performed by Hartelius and Morgan on Campbell's behalf prior to their discharge. The court then applied those facts to the guidelines set forth in *Tholkes* in determining the amount to be awarded as reasonable attorney fees. Furthermore, contrary to Campbell's contention, the court did not award attorney fees based solely on Hartelius' estimate of the number of hours he worked on the case or for the hours he estimated his paralegal worked on the case. Rather, the court determined that a reasonable fee for Hartelius was $6600. Based on the hourly fee of $110 stipulated to by the parties, the court determined that it was reasonable for Hartelius to have put in 60 hours on Campbell's case.

Accordingly, we hold that the District Court did not abuse its discretion in awarding attorney fees to Hartelius in the amount of $6600 and to Morgan in the amount of $2200.

. . .

Whether the District Court erred in failing to require that Campbell reveal the amount she received as settlement of her claim

Hartelius and Morgan contend that the District Court should have required Campbell to reveal the amount of the settlement. They argue that the court cannot effectively determine the amount of attorney fees owed until the settlement amount is known. We disagree. The amount of the settlement would only be necessary if the attorney fees were to be based on a percentage of that figure. Since we have already determined that Hartelius and Morgan are entitled only to the value of the services rendered, the amount of the settlement is immaterial.

Accordingly, we affirm the District Court's denial of Hartelius and Morgan's request to force Campbell to disclose the settlement amount.

Affirmed.

5.   Flat Fees

A **flat fee** is an arrangement in which the lawyer agrees to a set price for a particular piece of work. For instance, a price might be set for an uncontested divorce, for a bankruptcy, or for incorporating a business. The lawyer must do the work for the agreed-upon amount no matter how many hours the job takes.

6.   Prepaid Legal Services

Some employers, credit unions, and other groups offer an opportunity for their employees or members to have access to legal services at greatly reduced rates through a prepaid legal plan, in which the employee or member is charged a monthly fee and then can obtain legal services as needed for free or at relatively low rates.

7.   Retainers

A **retainer** is an upfront payment made by a client for work that a lawyer will perform in the future. Typically, a lawyer requires payment of a retainer when a client formally agrees to be represented by that lawyer. There are different types of retainers. A true nonrefundable retainer "is a fee that a lawyer charges the client not necessarily for specific services to be performed but, for example, to ensure the lawyer's availability whenever the client may need legal services."[9] A nonrefundable retainer is considered an earned fee that is not deposited into a lawyer's trust account but that becomes the property of the lawyer—so long as the fee is "reasonable" as required by Model Rule 1.5 and by state ethical rules. Some states have held that nonrefundable retainers are unethical because they limit the ability of a client to fire a lawyer.[10] A refundable retainer "is really payment in advance. Any funds which are part of a refundable retainer are credited against any services performed and any excess must be returned to the client when the attorney's obligation has been fulfilled."[11]

Whether a retainer is refundable or nonrefundable should be clearly explained in the attorney-client agreement.

8.   Court-Awarded Fees

Some statutes provide that a prevailing party may be awarded attorney fees. For example, consider section 505 of the Americans with Disabilities Act:

> In any action or administrative proceeding commenced pursuant to this Act, the court or agency, in its discretion, may allow the prevailing party, other than the United States, a reasonable attorney's fee, including litigation expenses, and costs, and the United States shall be liable for the foregoing the same as a private individual.[12]

Detailed records must be submitted to a court for attorney fees to be awarded in a case.

9. *Statutory Fees*

Some states limit the amount that an attorney can earn. For instance, fees for worker compensation claims might be limited to a percentage of the amount of compensation recovered. Similarly, the fee of an attorney appointed by a probate court to be an administrator of an estate may be limited to a percentage of value of the estate.

10. *Referral Fees*

Model Rule 7.2(b)(4) allows payment of a referral fee to another lawyer for referring a client so long as the referral agreement is not exclusive and the client is informed of the agreement.

F. Fee Collection

Lawyers are not really in the business of bill collection, and attempting to collect money from a long-time client who has suddenly fallen behind in payments can be somewhat stressful. At the same time, however, a firm must make sure that its own cash flow remains in balance so that it will not have to obtain loans to cover shortfalls.

1. *Overseeing the Process*

Ideally, a firm may appoint one person to oversee collections and to work with various partners to plan how clients might be pursued. Plans of approach will likely vary—a long-time business client that has slowed payments due to its own recessionary woes will probably not be treated in the same way as an insolvent individual going through a divorce. The amount of money owed can also influence the effort expended in getting paid. An outstanding bill of $100,000 deserves significantly more attention than one of $500. A certain measure of diplomacy is also necessary—a firm that acts in a heavy-handed manner risks losing a possibly valuable client that might be having only short-term problems.

A firm should establish a procedure for dealing with delinquent bills that begins with a follow-up notice, then a follow-up phone call from a member of the support staff to the client's support staff, and then a call from a partner directly to the client.

Such calls need not be combative. The caller might simply note that payment has not been received and indicate that he or she is calling to check whether the client received the bill. The caller can also express concern and ask whether everything is all right. Ultimately, of course, the caller can ask when to expect payment. The firm might also attempt to negotiate a payment plan with a client.

2. Delinquent Bills

If efforts to collect an overdue bill are not successful, a firm may need to take more drastic measures. The firm might be willing to reduce the amount of a bill in the hope that the client will actually pay the lower figure. Ultimately, a firm may have to file suit against a client for nonpayment of a bill. That risks negative publicity, however, as well as a possible countersuit from the client.

In addition, a firm must consider terminating the representation of a client. Model Rule 1.16(b)(5) allows lawyers to withdraw from representing a nonpaying client, but a court's permission may be necessary if a firm had been representing the client in a lawsuit and had taken substantial action in litigating that suit. A firm may be able to obtain a lien against the client to guarantee payment of the outstanding legal fees.[13]

G.   Client Trust Funds

A law firm handles more than just its own money; a firm often handles large sums of money for its clients. For example, the check from an award for damages in a personal injury case may be made payable to the client and the attorney, as might a settlement. After the client endorses, or signs, the check, the attorney may deposit such amounts in a client trust account, not in the attorney's or law firm's operating account. Client trust accounts are governed by rules of ethics. A client trust account is a bank account opened by a law firm solely for funds delivered to the firm in its capacity as a fiduciary.

Client trust accounts are required so that a client's money is protected. "Keeping client's funds separate from the attorney's funds protects the client's retainer from the attorney's creditors. Additionally, commingling of funds is often the first step towards conversion of those funds. Lastly, if the funds are commingled and the attorney dies, the funds are at risk of being lost."[14] Client funds and attorney funds may not be commingled. If a lawyer has deposited a client's refundable retainer into a client trust account, the lawyer then withdraws funds from that account when the lawyer has earned a legal fee and deposits that money into the firm's separate account for law firm operations.

States establish rules and programs for interest on lawyers' trust accounts (IOLTA). The interest from these accounts is pooled and used for charitable purchases, such as providing legal aid to indigent people. Most states require lawyers to participate in their IOLTA programs.[15]

H.   Escrow Funds

In addition to placing unearned retainers and money for expenses (such as court costs) that will be incurred in client trust accounts, lawyers sometimes place escrow funds in these accounts as well. Escrow funds are monies that the lawyer is holding on behalf of a client that are to be delivered to a third party when an event occurs. For instance, a lawyer might hold a client's down payment on a piece of property and then transfer that money to the seller when a contract is signed. A divorcing couple might disagree about the disposition of certain money they had; the lawyer for one of the parties might hold that money in a client trust account until the matter is resolved and ownership of the funds is determined.

I. Accounting

Given the amount of money a law firm handles and the varied sources from which the money comes, the accounting function within a law practice clearly is an important one. A firm may have a controller who handles a firm's accounting needs, prepares financial reports and analyses, and manages cash flow. Someone in the firm needs to address the firm's tax issues and also process and pay vendor bills. Large law firms might have an accounting staff to handle the accounting needs of clients, such as the preparation of estate tax returns and of judiciary fiduciary accountings for estates. Some functions might also be outsourced to an accounting firm.

Today, many accounting functions are automated. Examples of software that includes accounting functions are:

- CaseFox (http://www.casefox.com)
- Freshbooks (http://www.freshbooks.com)
- Intuit QuickBooks (http://quickbooks.intuit.com)
- OneSource (http://onesource.thomsonreuters.com)

Some law firms use the Microsoft Excel spreadsheet software that is available in Microsoft Office.

J. Safeguards

Sadly, theft can be a problem even at a law firm. Low-level employees, long-time trusted secretaries, and even associates and partners themselves are sometimes tempted to take what's not theirs. Consider these examples:

- A law office manager was sentenced to 10-plus years in prison for stealing more than $1 million from the firm across a seven-year time period.[16]
- A law-firm employee stole toner cartridges from a law firm with a value of $375,000 and was later convicted of that crime.[17]
- A lawyer pleaded guilty to stealing more than $300,000 from client trust accounts by having the money transferred to a personal checking account that the firm's accountant believed was a business checking account.[18]
- A paralegal who embezzled $300,000 from a New York law firm then moved to Pennsylvania and allegedly embezzled money from her new law firm employer to pay restitution to the previous firm.[19]
- A securities class action lawyer admitted to taking $9.3 million from client escrow accounts.[20]

Clearly, lawyers must protect themselves and their clients' funds by establishing procedures and safeguards designed to thwart such crimes. Even a trusted person may be the one who is stealing money, so firms must install safeguards for long-time, dedicated lawyers and staff. Checks and balances are clearly vital. Audits should be performed regularly and reviewed to prevent theft. Inventory of supplies should be taken, and duties involving financial operations should be divided so that no single person controls incoming or outgoing payments. For instance, checks above a certain amount might be signed by more than one person. A staffer responsible for purchasing supplies should not be the same person who takes inventory of them or issues payment for them.

Checklist

- A budget helps a firm plan for revenues and expenses. Even major law firms have declared bankruptcy. It is vital that a law firm pursue sound financial practices.
- A law firm must manage its cash flow. Steps can be taken to increase cash flow during economic hard times.
- Timekeepers at a firm must track and record the time they devote to work. Clients are billed for the time dedicated to their legal matters.
- Law firms require that attorneys and others meet specified billable-hour requirements.
- Clients are typically billed based on the hourly rate of a lawyer and other timekeepers at a firm. Some firms use alternative billing methods, such as task-based billing or incentive billing. Contingent fee arrangements are typically made in litigation involving money damages. Contingency fees are barred in cases that involve domestic relations or crimes.
- Attorneys must make collection efforts when clients do not pay their bills promptly. In extreme cases, a firm might file suit against a delinquent client or withdraw from representation of the client.
- Money that belongs to clients is deposited in a law firm's client trust fund, which is separate from the firm's operating account for its own business. Interest on lawyers' trust accounts is typically managed by a state program and used for charitable purposes, such as legal aid.
- A firm should institute proper accounting procedures and install safeguards to protect against theft.

Vocabulary

blended rate (p. 235)

budget (p. 228)

client activity report (p. 233)

flat fee (p. 242)

hourly rate (p. 233)

income budget (p. 229)

net profit (p. 229)

operating budget (p. 229)

realization rate (p. 229)

retainer (p. 242)

timekeeping (p. 230)

time-to-billing percentage (p. 228)

variance reporting (p. 229)

Career Preparation Tips

When considering prospective employers, you will want to assess the financial soundness of the organization to the extent that you can. Do your due diligence: Research lawsuits the employer has been involved in—search for media coverage and for disciplinary actions. Also try to learn about turnover at the organization and look to any recent changes in office space (whether downsizing or upsizing). In an interview, you might inquire directly about an organization's finances, or be more circuitous (e.g., "How has the firm weathered economic challenges? How has the firm remained competitive in these challenging times? Does the firm have any merger plans? How many lawsuits has the firm won in the past year?").

If you are already considering employers that you would like to work for, you might start following them now so you can remain abreast of their activities. You might set up a Google alert so that you will be notified by e-mail of any additions about the organization on Internet Web pages.

If You Want to Learn More

ABA Commission on Interest on Lawyers' Trust Accounts. http://www
.abanet.org/legalservices/iolta/home.html

The American Prepaid Legal Services Institute is a nonprofit clearinghouse
for the prepaid legal services industry. http://www.aplsi.org

The American Bar Association's Model Rules of Professional Conduct are
accessible online. http://www.americanbar.org/groups/professional_
responsibility/publications/model_rules_of_professional_conduct.html

News about electronic billing is provided by www.ebillingnews.com

Information about IOLTA programs may be found at www.iolta.org

Reading Comprehension

1. Why is the billable-hour system falling out of favor?
2. If a client is charged a blended rate, who benefits more: the law firm, or
   the client?
3. Read the excerpt from *Campbell v. Bozeman Investors of Duluth* in this
   chapter. What kind of agreement was at stake in this case? What is the
   "client discharge rule"? Was the outcome of the case fair? Would you still
   consider the outcome of the case fair if you learned that the settlement
   amount was $2 million? How can attorneys protect themselves if a client
   fires them and shortly thereafter settles a case?
4. As the client of a law firm, which type of billing arrangement would you
   prefer?
5. What are some ways that law firms are susceptible to embezzlement?

Discussion Starters

1. Suppose you go on a job interview and are told that you are required to
   bill 2,000 hours per year. Would you try to negotiate that figure?
2. Suppose your supervising attorney pulls you aside and tells you that you
   are not meeting your billable-hour requirements. What would you do?
3. Should a law firm pay bar association dues for its attorneys?
4. Why might some law firm clients prefer that bills contain only general
   information rather than specific details?

5. In what circumstances would someone other than a client pay that client's legal bill? What ethical considerations might arise in such cases?
6. Find one recent case in your state in which a lawyer was professionally disciplined for mismanaging client funds. What did the lawyer do? What punishment did the lawyer receive? Do you consider that punishment fair?
7. Research your state's rules on retainers. What types of retainers does your state allow? Do the rules specify whether a particular type of retainer is to be placed in a client trust account or in the lawyer's operating account?
8. Find one recent court decision in your state involving a law firm or lawyer that filed a lawsuit against a client over payment of fees. How much money was outstanding? Did the lawyer or the law firm win the case? Did the client file a countersuit? How much do you think the law firm spent litigating the matter?
9. Look up your state's rules on nonrefundable retainer agreements. Does your state allow them? Should nonrefundable retainer agreements be permissible? Whom do such agreements protect? Do they hurt anyone?

Case Studies

1. Suppose your supervising partner has asked you to research new timekeeping systems for your law firm, which has three partners, seven associates, four paralegals, and three legal secretaries. Which "off the shelf" software is best suited for the firm? What factors should be considered when choosing a software package? Compare and contrast the features of commercially available software and their prices.
2. You work in the accounting department of a large law firm that has 600 lawyers in five offices around the United States. The firm has corporate and litigation departments, and its clients are primarily businesses (both large and small ones). You have been asked to research new billing software for the firm. What software is commercially available, and what features might your firm be specifically interested in? How might your billing software needs differ from those of a two-lawyer firm dedicated to family law?
3. Consider the list of expenses in the sample law firm budget in Figure 9-1. During an economic downturn, which expenses would you try to reduce? How can a law firm prepare for future downturns during periods of economic growth?
4. Suppose you are a prospective client with a personal injury suit that could result in an award of damages up to $1 million. You are considering signing a contingent fee agreement. Look up sample contingency fee agreements. Which provisions of a contingency fee agreement would you definitely want to include?

5. Your supervising attorney is interested in advertising your law firm on sites like Groupon (http://www.groupon.com), which offer daily deals to prospective customers. Could the law firm's payment to a site like Groupon be considered an inappropriate referral fee payment to a nonlawyer? Is there a potential for any other ethics rules to be violated through the use of sites like Groupon for attorneys?

6. Compare and contrast annual revenue and profits per partner of three major law firms, and also research turnover at the firm in the last year. Did major practice groups join or leave? Which of the firms seems to be most financially stable and why? What questions might you ask during a job interview with the firm that seems to have the weakest financials?

7. Research the bankruptcies of two major law firms, Dewey & LeBoeuf and Howrey. What contributed to their collapses? How did the firms conduct themselves in the months preceding their bankruptcy filings? What other litigation occurred when the firms collapsed? How did partners at these firms fare? What happened to nonlawyer employees? How might these firms have taken measures to avoid bankruptcy?

Endnotes

1. Paul M. Barrett, *'American Lawyer' Revenue List Shows New No. 1 Firm: DLA Piper*, Bloomberg Businessweek (Apr. 26, 2013), *available at* http://www.businessweek.com/articles/2013-04-26/american-lawyer-revenue-list-shows-new-no-dot-1-firm-dla-piper.
2. *In re Dewey & LeBoeuf, LLP*, 478 B.R. 627, 632 (Bankr. S.D.N.Y. 2012).
3. Brian Baxter, *Dewey Filing Delineates Firm's Financial Affairs, Potential Merger Partners*, Am Law Daily (July 27, 2012), *available at* http://americanlawyer.com.
4. *See, e.g., In re Dewey & LeBoeuf, LLP*, 478 B.R. 627, 632 (Bankr. S.D.N.Y. 2012); *Entegra Power Group LLC v. Dewey & LeBoeuf, LLP (In re Dewey & LeBoeuf)*, No. 12-12321 (MG), 2013 WL 3327755 (Bankr. S.D.N.Y. July 2, 2013).
5. *See, e.g., How Small and Midsize Firms Weathered the Storm*, Law.com (Aug. 30, 2010), http://www.law.com/jsp/nlj/PubArticleNLJ.jsp?id=1202471122759.
6. *See, e.g.,* Building a Better Legal Profession, *An Investigation of the Billable Hour*, LexisNexis Legal newsroom Lexis Hub (Oct. 4, 2012), *available at* http://www.lexisnexis.com/legalnewsroom/lexis-hub/b/careerguidance/archive/2012/10/04/an-investigation-of-the-billable-hour.aspx.
7. Dee Crocker, *Managing Your Practice: Choices: Law Firm Billing and Accounting Software*, 69 Or. St. B. Bull. 34 (Dec. 2008).
8. Leigh Jones, *Revenues Up at Larger Law Firms*, Nat'l L.J., July 29, 2013, http://www.law.com/jsp/nlj/PubArticleNLJ.jsp?id=1202612599398&Revenues_Up_at_Larger_Law_Firms&slreturn=20130631051033.
9. State Bar of Wisconsin, Opinion E-93-4 Nonrefundable lawyer fees (1998), *available at* http://www.wisbar.org/AM/Template.cfm?Section=Home&TEMPLATE=/CM/ContentDisplay.cfm&CONTENTID=52814.
10. *See, e.g., In re Cooperman*, 187 A.2d 56 (N.Y. App. Div. 1993).
11. Suzan Herskowitz Singer, *Attorney Responsibilities & Client Rights: Your Legal Guide to the Attorney-Client Relationship* 44 (2003).
12. 42 U.S.C. §12205 (2013).

13. *See, e.g., Melnick v. Press*, No. 06-CV-6686 (JFB) (ARL), 2009 U.S. Dist. LEXIS 77609 (E.D.N.Y. Aug. 28, 2009).

14. Kate T. Hlava, *A Survey of Recent Illinois Ethics Law: Professionalism in Practice*, 33 S. Ill. U. L.J. 23, 38 (Fall 2008).

15. IOLTA.org, *IOLTA History,* http://www.iolta.org/grants/item.IOLTA_History (last visited Sept. 11, 2013).

16. Martha Neil, *Ex-administrator Gets Over 10 Years in $1M Law Firm Theft; All but $237K Was Recovered,* ABA J. online (Aug. 6, 2013), http://www.abajournal.com/news /article/ex-administrator_gets_over_10_years_in_1m_law_firm_theft_all_but_237k_ was/.

17. Mary E. Vandenack, *Preventing Theft and Fraud Within Your Law Firm,* 39(5) Law Practice online (Sept./Oct. 2013), http://www.americanbar.org/publications/law_ practice_magazine/2013/september-october/finance.html.

18. Press Release, U.S. Attorney's Office, Northern District of Georgia, *Atlanta Attorney Admits Stealing More Than $300,000 from Law Firm Clients* (Aug. 14, 2013), *available at* http://www.fbi.gov/atlanta/press-releases/2013/atlanta-attorney-admits-stealing- more-than-300-000-from-law-firm-clients.

19. Leigh Jones, *Law Firms Make Easy Pickings for Embezzlers,* Nat'l L.J., June 8, 2009, *available at* http://www.nlj.com.

20. *Id.*

10

File Management

Chapter Outcomes

By the end of this chapter, a student will be able to:

- Set up a new client file
- Establish and operate a filing system
- Draft a file retention policy
- Develop a file-destruction plan
- Write a conflict-of-interest waiver

Even a sole practitioner needs a system for accessing client files. Papers—or computer files—can quickly become voluminous and disorganized in offices both large and small. Paralegals and legal secretaries may need to pull information from the files. Without a system for organizing and maintaining the files, a law office can quickly—and devastatingly—devolve into chaos. Lawyers tend to represent more than one client at a time, and any given client may have more than one **client matter**, a legal problem needing resolution. There may be files on the client's divorce, the client's will, the client's real estate transactions. All of this material—whether in paper or digital format—must be easily accessible when needed.

client matter:
A client's legal problem; the subject of a given law firm representation.

People within the firm who are responsible for handling and maintaining files must understand the office's filing methods so that documents can be quickly retrieved. For instance, should a business client named A Better Baker be filed under *A* or under *B*? How should a file with a client name 21st Century Gold be placed? Under *T* for 21? Suppose a client is a real estate developer and the firm handles transactions for a number of different properties. Should client matters be filed under street number? Under the name of the street? Under the name of the apartment complex? Should all clients be assigned unique numbers and their materials filed by number?

Unless the firm has established a system, lawyers and others in the office may have difficulty accessing information when they most need it. Similarly, unless someone regularly maintains the files, client information will soon be in disarray. The potential for mayhem only increases as the law firm expands and more people need authorized access to information in files. When law firms merge, consideration must be given to how files will be handled and how different filing systems will be managed. Plans for turning over files either to clients or to another practitioner should be in place in case a law firm dissolves.

A.   Opening a New File

Whenever a prospective client comes into the office for a consultation, a file on that person or business should be created, or "opened," even if the client ultimately opts to use another firm or declines to be represented for any other reason. Meeting notes should be placed in the file. A client intake form should be completed, and a conflict of interest check should be conducted. A sample client intake form is shown in Figure 10-1. Information identified on the form, such as names of prospective witnesses and names of people affiliated with the prospective client, should be entered electronically into a database so potential conflicts can be easily identified, especially if future prospective clients list some of the same names.

If the prospective client wishes to retain the firm, or whenever a current client wishes to hire the firm to handle a new matter, a conflict of interest check must be performed. If a conflict is identified, a waiver of the conflict of interest might need to be obtained before the firm can represent the prospective client. If a conflict cannot be overcome, then the firm will be unable to represent the prospective client. In any event, a record should be kept of what transpired. A record that a conflict of interest search was initiated must be established, and the outcome of that search and any further action taken properly recorded. To initiate conflict of interest searches, a conflict of interest search form should be completed (see Figure 10-2).

Conflicts of interest can easily arise, as illustrated in the following case.

FIGURE 10-1
Sample Client Intake Form

CLIENT INTAKE FORM

Name: _____

Other names known as: _____

Home address: _____

Work address: _____

Where should bills and other correspondence be sent? _____

Phone numbers:

Office: _____ Cell: _____ Home: _____

Email_____
_____

Is your e-mail address a work e-mail address, or a personal e-mail address? _____
_____

How would you like us to correspond with you? Specify by order of preference.

E-mail

Call (specify number)

Text (specify number)

Employer: _____

Occupation: _____

Driver's license (state and number): _____

Social Security number: _____

Insurance information: _____

Name of insurance agent: _____

Type of insurance: _____

Policy number: _____

Why are you seeking legal advice?
_____

Are there any other parties involved?
_____

Name _____

Relationship _____

Have you been served with any papers in this case?
_____

What documents do you have concerning this case?
_____

Are there any witnesses to this case?
_____

What would you like to have happen?
_____

What is the urgency of this matter?
_____

Have you consulted other lawyers about taking this case?
_____

How did you learn about this law firm?
_____

If from a referral, obtain name and contact information.
_____

DATE: _____

ATTORNEY: _____

FIGURE 10-2
Sample Conflict of Interest Search Form

CONFLICT OF INTEREST SEARCH FORM

Client Number/Matter Number: _____

Client Name: _____

Address: _____

For individual clients:

Identify name of client, name of businesses owned by client, name of client's spouse, any other names client has been known by, name of businesses in which client is an executive, a shareholder, a principal, a partner, or a director.

_____

_____

For corporate clients:

Identify affiliates, parent companies, names of executive officers, shareholders who own more than 10 percent of stock, partners, and directors.

_____

_____

Lenders: Identify the name of client lenders if pertinent.

_____

Adverse parties: Identify all potential adverse parties.

_____

Conflict of interest search undertaken by _____

Date: _____

Attorney assigned to matter: _____

Date search results provided to attorney: _____

Abubakar v. County of Solano
No. Civ. S-06-2268 LKK/EFB, 2008 U.S. Dist. LEXIS 12173
(E.D. Cal. Feb. 4, 2008)

JUDGES: LAWRENCE K. KARLTON, SENIOR JUDGE
OPINION BY: LAWRENCE K. KARLTON

OPINION

ORDER
This is a Fair Labor Standards Act (FLSA) action for uncompensated over-time wages and other relief brought by various correctional officers against their employer, Solano County. Plaintiffs have filed a motion to disqualify defendant's

attorneys, one of whom allegedly established an attorney-client relationship with nine of the plaintiffs in this action while representing the county in a separate suit. The court resolves the matter upon the parties' papers and after oral argument. For the reasons explained below, the court denies the motion.

I. BACKGROUND

This is an FLSA action filed in October 2006 by Solano County correctional officers. The complaint alleges that the county failed to pay overtime for certain pre- and post-shift activities. First Am. Compl. (FAC) P 1. At present, there are approximately 160 plaintiffs in the action. Mr. Terence Cassidy and Mr. John Whitefleet of the law firm of Porter Scott represent the county.

A. Events Giving Rise to Asserted Conflict of Interest

In April 2007, the county retained one of these same attorneys, Mr. Cassidy, to represent it in another action filed in this district, *Todd v. County of Solano,* No. 07-CV-726 FCD/EFB. Decl. of Terence Cassidy ("Cassidy Decl.") P 5. *Todd* is a currently pending class action arising from the strip search policies and practices of the Solano County Adult Jail.

In connection with that case, on October 10, 2007, Mr. Cassidy requested that the Sheriff's Department coordinate meetings with the officer-witnesses identified in the *Todd* defendants' mandatory initial disclosures. *Id.* P 6. The following day, on October 11, 2007, Mr. Cassidy met with a total of approximately fifteen officers. *Id.* P 8. He met with them in groups of four or five for approximately forty-five minutes to an hour and fifteen minutes each. *Id.*

During each meeting, Mr. Cassidy explained that he was representing the county in a lawsuit regarding its strip search policies and practices. *Id.* P 8. He also volunteered to represent the officers for the specific and limited purpose of defending them as witnesses in the *Todd* case and for purposes of depositions. *Id.* During the meetings, Mr. Cassidy and the officers discussed the operating procedures regarding strip searches of inmates at the main jail. *Id.* Not discussed, according to Mr. Cassidy, was this case, nor the officers' wages, overtime, or compensation. *Id.* P 9. In addition, Mr. Cassidy maintains that he did not obtain any information from the officers regarding strip searches that could not have been obtained through deposition. *Id.* P 8.

Of the approximately fifteen officers who met with Mr. Cassidy, nine were plaintiffs in this suit.

B. Events After Officer Meeting

Later in the day after the meetings had concluded, Mr. Cassidy realized for the first time that some of the officers with whom he had met might also be plaintiffs in this action. Cassidy Decl. P 10. Upon confirming that his suspicions were accurate, Mr. Cassidy immediately informed plaintiffs' counsel. *Id.* Both parties then conducted research on the ethical obligations under the circumstances. *Id.*

Approximately a week later, Mr. Cassidy wrote to each of the nine officers to inform them that he had "a conflict of interest in representing [them] as [] witness[es] in the *Todd* case." Carr Decl., Ex. C. This correspondence was copied to counsel. Cassidy Decl. P 11.

On November 6, 2007, plaintiffs sent Mr. Cassidy a written letter requesting that he (and all other Porter Scott attorneys, including Mr. Whitefleet) voluntarily recuse themselves from continued representation of the county in this action. *Id.,* Ex. A. Then, on November 12, 2007, plaintiffs contacted Mr. Whitefleet about potentially adding a new plaintiff. Decl. of John Whitefleet P 7. At that point, Mr. Whitefleet informed plaintiffs that given the recusal request, and in an abundance of caution, Porter Scott would not be conducting any further activity on the case. *Id.*

On November 15, 2007, Mr. Cassidy explained in writing the reasons why he felt that recusal was not required under the circumstances. Cassidy Decl., Ex. B. Plaintiffs did not respond to this correspondence; instead, on December 10, 2007, they inquired about the inspection of documents that had previously been scheduled for that date (before Mr. Cassidy's meeting with the nine officer plaintiffs). *Id.* P 9. Defendant stated that it would not produce documents because the conflict of interest issue appeared to remain pending. Carr Decl., Ex. D. Plaintiffs responded that defense counsel was improperly conditioning the production of documents, as well as its stipulation to add new plaintiffs, upon a waiver of the conflict of interest issue. Carr Decl. P 15.

Following this exchange, plaintiffs filed a motion to compel on December 18, 2007. The magistrate judge assigned to this case ruled that if the present motion to disqualify were denied, the county would have 30 days to produce the documents, and that if the present motion were granted, the county would have 30 days to produce the documents from the date it obtained new counsel.

II.   DISCUSSION

Motions to disqualify are decided under state law. *See In re County of Los Angeles,* 223 F.3d 990, 995 (9th Cir. 2000); L.R. 83-180(e) ("[T]he Rules of Professional Conduct of the State Bar of California . . . are hereby adopted as standards of professional conduct in this court."). Whether an attorney should be disqualified is within the discretion of the trial court. . . . Disqualification, however, is a drastic remedy that courts should hesitate to impose unless necessary. . . . An appearance of impropriety by itself is generally not sufficient to warrant disqualification. . . .

Here, plaintiffs argue that defense counsel violated two California Rules of Professional Conduct. First, plaintiffs maintain that defense counsel violated the rule against concurrent representation of adverse interests. *See* Cal. Rules of Prof'l Conduct 3-310(C) (stating that an attorney "shall not, without the informed written consent of each client . . . [r]epresent a client in a matter and at the same time in a separate matter accept as a client a person or entity whose interest in the first matter is adverse to the client in the first matter"). Second, plaintiffs contend that defense counsel violated the rule prohibiting ex parte contact with represented parties without consent. *See* Cal. Rules of Prof'l Conduct 2-100(A) (stating that an attorney "shall not communicate directly or indirectly about the subject of the representation with a party the member knows to be represented by another lawyer in the matter" without obtaining that lawyer's consent).

A. Waiver

As an initial matter, defendant argues that plaintiffs have waived any right to move to disqualify. In general, waiver occurs where one evinces the intention to relinquish a right, or engages in conduct so inconsistent with that right as to induce a reasonable belief that it has been relinquished. . . . "Implied waiver, especially where it is based on conduct manifestly inconsistent with the intention to enforce a known right, may be determined as a matter of law where the underlying facts are undisputed." *Oakland Raiders v. Oakland–Alameda County Coliseum, Inc.*, 144 Cal. App. 4th 1175, 1191, 51 Cal. Rptr. 3d 144 (2006).

Here, defendant argues that plaintiffs have impliedly waived the right to seek disqualification based upon their conduct. Specifically, defendant points to the fact that after plaintiffs' initial recusal request and defendant's response (on November 6 and 15, 2007, respectively), plaintiffs did not pursue the conflict issue any further but instead pressed forward with its request for production of documents (on December 10, 2007). In defendant's view, it is inconsistent to argue that there has been an ethical violation warranting disqualification but then demand that defense counsel continue litigating the case.

Plaintiffs, on the other hand, maintain that unless the very utterance of an ethical objection operates as an automatic stay of all proceedings, Mr. Cassidy and Mr. Whitefleet still had a continuing duty to represent the county, which included responding to discovery requests. In addition, plaintiffs contend that their conduct has been no more inconsistent than defendant's position that there has been no ethical violation but that it has no obligation to honor its discovery obligations pending a resolution of the ethical objections.

. . .

Throughout this entire dispute, plaintiffs consistently maintained the position that they were not waiving the conflict of interest issue—and defendant was aware of this fact. Given this context, plaintiffs' conduct in pressing forward with discovery would not induce a reasonable belief that plaintiffs were relinquishing their rights. More fundamentally, the conduct at issue—a request for production of documents—is not sufficiently clear to constitute implied waiver. . . . This is not a case, for example, where a party knowingly refrained from raising a grounds for disqualification, . . . or where a party unreasonably delayed in raising the objection. . . . Rather, plaintiffs timely expressed their opinion that defense counsel should be disqualified from this action. Accordingly, the court finds that plaintiffs have not waived the right to bring the present motion.

B. Conflict of Interest

1. *Concurrent Versus Successive Adverse Representations*

Turning to the merits, plaintiffs first argue that Mr. Cassidy created a conflict of interest by representing clients with adverse interests: the county, in this action, and the officers, in *Todd*. Conflicts of interest may arise in one of two ways. First, an attorney may successively represent clients with adverse interests.

Flatt v. Superior Court, 9 Cal. 4th 275, 283, 36 Cal. Rptr. 2d 537, 885 P.2d 950 (1994). Under those circumstances, the chief fiduciary value at jeopardy is that of confidentiality. Accordingly, the legally relevant question is whether there is a substantial relationship between the former and subsequent representations; if so, access to confidential information by the attorney in the course of the first representation is presumed and disqualification in the second representation is required. *Id.* at 283.

Second, an attorney's duty of loyalty may be violated when he or she simultaneously represents clients with adverse interests, which is what plaintiffs contend happened here. Under this second set of circumstances, the chief fiduciary value at stake is not one of confidentiality but that of loyalty. *Id.* at 284 ("The primary value at stake in cases of simultaneous or dual representation is the attorney's duty—and the client's legitimate expectation—of loyalty, rather than confidentiality."). Accordingly, there is no requirement that the two representations be substantially related. Instead, unless an exception applies,[1] "the rule of disqualification in simultaneous representation cases is a per se or 'automatic' one." *Id.* at 285. Merely converting a present client into a former client is, under the aptly-named "hot potato rule," insufficient to cure the conflict. *Id.* at 288.

2.   Existence of Attorney-Client Relationship

In analyzing the conflict of interest issue, the initial question that must be answered is whether Mr. Cassidy formed an attorney-client relationship with the nine plaintiff officers during the meeting.[2] *See Civil Service Comm. v. Superior Court,* 163

---

[1] These exceptions include instances where an attorney "immediately withdraws from an unseen concurrent adverse representation which occurs by 'mere happenstance,'" *Florida Ins. Guaranty Assn. v. Carey Canada, Inc.,* 749 F. Supp. 255, 261 (S.D. Fla. 1990), and where the attorney played no role in creating the conflict of interest, such as when a corporate client is acquired by another company. . . . Also, as contemplated by the text of Rule 3-310(C), no disqualification is required where there is informed written consent by both clients. Cal. Rules of Prof'l Conduct 3-310(C). . . .
. . . I need not reach the issue of whether an exception applies given that I ultimately conclude that no attorney-client relationship was formed for conflict of interest purposes. . . .

[2] Not all courts have framed this requirement in terms of whether an attorney-client relationship has been formed. For example, other courts have required "standing" to bring disqualification motions, which is conferred by "a breach of the duty of confidentiality owed to the complaining party, regardless of whether a lawyer-client relationship existed." *DCH Health Services Corp. v. Waite,* 95 Cal. App. 4th 829, 832, 115 Cal. Rptr. 2d 847 (2002) (noting that a lawyer may be disqualified after improper contacts with an opposing party's expert witness); *see also Am. Airlines v. Sheppard, Mullin, Richter, & Hampton,* 96 Cal. App. 4th 1017, 1033-34, 117 Cal. Rptr. 2d 685 (2002) (holding that conflict may arise from an attorney's relationship with a non-client where confidential information has been disclosed or there is an expectation that the attorney owes a duty of fidelity); *Colyer v. Smith,* 50 F. Supp. 2d 966, 971 (C.D. Cal. 1999) (holding that non-clients have standing to raise serious ethical breaches). The difference in approach, however, is oftentimes "largely semantic." *Dino v. Pelayo,* 145 Cal. App. 4th 347, 353, 51 Cal. Rptr. 3d 620 (2006) (finding that so long as "some sort of confidential or fiduciary relationship" existed, disqualification motion is proper).

Cal. App. 3d 70, 76–77, 209 Cal. Rptr. 159 (1984) ("Before an attorney may be disqualified . . . because his representation . . . is adverse to the interest of a current or former client, it must first be established that the party seeking the attorney's disqualification was or is 'represented' by the attorney in a manner giving rise to an attorney-client relationship.").

Under the California Supreme Court's decision in *SpeeDee Oil,* the formation of an attorney-client relationship for conflict of interest purposes turns on "whether and to what extent the attorney acquired confidential information." *People ex rel. Dept. of Corporations v. SpeeDee Oil Change Systems, Inc.,* 20 Cal. 4th 1135, 1148, 86 Cal. Rptr. 2d 816, 980 P.2d 371 (1999). "An attorney represents a client—for purposes of a conflict of interest analysis—when the attorney knowingly obtains material confidential information from the client and renders legal advice or services as a result." *Id.* When one seeking legal advice consults with an attorney and secures that advice, an attorney-client relationship is presumed. *Id.* An attorney-client relationship may be formed even when the conversation between the lawyer and client is brief, or where there has been no fee agreement or retainer. *Id.*

As noted above, the primary fiduciary value at stake in concurrent representation cases is that of loyalty rather than confidentiality, but the court must nevertheless consider whether Mr. Cassidy obtained confidential information for the limited purpose of ascertaining whether an attorney-client relationship was formed.[3] Plaintiffs have submitted the declarations of two of the nine officers who met with Mr. Cassidy. Both officers declared that the discussion with Mr. Cassidy at the October 11, 2007 meeting "generally involved the operating procedures regarding strip-searches of inmates in the jails." Decl. of David Holsten ("Holsten Decl.") P 6; Decl. of Thomas Schlemmer ("Schlemmer Decl.") P 6. They also stated that Mr. Cassidy discussed the general aspects of a deposition. Holsten Decl. P 7; Schlemmer Decl. P 7. Neither officer, however, stated that they divulged confidential information. Mr. Cassidy has also affirmed that the officers did not disclose confidential information, and that he did not render any legal advice during the meeting. Cassidy Decl. P 8. Plaintiffs respond that the nine officers had a reasonable belief that Mr. Cassidy was their attorney, based on both his verbal promise to represent them as witnesses, as well as his subsequent letter terminating any attorney-client relationship with the officers. Carr Decl., Ex. C ("[W]e hereby withdraw our representation of you as a witness in the *Todd* case."). But the "reasonableness" of their beliefs ultimately turns on a question of law: when is an attorney-client relationship formed for conflict of interest purposes? Under *SpeeDee Oil,* the answer is whenever confidential information is disclosed. Here, the silence of the officer declarations on that issue is telling. While certainly not dispositive, the short length of the meetings (approximately

---

[3] This initial focus on whether confidential information has been disclosed is therefore somewhat anomalous. Nevertheless, the relationship between an attorney and a client must mature to a sufficiently serious stage before courts will intervene to protect a would-be client's trust in his or her attorney — particularly with the harsh remedy of disqualification. The disclosure of confidential information may not be a perfect barometer of that maturation, but it is not an irrational line to draw. In any event, this court is bound to follow the California Supreme Court's holding in *SpeeDee Oil.*

one hour), combined with the fact that Mr. Cassidy did most of the talking, also supports the inference that no confidential information was disclosed.[4]

Moreover, the court's present finding dovetails with the practical reality that any harm suffered by plaintiffs is likely minimal. Even if the nine officers believed that Mr. Cassidy was their attorney, Mr. Cassidy disabused them of this belief a week later when he sent his letter. This absence of practical harm is juxtaposed against the serious consequences that would flow from disqualification, including financial burdens on the county and interference with its choice of counsel.

Accordingly, the count finds that plaintiffs never formed an attorney-client relationship with Mr. Cassidy for conflict of interest purposes.

C.   Ex Parte Contacts

Plaintiffs next argue that Mr. Cassidy violated the rule against communicating with a represented party without the consent of that party's lawyer. Cal. Rules of Prof'l Conduct 2-100(A) ("While representing a client, a member shall not communicate directly or indirectly about the subject of the representation with a party the member knows to be represented by another lawyer in the matter, unless the member has the consent of the other lawyer.").

Here, both officers have stated that strip searches were performed "prior to and/or immediately after the end of the scheduled work shift without compensation" and that strip searches constitute part of their overtime claim in this action. Schlemmer Decl. P 11; Holsten Decl. P 11. Curiously, there is no allegation in the complaint that the plaintiffs conducted strip searches as part of their uncompensated overtime work.[5] *See* FAC PP 38-39 (discussing pre- and post-shift activities, such as obtaining assignment information, gathering paperwork, logging in/out of computers, returning keys, and briefings). Nevertheless, plaintiffs need not recite every single fact in support of their claims, *see* Fed. R. Civ. P. 8 (requiring only a "short and plain statement of the claim"), and the present complaint can be fairly read to encompass strip searches.

Mr. Cassidy's October 11, 2007 meeting therefore violated the rule against ex parte communication. But, given that his communication was obviously inadvertent, and that no confidential information was disclosed during this contact, the harsh penalty of disqualification would not be appropriate.

Generally, disqualification for ex parte communication is only appropriate where the misconduct will be certain to have "continuing effect" on the judicial proceedings. *See Marcum v. Channel Lumber Co.,* No. 94-2637, 1995 U.S. Dist. LEXIS 3799, 1995 WL 225708, at *2 (N.D. Cal. Mar. 24, 1995); *Chronometrics, Inc. v. Sysgen, Inc.,* 110 Cal. App. 3d 597, 607, 168 Cal. Rptr. 196 (1980). Here,

---

[4] Although plaintiffs argue that the exchange of confidential information may be presumed where the two actions are substantially related, *Civil Service Commn.,* 163 Cal. App. 3d at 79, that is not the case here, *see infra* n.5, and this presumption applies in successive as opposed to concurrent adverse representation cases.

[5] Although the court need not resolve the issue of whether there was a substantial relationship between Mr. Cassidy's representation of the county in this action and his brief representation of the officers in *Todd,* the omission of any mention of strip searches in the complaint in this case would counsel against such a finding.

plaintiffs argue that they are prejudiced by virtue of the fact that Mr. Cassidy had the opportunity to examine the credibility of the nine officer plaintiffs. They contend that where an employer fails to record time and keep proper records, an employee's testimony is relevant to proving damages. *See, e.g., Brock v. Seto,* 790 F.2d 1446 (9th Cir. 1986). But this same credibility assessment can also be made during the course of depositions. *See Marcum,* 1995 U.S. Dist. LEXIS 3799, 1995 WL 225708, at *2. ("Nothing was discussed which could not have been learned through [] depositions."). More fundamentally, it does not rise to the level prejudice warranting disqualification.

III. Conclusion

For the reasons explained above, the motion to disqualify (Dock. No. 64) is DENIED.

IT IS SO ORDERED.

When a firm does take on a new client, a memo or form announcing that fact should be sent to the firm's managing partner, other lawyers who need to know about the representation, the attorneys responsible for handling the client's matter, and the firm's accounting office. Essentially, when a firm gets a new client, appropriate people must be informed so that the client is provided with the service he needs. The firm must also make sure that the client is billed for the services the firm provides and that the client pays for those services. None of this can happen unless information about the client is entered into the firm's filing and accounting systems.

B. Contents of Client Files

Lawyers might speak about "opening a new client file," but they really mean that a series of standard files are prepared whenever a new client retains the firm or a prospective client contacts the firm with a potential case. Although little more than the client intake form, the results of a conflict of interest search, and notes from meetings and conversations might be placed in a prospective client's file if that contact does not ultimately retain the firm, more information—and a greater number of files—is prepared for a new client or a new client matter.

The standard set of files to be prepared for any new client depends on the type of case involved—criminal, divorce, hazardous waste site cleanup, and so forth. A primary file on the client should contain basic information about the client and the terms of the firm's retention. Such a file would likely include basic information on a new client sheet stapled inside the file itself:

- Name and contact information for the client
- Date the matter was opened

- Date of any relevant statute of limitations
- Fee agreement terms
- Billing statement requirements
- Legal team information
  - Name of the originating attorney (attorney who brought the client to the firm)
  - Name of the lawyers assigned to work on the case
- Results of a conflict of interest check

This form would also contain an entry, to be filled in later, when a matter is closed, or concluded.

A copy of the engagement letter should also be included in the client file. The engagement letter itself might explain the firm's file retention policy. For instance, it may indicate that files will be returned to the client after a specified period of time, or that files are automatically destroyed after ten years.

During the course of representation, any number of actual file folders will be used. An index of files should be created. There may be standard hierarchy ones for all clients and for certain types of matters. For instance, a standard set of files for all clients might include:

- Attorney-Client Correspondence
- Third-Party Correspondence
- Meeting Notes

For an individual type of matter, standard files are also generated. For instance, for divorce, standard files created might be Court Documents, Mediation, Financial Information, Depositions, Transcripts, Settlement, Custody Agreement. Within each of those categories, there may be subcategories. For example, files might be labeled Court Documents–Complaint; Court Documents–Answer, Court Documents–Response, and so on. How many files, and how specifically each file is labeled, will depend on the size of the case and the scope of the representation. Original documents might be kept in specially labeled files and copies of those documents placed in other files as needed. Files on litigation might include a case cover sheet documenting the progress of the litigation, such as dates pleadings were filed, dates discovery was conducted, and dates of hearings and trials. Opposing parties and their lawyers might also be identified. These cover sheets are meant to make use of the file easier for the attorney, paralegal, or other employee who needs materials found in the files.

Materials in each file are typically filed in reverse chronological order, with the most recent document on top. All correspondence received by a law firm is logged, and the date a document is received is noted on the document, typically with the initials of the person who logged the document into the firm's master log.

C. File Management Systems

Files must be carefully maintained, both so clients can be serviced well by lawyers and because lawyers owe a duty of confidentiality to the client. A single client might generate hundreds of actual file folders within a law firm. Multiply that by 10 clients, or 100, or 1,000, and the potential for chaos is easy to understand. For that reason, careful attention must be paid to labeling and organizing files so that people who need them can retrieve them and have easy access to them. At the same time, though, files must be protected so that no one with unauthorized access views them.

1. Filing Conventions

As important as having a well-organized filing system is communicating the organization of that system to members of the law firm office who are responsible for maintaining and using the files. Ideally, training of law office personnel should be conducted periodically. At the very least, a written explanation of a firm's filing system should be maintained and distributed to employees who work with the files.

An **alphabetic filing system** is one in which files are stored alphabetically, by last name of individuals or by business name of corporate clients. In a **numerical filing system**, a unique number is assigned to each client and an additional number is assigned to each client matter. An **alphanumeric filing system** combines elements of both. For instance, a responsible attorney's initials might be included in a matter number, or an abbreviation for the type of matter involved might be included. An environmental matter might be slugged ENV; a criminal case might be labeled CRIM. Law firm personnel responsible for creating files must be aware of the firm's naming conventions. For ease of use, folders in which documents are stored might be assigned a unique color based on the type of matter or, if the law firm is small enough, the lawyer handling the case. Colored file labels might also be used for similar reasons.

A master list of files should be maintained, along with the opening and closing dates of the files, the storage location of the files, and the destruction date of the files.

Numbered files should be filed sequentially, first by client code and then by matter code. Firms using an alphabetic filing system should place files in alphabetical order. Files in firms using an alphanumeric system should have materials beginning with numbers, from lowest to highest, and then in alphabetical order. Files themselves are filed according to the "unit" on each file. For example, a file might be labeled *Bedford Bakery*. Unit 1 in this file is *Bedford*, and Unit 2 is *Bakery*. In a file labeled *3 Big Brothers Construction*, Unit 1 is *3*, Unit 2 is *Big*, Unit 3 is *Brothers*, and Unit 4 is *Construction*. Individuals are identified on files with last name first, so a client named Ada B. Codding would have a filed labeled *Codding, Ada B*. Unit 1 is *Codding*, Unit 2 is *Ada*, Unit 3 is *B*. These files would be placed in the following order in a filing cabinet:

3 Big Brothers Construction
Bedford Bakery
Codding, Ada B.

---

alphabetic filing system: A system in which files are stored alphabetically, by last name of individuals, or by business name of corporate clients.

numerical filing system: A system in which a unique number is assigned to each client and an additional number is assigned to each client matter.

alphanumeric filing system: A system that combines elements of both alphabetic and numerical filing systems.

In what order should the following files be placed?

Bedford Bakery
Laino, Victor Lorenzo
Laino, Victor L.
The Laino Group, Ltd.
A Smarter Vegan Frozen Foods
Heuess-Barber, Hadley
Heuess, Helen
Heuess Baker, Amara
Mt. Kisco Medical Associates
Mount Kisco Hospital
3 Big Brothers Construction
L. Tripoli & Sons
The George Washington University

A look at the list demonstrates the need for certain filing conventions. How should the word *The* be handled when it begins a company name? What if the word *A* begins the company name? What if a company's name includes an ampersand rather than the word *and*? Where should a file for a client with a hyphenated name be filed? If an organization's formal name includes an abbreviation, should a document be filed using the abbreviation or the complete word?

Many firms observe the following conventions:

- When an organization's name begins with the word *The*, file the material using the second word in the name. In creating a file label, the word *The* is placed at the end of the label, not the beginning: George Washington University, The
- When an organization's name begins with the word *A*, file under *A*.
- When an individual's name is included in an organization's name, file according to the first unit in the name: L. Tripoli & Sons is filed under *L*.
- When an organization's name includes an ampersand, file as if the word *and* appeared in place of the ampersand.
- When an organization's formal name includes an abbreviation, file according to the abbreviation.
- If a client's name is hyphenated, ignore the hyphen and treat the hyphenated name as a single unit.
- If a client's name begins with a numeral, such as *3*, file in numerical order if the firm uses an alphanumeric system. Files begin with 1, 2, 3, and then proceed to alphabetical order for clients whose names begin with letters. If the firm uses an alphabetical system, file in the appropriate place alphabetically. A client's name that begins with the numeral *3* is filed under the letter *T*.

With these conventions and following an alphanumeric system, the files in the list above should be placed in the following order using the file names given below:

3 Big Brothers Construction
A Smarter Vegan Frozen Foods
Bedford Bakery

George Washington University, The
Heuess Baker, Amara
Heuess, Helen
Heuess-Barber, Hadley
L. Tripoli & Sons
Laino, Victor L.
Laino, Victor Lorenzo
Laino Group, Ltd., The
Mount Kisco Hospital
Mt. Kisco Medical Associates

Ultimately, the filing conventions that any given firm uses will vary by firm. The important point is that conventions be established and effectively communicated. A firm might also adapt standard naming conventions to its own needs. For instance, a firm that handles a high volume of real estate transactions might organize the files according to the address of the building involved, such as 123 Park Avenue, 45 Cheswell Way, and so on. Naming conventions for files involving street addresses might be modified so that addresses with hyphenated numbers, such as 305-315 West 57 Street, are filed under the first number before the hyphen. File systems can be adapted to fit the needs of the law firm.

2.   *Storage and Tracking*

The location of files must be tracked so that a file can be easily found if someone needs to access it. Firms that have a **centralized file system** keep all their files in one file room. In a **decentralized file system**, files are placed in various locations in an office, such as with individual attorneys or specific departments. A decentralized file system is also referred to as a *local filing system*. However files are located and stored, their placement in certain areas must make sense for the law firm. An office map indicating where files are located should be created and posted at useful points throughout the firm.

Bar coding is a method in which files are tracked using a bar code assigned to each file. The bar code must be scanned into a computer when someone removes the file from the repository. The name of the person withdrawing the file is recorded in the computer as well, perhaps with a firm identification bar code assigned to that individual. Bar coding systems make tracking files easy. Reports can be generated indicating where various files are. Bar code systems can also be used for recording the time when someone begins work on a file. Even with a bar code system, a file should have a label indicating the file name (client number and matter number or client name and subject name of the file).

Even where bar coding is not used, a file checkout system must be established. Files might be signed out from a central repository, or large, brightly colored cards (similar to cards used to check out library books) might be inserted in the location from which the file was taken. The person who took the file records his or her name and location on the card along with the date the file was removed.

Paralegals are often responsible for maintaining files. They should never purge material from a file unless given explicit instructions from an attorney to do so. Even seeming irrelevant materials, such as scribbled-on sticky notes or

centralized file system:
An arrangement in which all the files are located in one file room.

decentralized file system:
Also called a local filing system, an arrangement in which files are in various locations in an office, such as with individual attorneys or specific departments.

bar coding:
A method that tracks files using a bar code assigned to each file.

handwritten pages, may contain something relevant for the lawyer working on the case.

Firms must establish procedures for marking documents to be placed in certain files. For instance, each lawyer might have a "To File" box that is regularly checked by a secretary or paralegal. Lawyers might write the client number and matter number on the top-right corner of a document along with the name of the file in which the document is to be placed.

Lawyers tend to like to have their frequently used materials around them. They don't want to have to walk up three floors to a central location to sign out a file. Typically, active files on which lawyers are regularly working are stored in or near their offices or near those of their secretaries. Active files that are not being worked on are stored in their designated storage area. When files are closed, they are typically deposited in a centralized location or moved off-site for longer-term storage.

Files are too voluminous to be maintained indefinitely. There's no real need to keep a file on-site for a client who saw the firm for a single matter ten years ago. Files for closed matters might be returned to the client or sent into storage at an off-site facility, and they might be destroyed after a certain number of years. Before a paper file is destroyed, though, a firm might opt to store digital copies of the materials in the file.

3. *Paperless Files*

Lawyers and those who work for them can appreciate the space-saving advantages of paperless files. If records are digitized rather than printed out on paper, far less office real estate needs to be dedicated to storing them. Digital files, which can be searched by name or by key word, provide easier access to attorneys, paralegals, and others within the office who need access to the materials. Electronic files might also be created as backups to paper files.

A firm must have a scanner to transfer paper files to digital form, typically a PDF, or portable document format. A firm should also establish conventions for retaining the originals of certain documents, such as contracts, wills, and deeds. These conventions might be modified as courts expand their willingness to accept electronic versions of certain materials.

Even if a firm still relies extensively on paper files for must client records, a number of computer files are generated as lawyers and others prepare documents related to a client's matter. For example, ten drafts of a document may be prepared before it is finalized.

A firm should establish protocols for naming digitized documents and newly created electronic files. In addition, the personnel who create such files may add appropriate key words to the metadata in these files so that the materials can be easily searched and retrieved. **Metadata** is information embedded in an electronic file about the creation and modification of that file. Examples of metadata are key words and dates that files were edited.

metadata:
Information embedded in an electronic file about the creation and modification of that file.

Although metadata is very useful for retrieving data, firms must also take care not to transmit such data when documents are provided to others outside the firm. Confidential information can sometimes be inadvertently transmitted in metadata. Metadata can be removed, or "scrubbed" from documents using software. Ethical rules on metadata and an attorney's obligation with respect to it vary by state.[1]

A firm must establish naming conventions for directories and files so that these materials can easily be retrieved by those in the firm who need them. For instance, a firm might determine that the date on each document must precede every file name within a client and matter file in a computer. A computerized version of a letter might be named as follows:

06062013 ltr fr LTripoli to VLaino

If the firm has procedures set up and educates its personnel on appropriate naming conventions, documents can be retrieved easier and more quickly.

4. File Ownership

If a client fires a lawyer, typically, the attorney has an obligation to provide the client's file to the client. State requirements vary, though, as to whether the file must be provided if the client still owes the lawyer money. Rule 1.15(a) of the ABA's *Model Rules of Professional Conduct* obligates lawyers to safeguard property that belongs to clients.

Some states allow lawyers to hold on to client files until their fees are paid. For instance, in Nevada, "an attorney who has been discharged by his client shall, upon demand and payment of the fee due from the client, immediately deliver to the client all papers, documents, pleadings and items of tangible personal property which belong to or were prepared for that client."[2]

Whether a client is entitled to the return of an entire file or only some of its contents also varies by state.[3]

A firm might prevent later disputes by including a standard file retention policy provision in its retainer agreement about the contents of files and the charges associated with maintaining files or returning them to the client. The policy should clearly specify when a firm will destroy files after a matter is closed. Whether a lawyer can charge a client to prepare and deliver the contents of the client's file varies by state.[4]

If a lawyer leaves a law firm, it should be clarified whether the lawyer or the original law firm is responsible for retaining the client files. A firm's employment or partnership agreement might clarify this, as might a retainer agreement with the client.[5] The client should be informed who is retaining the files.

5. Proper Disposal of Files

Whether paper or electronic, proper precautions must be taken to safely dispose of information marked for deletion in files. Sensitive materials could easily get into the wrong hands. Lawyers and people who work for them must take measures to ensure that confidential information is not disclosed inappropriately. Consider, for example, the following case.

Disciplinary Counsel v. Shaver
904 N.E.2d 883 (Ohio 2009)

JUDGES: MOYER, C.J., AND PFEIFER, LUNDBERG STRATTON, O'CONNOR, O'DONNELL, LANZINGER, AND CUPP, J.J., CONCUR.

OPINION
Per curiam.

Respondent, David Brian Shaver of Pickerington, Ohio, Attorney Registration No. 0036980, was admitted to the practice of law in Ohio in 1986. The Board of Commissioners on Grievances and Discipline recommends that we publicly reprimand respondent, based on findings that he failed to properly dispose of confidential client files and other materials, in violation of the Rules of Professional Conduct. We agree that respondent committed professional misconduct as found by the board and that a public reprimand is appropriate.

Relator, Disciplinary Counsel, charged that respondent had violated *Model Rules of Professional Conduct* Rules 1.6(a) (prohibiting, with exceptions not relevant here, a lawyer from revealing information relating to the representation of a client) and 1.9(c)(2) (prohibiting, with exceptions not relevant here, a lawyer who has formerly represented a client from revealing information relating to that representation). A panel of board members considered the case on the parties' stipulations, found the cited misconduct, and recommended the public reprimand proposed by the parties. The board adopted the panel's findings of misconduct and recommendation.

MISCONDUCT

At all times relevant to this case, respondent served as the mayor of Pickerington. In the spring of 2007, respondent moved his law office from a Columbus Street location to another location in that city. He continued to lease the garage behind the Columbus Street address, storing an estimated 500 boxes of records in that space on a month-to-month basis.

In late June 2007, the owner of the Columbus Street property sold the garage and advised respondent to remove the records from it. The new owner and her tenant took possession shortly thereafter and immediately began preparing the space for their businesses. In early July 2007, respondent brought a crew to assist him in removing the many boxes. He took some boxes with him, placing them in a moving truck; but he put some boxes in a nearby dumpster and left approximately 20 other boxes beside the dumpster.

The new tenant, who had worked as a paralegal for a law office, had misgivings about the propriety of respondent's disposal method. She examined the contents of several of the boxes left by the dumpster and realized that they contained client materials including confidential information. Concerned that those boxes might not be taken away with the others in the dumpster and that client confidences might be compromised, the tenant and her husband returned them to the garage later that evening.

Upon receiving notice that respondent had left not only the boxes of client records but also furniture and computers in the garage, the former owner paid to have those items hauled away. Neither of the property owners nor the new tenant contacted respondent again about his failure to remove all the contents of the garage. An anonymous tipster, however, contacted a television station about the incident, and the tip led to television news and newspaper stories.[1]

Respondent admitted that he failed to ensure the proper disposal of client files, records, and related materials. The panel and board thus found him in violation of *Model Rules of Professional Conduct* Rules 1.6(a) and 1.9(c)(2). We accept these findings of misconduct.

SANCTION

In recommending a sanction for this misconduct, the panel and board weighed the aggravating and mitigating factors of respondent's case. See BCGD Proc. Reg. 10(B). The panel and board found no aggravating factors. Mitigating factors were respondent's history of public service and the absence of a prior disciplinary record. See BCGD Proc. Reg. 10(B)(2)(a).

We accept the board's recommendation of a public reprimand. Respondent is hereby publicly reprimanded for his violations of *Model Rules of Professional Conduct* Rules 1.6(a) and 1.9(c)(2). Costs are taxed to respondent.

Judgment accordingly.

---

[1] A television reporter took two boxes of files to her office for the story but has since turned them over to relator.

To properly dispose of papers, a firm might purchase a shredder. Originals of some documents may be returned to the client. To properly scrub, or delete, electronic records, a firm might need to hire an information technology consultant to ascertain that material is permanently deleted and cannot be retrieved.

Checklist

- A client may retain a law firm to handle more than one matter.
- Materials relevant to a client's representation are stored in a client file, which may be in paper format, digital format, or some mix of the two.
- Files must be properly maintained, organized, and easily retrievable.
- A new file is opened for prospective clients and when current clients hire the firm to handle an additional matter. Conflicts of interest checks must be performed whenever a prospective client wishes to hire the firm and when a current client asks the firm to handle an additional matter.

- A record that a conflict of interest search was initiated must be established, and the outcome of that search and any further action taken properly recorded.
- A firm might be able to obtain a waiver from a client who presents a conflict of interest.
- A standard set of files should be prepared for each new client.
- Given the vast number of documents that can be generated for a single client, a firm must have a file management system in place. Files must be labeled and organized so that they are easily retrievable.
- Numbered files should be filed sequentially, first by client code and then by matter code. Firms that use an alphabetic filing system place files in alphabetical order. Firms that use an alphanumeric system file materials beginning with numbers, from lowest to highest, and then in alphabetical order. Files themselves are filed according to each "unit" on the file.
- Files for closed matters may be returned to the client or put in storage at an off-site facility, and they may eventually be destroyed after a certain number of years. Before destroying a paper file, a firm might opt to store digital copies of the materials in the file.
- Digital files, which can be searched by name or by key word, can provide easier access to attorneys, paralegals, and others in the office who need the materials. Electronic files might also be created as backups to paper files.
- Although metadata is useful to lawyers and others as they retrieve and use electronic files, precautions should be taken to remove such data, as appropriate, so that confidential information is not inadvertently disclosed to outsiders when electronic documents are disseminated outside the firm.
- Lawyers who are fired by clients generally have an obligation to give the client's file back to the client. Some states allow lawyers to hold on to client files until their fees are paid.
- The firm's file retention policy should be provided to clients in the retainer agreement. The policy should clearly specify when a firm will destroy files after a matter is closed.
- Model Rule 1.15(a) obligates lawyers to safeguard property that belongs to clients.
- Whether files are paper or electronic, proper precautions must be taken to safely dispose of information marked for deletion in files.

Vocabulary

alphabetic filing system
(p. 265)

alphanumeric filing system
(p. 265)

bar coding (p. 267)

centralized file system (p. 267)

client matter (p. 253)

decentralized file system
(p. 267)

metadata (p. 268)

numerical filing system
(p. 265)

Career Preparation Tips

File management really depends on good organization. Develop and enhance your own organizational skills by applying some of the concepts learned in this chapter to your personal life. You might practice scrubbing metadata from personally created documents and set up naming and filing conventions for your own personal documents and records. Consider how different versions of the same documents should be named. Focus, too, on easy, quick retrievability of documents.

If You Want to Learn More

International Legal Technology Association. http://www.iltanet.org

Legal files case and matter management software. http://www.legalfiles.com/

PDF for Lawyers is a blog about PDFs. http://www.pdfforlawyers.com

The American Bar Association's Model Rules of Professional Conduct are accessible online. http://www.americanbar.org/groups/professional_responsibility/publications/model_rules_of_professional_conduct/model_rules_of_professional_conduct_table_of_contents.html

Reading Comprehension

1. When must a client intake form be filled out?
2. If a firm identifies a conflict of interest after conducting a search, what should the firm do?
3. Read the excerpt from *Abubakar v. County of Solano*. Why did the plaintiffs in the case believe a lawyer representing the defendant had a conflict of interest? Did the court agree that there was a conflict of interest? How might the lawyer have avoided litigation over this alleged conflict of interest?
4. Prepare file name labels for each of the clients listed here, and then place the file names in alphabetical order:

> Pinky Ring Jewelers, Co.
> Pink Moon Dust Paper Products
> Pinkmoondust Petroleum
> Pink Moon, Inc.
> Pink, Moon & Rainbow
> A Pink Moon
> Leon A. "Pinky" Pink
> Priscilla Pink
> Patty-Ann Pink Potter
> Patricia Pink
> Patrick B. Pink
> Amy Pink-Fink
> Amy Pink Fasselback
> Amy Jo Pinfass
> Pink Holding Corp.
> The Pink and Blue Babywear Co.
> Pink & Blue Baby Bottles, Inc.
> Leon A. "Pinky" Pink, Jr.
> Leon A. "Pinky" Pink, III
> Leon A. "Pinky" Pink, IV
> Lori World
> Lori's World Roller Rink
> The World of Lori Stationery Co.
> Lori Wayne
> Lorri Wade
> L'Ree Wooster
> L. R. Wooster-Brewster
> Lawrence Wooster-Brewster
> Lorenzo Wooster-Brewster
> Lauri Wooster Brewster
> Lorri B. Wooster
> Lori Wooster Brewster
> City of Wooster

Pink House Trailer Park
Little Pink Houses Toy Co.
Pinkerton Fire Arms
Pickled Pink Plateware Corp.
A Pinker Pink Party House
The Pink Family Trust

What filing conventions did you use in ordering the files?

5. Under what circumstances should files be destroyed?

Discussion Starters

1. Review the client intake form in Figure 10-1. How might this form be improved?
2. Consider the case of *Disciplinary Counsel v. Shaver*. Why was the lawyer involved in the controversy being professionally disciplined? How might that lawyer have avoided the situation? What impact might the disciplinary proceeding have had on the lawyer's client base? If you had hired that lawyer to work on one of your matters and you found out about the disciplinary action, what would you do? What would you tell your friends and colleagues about the lawyer? What impact do you suppose this disciplinary proceeding had on the lawyer's practice? Ultimately, the lawyer was just publicly reprimanded. Does that seem to imply that improper disposal of client records is not a significant infraction?
3. What set of standard files should be prepared for the following?

   a personal bankruptcy case?
   a closing on a house for an individual client?
   an immigration case involving deportation?
   a landlord-tenant dispute?
   a car accident case?

4. Create a one-page filing conventions sheet to be posted by each filing station in a law firm. The sheet should identify the 25 most significant filing conventions used by the firm.
5. Research your jurisdiction's ethical rules on metadata in electronic files. How can a lawyer in your jurisdiction take care not to violate rules on metadata?
6. Research language that should be included in a file retention policy. Craft an appropriate file retention provision for inclusion in a retainer agreement that complies with professional conduct rules in your jurisdiction.
7. Look up a recent legal decision or disciplinary action involving an attorney conflict of interest. Consider whether and how a better file management system might have prevented the problem from arising.

Case Studies

1. Cynthia Smith wants to retain your firm to handle her divorce from Mark Jones. A conflict of interest search reveals that, 15 years ago, the firm represented Mark Jones's business partner in a civil suit brought against the partner stemming from a car accident he'd had during nonbusiness hours. Does this pose a conflict of interest for the firm? Why or why not? Suppose the firm had represented the business partner in a divorce proceeding. Would a conflict of interest exist then?

2. Mariel Carter and Jennifer Hayes wish to hire your firm to incorporate their business, Sew Little Time, a yarn retailer. Your firm represents the landlord of the building where their yarn shop is located. The landlord is the defendant in a criminal case in which he was charged with driving while intoxicated. Does the representation of the landlord prevent the firm from representing Carter and Hayes? Draft a letter from the firm asking the landlord to waive any conflict of interest.

3. You work for a ten-lawyer, single-office law firm in your state, and you have been charged with drafting the firm's file destruction policy. What factors should be considered before files are destroyed? How should files be destroyed?

4. Research shredders and their capacities and abilities, and make recommendations about which one to purchase for a sole practitioner.

5. Your firm must either place 2,000 boxes of documents in off-site storage or create electronic images of all the documents. Compare and contrast the merits of each option, including the costs. Which do you recommend? Why?

6. You are a paralegal at a law firm charged with maintaining client files. You realize you just accidentally shredded the last will and testament of a firm client, who died last week. What do you do?

7. Suppose you are a paralegal at a law firm that represents a famous singer. A reporter for a major newspaper calls you and asks whether the firm represents the singer. You explain that you cannot disclose whether or not the firm represents the singer. The reporter then says that she found a copy of the singer's recording contract in a trash bin in your office building and wants to confirm that the singer will earn $10 million for her next album. What should you say?

Endnotes

1. *See, e.g.,* ABA Law Practice Division Legal Technology Resource Center, *Metadata Ethics Opinions Around the U.S., available at* http://www.americanbar.org/groups /departments_offices/legal_technology_resources/resources/charts_fyis/metadatachart .html (last visited Sept. 13, 2013).
2. Nev. Rev. Stat. Ann. §7.055(1) (2013).
3. *See, e.g.,* Maine Board of Overseers of the Bar, Opinion #187 (Nov. 5, 2004), http://www.maine.gov/tools/whatsnew/index.php?topic=mebar_overseers_ethics_ opinions&id=89446&v=article.
4. *See, e.g., Sage Realty Corp. v. Proskauer Rose Goetz & Mendelsohn LLP,* 9 N.Y.2d 30, 38 (1997).
5. *See, e.g.,* Maine Board of Overseers of the Bar, Opinion #201 (Nov. 1, 2010), http://www.maine.gov/tools/whatsnew/index.php?topic=mebar_overseers_ethics_ opinions&id=152001&v=article.

11

Docket Management

Chapter Outcomes

By the end of this chapter, a student will be able to:

- Explain calendaring
- Specify information needed to make a calendar entry
- Identify ethical implications of incompetent docket management
- Understand and apply different methods for determining deadlines
- Compare and contrast features of different case management programs

A law firm should have a system in place for tracking and overseeing each case that the firm is involved in on behalf of a client. Lawyers must appear in court, at depositions, in conferences, at informal meetings. Sometimes, they need the additional support of paralegals or others in a law firm. Of course, activities involving litigation are not the only ones lawyers are involved in. They are also working on other matters not necessarily destined for court—contracts, mergers and acquisitions, compliance counseling, commenting on proposed regulations, and so on. Without a procedure in place to track who is doing what, where, when, and by what deadline, a firm's business can easily become chaotic given the number of clients, client matters, and professional activities with which lawyers and support staff are involved.

A. Calendaring

master calendar:
A calendar on which important dates for an entire law firm are recorded.

At the very least, a firm should have a **master calendar** listing all of the litigation-related activities (such as filing deadlines and hearing dates) scheduled for lawyers and staff at the firm. Some firms also track other important client events that are not involved in litigation, such as real estate closings, deadlines for submitting comments on proposed rulemakings, and the like. Reminders about upcoming due dates should also be entered in a calendar.

> Calendar systems provide lawyers with advance notice of due dates for matters requiring legal action. The advance notice is provided by "ticklers" that identify that an action date is approaching. The "tickler" can be preset to the amount and frequency of notices, i.e., a single (e.g., 10 day or 7 day) notice or multiple (e.g., 30 day, 7 day, 1 day) notices. Calendar systems help insure that the lawyer's attention and the client's file are brought together sufficiently in advance of the date action is required so that a conscientious lawyer does not fail to do the work. Calendar systems cannot ensure good work, but they permit lawyers the opportunity to do good work through appropriate time management. Not surprisingly, insurers are true believers in the efficacy of calendaring, and it is inconceivable that a policy would be written today for a firm that did not have a calendaring system and trained personnel and office procedures to insure that it is implemented properly.[1]

calendaring:
The act of recording important information on a calendar.

As simple as **calendaring** seems to be, about one-sixth of malpractice claims are attributable to calendar, deadline, and time-management mistakes.[2] Consider the following case involving a single attorney.

Daniels v. Sacks
No. E041543, 2008 Cal. App. Unpub. LEXIS 6316
(Cal. Ct. App. July 29, 2008)

JUDGES: GAUT, J.; MCKINSTER, ACTING P. J., MILLER, J. CONCURRED.
OPINION BY: GAUT

OPINION

Defendant Dennis Michael Sacks appeals a default judgment entered on May 31, 2006, in favor of plaintiff Clifford R. Daniels in the amount of $228,896.52. Defendant, an attorney who represented himself in this matter, contends the trial court abused its discretion in denying his motions to set aside the default judgment. He claims default was entered due to defendant's and his staff's inadvertence.

We conclude there was no abuse of discretion in denying defendant's motions to set aside default. . . . We affirm the judgment.

Unless otherwise noted, all statutory references are to the Code of Civil Procedure.

FACTUAL AND PROCEDURAL BACKGROUND

On November 16, 2004, plaintiff filed a complaint for damages against defendant. The complaint contained the following causes of actions: (1) negligence—legal malpractice; (2) intentional breach of fiduciary duty; (3) negligent breach of fiduciary duty; and (4) unjust enrichment.

Plaintiff alleged in his complaint that he and defendant entered into an agreement, which was partially oral and partially written, whereby defendant was to provide plaintiff with legal services consisting of recovering proceeds due plaintiff from a foreclosure trustee company, after the foreclosure sale of plaintiff's home. Plaintiff further alleges defendant committed legal malpractice and breached his fiduciary duty owed to plaintiff by not disclosing to plaintiff that the trustee was required to release to plaintiff those funds from the foreclosure sale of plaintiff's home that exceeded the mortgage and liens on plaintiff's home. Defendant charged plaintiff an unconscionable fee for legal services since recovery of the funds was certain and required very little work. By not disclosing this to plaintiff, defendant allegedly tricked plaintiff into executing an unconscionable contingency fee agreement. Defendant was thus unjustly enriched in the amount of at least $40,000 paid for legal fees.

Plaintiff further alleged in his complaint that in a separate matter defendant agreed to defend plaintiff in an unlawful detainer action, arising from plaintiff renting back his foreclosed home from the new owner for 60 days after the foreclosure. Defendant negligently defended plaintiff in the unlawful detainer action by failing to obtain a rental agreement in writing, which resulted in plaintiff being locked out of his home.

Defendant failed to file a timely answer to plaintiff's first amended complaint. Accordingly, plaintiff filed a request for entry of default, which the trial court entered on April 29, 2005.

On May 4, 2005, defendant filed a motion to set aside entry of default. Defendant's notice of motion stated the motion was brought under section 473.1 and was based on surprise, mistake or excusable neglect. Defendant attached his own nonsensical declaration stating, "Counsel for Plaintiff inadvertently missed the deadline to respond to defendant's Cross-Complaint, but has moved quickly to correct the error so that no prejudice should have occurred as to Defendant. [P] Plaintiff has attached his proposed Answer to Cross-Complaint clearly indicating a probability of successfully defeating t[sic], other than where both Complaint and Cross-Complaint are seeking virtually the same causes and the same results as to the Dissolution of Partnership, Partition of Real Estate, and Accounting."

On June 13, 2005, the trial court denied defendant's first motion without prejudice to defendant refiling his motion, noting the motion was incomprehensible. Defendant acknowledged the motion cited the wrong code section and needed to be redrafted.

In defendant's third attempt to set aside the default, on August 12, 2005, defendant filed an ex parte application for an order shortening time for a hearing on his refiled motion to set aside default pursuant to section 473.2. Defendant asserted he inadvertently missed the deadline to respond to plaintiff's complaint due to his heavy case load. The trial court denied defendant's ex parte application without prejudice to refiling the motion. The court noted there was no section 473.2 statute and the motion therefore needed to be corrected and refiled.

On August 22, 2005, defendant refiled his ex parte application to shorten time for hearing defendant's motion to set aside default pursuant to section 473. Defendant stated in his attached declaration that he was representing himself in the case and inadvertently missed the deadline to respond to plaintiff's complaint due to his heavy case load. Defendant requested shortened notice "due to impending default judgment." Plaintiff filed opposition.

On September 14, 2005, the trial court denied defendant's motion without prejudice. The trial court explained it was denying the motion because merely stating defendant did not timely respond to plaintiff's amended complaint was too general: "The excuse, i.e., heavy case load, is very non specific."

On October 21, 2005, defendant again filed an application for an order shortening time, along with a fourth notice and a motion to set aside default pursuant to section 473. Defendant erroneously stated in his notice of motion that attached to his motion was a proposed demurrer and motion to strike the amended complaint. Rather, defendant attached a proposed "answer to complaint." Defendant asserted he inadvertently missed the deadline to respond to plaintiff's complaint due to failing "to properly calendar the date for the response to the first amended complaint." The court set the motion for a hearing on November 29.

After plaintiff filed opposition, defendant filed additional points and authorities, asserting that the motion was brought under section 473. Defendant argued in his supplemental points and authorities that his secretary erroneously and improperly calendared the hearing date for the demurrer of the original complaint, and therefore failed to notify defendant of the due date for the response. Defendant's secretary, Minerva Soto, provided a declaration attached to the supplemental points and authorities, stating defendant informed her of the due date for filing a response to the amended complaint but Soto inadvertently failed to properly calendar the date, resulting in entry of default against defendant.

Plaintiff filed supplemental opposition. Plaintiff argued in his opposition and supplemental opposition that defendant's motion to set aside default was in effect an improper, untimely motion for reconsideration.

On November 29, 2005, the trial court denied defendant's motion to set aside the default. . . . The court . . . noted that defendant initially failed to provide in his earlier motion sufficient details explaining why he missed the filing deadline due to a heavy case load. Then, not until his supplemental brief in his fourth motion did he attach his secretary's declaration and blame the failure to file a timely response on his secretary. This contradicted his previous declarations and there was no explanation as to why he did not provide his secretary's declaration sooner.

On December 9, 2005, defendant filed a motion for reconsideration of the November 29 ruling denying his motion to set aside default. . . . Defendant did not state in his motion any grounds for granting reconsideration.

Defendant, however, attached his own declaration stating that he inadvertently failed to calendar properly the deadline to file a response to the amended complaint. When his office received the amended complaint, his secretary brought it to his attention but defendant was in the middle of another matter. He told his secretary to calendar the response date and bring the amended complaint back to him later. She neglected to do so. Defendant explained in his declaration that, because defendant's office is so busy, he relies on his staff to calendar matters. His calendaring system failed in this instance. Defendant further stated in his declaration the factual basis for his defense in the case.

On January 9, 2005, the trial court continued defendant's motion for reconsideration and because plaintiff claimed he had not been served with defendant's motion. The trial court also permitted plaintiff to file opposition. Thereafter, plaintiff filed opposition.

On January 26, 2006, the trial court denied defendant's motion for reconsideration and entered judgment on May 31, 2006. The trial court noted during the hearing on January 26, that defendant had not complied with the requirements of section 1008. There were no new facts or law, including no new facts explaining why defendant did not provide his secretary's supporting declaration earlier.

Deficient Record and Failure to Cite Clerk's Transcript

We begin by noting that defendant's appellate brief is in violation of *California Rules of Court*, Rule 8.204(1)(C) in that it contains no citations to the record on appeal. Furthermore, defendant violated *California Rules of Court*, Rules 8.120 and 8.122, by failing to request in his notice to prepare the clerk's transcript the following documents: (1) the underlying complaint, (2) amended complaint, and (3) April 29, 2005, request and entry of default. These are court documents that are critical to defendant's appeal. The exclusion of these documents, as well as the failure to cite to the court record, are sufficient grounds alone to dismiss defendant's appeal or return the appellate brief for corrections. (*Cal. Rules of Court*, Rules 8.276, 8.204(e)(2).)

In addition, defendant's appellate brief violates *California Rules of Court*, Rule 8.204(a)(2), in that it does not: "(A) State the nature of the action, the relief sought in the trial court, and the judgment or order appealed from; (B) State that the judgment appealed from is final, or explain why the order appealed from is appealable; and (C) Provide a summary of the significant facts limited to matters in the record."

Despite these significant deficiencies in defendant's appeal, which impede our ability to review efficiently and decide the matter, we nevertheless will disregard defendant's noncompliance and decide the appeal on the merits. Plaintiff has assisted us in the review of this matter by augmenting the record to include the complaint and amended complaint. In addition, the register of actions contains sufficient additional information upon which to decide this appeal. (*Cal. Rules of Court*, Rule 8.204(e)(2)(C).)

Motions to Set Aside Default Judgment

Defendant contends the trial court abused its discretion in denying his motions to set aside default. We disagree.

. . .

Discussion

Defendant argues that his supporting declaration attesting to his mistake in not filing a timely response was all that was required for the court to grant his motion to set aside default, particularly since he was diligent in seeking relief and the courts favor trial on the merits, as opposed to default judgments. We conclude the trial court did not abuse its discretion in denying defendant's five motions seeking to set aside default.

Irst and Second Motions

As to defendant's first and second motions to set aside default, it is quite clear the trial court did not abuse its discretion in denying them. The first motion was incomprehensible. The second motion, while somewhat comprehensible, was based on incorrect statutory authority. For this reason, the trial court denied the motion without prejudice and indicated that defendant could refile his motion.

Third Motion

The trial court's denial of defendant's third motion to set aside default was also not an abuse of discretion. Defendant's excuse was that he failed to file a response to the amended complaint due to his heavy case load. The courts have routinely rejected this as a valid excuse for setting aside a default judgment.

As stated in *Martin v. Taylor,* 267 Cal. App. 2d 112, 117 (1968), "The 'busy attorney' reason for delay has been almost uniformly rejected by the courts as a ground for failure to seek relief from a default within a reasonable time. For example, in *Smith v. Pelton Water Wheel Co.,* 151 Cal. 394 (1907), the delay was only four months—the defendant pleaded that his attorney was ill for over two months and under the pressure of 'other business' for some weeks thereafter—yet the court held the reason was insufficient ground for granting relief under section 473. In *Schwartz v. Smookler,* 202 Cal. App. 2d 76, the defendant delayed moving to set aside a default for three and a half months and the attorney alleged 'pressure of other business in my office.' The court held this did not constitute legal justification for the delay."

Here, such an excuse is even less persuasive since defendant was representing himself and thus he was directly responsible for failing to file his own response to the amended complaint.

The court in *Martin* explained that "The reason 'press of business' is not usually accepted as a ground for relief under section 473 is found in *Willett v. Schmeister Manufacturing Co.,* 80 Cal. App. 337 at 340: 'Nor is unusual press of business a legal excuse. To accept this as a legal justification for the failure to comply with the statute would be to discourage diligence in the prosecution of appeals and establish a precedent that might lead to vexatious delays.' [P] Moreover, there is some indication here that defendants themselves were inexcusably negligent." (*Martin v. Taylor, supra,* 267 Cal. App. 2d at 117.) This is the case here. Defendant, representing himself, had full knowledge that he was required to respond to the amended complaint and failed to do so.

Fourth Motion

Realizing the press of business was not an adequate basis for setting aside the default, defendant filed his fourth motion, claiming he failed to file a timely response because his secretary failed to calendar the due date properly. The trial court did not abuse its discretion in rejecting this excuse as well, since it was completely different from defendant's original press-of-business excuse and defendant failed to provide any justification for failing to mention previously his new excuse.

Fifth Motion

As to defendant's fifth attempt to set aside default, defendant brought a motion for reconsideration of the trial court's November 29, 2005, ruling denying his motion to set aside default. We first note that there is a split of authority over whether orders denying reconsideration (§1008) are appealable. . . . Some courts have held that motions for reconsideration are appealable only if the underlying orders are appealable and if the reconsideration motions are based on new or different facts. . . .

The trial court's order denying defendant's reconsideration motion is not appealable for the simple reason that the motion was not based on new or different facts. For the same reason, even assuming it is appealable, there was no abuse of discretion in denying the motion for reconsideration. There was no explanation as to why defendant initially said he failed to file a timely response because of the press of business, and then in his supplemental brief filed in connection with his fourth motion he asserted for the first time that his secretary was responsible for the omission. We do not find compelling defendant's explanation that his initial excuse and most recent excuse were compatible and that his most recent explanation merely elaborated on his initial press-of-business excuse.

We conclude there was no abuse of discretion in the trial court denying defendant's four motions to set aside default and motion for reconsideration.

Disposition

The judgment is affirmed. Plaintiff is awarded his costs on appeal.

No matter what size a law firm, someone at the firm should be designated to record appointments and deadlines on a master calendar. At some firms, calendaring events and filing and tracking documents can be a full-time job.

Today's law firms tend to use computerized calendars, which make changing entries and printing out daily, weekly, and monthly calendars very easy. Thus, lawyers—and sometimes trusted paralegals—might update and maintain their own entries on the master calendar rather than submitting requests to calendar clerks to update the system.

As modifications to the calendar are made, lawyers and staff must be alerted to the revisions. Some firms use electronic calendars but keep a paper backup as well. No matter what sort of calendar is used, updating the calendar on a daily basis and actually referring to it are vital. A calendar can be perfectly up to date, but unless a lawyer takes a look at it, the calendar will be of little use.

At a minimum, entries in a master calendar should include the following information:

- time of event
- location of event
- name of case
- client name and matter
- short description of the entry
- name or initials (depending on firm size) of the firm's lawyers and/or staff involved in the event

So, an entry for June 6 might look like this:

> 10 a.m.
> Westchester County Courthouse
> Conference Room 3
> *Ciavardini v. Fox Run*
> Lorenzo Ciavardini—personal injury case
> Settlement conference with defendant and magistrate
> LNT, VLL, H2H

As entries are added to or revised, appropriate personnel within the firm should be alerted to the changes. This might be done by circulating an updated paper version of the calendar, by e-mail, or by automatically generated communications that inform personnel of the modification.

Firms that identify lawyers and staff using their initials should have a system in place in case two or more people at the firm have the same initials. A firm might assign a number as the middle initial for a person with the same initials who is hired later. So, a lawyer named Harry Alders Haight would be identified with the initials HAH. When a new lawyer named Hadley Alison Heuess joins the firm, she will be identified with the initials H2H. When a paralegal named Henderson Aimes Hill joins, he will be identified as H3H. Consistency in entering lawyer and staff identities is important, especially in large firms. Care must be taken to accurately identify people who go by nicknames. Someone named Robert T. Jones who goes by "Bob" must still be identified by the first initial of his given name to avoid confusing him with Brian T. Jamison, a lawyer whose first initial is B.

personal calendar:
A calendar maintained for an individual's own use.

Lawyers' and staff members' **personal calendars** may contain more detailed information about "officially" calendared events along with activities, such as bar association luncheons, speaking engagements, and continuing legal education classes, that may not merit inclusion on the master calendar that is widely circulated to members of the firm and staffers in need of it. In addition to fleshing out entries on the master calendar in an individual one, entries for other important deadlines involving legal action that may not be in litigation (such as a deadline for submitting comments on proposed rulemaking to a government agency) should be made in an individual calendar.

Calendaring practices vary by firm and even by attorney. A lawyer who is very comfortable using technology may have no problem using an individual calendar that is computerized. One who is not quite so technically savvy may prefer to maintain a paper-calendar backup. Most important, calendars should not be limited to "one set of eyes"—if they are, it is easy to overlook or forget about an important deadline. A lawyer, her paralegal, and her legal secretary should check entries in the firm's master calendar that pertain to matters the lawyer is working on. The human element involved in calendaring and alerting appropriate people to significant events cannot be overlooked.

B.   Docket Control

Whereas an individual calendar contains networking meetings, client meetings, scheduled conference calls, and other matters, master calendars tend to identify major events in litigation with which the firm is involved. Keeping close track of matters in litigation, or a firm's **docket,** is especially important, because failure to make an appearance or to meet a deadline can have serious repercussions, both for a client and for the lawyer who made a mistake. A client might automatically lose a case because her lawyer neglected to file an answer on time.

docket:
A list of matters in litigation; caseload.

1.   Deadlines

Automated docketing programs can incorporate court rules by, for instance, calculating a response date if one is required within 14 days of receipt of a document. Computerized docketing programs can also generate reminders about important upcoming deadlines. Such computer programs are also valuable because they can easily generate reports identifying activities by lawyer, by date, by practice group, by case, and so forth. Automated docketing programs can often be synchronized with smartphones and tablets (small handheld computers such as the iPad). Using an automated calendar can result in lower malpractice insurance premiums.[3] Automated docketing programs are not without their drawbacks, though. They can be expensive for small firms and pose management challenges for very large firms practicing in multiple jurisdictions.[4]

No matter what type of calendar (automated or paper) a firm uses, of necessity, a firm must establish a process for making entries into the master calendar. The firm might generate a docket request form to ask that an item be added to the firm's master calendar. At minimum, the form should identify the requester, the responsible attorney, the case name, the event being scheduled, and the client and matter numbers. The law firm must establish a process for entering the data on the forms into the computer and for verifying that the information was entered accurately.

If the firm does not have an automated calendar program that calculates dates, someone must do so manually. A **trigger date** is the date that launches the time clock. For instance, suppose an answer must be filed within 30 days from the filing of a complaint; then the trigger date is the filing date. Care must be taken to distinguish between events that are triggered upon the filing of a document and those that are triggered upon the receipt of a document. A **deadline** is the date on which a specified document is due. A **mailing date** is the date on which a document must be sent in order to be received by a deadline. A **default date** is the date an opposing party will be considered to have defaulted if an answer is not filed by the appropriate deadline.

trigger date:
The date that launches a specified amount of time by which another event must occur.

deadline:
The date on which a specified document is due.

mailing date:
The date on which a document must be sent in order to be received by a deadline.

default date:
The date an opposing party will be considered to have defaulted if an answer is not filed by the appropriate deadline.

FIGURE 11-1
Federal Rules of Civil Procedure

Rule 6: Computing and Extending Time; Time for Motion Papers

(a) Computing Time. The following rules apply in computing any time period specified in these rules, in any local rule or court order, or in any statute that does not specify a method of computing time.

    (1) *Period Stated in Days or a Longer Unit.* When the period is stated in days or a longer unit of time:

        (A) exclude the day of the event that triggers the period;

        (B) count every day, including intermediate Saturdays, Sundays, and legal holidays; and

        (C) include the last day of the period, but if the last day is a Saturday, Sunday, or legal holiday, the period continues to run until the end of the next day that is not a Saturday, Sunday, or legal holiday.

    (2) *Period Stated in Hours.* When the period is stated in hours:

        (A) begin counting immediately on the occurrence of the event that triggers the period;

        (B) count every hour, including hours during intermediate Saturdays, Sundays, and legal holidays; and

        (C) if the period would end on a Saturday, Sunday, or legal holiday, the period continues to run until the same time on the next day that is not a Saturday, Sunday, or legal holiday.

    (3) *Inaccessibility of the Clerk's Office.* Unless the court orders otherwise, if the clerk's office is inaccessible:

        (A) on the last day for filing under Rule 6(a)(1), then the time for filing is extended to the first accessible day that is not a Saturday, Sunday, or legal holiday; or

        (B) during the last hour for filing under Rule 6(a)(2), then the time for filing is extended to the same time on the first accessible day that is not a Saturday, Sunday, or legal holiday.

    (4) *"Last Day" Defined.* Unless a different time is set by a statute, local rule, or court order, the last day ends:

        (A) for electronic filing, at midnight in the court's time zone; and

        (B) for filing by other means, when the clerk's office is scheduled to close.

    (5) *"Next Day" Defined.* The "next day" is determined by continuing to count forward when the period is measured after an event and backward when measured before an event.

    (6) *"Legal Holiday" Defined.* "Legal holiday" means:

        (A) the day set aside by statute for observing New Year's Day, Martin Luther King Jr.'s Birthday, Washington's Birthday, Memorial Day, Independence Day, Labor Day, Columbus Day, Veterans' Day, Thanksgiving Day, or Christmas Day;

        (B) any day declared a holiday by the President or Congress; and

        (C) for periods that are measured after an event, any other day declared a holiday by the state where the district court is located.

(b) Extending Time.

    (1) *In General.* When an act may or must be done within a specified time, the court may, for good cause, extend the time:

        (A) with or without motion or notice if the court acts, or if a request is made, before the original time or its extension expires; or

        (B) on motion made after the time has expired if the party failed to act because of excusable neglect.

    (2) *Exceptions.* A court must not extend the time to act under Rules 50(b) and (d), 52(b), 59(b), (d), and (e), and 60(b).

(c) Motions, Notices of Hearing, and Affidavits.

    (1) *In General.* A written motion and notice of the hearing must be served at least 14 days before the time specified for the hearing, with the following exceptions:

(continued)

(A) when the motion may be heard ex parte;

(B) when these rules set a different time; or

(C) when a court order—which a party may, for good cause, apply for ex parte—sets a different time.

(2) *Supporting Affidavit.* Any affidavit supporting a motion must be served with the motion. Except as Rule 59(c) provides otherwise, any opposing affidavit must be served at least 7 days before the hearing, unless the court permits service at another time.

(d) Additional Time After Certain Kinds of Service. When a party may or must act within a specified time after service and service is made under Rule 5(b)(2)(C), (D), (E), or (F), 3 days are added after the period would otherwise expire under Rule 6(a).

Source: Fed. R. Civ. P. 6

The person calculating a deadline must know how a given court establishes various deadlines. Some courts calculate deadlines by calendar days; other courts calculate deadlines using workdays (days when the court is open) and do not include weekends, holidays, and other days when the court is closed (such as election day). Federal, state, and local court rules can vary significantly, and the person responsible for calculating due dates must take great care in determining the dates. Federal Rules of Civil Procedure Rule 6 governs how time is computed in federal district courts (see Figure 11-1 on page 288). The calculations vary somewhat for federal appeals courts (see Figure 11-2). A state statute specifying that workdays are to be used when calculating deadlines is presented in Figure 11-3.

FIGURE 11-2
Federal Rules of Appellate Procedure

Rule 26: Computing and Extending Time

(a) Computing Time. The following rules apply in computing any time period specified in these rules, in any local rule or court order, or in any statute that does not specify a method of computing time.

(1) Period Stated in Days or a Longer Unit. When the period is stated in days or a longer unit of time:

(A) exclude the day of the event that triggers the period;

(B) count every day, including intermediate Saturdays, Sundays, and legal holidays; and

(C) include the last day of the period, but if the last day is a Saturday, Sunday, or legal holiday, the period continues to run until the end of the next day that is not a Saturday, Sunday, or legal holiday.

(2) Period Stated in Hours. When the period is stated in hours:

(A) begin counting immediately on the occurrence of the event that triggers the period;

(B) count every hour, including hours during intermediate Saturdays, Sundays, and legal holidays; and

(C) if the period would end on a Saturday, Sunday, or legal holiday, the period continues to run until the same time on the next day that is not a Saturday, Sunday, or legal holiday.

(3) Inaccessibility of the Clerk's Office. Unless the court orders otherwise, if the clerk's office is inaccessible:

(continued)

it is a Saturday or a legal holiday, including Sunday, in which event the period runs until the end of the next day which is not a Saturday or a legal holiday. If the period so computed relates to serving a public officer or filing a document at a public office, and if the last day falls on a day when that particular office is closed before the end of or for all of the normal work day, the last day shall be excluded in computing the period of time within which service is to be made or the document is to be filed, in which event the period runs until the close of office hours on the next day the office is open for business. When the period of time prescribed or allowed (without regard to section C. of this rule) is less than 7 days, intermediate Saturdays and legal holidays, including Sundays, shall be excluded in the computation. As used in this rule, "legal holiday" means legal holiday as defined in ORS 187.010 and 187.020. This section does not apply to any time limitation governed by ORS 174.120.

Source: Or. R. Civ. P. 10

Review the calendar in Figure 11-4. If a document was due 14 calendar days from a trigger date on December 1, the document would have to be filed by December 15 in a court that uses calendar days to calculate deadlines. In a state court that uses workdays, however, the document would not have to be filed until December 16 (because weekends and other days when the court is closed are excluded). The trigger date is not included in the calculation; begin counting on the next day.

FIGURE 11-4
Sample Calendar

| November 2010 | | | | | | | | December 2010 | | | | | | January 2011 | | | | | | |

December 2010

Sunday	Monday	Tuesday	Wednesday	Thursday	Friday	Saturday
			1	2	3	4
5	6	7	8	9 STATE ELECTIONS-STATE COURTHOUSE CLOSED	10	11
12	13	14	15	16	17	18
19	20	21	22	23	24 FEDERAL HOLIDAY STATE HOLIDAY	25 CHRISTMAS
26	27	28	29	30 STATE HOLIDAY	31 FEDERAL HOLIDAY STATE HOLIDAY	Jan. 1-NEW YEAR'S DAY

statute of limitation:
A law barring lawsuits after a certain period of time after the activity (such as a car accident) that gave rise to the legal action occurred.

In addition to filing deadlines, statutes of limitations dates should be included as calendar entries. A **statute of limitation** bars lawsuits after a certain period of time after the occurrence of the activity (such as a car accident) that gave rise to the legal action. The time after which an action is time-barred varies by the type of claim involved. See Figure 11-5 for a sample statute of limitations.

The importance of maintaining and updating a calendar cannot be overstated.

2. Reminders

tickler:
A reminder about an upcoming deadline.

Because deadlines can be missed even when they are properly noted on a calendar, firms post reminders, or **ticklers,** to alert lawyers to upcoming deadlines.

FIGURE 11-5
Sample Statute of Limitations

New York Civil Practice Law and Rules 214 (2013)

§214. Actions to be commenced within three years: for non-payment of money collected on execution; for penalty created by statute; to recover chattel; for injury to property; for personal injury; for malpractice other than medical, dental or podiatric malpractice; to annul a marriage on the ground of fraud.

The following actions must be commenced within three years:

1. an action against a sheriff, constable or other officer for the non-payment of money collected upon an execution;

2. an action to recover upon a liability, penalty or forfeiture created or imposed by statute except as provided in sections 213 and 215;

3. an action to recover a chattel or damages for the taking or detaining of a chattel;

4. an action to recover damages for an injury to property except as provided in section 214-c;

5. an action to recover damages for a personal injury except as provided in sections 214-b, 214-c and 215;

6. an action to recover damages for malpractice, other than medical, dental or podiatric malpractice, regardless of whether the underlying theory is based in contract or tort; and

7. an action to annul a marriage on the ground of fraud; the time within which the action must be commenced shall be computed from the time the plaintiff discovered the facts constituting the fraud, but if the plaintiff is a person other than the spouse whose consent was obtained by fraud, the time within which the action must be commenced shall be computed from the time, if earlier, that that spouse discovered the facts constituting the fraud.

Automated calendars can also send e-mail reminders automatically or display pop-up boxes on a computer. Apps for smartphones can synchronize with a lawyer's automated calendar. A tickler for any given event might be set at 30 days, 14 days, 7 days, and the day before a deadline. Some firms even color code their ticklers, so events might reach "red alert" level as the date of a deadline gets closer.

Ultimately, the responsibility for meeting deadlines rests with the lawyer. But, inevitably, lawyers still miss deadlines. When they do, they might face a malpractice lawsuit from the client whose deadline was overlooked. Even if the client does not sue the lawyer, the client is likely to fire the lawyer.

Although people may agree that "everyone makes mistakes," courts are not necessarily so forgiving of casual errors. In certain circumstances, a court will forgive a lawyer's calendaring error if the court finds there has been "excusable neglect." Excusable neglect is defined as:

> a failure—which the law will excuse—to take some proper step at the proper time (esp. in neglecting to answer a lawsuit) not because of the party's own carelessness, inattention, or willful disregard of the court's process, but because of some unexpected or unavoidable hindrance or accident or because of reliance on the care and vigilance of the party's counsel or on a promise made by the adverse party.[5]

Simply making a mistake, or failing to catch the mistake of a staff person, generally will not absolve the lawyer before a court:

> Lawyers must assume that courts will treat the failure to read rules, failure to understand rules and failure to properly apply rules as *in*excusable neglect. Few courts are likely to hold otherwise where a lawyer delegates responsibility for rules interpretations to non-lawyer staff. The bottom line is that lawyers must be responsible for reading appropriate rules and deciding upon appropriate deadlines, even if the task of calendaring such deadlines and ministerial acts designed to ensure compliance are delegated to non-lawyers.[6]

Of course, there is an exception to every rule. Consider the following case, where a court did allow a lawyer who had missed a deadline to obtain an extension of time. Notice the reasons for the mistake that the lawyer provided.

Pincay v. Andrews
389 F.3d 853 (9th Cir. 2004)

Counsel: Neil Papiano and Patrick McAdam, Iverson, Yoakum, Papiano & Hatch, Los Angeles, California, for the plaintiffs-appellants.

David Boies and Robert Silver, Boies, Schiller & Flexner, LLP, Armonk, New York, for the defendants-appellees.

Judges: Before: Mary M. Schroeder, Chief Judge, Alex Kozinski, Pamela Ann Rymer, Andrew J. Kleinfeld, Sidney R. Thomas, Barry G. Silverman, M. Margaret McKeown, Ronald M. Gould, Marsha S. Berzon, Johnnie B. Rawlinson, and Consuelo M. Callahan, Circuit Judges. Opinion by Chief Judge Schroeder; Concurrence by Judge Berzon; Dissent by Judge Kozinski.

OPINION BY: MARY M. SCHROEDER

OPINION

This appeal represents a lawyer's nightmare. A sophisticated law firm, with what it thought was a sophisticated system to determine and calendar filing deadlines, missed a critical one: the 30-day time period in which to file a notice of appeal under Federal Rule of Appellate Procedure 4(a)(1)(A). The rule, however, provides for a grace period of 30 days within which a lawyer in such a fix may ask the district court for an extension of time, and the court, in the exercise of its discretion, may grant the extension if it determines that the neglect of the attorney was "excusable."[1] Here an experienced trial judge found excusable neglect, and the appellee asks us to overturn that ruling.

The underlying dispute began in 1989 when Laffit Pincay, Jr. and Christopher McCarron (Pincay) sued Vincent S. Andrews, Robert L. Andrews, and Vincent Andrews Management Corp. (Andrews) for financial injuries stemming from alleged violations of the Racketeer Influenced and Corrupt Organizations Act (RICO) and California law. In 1992, a jury returned verdicts in Pincay's favor on both the RICO and the California counts. Pincay was ordered to elect a remedy, and he chose to pursue the RICO judgment. This judgment was reversed on appeal on the ground that the RICO claim was barred by the federal statute of limitations. *Pincay v. Andrews*, 238 F.3d 1106, 1110 (9th Cir. 2001). On remand, Pincay elected to pursue the remedy on his California law claim. Judgment was entered in his favor on July 3, 2002.

Andrews's notice of appeal was due 30 days later, but a paralegal charged with calendaring filing deadlines misread the rule and advised Andrews's attorney that the notice was not due for 60 days, the time allowed when the government is a party to the case. *See* Fed. R. App. P. 4(a)(1)(B). Andrews's counsel learned about the error when Pincay relied upon the judgment as being final in related bankruptcy proceedings, and Andrews promptly tendered a notice of appeal together with a request for an extension within the 30-day grace period. By that time the matter had been in litigation for more than 15 years. Everyone involved should have been well aware that the government was not a party to the case, and any lawyer or paralegal should have been able to read the rule correctly. The misreading of the rule was a critical error that, had the district court viewed the situation differently, would have ended the litigation then and there with an irreparably adverse result for Andrews. The district court, however, found the neglect excusable and granted the motion for an extension of time to file the notice of appeal.

Pincay appealed to this court, and a majority of the three-judge panel concluded that Andrews's attorney had improperly delegated the function of calendaring to a paralegal, and held that the attorney's reliance on a paralegal was inexcusable as a matter of law. . . . It ordered the appeal dismissed. The dissent

---

[1] The rule provides in relevant part: "The district court may extend the time to file a notice of appeal if: (i) a party so moves no later than 30 days after the time prescribed by this Rule 4(a) expires; and (ii) . . . that party shows excusable neglect or good cause." Fed. R. App. P. 4(a)(5)(A).

would have applied a more flexible and deferential standard and affirmed the district court. . . .

A majority of the active non-recused judges of the court voted to rehear the case en banc to consider whether the creation of a per se rule against delegation to paralegals, or indeed any per se rule involving missed filing deadlines, is consistent with the United States Supreme Court's leading authority on the modern concept of excusable neglect, *Pioneer Investment Services Co. v. Brunswick Associated Ltd. Partnership*, 507 U.S. 380, 123 L. Ed. 2d 74, 113 S. Ct. 1489 (1993). We now hold that per se rules are not consistent with *Pioneer*, and we uphold the exercise of the district court's discretion to permit the filing of the notice of appeal in this case.

The *Pioneer* decision arose in the bankruptcy context and involved the "bar date" for the filing of claims. The Court in *Pioneer* established a four-part balancing test for determining whether there had been "excusable neglect" within the meaning of Federal Rule of Bankruptcy Procedure 9006(b)(1). The Court also reviewed various contexts in which the phrase appeared in the federal rules of procedure and made it clear the same test applies in all those contexts. The *Pioneer* factors include: (1) the danger of prejudice to the non-moving party, (2) the length of delay and its potential impact on judicial proceedings, (3) the reason for the delay, including whether it was within the reasonable control of the movant, and (4) whether the moving party's conduct was in good faith. 507 U.S. at 395.

In this case, the district court analyzed each of the *Pioneer* factors and correctly found: (1) there was no prejudice, (2) the length of delay was small, (3) the reason for the delay was carelessness, and (4) there was no evidence of bad faith. It then concluded that even though the reason for the delay was the carelessness of Andrews's counsel, that fact did not render the neglect inexcusable. The district court relied on this court's decision in *Marx v. Loral Corp.*, 87 F.3d 1049 (9th Cir. 1996), in which we affirmed an order granting an extension of time in a case that involved an attorney's calendaring error.

Because the panel majority decided the case in part on the issue of delegation of calendaring to a paralegal, we consider that issue first. This issue was not presented to the district court, and it was raised *sua sponte* by the three-judge panel.

In the modern world of legal practice, the delegation of repetitive legal tasks to paralegals has become a necessary fixture. Such delegation has become an integral part of the struggle to keep down the costs of legal representation. Moreover, the delegation of such tasks to specialized, well-educated non-lawyers may well ensure greater accuracy in meeting deadlines than a practice of having each lawyer in a large firm calculate each filing deadline anew. The task of keeping track of necessary deadlines will involve some delegation. The responsibility for the error falls on the attorney regardless of whether the error was made by an attorney or a paralegal. We hold that delegation of the task of ascertaining the deadline was not per se inexcusable neglect.

The larger question in this case is whether the misreading of the clear rule could appropriately have been considered excusable. . . .

. . .

In this case the mistake itself, the misreading of the Rule, was egregious, and the lawyer undoubtedly should have checked the Rule itself before relying on the paralegal's reading. Both the paralegal and the lawyer were negligent. That, however, represents the beginning of our inquiry as to whether the negligence is excusable, not the end of it. The real question is whether there was enough in the context of this case to bring a determination of excusable neglect within the district court's discretion.

We therefore turn to examining the *Pioneer* factors as they apply here. The parties seem to agree that three of the factors militate in favor of excusability, and they focus their arguments on the remaining factor: the reason for the delay. Appellee Andrews characterizes the reason for the delay as the failure of a "carefully designed" calendaring system operated by experienced paralegals that heretofore had worked flawlessly. Appellant Pincay, on the other hand, stresses the degree of carelessness in the failure to read the applicable Rule.

We recognize that a lawyer's failure to read an applicable rule is one of the least compelling excuses that can be offered; yet the nature of the contextual analysis and the balancing of the factors adopted in *Pioneer* counsel against the creation of any rigid rule. Rather, the decision whether to grant or deny an extension of time to file a notice of appeal should be entrusted to the discretion of the district court because the district court is in a better position than we are to evaluate factors such as whether the lawyer had otherwise been diligent, the propensity of the other side to capitalize on petty mistakes, the quality of representation of the lawyers (in this litigation over its 15-year history), and the likelihood of injustice if the appeal was not allowed. Had the district court declined to permit the filing of the notice, we would be hard pressed to find any rationale requiring us to reverse.

Pioneer itself instructs courts to determine the issue of excusable neglect within the context of the particular case, a context with which the trial court is most familiar. Any rationale suggesting that misinterpretation of an unambiguous rule can never be excusable neglect is, in our view, contrary to that instruction. "The right way, under *Pioneer*, to decide cases involving ignorance of federal rules is with an 'elastic concept' equitable in nature, not with a per se rule." *Pincay v. Andrews*, 351 F.3d 947, 953 (9th Cir. 2003) (Kleinfeld, J., dissenting).

We are also mindful that Rule 4 itself provides for leniency in limited circumstances. It could have been written more rigidly, allowing for no window of opportunity once the deadline was missed. Many states' rules provide for an extension of the time for filing a notice of appeal under few, if any, circumstances. . . . The federal rule is a more flexible one that permits a narrow 30-day window for requesting an extension, and the trial court has wide discretion as to whether to excuse the lapse.

We understand several of our sister circuits have tried to fashion a rule making a mistake of law per se inexcusable under Rule 4. We agree that a lawyer's mistake of law in reading a rule of procedure is not a compelling excuse. At the same time, however, a lawyer's mistake of fact, for example, in thinking the government was a party to a case and that the 60-day rule applied for that reason, would be no more compelling.

We are persuaded that, under *Pioneer*, the correct approach is to avoid any per se rule. *Pioneer* cautioned against "erecting a rigid barrier against late filings attributable in any degree to the movant's negligence." 507 U.S. at 395 n.14. There should similarly be no rigid legal rule against late filings attributable to any particular type of negligence. Instead, we leave the weighing of *Pioneer*'s equitable factors to the discretion of the district court in every case.

We hold that the district court did not abuse its discretion in this case. Therefore, the district court's order granting the defendant's motion for an extension of time to file the notice of appeal is AFFIRMED. The merits of the appeal are before the three judge panel in appeal number 02-56491. The panel should proceed to decide that appeal.

C.   Case Management

Although the concepts are related, case management is broader than docket control and includes cases and client matters as well as calendars, notes, time reports, documents, and other materials. Such a system really is practice management software that helps lawyers organize and track many of the materials they generate or use in support of their work for clients.

Case management systems may be customized for an individual firm. Off-the-shelf systems are also available. A case management system is helpful to attorneys and their staffs only if people within the firm know how to use the system and how to update and maintain it. Training on the system is vitally important for support staff as well as for attorneys. Law firm leadership must also consistently send a message that the case management system is important to the ultimate success of the firm and should be updated and referred to often.

case management systems: Law firm management programs that include information about lawsuits involving clients and other client matters, along with other documents, calendars, lawyers' notes, and timekeeping elements.

Checklist

- A law firm should have a system in place for tracking and overseeing each case that the law firm is involved in on behalf of a client.
- A master calendar lists all of the litigation-related activities (such as filing deadlines, hearing dates, and the like) scheduled for lawyers and staff at the firm. Some firms also track other important client events that are not part of litigation.
- Lawyers and staff also maintain their own personal calendars, which tend to flesh out entries on the master calendar with which they are involved and include other activities not listed in the master calendar, such as bar association luncheons, continuing legal education classes, and so forth.
- Automated docketing programs can incorporate court rules and calculate response dates.

- Whether or not a calendar or docket control program is computerized, it must be constantly updated and referred to.
- If the firm does not have an automated calendar program that calculates dates, someone must calculate dates manually. A trigger date is the date that launches the time clock. Care must be taken to distinguish between events that are triggered upon the filing of a document and events that are triggered upon the receipt of a document. A deadline is the date on which a specified document is due. A mailing date is the date on which a document must be sent in order to be received by a deadline. A default date is the date an opposing party will be considered to have defaulted if an answer is not filed by the appropriate deadline.
- The person calculating a deadline must know how a given court establishes various deadlines. Some courts calculate deadlines by calendar days; other courts calculate deadlines using workdays (days when the court is open) and do not include weekends, holidays, and other days when the court is closed (such as election day).
- The responsibility for meeting deadlines rests with the lawyer.
- When lawyers miss deadlines, they might face a malpractice lawsuit from the client whose deadline was overlooked. Even if the client does not sue the lawyer, the client is likely to fire the lawyer.
- Lawyers who miss deadlines might blame their staff for their error.
- Courts are not necessarily forgiving of casual errors. In certain circumstances, a court may forgive a lawyer's calendaring error if the court finds there has been "excusable neglect."

Vocabulary

calendaring (p. 280)

case management systems (p. 297)

deadline (p. 287)

default date (p. 287)

docket (p. 287)

mailing date (p. 287)

master calendar (p. 279)

personal calendar (p. 286)

statute of limitation (p. 292)

tickler (p. 292)

trigger date (p. 287)

Career Preparation Tips

You don't need to be working in the legal field to develop your docket management skills. Apply the principles you have learned here to your personal life, to your volunteer activities, or to your current career. Practice calendaring events and setting up ticklers. For instance, suppose you were invited to a wedding to take place in two months. You might set that up, and then calendar certain tasks (and set up accompanying ticklers) that you need to accomplish, such as returning the response card, purchasing a gift, making travel arrangements, buying a wedding outfit, and so on. Become familiar with free or low-cost software and applications that can aid you in the management of your personal docket.

If You Want to Learn More

Association of Legal Administrators. www.alanet.org

National Institute for Trial Advocacy. http://www.nita.org

Texas Lawyers' Insurance Exchange Self-Audit Docket Control Evaluation. http://www.tlie.org/prevention/self-audit-docket.php

Calendar/docket management/case management software:

http://www.abacuslaw.com

http://www.activecollab.com

http://www.amicusattorney.com

http://basecamphq.com

http://www.aderant.com/products/aderant-compulaw/

http://www.deadlines.com

http://www.elite.com

http://www.lawfirmadvisor.com

https://www.ma3000.com

http://www.perfectpractice.com

http://www.projectpier.org

http://www.elite.com/prolaw/

http://www.theombudsman.com/wp_site/

Reading Comprehension

1. What is the difference between a master calendar and a personal calendar?
2. What types of events are recorded in a master calendar?
3. What information should be included in an entry in a master calendar?
4. Who is responsible for maintaining a master calendar?
5. What does a calendar clerk do?
6. What is the difference between calendar days and workdays, and why is this difference important for calendaring events?
7. Will courts allow lawyers to file documents after deadlines have passed?
8. What factors does a court consider in assessing whether a lawyer should be allowed to file a document after a deadline has been missed?
9. What are some drawbacks to automated calendaring and case management systems?

Discussion Starters

1. Review *Daniels v. Sacks*. Who brought the lawsuit? What excuses did the defendant give for his failure to meet important deadlines? Why didn't the court accept those excuses?
2. Compare *Pincay v. Andrews*. Who did the lawyer who missed the important deadline blame for the error? Did the court accept the lawyer's excuse? What was the result of the case? In what ways is this case similar to *Daniels v. Sacks*? In what ways is it different? Why do you suppose the U.S. Court of Appeals for the Ninth Circuit decided *Pincay* as it did? Who was the attorney who represented the defendants/appellees? At what firm did the lawyer who made the mistake work? Do you think the law concerning mistakenly missed deadlines is evolving? Do you think the law is changing for the better? Do you think lawyers should delegate calendaring responsibilities to staff?
3. Lawyers seem to blame their paralegals or other staff when they miscalculate deadlines or miss important deadlines. Why do you suppose they do that? How might a paralegal or other staff person protect himself from such an accusation? What should a staff person do if she realizes that she miscalculated an important deadline and the law firm failed to take action by the "real" deadline?
4. Do you think the U.S. Court of Appeals for the Ninth Circuit in *Pincay* displayed favoritism toward the lawyer who had made the mistake? Why do you think the lawyer's law firm was not mentioned in the body of the decision? How might you find out at what law firm the lawyer worked at

the time the mistake was made? If you think favoritism did occur, what does that tell you about the importance of a law firm's reputation and a lawyer's good relationship with judges and court clerks?

5. What do you consider to be the difference between excusable negligence and inexcusable negligence?

6. How might docket management skills be transferred to organizations other than law firms?

Case Studies

1. Suppose you work for a single-office, three-lawyer general practice firm. Identify three case management programs that the firm might purchase. What features of each program would work well for the firm? Are there a lot of superfluous features that the firm might not need or use? Compare and contrast the programs, and recommend one the firm should buy.

2. Suppose you work for a major law firm with 1,500 lawyers in ten offices: seven in the United States, one in London, one in Hong Kong, and one in Dubai. Identify three case management programs that the firm might purchase. What features of each program would work well for the firm? Are there a lot of superfluous features that the firm might not need or use? Compare and contrast the programs, and recommend one the firm should buy.

3. How are court deadlines computed in your state's courts? Look up your state's statute on computation. Is the statute clearly written? Could it be improved to eliminate possibilities for errors?

4. You are the docket clerk at a law firm, and you must calculate the deadlines for the following items. Use the calendar in Figure 11-4 in calculating the deadlines.

> Answer due 15 days after a complaint's filing on Dec. 3 in federal court
> Answer due 15 days after a complaint's filing on Dec. 3 in state court
> Appeal due in federal court seven days after court's decision was filed on Dec. 23
> Appeal due in state court seven days after court's decision was filed on Dec. 23
> Complaint to be filed in federal court by statute of limitations deadline on Dec. 30
> Complaint to be filed in state court by statute of limitations deadline on Dec. 9

What ticklers for each of these items would you add to the calendar?

5. You are the docket clerk at a law firm, and you must enter the following items on your firm's master calendar. Prepare a calendar with each of these entries; include only pertinent material.

Smith v. Jones oral argument on Dec. 20
Second U.S. Circuit Court of Appeals
11:30 A.M.
Client: Samantha Strahern, who filed an amicus curiae brief on behalf of respondent Jones
Attorneys: Carrie Diane Kearns, Juana Marie Lopez, George Mario Letterer
Paralegal: Mindy Starr Osmond

Dec. 20
Apple v. Dell
answer due
Second U.S. Circuit Court of Appeals
Client: Wilhelmina Dell
Attorneys: Carrie Diane Kearns, Juana Marie Lopez
Paralegal: Mindy Starr Osmond

Dec. 20
response to motion for summary judgment due
Dell v. Smith Bank
Client: Wilhelmina Dell
Attorneys: Juana Marie Lopez, George Mario Letterer
Paralegal: Mindy Starr Osmond

Dec. 20
deadline for any appeal to be filed
Dell Holding Co. v. Dell
Client: Wilhelmina Dell
Attorney: Mark Landers Christian
Paralegal: Marcia Lynne Cheney
contract claim

Keller v. Keller
conference with mediator on Dec. 21
2 P.M.
Westchester County Courthouse
Room 8
Client: Ryan Keller (plaintiff)
Attorney: Mark Landers Christian
Paralegal: Marcia Lynne Cheney
divorce action

Dec. 15
Simonetti v. Garfunkle
jury selection
Monroe County Courthouse
Courtroom 10

Client: Justicia Simonetti
Attorney: Mark Landers Christian
personal injury case

6. What ticklers for each of these events should also be added to the master calendar? What other information, if any, should be added to the master calendar for each of these entries? What additional information, if any, should be added to the personal calendars of each of the people involved in these activities?

7. Research "help wanted" ads for docket/calendar/case management clerks in your area. Are many positions available? What pay levels are given? Would you like to be a docket/calendar/case management clerk? Do you think there's much promotion potential for someone with that job?

Endnotes

1. James M. Fischer, *External Control over the American Bar*, 19 Geo. J. Legal Ethics 59, 76-77 (Winter 2006).
2. Dan Pinnington, *Avoid a Malpractice Claim Using Time Management Tools*, 38(3) Law Prac. online, May/June 2012, http://www.americanbar.org/publications/law_practice_magazine/2012/may_june/avoid-a-malpractice-claim-using-time-management-tools.html.
3. *See, e.g.*, Gerald J. Hoenig, *Selecting Practice Management Software, a Daunting Task*, 22 Prob. & Prop. 57 (Oct. 2008).
4. *See, e.g.*, Joseph C. Scott, *Test Your Court Calendaring IQ*, 51 Orange County Law. 35 (May 2009).
5. Black's Law Dictionary 1061 (2004).
6. Douglas R. Richmond, *Neglect, Excusable and Otherwise*, 2 Seton Hall Cir. Rev. 119, 136 (Fall 2005).

12

Knowledge and Records Management

Chapter Outcomes

By the end of this chapter, a student will be able to:

- Distinguish between knowledge management and records management
- Describe the elements of a records management system
- Identify ethical issues associated with knowledge and records management
- Propose means to prevent ethical violations from occurring

Think about all of the information that arrives at a law firm every single day, whether by delivery, e-mail, regular mail, messenger, FedEx or UPS, phone, voice mail, or download from the Internet. Much of that information must be retained, remembered, followed up, and retrieved at some future date. **Records management** is the process in which all of these materials are organized, handled, and stored. As tedious as supervising a paper trail (much of which is no longer actually on paper but is in various electronic forms) might seem to some people, it's a vitally important responsibility. Without some sort of system in place, a law firm's business—its very reason for existence—can easily go astray. Think for a moment about a private individual's life. A person probably has established his or her own systems for dealing with the information that arrives each day: She might place bills received in the mail into a basket for handling before the end of the month, she might enter appointments on a family calendar, she might listen to voice mail messages after she comes home from work and then return calls later in the evening, she might place paychecks that arrive directly into her wallet for later deposit at her bank. If she stops doing any of these activities, bills can pile

records management:
The process by which materials containing information are organized, handled, and stored.

up, utilities can be turned off, appointments can be missed, friends and family can become mad, and, in short, chaos ensues.

Law firms are constantly barraged by an overwhelming amount of information. It is very easy for some to slip away, to be overlooked, accidentally discarded, or simply forgotten. Law firms must establish their own practices for handling all of the information they receive, they must educate their lawyers and staff about the practices, and they must make sure that the practices are followed accurately. If they are not, the same negative events that can happen to an individual can happen to a law firm: Bills can pile up, utilities can be turned off, appointments can be missed, clients can become mad, and chaos ensues. Sometimes clients sue their lawyers for malpractice. Then the law firm's reputation suffers, it loses clients and fails to attract more of them, and, in a worst-case scenario, the law firm might become insolvent and shut down.

Ultimately, of course, just about everyone at a law firm must be responsible for managing the firm's records in some way. Documents must be retrievable, and the system for managing them must be understood and used by everyone at the firm. A law office manager, an information technology employee, a records administrator, or even a librarian employed by the firm might be responsible for developing, implementing, and enforcing a records management program.

Dealing efficiently and effectively with records is no small matter for a law firm. Think of the many activities that take place on any given day at a law firm: Lawyers prepare work products for clients, paralegals conduct research, prospective clients visit the firm, new employees begin their first day on the job, practice groups depart, marketers place advertisements about the firm, payroll is met, the rent is paid, the utilities remain on, and so on. All of these activities must occur seamlessly on an ongoing basis. The ability to function well begins with a strong records management system.

A. What Is Records Management?

Records management is a broader activity than file management and docket management. Records management really refers to systems a law firm establishes to manage all of the materials it receives. One useful definition of records describes them as

> books, papers, maps, photographs, machine readable materials, or other documentary materials, regardless of physical form or characteristics, made or received . . . or in connection with the transaction of . . . business and preserved or appropriate for preservation . . . as evidence of the organization, functions, policies, decisions, procedures, operations, or other activities . . . or because of the informational value of data in them.[1]

File management and docket management may be considered subsets of records management, although in some ways they overlap. File management refers primarily to client files, whereas docket management involves mostly the actual lawsuits a firm is involved in on behalf of clients. Records management encompasses files, dockets, and all of the other records flowing through a firm.

Dealing with records can be very costly. Hours and hours might be dedicated to creating record management policy, procuring software for managing it, implementing the policy, training staff on records management, arranging for physical storage space, and hiring a record destruction service.

Remember that more than **"front-office" activities**—which support the law practice itself—are included in records management. **"Back-office" activities**, such as accounting, human resources, marketing, and facilities management, also generate plenty of records that have to be protected from inappropriate disclosure.

A records management policy developed by a firm should identify the various types of records that are being tracked, establish handling requirements for each type, determine who has access to various types of records, and safeguard the handling of records. Arrangements must also be made for storage, whether electronic, physical on-site, or long-term off-site storage. A records destruction policy and procedure should also be an element of a records management policy.

"front-office" activity: Work that supports the law practice itself.

"back-office" activity: Work that deals with the business administration side of the law firm.

1. Records Retention

Records retention—the length of time an item is kept—should be an element of any records management policy. Some records must be kept for a certain number of years as specified by statute. For instance, tax laws and unemployment insurance laws might require that records be available for a certain number of years. It's a good idea to retain other records as well. Remember that law firms today are not static entities. People are constantly moving into and out of them—working there for a period of time and then departing. The institutional memory that might have existed in firms of a century ago, when lawyers tended to stay at a single firm for their entire professional lives, does not exist today—unless a well-developed records management policy is set up to preserve it. For instance, although a firm might not be legally required to maintain records about its advertising campaign in perpetuity, the firm still might want to keep them. Five years, 10 years, 15 years from now, firm employees are not likely to remember approaches the firm tried today that backfired, or slogans that were considered and rejected. As even more time goes by, the firm might want to preserve these records for use in a firm history.

records retention: The length of time a piece of information should be kept.

The important point is that a firm must set up a policy for records retention, and its employees must then follow that policy. Areas must be designated for the storage of records on-site, either in a centralized records room or at decentralized areas near lawyers and personnel who will frequently use them. Procedures for shipping records to off-site storage and for accessing those records in off-site storage must also be established.

Records retention policy will likely vary for client files as opposed to administrative files of the law firm. Here are some examples of administrative records a law firm is likely to have:

- payroll data
- health insurance information
- employee files
- records on job applicants

- performance evaluations
- contracts
- hiring letters
- offer letters
- background checks
- information about salaries
- references
- vacation request forms
- information on garnishments
- disability claims
- attendance records
- time cards for staff
- recruiting materials
- family and medical leave materials
- accounts payable
- accounts receivable
- affirmative action/diversity information
- discrimination claims
- benefits information
- independent contractor records
- data on marketing efforts
- research on prospective clients
- insurance carriers, policies, and premiums
- workers' compensation claims
- material safety data sheets
- Occupational Safety and Health Administration information
- injury reports
- retirement policies

In addition, a firm is likely to establish its own databases, or storehouses of knowledge, on legal subjects that lawyers and others at the firm frequently research. These databases may include templates and copies of work the firm has done for other clients. For instance, a real estate firm is unlikely to draw up a new contract of sale for every single real estate transaction. It will likely use a template or pull up samples of contracts prepared for similar clients and then customize individual parts. Publicly available documents might also be stored in these databases, such as comments on proposed regulations, complaints, answers, and so on.

A records retention policy must address how all of these different types of records are to be handled and retained and must also specify when they are to be destroyed. Such a policy should identify the people who are responsible for determining the records' fate.

cloud computing:
Use of remote servers for data and management allowing users to access data from any computer with an Internet connection (rather than programs and other materials being stored directly on one's personal computer or internal network).

Of necessity, technology plays a role here. Increasingly, more records are electronic. Technological developments are likely to affect a firm's records management policies, especially as phenomena like **cloud computing**—which uses remote servers for data storage and management rather than programs and other materials for storage directly in one's personal computer—become more accepted and mainstream.

Practical matters must also be attended to. As anyone who has worked for a law firm knows, there is likely to always be at least one lawyer at a firm who has a "leaning tower of Pisa" inbox, with documents piled almost to the tipping point. Lawyers may not spend a whole lot of time managing records they keep in their own offices, and these can fall into disarray. Actual storage space—meaning filing cabinets—can be highly coveted within a firm, and lawyers, paralegals, and others sometimes battle in an effort to stake out convenient storage space. A records management procedure, which clearly sets out how any newly available storage space is to be parceled out, can alleviate some of these disturbances.

A law firm must have appropriate materials for storing all of these records: filing cabinets, file folders, labels, bar coding systems, and such. Unfortunately, these supplies do not just magically appear when a lawyer or paralegal needs them. Someone at the firm must be responsible for ordering and reordering them and for monitoring new developments that will make records management easier.

Perhaps the most important attribute of any records management system is being able to find a document when you need it.

2.   *Indexing and Records Retrieval*

One sign that a firm has a less than optimal records managements system is when paralegals or legal secretaries have to call former lawyers and other employees asking where they left certain files. Simply put, a firm must have a records management system in place, and the firm's leaders must make sure people are aware of it! Also important is cataloging information so that it can be retrieved easily. Probably all of us have had the experience of using a book with a poorly crafted index—one with few entries, where seemingly obvious topics are omitted, and information cannot be easily found. No matter how punctilious a firm is in logging in new documents and storing them promptly, its efforts will be of little use if the very people who must access the information are unable to locate it.

Records may be organized in a number of ways: by subject matter, by practice area, by author, by a unique number assigned to the record, by client and matter number, by other numbers assigned to materials generated within the firm, and so on. An index of these categories and subcategories should be created, and guidelines on how to categorize various types of documents must be established. An index is "a structured hierarchy of terms developed for the purpose of locating specific objects within a larger collection."[2] In short, an index is essentially a map to all of a firm's records. It largely resembles an outline and becomes increasingly detailed.

What does this mean for the law office manager or the records manager, if the firm has one? Someone needs to set up the system and then implement it. Employees must be trained in using the system, and someone must follow up to make sure that materials are properly categorized so that the system is actually useful. Remember that records are retrieved for different purposes. For instance, a paralegal might be looking for a specific deed the law firm has worked on. Alternatively, the paralegal might be looking for copies of all deeds that have a certain phrase in them or that are in a certain geographic area. Users of the records management system must be able to retrieve very specific information as well as more general information.

Of necessity, much of the information—and the index itself—is stored electronically. Key words can be assigned to electronic records, and even to paper ones, to make them more easily retrievable. When key words are assigned to a document, consistent terms must be used. For example, a search engine might not retrieve a document to which the key word *Superfund* had been spelled *Super Fund*. The search engine would not retrieve a search for the key word *radioactive* if the word *nuclear* had been assigned to a document itself. Conventions must be established for assigning key words and for spelling them. For example, a search engine might be unable to retrieve a document labeled *N.Y. D.E.C.* if someone had searched for *NYDEC*.

Naming conventions should be established for documents. Here, too, there are many methods. Documents might be slugged first by client name and matter and then by document type, version, the initials of the person who wrote the most recent revision, and the date. For example, the following are some document names:

- ManhattanNetworkInc-NYCtransactions-305E86St9JWcontractofsale-LNT-06152010
- PinkmoondustProductions-Connecticutstore-interiordesigncontract-v2-VLL-04302009
- GreggFarms-roadsidestandfranchise-storespecs-v4-RSD-06062010

The ability to track documents is vital. Untold hours could be wasted drafting a new work product from scratch when a prior effort is not remembered or recovered. Earlier projects can serve as templates for later ones. New contracts are not written each time a client needs an agreement drawn up; a lawyer or staff person begins with a prototype and then tailors it to the individual client's needs.

Not only must a firm's lawyers be able to locate documents previously prepared by themselves or by others at the firm, but also knowing who worked on those materials can also be enormously helpful. The lawyer can then consult these earlier drafters, as needed, for suggestions and input about various elements of a document. Why did they craft a phrase a certain way? Why was a standard clause omitted? Unless a later user can retrieve this earlier work, much valuable insight may well be lost.

3. Record Destruction

At some point, certain records are no longer needed. The trick is deciding what is unnecessary and when it becomes unnecessary. No one wants to deliberately destroy an important document. A firm should develop a records destruction policy in which records are reviewed periodically and slated for destruction provided that such measure is approved. For instance, a records clerk might identify certain materials that have been unused for a period of time, such as ten years, then circulate a list of materials to lawyers and others in the firm who once worked on them, and indicate that, unless there is an objection, the records will be destroyed on a certain date. Even if there is no objection, a lawyer should review the records to be destroyed. Other firms might choose to take greater precautions and require a lawyer to sign a request for records destruction.

If the records at issue are client files, the client should be informed that the firm no longer wishes to store the records for the client. The firm should offer to deliver the files to the client and should explain that if the client does not get back in touch with the firm by a certain date about the disposition of the files, the files will then be destroyed.

Factors to consider before files are destroyed include whether the statute of limitations period on any prospective malpractice claim has run and whether a case involves an unsatisfied judgment.

Certain documents should be retained, such as wills, files on a structured settlement if the settlement is not yet final, deeds, and other vital documents.

Precautions should be taken in actually destroying the documents, whether they are in digital form or in hard copy. Papers should not merely be deposited in garbage cans; they should be shredded first. Electronic files can often be recovered even if someone hits the "delete" key. A disk wiping program or other technological approach should be taken to permanently erase the existence of a file from a computer.

4. *Lawyer and Staff Training*

Personnel at law firms need to be told how to handle records. If they are not properly trained, documents will not be properly recorded, acted upon, filed, stored, retrieved, or disposed of, and a law firm will struggle as lawyers and others waste valuable time trying to find materials or to "reinvent the wheel" and generate new documents needlessly.

Undoubtedly, learning about records management procedures can be a bit tedious. Lawyers have a tendency to delegate such responsibilities to their support staff. Lawyers might put off going to training classes themselves or attend only briefly. New law clerks at large firms may be given no training and may have no idea where work they generate should be stored or how it should be filed. This is a mistake. How expensive is it on a day-to-day basis as they hunt for materials? Top-down demonstrations that records management is a vital activity for everyone at the firm are necessary in order for both lawyers and staff people to take the chore seriously.

Not only must everyone at the firm be trained on records management, but also a records supervisor must conduct quality control activities to make sure that materials are properly recorded and managed. A firm that is lax in its records management will find itself in disarray and exposed to malpractice lawsuits.

If a firm opts to delegate records management responsibilities to a revolving team of paralegals or other staffers, not much attention may be paid to quality control. Documents must still be retrievable when the primary person responsible for managing them is not in the office. To get people to follow appropriate records management procedures, the procedures should be user friendly, easy to explain, and easy to learn and use.

To encourage lawyers and staff people to take records management duties seriously, a firm might provide them with an opportunity to have input into its records management procedures. The suggestions of staff, in particular, should be sought. After all, they are the people who most often manage records. Lawyers must delegate appropriate records management tasks. Why should a lawyer who charges $500 per hour organize files when a files clerk making $40 per hour can do the task more efficiently? Even though staffers are likely to be better acquainted with records management tasks, lawyers must still be able to retrieve information, especially after-hours when support staff have gone home.

B.   Records Management Systems

Every law firm must have a records management system—a standardized means for recording, using, retaining, and destroying materials that can be taught to and used by others and revised as needed. Mail and packages must be appropriately routed, faxes must be delivered to the right person, client lists must be maintained, client contact information must be updated, copies of complaints or answers or other documents filed in a lawsuit must be responded to, documents associated with being in business must be addressed: utility bills, credit card bills, information about health insurance and claims, information about workers' compensation. The information coming into a firm must be organized and tracked so it can be followed up on, used, stored, and retrieved when necessary.

The need for duplicating some records must be addressed. If a letter from a client to a partner arrives, does a secretary log that letter into a master list of documents? Does she deliver it directly to the partner's inbox, or does she make a copy for the associate who is also working on the case? Does she place a copy of the letter in a client file? Does she scan a copy of that letter so it can be stored electronically? Who will follow up to determine that a response to the letter is sent?

So many different types of documents come into a firm that a clear line of authority must be established. Some materials must be circulated and acted upon or responded to, while others must be stored for future reference. Will all bills received be directed to the head of the accounting department? Or should they instead be routed to an overseeing partner, who will review them before forwarding them to accounting?

Although many records are stored electronically, these items, too, must be tracked and acted upon or stored appropriately so they can be easily retrieved at a future date. A firm's chief information officer may be closely involved with electronic records management, and a firm's librarian may share responsibilities for establishing and maintaining the firm's records management system. If a staff person is out of the office or on leave, others in the office must be able to maintain the records management system with no, or minimal, interruption. A system is necessary so that decision making is uniform: One person who is handling a document will route it to the appropriate destination just as another person who is handling it will.

A records management system can ensure an orderly business process. Without such a system, lawyers risk some fairly negative consequences. They can be subject to court sanctions and to legal malpractice claims.[3] Through the use of routing forms and software, records can be organized and stored. Using software will allow people to retrieve documents by key word and by other searchable features.

Before a records management system is established, modified, or expanded, an audit should be conducted to determine how records are used and managed and where problems currently exist. A new or modified system can correct failures associated with earlier ones the firm used.

Firms might either use commercially available software or have a custom-developed system created. In deciding whether to choose an "off-the-shelf" product or pay for someone to personalize one, a law firm should consider the following questions:

- How easily can the product be integrated with other systems, such as the firm's calendar or docket control system?
- How popular is the product? Are other users, especially other law firms, pleased with the product, or does it contain serious flaws?
- Are upgrades frequently and regularly available? Are they free, or is there a charge?
- How reputable is the company selling or developing the software? Is the company likely to be in existence and to create future generations of the product?
- How easily will new employees be able to learn and use the system successfully? What is the likelihood they will already be familiar with it?
- Is technical support available, and what does it cost?
- What does the product itself cost?

C. The Importance of Knowledge Management

Just as file management and docket management are subsets of records management, records management itself is a subset of the broader **knowledge management.** Knowledge refers both to explicit knowledge (that which is easily articulated and recorded) and to tacit knowledge (the knowledge that is in people's heads, such as insights).

knowledge management: The means by which knowledge is provided to allow people to perform their jobs.

Tacit knowledge—the sort that is unspoken—can be exceedingly valuable to a lawyer's practice. For instance, a firm might have, on behalf of a client, a copy of an application for a wetlands permit that it filed with a state department of environmental management. That is a record (explicit knowledge). The client might want to know when the application will be approved or, if it is not, when requests for additional information will be made. The state agency might not yet be able to provide a formal date for when it will make its decision or seek additional materials. A lawyer at the firm might know someone who works in the wetlands program who might be able, via a phone call, to found out whether this particular permit application will be deemed complete soon, or if additional information is likely to be sought. The agency contact might even be able to provide an informal time frame for when the agency will respond to the applicant. The lawyer with the contact could be in another office and might not even work in a firm's environmental group. Perhaps the lawyer went to graduate school with the state agency contact. The ability to determine that the firm and this particular lawyer have this resource—and the ability to retrieve and use it when appropriate—is knowledge management. Other lawyers at a firm might know that a certain judge likes to golf on Wednesdays or that another judge is very formal and prefers that lawyers who appear before him dress very conservatively. Knowledge management—via databases, SharePoint sites, intranets, and so forth—can provide a means to record, retrieve, and share this information. This is especially important for large firms with multiple offices.[4]

> The fundamental problem of managing knowledge has been with the profession since the earliest legal proceedings at Westminster, through the print era and has carried forward into the digital age. It is a challenge that lawyers will face far into the future. The prevailing modes of information transfer that are available to lawyers often dictate the methods we choose to preserve knowledge. In the early days of Anglo-American law practice, lawyers relied on being physically present and utilized their memory or their capacity for note taking as a way of building expertise. With the advent of the printing press, text became the dominant method for acquiring and preserving knowledge. Now, at what are still the early stages of the digital age, new tools of knowledge management are available to us. Our methods may change, but the problem remains the same.
>
> The challenge of finding new and better ways to develop, retain, and share expertise has never been more pressing.[5]

Knowledge should be organized, retrievable, shared, and maintained so that it remains even when there are departures from the firm. A firm should provide both internal knowledge management for information to be used by lawyers and staff, and client-facing knowledge management so that pertinent and appropriate information can be shared with specific clients. In setting up knowledge management systems, firms should be aware that some lawyers prefer to protect their knowledge. They feel their value to the firm might diminish if their insights are widely disseminated within the firm. Steps should be taken to reward lawyers and others for sharing their information to prevent this sort of knowledge hoarding.

D.   Ethical Issues

Like client files, many records must be properly safeguarded and protected from inadvertent disclosure. Personnel files contain sensitive information that should not be treated casually. Similarly, a firm is unlikely to want outsiders to know its income, expenditures, and the draw each partner gets. The same precautions accorded client files should also be given to firm records. Sensitive material in those files should be safeguarded and confidentiality maintained.

1.   Security

A firm should delineate clear lines of access to certain records. A random paralegal should not be able to access a senior associate's health care reimbursement claims. Should a summer associate be able to obtain every partner's home phone number and address? Should a new hire be able to access all prospective client intelligence data? Access to various types of information should be limited.

Protection of records may require the use of data encryption and passwords. A large firm that has an information technology employee should be able to discover potential problems with a records management system easily. For instance, an inquiry might be made if someone tries to access or duplicate thousands of files.

Precautions should likewise be taken when disposing of old records. Sensitive materials should not simply be placed in a wastebasket. Confidential materials should be shredded. A disk-wiping program should be used to rid old computers of sensitive data.

Appropriate precautions must also be taken to preserve records currently in use. Electronic records should be protected with antivirus software that is regularly updated. A firm should also have a procedure to alert appropriate people and take action should a security breach occur. Clear lines of authority should specify the people to be notified of a security breach, and decision-making authority should be established. Who decides whether the police should be notified of a security breach? It is best to anticipate such crises before they actually occur so lawyers and employees will understand their responsibilities if an unfortunate situation arises.

Likewise, a firm must have a disaster plan in place. If a fire or flood occurs in the office, the firm must be able to recover and to begin operating again as soon as possible. Electronic copies of vital records should be made and backed up at a remote location, so if an in-house computer service is destroyed, copies of the documents can still be recovered. Lawyers learned the importance of disaster planning after the 9/11 terrorist attacks on the World Trade Center in New York City. Several major law firms were housed in and around the World Trade Center. Buildings that were not destroyed by the attack were closed for a period of time after the attack occurred. Some firms had realized the importance of backing up important documents after the first attack on the World Trade Center in 1993.[6]

In addition to plans for a disaster, plans should be made for the disposition of records should the law firm dissolve or, in the case of a sole practitioner, should an attorney become incapacitated.

2. When Lawyers Leave Law Firms

In this age of mobility and transition, law firms merging, practice groups departing, and associates leaping from firm to firm, a law office must have a clear policy addressing the ownership of records that do not belong to clients. A lawyer who is thinking about leaving a firm may surreptitiously make copies of documents, such as sample forms, publicly available information that the firm has obtained, and prospective client intelligence. The lawyer might intend to take these materials with him or her to a new law firm. If leadership at a firm becomes aware that a lawyer, or practice group, may be departing, the firm might want to limit access to records. Ideally, a computerized records management system would flag instances of massive duplication of records and be able to identify such activities by user. A lawyer who is leaving may well begin to copy materials before he or she has given formal notice of departure.

Consider the following case involving lawyers who moved from one firm to another.

Gibbs v. Breed, Abbott & Morgan
271 A.D.2d 180 (N.Y. App. Div. 2000)

OPINION

MAZZARELLI, J.

Plaintiffs Charles Gibbs and Robert Sheehan are former partners of Breed, Abbott & Morgan (BAM) who specialize in trust and estate law. They withdrew from BAM in July 1991 to join Chadbourne & Parke (Chadbourne), and brought this action for monies due to them under their BAM partnership agreement. Defendants asserted various counterclaims alleging that plaintiffs breached their fiduciary duty to BAM. The counterclaims were severed and tried without a jury. Plaintiffs appeal from the trial court's determination that, in the course of both partners' planning and eventually implementing their withdrawal from BAM, they breached their fiduciary duty to the partnership.

From January 1991 until July 1991, plaintiffs were the only partners in the trusts and estates department (T/E) at BAM; plaintiff Gibbs was the head of the department. A third partner, Paul Lambert, had been the former head of the department, and he had obtained many, if not most, of the department's clients. In 1989 he had left the firm to become the United States Ambassador to Ecuador and was still on leave in 1991. Lambert intended to return to the firm upon completion of his term as ambassador. The BAM trusts and estates department also employed three associate attorneys, Warren Whitaker (fifteenth year), Austin Wilkie (fourth year), and Joseph Scorese (first year); two accountants, Lois Wetzel and Ellen Furst; and two paralegals, Lee Ann Riley and Ruth Kramer.

Gibbs had become dissatisfied with BAM, and in January 1991 he began interviews to locate a new affiliation. He also approached Sheehan to persuade him to move with him. Sheehan and Gibbs subsequently conducted a number of joint interviews with prospective employers. In May 1991, Ambassador Lambert visited BAM, and Gibbs told him that he had been interviewing. Lambert relayed this information to the other partners. In early June, plaintiffs informed the executive committee that they had received an offer from two firms: McDermott, Will & Emory and Bryan Cave.

On June 19, 1991, both plaintiffs informed Stephen Lang, BAM's presiding partner, that they had accepted offers to join Chadbourne. Lang asked Gibbs not to discuss his departure with any of the T/E associates, and Gibbs agreed not to do so. On June 20, 1991, Lawrence Warble, a BAM partner who was named temporary head of the T/E department, met with its associates and nonlegal personnel to inform them that plaintiffs were leaving the firm.

On June 24, 1991, Gibbs and Sheehan sent Chadbourne a memo listing the names of the personnel in the T/E department at BAM, their respective salaries, their annual billable hours, and the rate at which BAM billed out these employees to clients. The memo included other information about the attorneys, including the colleges and law schools they attended and their Bar admissions. This list had been prepared by Sheehan on April 26, 1991, months before the partners announced they were leaving. Sheehan specifically testified that the memo was prepared in anticipation of discussions with prospective firms, and both Gibbs and Sheehan testified at trial that the recruitment of certain associates and support personnel was discussed with different firms between March and May, as the partners were considering various affiliations. While Gibbs and Sheehan were still partners at BAM, Chadbourne interviewed four BAM employees that Gibbs had indicated he was interested in bringing to Chadbourne with him. On June 27, 1991, plaintiffs submitted their written resignations. Before Gibbs and Sheehan left BAM, they wrote letters to clients served by them, advising that they were leaving BAM and that other attorneys at BAM could serve them. These letters did not mention the fact that the two partners were moving to Chadbourne. Although the partnership agreement required 45 days' notice of an intention to withdraw, BAM waived this provision upon plaintiffs' production of their final billings for work previously performed.[1] Gibbs left BAM on July 9, 1991, and Sheehan left on July 11, 1991, both taking various documents, including their respective "chronology" or desk files.[2] With the assistance of his chronology file, Gibbs began to contact his former clients on July 11, 1991. On July 11th, Chadbourne made employment offers to Whitaker, Wilkie, Wetzel, and Riley. Wilkie, Wetzel, and Riley accepted that same day; Whitaker accepted on July 15, 1991. In the following weeks, 92 of the 201 BAM T/E clients moved their business to Chadbourne.

After hearing all the testimony and the parties' arguments, the trial court determined that Gibbs' actions in persuading his partner Sheehan to leave BAM, "and the way in which the leave was orchestrated, were done, at least partially, with the intention of crippling BAM's trusts and estates (T/E) department," (181 Misc 2d 346, 348) and constituted a breach of loyalty to BAM. The court also found that Gibbs and Sheehan had breached their fiduciary duties to BAM by sending Chadbourne the April 26, 1991 memo detailing personal information about the individuals in the T/E department at BAM, because this gave Chadbourne a competitive advantage in offering employment to other members of the department. Finally, the court found that Gibbs and Sheehan breached their fiduciary duties to BAM by taking their chronology files with them to Chadbourne. Specifically, the court concluded that by taking their respective chronology files, the partners "to a large degree hobbled their former partners in their effort to rebuild the Trusts and Estates department, in order to maintain a viable department, and in their ability to serve clients without undue disruption."

With respect to damages, the court concluded that both Gibbs and Sheehan were entitled to recover their share of BAM profits accruing until the end of July 1991, and that Sheehan was entitled to the remainder of his capital account with the firm. Although there was no evidence that the partners had improperly solicited former BAM clients, the court found that despite BAM's efforts to mitigate

---

[1] AM did not attempt to prepare a joint letter with Gibbs and Sheehan, announcing their departure, as recommended by the American Bar Association (ABA) Committee on Ethics and Professional Responsibility (*see* ABA Comm. on Ethics & Prof'l Responsibility, Informal Op. 1457 [1980]).

[2] The "chronology" or desk files contained copies of every letter written by the respective attorneys during the previous years. The letters included those written to adversaries about pending legal matters, letters written to clients, and letters written to others about ongoing BAM matters. These letters were duplicates of those kept in BAM's regular client files, but defendants allege that due to the fact that the files are arranged chronologically, active matters are more easily referenced. The original correspondences, left with the firm, have been filed by client and are dispersed throughout the department.

damages by hiring a new partner and two associates into the T/E department, that department suffered financial losses as a result of plaintiffs' conduct, and concluded that it was entitled to recover lost profits for a reasonable period following plaintiffs' departure. The court directed that lost profits be calculated from July 1991, when the partners left the firm, to November 1993, when BAM dissolved. Gibbs and Sheehan were held jointly and severally liable for $1,861,045. The court also awarded defendants prejudgment interest and attorneys' fees. The court's liability finding should be modified, the damage award vacated, and the matter remanded for a determination of the financial loss, if any, occasioned by plaintiffs' disloyal act of supplying competitors with BAM's confidential employee data.

The members of a partnership owe each other a duty of loyalty and good faith, and "[a]s a fiduciary, a partner must consider his or her partners' welfare, and refrain from acting for purely private gain" (*Meehan v. Shaughnessy*, 404 Mass. 419, 434, 535 N.E.2d 1255, 1263). Partners are constrained by such duties throughout the life of the partnership and "[t]he manner in which partners plan for and implement withdrawals . . . is [still] subject to the constraints imposed on them by virtue of their status as fiduciaries" (Robert Hillman, *Loyalty in the Firm: A Statement of General Principles on the Duties of Partners Withdrawing from Law Firms*, 55 Wash. & Lee L. Rev. 997, 999 [1998]). According the trial court's findings on issues of fact and credibility appropriate deference, we uphold that portion of the court's liability determination which found that plaintiffs breached their fiduciary duty as partners of the firm they were about to leave by supplying confidential employee information to Chadbourne while still partners at BAM. However, we find no breach with respect to Gibbs' interactions with Sheehan, or with respect to either partner's removal of his desk files from BAM.

Defendants did not establish that Gibbs breached any duty to BAM by discussing with Sheehan a joint move to another firm, or that Sheehan's decision was based upon anything other than his own personal interests. In addition, while in certain situations "[A] lawyer's removal or copying, without the firm's consent, of materials from a law firm that do not belong to the lawyer, that are the property of the law firm, and that are intended by the lawyer to be used in his new affiliation, could constitute dishonesty, which is professional misconduct under [Model] Rule 8.4 (c)" (DC Bar Legal Ethics Comm. Op. 273, at 192), here, the partners took their desk copies of recent correspondence with the good faith belief that they were entitled to do so.

Contrary to the finding of the trial court, and applying the principle that "[t]he distinction between motive and process is critical to a realistic application of fiduciary duties" (Hillman, *op. cit.* at 999), we find no breach of duty in plaintiffs taking their desk files. These were comprised of duplicates of material maintained in individual client files, the partnership agreement was silent as to these documents, and removal was apparently common practice for departing attorneys.

However, the record supports the court's finding that both partners committed a breach of their fiduciary duty to the BAM partners by supplying Chadbourne, and presumably the other partnerships they considered joining, with the April 26, 1991 memorandum describing the members of BAM's T/E department, their salaries, and other confidential information, such as billing rates and average billable hours, taken from personnel files. Moreover, a closer examination of the record does not support the dissent's conclusion that these partners did not engage in surreptitious recruiting. The partners may not have discussed with firm employees the possibility of moving with them prior to June 20, 1991, but they indicated to Chadbourne the employees they were interested in prior to this date, and Gibbs specifically testified that he refrained from telling one of his partners, to whom he had a duty of loyalty, about his future plans to recruit specific associates and support staff from the partnership.

There is no evidence of improper client solicitation in this case, nor is it an issue on this appeal. Although the analogy could be useful in concluding that Gibbs did not breach his fiduciary duty to the partnership by working with Sheehan to find a new affiliation, the fiduciary restraints upon a partner with respect to client solicitation are not analogous to those applicable to employee recruitment. By contrast to the lawyer-client relationship, a partner does not have a fiduciary duty to the employees of a firm which would limit his duty of loyalty to the partnership. Thus, recruitment of firm employees has been viewed as distinct and "permissible on a more limited basis than . . . solicitation of clients" (Hillman, *op. cit.* at 1031). Prewithdrawal recruitment is generally allowed "only after the firm has been given notice of the lawyer's intention to withdraw" (*ibid.*).

However, here Sheehan prepared a memo in April of 1991, well in advance of even deciding, much less informing his partners of his intention to withdraw. There is ample support in the record for the trial court's finding that the preparation and sending of the April 26, 1991 memo, combined with the subsequent hiring of certain trusts and estates personnel, constituted an egregious breach of plaintiff's fiduciary duty to BAM. Moreover, it is not speculative to infer more widespread dissemination given Sheehan's trial testimony that the memo "was prepared in connection with talking to other firms," and that "he was sure the subject of staffing was discussed at firms other than Chadbourne." Sheehan's disclosure of confidential BAM data to even one firm was a direct breach of his duty of loyalty to his partners. Because the memo gave Chadbourne confidential BAM employment data as well as other information reflecting BAM's valuation of each employee, Chadbourne was made privy to information calculated to give it an unfair advantage in recruiting certain employees.

While partners may not be restrained from inviting qualified personnel to change firms with them, here Gibbs and Sheehan began their recruiting while still members of the firm and prior to serving notice of their intent to withdraw. They did so without informing their partners that they were disseminating confidential firm data to competitors. Their actions, while still members of the firm, were intended to and did place BAM in the position of not knowing which of their employees were targets and what steps would be appropriate for them to take in order to retain these critical employees. The dissent's analysis, that once the firm was notified of the partners' departure, there was no breach of fiduciary duty, is flawed. The breach occurred in April of 1991 and could not be cured by any after-the-fact notification by the fiduciary who committed the breach that he was withdrawing from the firm. Chadbourne still had the unfair advantage of the confidential information from the April 1991 memo, and still had the upper hand, which was manifested by its ability to tailor its offers and incentives to the BAM recruits.

Contrary to the dissent, I would characterize the memo distributed to prospective competitors as confidential. The data was obtained from BAM personnel files which Sheehan had unique access to as a BAM partner. The dissent's statement that such financial information is generally known to "headhunters" is without foundation. While the broad outlines of the partners' profits at a select number of large New York firms and the incremental increases in the base compensation of young associates at some firms are published in professional publications such as the New York Law Journal, or known to some recruitment firms, the available figures often vary substantially from the actual compensation received by specific individuals.

For example, the BAM partnership agreement, which is included in the record, reveals that the approximately 40 partners in the firm earn substantially different percentages of the firm's earnings. No professional publication would be privy to these financials. With respect to the specific associates and support staff whose compensation was disseminated in the April 1991 memo, the information disclosed to Chadbourne incorporated these individuals' bonuses. Bonus payments are confidential, often voted by the partnership, based upon the unique quality of an individual's work, the number of hours billed, and many other intangible factors. These lump-sum payments often constitute a substantial portion of an associate's salary, and the payments are certainly not available to the public. Finally, support staff also receive bonuses paid to them at the discretion of the individual partners, from their personal accounts. This information is highly individualized and also privileged. Sheehan abused his fiduciary duty to the partnership by accessing personnel files to obtain the actual gross compensation of the associates and support staff he and Gibbs wished to bring with them, including bonuses, and disclosing this information to Chadbourne.

Moreover, the memo contained more than a list of salaries. It itemized each of the employee's annual billable hours, and the rates at which BAM billed these employees out to their clients, information which was not otherwise publically available. These facts go directly to a potential employee's value and were accessible only to members of the BAM partnership. Selected partners providing BAM's confidential information, which they were able to obtain by virtue of their position as fiduciaries, to Chadbourne was an act of disloyalty to their partnership. The confidential information placed Chadbourne, as a competing prospective employer, in the advantageous position of conducting interviews of the associates and support staff with more knowledge than any firm could obtain through independent research, as well as providing it with information BAM partners did not know it had, thereby prejudicing their own efforts to retain their associates and support staff.

The calculation of damages in cases such as this is difficult. "[B]reaches of a fiduciary relationship in any context comprise a special breed of cases that often loosen normally stringent requirements of causation and damages" (*Milbank, Tweed, Hadley & McCloy v. Chan Cher Boon*, 13 F.3d 537, 543 [2d Cir. 1994]; *see Wolf v. Rand*, 258 A.D.2d 401). This is because the purpose of this type of action "is not merely to *compensate* the plaintiff for wrongs committed . . . [but also] 'to *prevent* them, by removing from agents and trustees all inducement to attempt dealing for their own benefit in matters which they have undertaken for others, or to which their agency or trust relates'" (*Diamond v. Oreamuno*, 24 N.Y.2d 494, 498 [emphasis in original], quoting *Dutton v. Willner*, 52 N.Y. 312, 319). However, the proponent of a claim for a breach of fiduciary duty must, at a minimum, establish that the offending parties' actions were "a substantial factor" in causing an identifiable loss (*Millbank, Tweed, Hadley & McCloy v. Chan Cher*

Boon, supra at 543; *see 105 E. Second St. Assocs. v. Bobrow,* 175 A.D.2d 746 [awarding amount of loss sustained by reason of the faithless fiduciary's conduct]).

A reasonable assessment of lost profits has been deemed an appropriate measure of damages in cases where there was evidence that the fiduciary improperly solicited clients to move with him or her (*see Meehan v. Shaughnessy, supra,* 404 Mass. at 435, 535 N.E.2d at 1264), or where the fiduciary's acts could otherwise be connected to a subsequent loss of business (*see Duane Jones Co. v. Burke,* 306 N.Y. 172, 192; *Bruno Co. v. Friedberg,* 21 A.D.2d 336, 341; *see also Wolf v. Rand, supra* at 402 [lost profits awarded where defendants in closely held corporation misappropriated company profits to themselves]). Here, the court based its damage award on what it believed to be a series of disloyal acts. Defendants did not establish how the only act of plaintiffs which this Court finds to be disloyal, that of supplying employee information to Chadbourne, in and of itself, was a substantial cause of BAM's lost profits (*see Stoeckel v. Block,* 170 A.D.2d 417 [no demonstration that the decline in defendant's business was attributable to plaintiffs' alleged wrongful conduct during the term of their employment]). We therefore vacate the court's award to defendants of the total profits lost by BAM between the time of plaintiffs' departure in July 1991 and BAM's dissolution in November 1993, and remand for consideration of the issue of whether plaintiffs' disloyal act of sending Chadbourne the April 26, 1991 memorandum was a significant cause of any identifiable loss, and, if so, the amount of such loss.

Accordingly, the order, Supreme Court, New York County (Herman Cahn, J.), entered October 1, 1998, which, after a nonjury trial on defendants' counterclaims, determined that plaintiffs had breached their fiduciary duty to defendants, should be modified, on the law, to limit such conclusion to the act of disseminating confidential employee information, and otherwise affirmed, without costs. Order, same court and Justice, entered on or about June 29, 1999, which, to the extent appealed from as limited by the parties' briefs, directed that defendants shall recover $1,861,045, plus prejudgment interest, on their counterclaims, should be reversed, on the law, without costs, the damage award vacated, and the matter remanded for recalculation of damages in accordance with this Opinion.

CONCUR BY: SAXE (IN PART)

Dissent by: SAXE (In Part)

E.   Special-Interest Area: E-mail

Rule 1.6 of the ABA's *Model Rules of Professional Conduct* directs lawyers to ensure that their communications regarding representation of clients are confidential. A law firm should take precautions to protect its e-mail communications. A firm should draft an e-mail policy addressing the use of e-mail and its handling and storage. Such a policy might specify that all e-mail messages should have a confidentiality notice indicating that the message is intended for only a specified recipient. The policy might also standardize how e-mail messages should be "slugged," or named, in the "Re" line so they can be tracked easily and retrieved later.

A system for storing e-mail messages should be established. Will e-mail messages be filed according to client and matter? Will certain ones be directed to others for follow-up? How will such correspondence be logged and tracked? E-mail messages might also be separated into subject matter files with copies stored in client files. Ideally, any e-mail system will have a search capability. If an e-mail program is incapable of storing large volumes of material, then options for storing and retrieving older e-mail messages should be explored.

Care must be taken not to misdirect e-mail messages by, for instance, hitting "Reply all" when responding to a message, if that is not the sender's intention. "Reply all" might be disabled or "Reply sender" might be made the default option. Caution should also be exercised when an e-mail program automatically fills in an addressee's name after a few letters have been typed in the "To" box. A message can easily be misdirected simply because two people have names that begin with the same letters.

Access to e-mail messages should be appropriately limited through the use of passwords, firewalls, and antivirus software. At the same time, such protections should be monitored and checked that they are allowing necessary correspondence to be received.

Checklist

- A law firm must have a records management system in place to deal with all the materials it receives on a daily basis.
- A firm's record management policy should identify the various types of records that are being tracked, establish handling requirements for each type, determine who has access to various types of records, and safeguard the handling of different types of records.
- A firm should also have a broader knowledge management system that incorporates both explicit knowledge, such as records, and tacit knowledge, such as lawyers' insights about judges. The information in a knowledge management system should be retrievable and able to be shared both internally and with clients, as appropriate.
- Arrangements must also be made for knowledge and records storage, whether electronic, physical on-site, or long-term off-site storage.
- A records destruction policy and procedure should also be an element of a records management policy.
- The firm's leadership should support the firm's knowledge and records management systems and ensure that other lawyers and employees are aware of them and contribute to them.
- An index identifying the categories by which records are organized must be created and maintained.

- Users of the knowledge and records management systems must be able to retrieve very specific information as well as more general information.
- Key words can be assigned to electronic records, and even to paper ones, to make them more easily retrievable.
- Conventions must be established for assigning key words and for spelling them.
- Through the use of routing forms and software, records can be organized and stored. Using software allows documents to be retrieved by key words and other searchable features.
- Before a records management system is established, modified, or expanded, an audit should be conducted to determine how records are used and managed and where problems exist.
- Records must be protected so that sensitive or confidential information is not accessible by inappropriate people within or outside the firm.
- Law firms should have a disaster preparedness plan in place and should also provide for the disposition of records should the law firm dissolve or, in the case of a sole practitioner, should an attorney become incapacitated.
- Given the amount of correspondence by e-mail today, a firm should also have a policy in place to protect e-mail correspondence and to store and retrieve it.

Vocabulary

"back-office" activity (p. 307)	**knowledge management** (p. 313)
cloud computing (p. 308)	**records management** (p. 305)
"front-office" activity (p. 307)	**records retention** (p. 307)

Career Preparation Tips

Much of the knowledge that you are acquiring as you work your way through this textbook can be applied and used in a future career in the legal field. As you gain knowledge and insight about the legal market and those who work in it, you might want to organize it into your own personal knowledge management system. Rather than taking notes on paper by hand, you might want to take notes electronically using your computer so that you can file these notes and retrieve them easily at some future point. As you take other courses about law and the legal industry, you can add to your knowledge management system so that you will be better prepared when you are seeking a position in the legal field and going on job interviews. Learn how to assign key words to documents and to store them in various places in your computer or in the cloud so that they can be retrieved easily at some future point.

If You Want to Learn More

ABA Law Practice Division. http://www.americanbar.org/groups/law_practice.html

Association of Legal Administrators Legal Management Resource Center. http://www.alanet.org/research/directory.asp

Association of Records Managers and Administrators. http://www.arma.org

Florida Bar, Member Services, Law Office Management Assistance Service (LOMAS). http://www.floridabar.org/LOMAS

U.S. National Archives and Records Administration. http://www.archives.gov

A2J Author, a software tool to assist pro se litigants that allows courts and others to create guided interviews to help these litigants complete forms. http://www.a2jauthor.org/drupal/ or http://www.youtube.com/a2jauthor

HotDocs, a document generation platform that includes document generation interviews so a client can provide much information himself. http://www.hotdocs.com

Reading Comprehension

1. How does records management differ from file management and docket management?
2. Which is more challenging to record, explicit knowledge or tacit knowledge?
3. What equipment is needed for records management?
4. For how long should a law firm retain records?
5. How does an index help support a law firm's record management system?
6. When should client files be destroyed?
7. Who is responsible for records management at a law firm?

8. What are some precautions that can be taken to protect physical records?
9. What are some precautions that can be taken to protect electronic records?
10. Who owns law firm records that do not belong to the law firm's clients?
11. How can the confidentiality of e-mail messages be protected?

Discussion Starters

1. Consider the documents you have stored in your own computer. Would a stranger be able to retrieve a paper you had written for one of your courses? Would the stranger be able to determine which version was the final one if you had drafted more than one? How do you name documents?

2. Consider e-mail messages slugged with the following words:

   Us
   Today's Meeting
   Thanx
   Snuggy Bear v. Puffinstuff Expert Witness

   a. Which one is the most informative?
   b. Which one is too casual?
   c. Which ones are appropriate for lawyer-client correspondence?
   d. Which ones are appropriate for paralegal-client correspondence?

3. Consider the following types of administrative records a law firm is likely to have in its possession. Who should have access to each type of record, and why?

   - payroll records
   - health insurance information
   - employee files
   - forms completed by job applicants
   - performance evaluations
   - contracts
   - hiring letters
   - offer letters
   - background checks
   - information about salaries
   - references
   - vacation request forms
   - information on garnishments
   - disability insurance claims
   - attendance records
   - time cards for staff
   - recruiting materials
   - family and medical leave materials

- accounts payable
- accounts receivable
- affirmative action/diversity information
- discrimination claims
- benefits information
- independent contractor records
- data on marketing efforts
- research on prospective clients
- insurance carriers, policies, and premiums
- workers' compensation claims
- material safety data sheets
- Occupational Safety and Health Administration information
- injury reports
- information on retirement benefits

4. Suppose you had to teach a four-hour seminar on your law firm's records management policy to new hires, both lawyers and support staff. What areas would you cover? How would you make the seminar interesting? How would you ensure that the new hires follow the records management policy?

5. Review the excerpt from *Gibbs v. Breed, Abbott & Morgan* in the chapter. Who brought the lawsuit? Why? What was the court's holding in the case? Do you think the decision was correctly decided? Did any aspect of the decision surprise you? How did the dissenting opinion differ from the majority one?

6. Look up and read *Pace v. United Services Automobile Assn.*, No. 05-cv-01562-LTB-MJW, 2007 U.S. Dist. LEXIS 49425 (D. Colo. July 9, 2007). Why did the plaintiff's counsel in the case fail to appear for a settlement conference? What excuse for their failure to appear did they provide to the court? Was this an adequate excuse? What was the result of their failure to appear?

Case Studies

1. Suppose you work for the law firm that represented the plaintiffs in *Gibbs v. Breed, Abbott & Morgan* (see the excerpt in this chapter). What key words would you assign to the case so that the opinion would be retrievable in your firm's electronic database? If you were setting up client files for these plaintiffs, what would you name the files? Create a master list of files, and then create an index for those files.

2. Imagine that you are an information manager at a major law firm that wants to expand the tacit knowledge in its knowledge management system as the firm has expanded and has many lawyers in multiple offices

around the globe. Develop a questionnaire for attorneys and staff to complete that will provide useful, tacit knowledge. Consider specifically how questions might be phrased to provide more thorough, candid responses. Also research change management plans and develop a change management plan appropriate for the legal field to persuade lawyers and others to contribute regularly to the knowledge management system.

3. Consider all of the subjects discussed in this chapter and establish naming conventions for them. For instance, should the phrase "records management" include an *s* on the end of records, or should there be no *s*? Should the law firm Breed, Abbott & Morgan be identified by that name, by the name Breed Abbott and Morgan, by the initials BAM, or by the initials B.A.M.? Write a short naming conventions manual including the letters *A* through *Z* for which names or words should be standardized.

4. Research several commercially available records management systems programs. Compare and contrast their features. Which would work best in a firm with 10 or fewer lawyers? Which would work with a 30-lawyer firm that has offices in three states? Which would work with a 1,000-lawyer firm that has seven offices in the United States and eight other offices around the world? The programs you might research include Accutrac, Elite, FileSurf, iManage, LegalKey, ProLaw, and Worldox.

5. Find a recent newspaper account of a lawyer or law firm employee who got into trouble involving e-mail. What activity is covered in the newspaper account? How might this situation have been avoided? What would your reaction to this account be if you were a client of this particular firm? In what way should the lawyer or law firm employee have been reprimanded for getting into this trouble?

Endnotes

1. 44 U.S.C. §3301 (2013).
2. George C. Cunningham & John C. Montaña, *The Lawyer's Guide to Records Management and Retention* 120 (2006).
3. *See, e.g.,* Anthony E. Davis & David J. Elkanich, *The Risk Management Challenges of Record Retention and Destruction — Developing Records Management Policies That Protect Both Law Firms and Their Clients,* 19 A.B.A Prof. Law. 1 (2008).
4. *See, e.g.,* Robert Denney, *Can All the Multinational Firms Survive?,* 63 The Advoc. (Texas) 27 (Summer 2013).
5. Conrad Johnson & Brian Donnelly, *If Only We Knew What We Know,* 88 Chi.-Kent L. Rev. 729, 729–30 (2013) (footnote omitted).
6. *See, e.g.,* Jonathan D. Glater, *After the Attacks: The Records; Corporate Paper Trails Lie Buried in Soot,* N.Y. Times, Sept. 13, 2001, *available at* http://www.nytimes .com/2001/09/13/business/after-the-attacks-the-records-corporate-paper-trails-lie-buried-in-soot.html?scp=6&sq=law%20firm%20records%20&st=nyt&pagewanted=1.

13

○ ○ ○

Law Firm Library Management

○ ○ ○

Chapter Outcomes

By the end of this chapter, a student will be able to:

- Understand the importance of competent and thorough legal research to a law practice and clients
- Discuss the importance of competitive intelligence to the growth of a legal business
- Identify different types of primary and secondary sources of law
- Locate pertinent legal materials using different resources
- Research and compile lists of pertinent legal resources

Prospective lawyers and paralegals may envision law firm libraries like those featured in films: grand, stately rooms furnished with mahogany tables and chairs, brass lamps with shades made of green glass, and shelving featuring rows and rows of, if not leather-bound, serious-looking books with uniform bindings. Some libraries—especially law school libraries—do look like that. A law firm's library probably does not look quite so impressive, though. It's likely to be multifunctional and may be more cramped. But the law firm library serves a vital function as a repository and disseminator of materials to which lawyers and staff need access.

Although pleasant surroundings are nice to work in, more important, as far as libraries go, are materials that are well organized and retrievable. A library in disarray or databases that go unused do not help lawyers do their jobs and may cause them and their staff to squander precious time tracking down materials that should have been properly identified, distributed, and tracked.

Technological advances mean that law firm libraries today include far more than bookcases, tables, and shelves. As firms transition from print materials to electronic ones and downsize the physical space allocated to libraries[1] and lower budgets, librarians are conducting more training, managing vendor relationships, and conducting research about competitors and prospective clients. Librarians tend to be very efficient researchers, especially compared to junior associates.

The contents of a law firm's library vary depending on the size of the firm and the practice areas it hosts. A small firm in Albany, N.Y., is likely to use *New York Reports* (covering decisions issued by the state's highest court) but probably won't have much need for *California Reports*. Likewise, a small firm in Sacramento will probably use *California Reports* but not *New York Reports*. Large law firms with varied practices in multiple jurisdictions will, of course, have more extensive information needs.

Increasingly, lawyers are using electronic databases, Web-based applications, and ebooks for research rather than printed materials. Lawyers are likely to use an integrated library system, or computerized database, to search for materials accessible via the library.[2] In a survey by a technical services manager in the library and knowledge management department of a major law firm, almost 27 percent of law firms purchased ebooks for lawyers in 2012, and 43 percent planned to do so in 2013.[3] Rather than having to spend a lot of time labeling and cataloging books, law firm librarians are undertaking very different tasks.

curate:
Care for or oversee the items in a collection.

A librarian's role differs given the type of firm, its culture, its size, and the materials in its library. **Curating,** or overseeing, a firm's collection, with input from lawyers and others, is a primary function of a librarian. Librarians' roles have changed as libraries have become more automated. Large firms may have a librarian or even a team of them, along with support staff. Some firms might embed a librarian within a practice group so the group can work as a team and the librarian can build good working relationships with the lawyers and paralegals in that group. A librarian is likely to review periodicals for articles that might be useful to the firm's lawyers and will need to maintain routing lists to circulate materials accordingly. The librarian may work with a network of other firm and agency libraries to coordinate interlibrary loans and to oversee access to the library by personnel outside the firm.

A librarian helps to locate needed information. The methods by which librarians find and retrieve materials have evolved significantly:

> In the twenty-first century, the law librarian is neither a solitary explorer nor a bridge. The intersection of technology and source material has triggered a reconsideration of the figure. Now, the law librarian is a multi-faceted nodule on a three-dimensional network, accessible through multiple points of entry and connected to a constellation of source material derived from personal and educational experiences. Diversity of experience is a strength, and specialization is expected.[4]

Outreach to members of the firm is important so that lawyers and others are comfortable using the library and finding materials there. A law librarian might develop a guide to the library and its resources to make it more user friendly, especially for new hires. Increasingly, librarians are called upon to help train staffers, summer associates, and even lawyers, some of whom are ill prepared to conduct legal research.

Beyond educating new hires about a firm's information resources, a librarian may well provide frequent training sessions to personnel, even for those whose capabilities are at the intermediate or advanced level. New technologies and new means for conveying and retrieving information make "continuing library education" a must for lawyers and staff members at all levels. The importance of being able to do legal research cannot be underestimated. A librarian is also likely to provide research support as practitioners approach the librarian for help with research needs. It is possible that a librarian might also bill for time spent on specific research projects. While, ultimately, a lawyer is responsible for being a competent legal researcher, a capable librarian can be invaluable. Lawyers, after all, can be subject to sanction if they are sloppy in their legal research.

Golden v. Helen Sigman & Associates, Ltd.
No. 08-1506, 2010 U.S. App. LEXIS 13585
(7th Cir. July 2, 2010)

JUDGES: BEFORE CUDAHY, WOOD, AND SYKES, CIRCUIT JUDGES

OPINION BY: WOOD

WOOD, *Circuit Judge*. In 2004, Bruce Golden's wife Jody Rosenbaum filed for divorce in Illinois state court. The proceedings that followed were fraught with hostility as the parties engaged in a bitter dispute over division of assets and custody of Dale, their only child. After a year of setbacks in state court, Golden filed a multi-count federal lawsuit. He seems to have named anyone who advocated for Rosenbaum in state court as a defendant, including Nancy Thomas, Rosenbaum's friend and neighbor; Helen Sigman, the court-appointed representative for the child; Rosenbaum's counsel; and two of Rosenbaum's business associates.

The district court abstained with respect to Golden's claim that he owned certain copyrights, on the theory that the ownership of assets in general would be resolved in the state divorce proceedings; it granted defendants' motions to dismiss on all other counts. A couple of years later, the district court sanctioned Golden pursuant to Fed. R. Civ. P. 11(b)(2), requiring him to pay defendants' attorneys' fees and expenses. Golden has now appealed, and we affirm.

I

On January 18, 2005, Golden sued the defendants in federal court, raising claims under federal copyright law, 17 U.S.C. §§501 *et seq.*, civil RICO, 18 U.S.C. §§1962(c) and (d), and 42 U.S.C. §1983, as well as a variety of state-law theories. Golden's allegations revolve around his stormy divorce. He is convinced that the defendants have acted in concert to damage his relationship with his daughter Dale, impugn his reputation, and destroy his financial well-being.

Golden's complaint alleges that Rosenbaum's attorneys at Nadler, Pritikin & Mirabelli, LLC (collectively "Nadler") wrote letters defaming him and sought to disrupt his business relationships. He also accused Nadler, along with two of Rosenbaum's business associates, of deliberately infringing his copyright to a real estate listing system. Sigman, Golden asserts, maligned his reputation and abdicated her duty of neutrality by favoring Rosenbaum in the custody proceedings. Finally, he believes that Thomas violated his rights when, in an effort to assist

Rosenbaum's claim for child custody, she called 911 to report (falsely, he says) that Golden had abused his daughter.

After Golden amended his complaint, the defendants filed motions to dismiss for failure to state a claim upon which relief may be granted. See Fed R. Civ. P. 12(b)(6). On November 1, 2005, the district court granted these motions with one exception: it stayed proceedings for Count I, which alleged copyright infringement. For that claim, the court decided to abstain and to stay the federal action pending the resolution of ongoing state proceedings. In dismissing Golden's civil RICO claim, the court concluded that he had not properly pleaded the requisite predicate acts and pattern of racketeering activity necessary to state a claim. Golden was not entitled to relief under §1983, the court found, because Sigman had not acted under color of state law and she enjoyed absolute immunity from suit. As Golden's state-law claims were unrelated to the remaining copyright count, the district court relinquished supplemental jurisdiction over them.

A month later, Nadler filed a motion for Rule 11 sanctions. The magistrate judge issued a report on July 15, 2008, recommending that Nadler's motion be granted. The following week, Sigman and Thomas jumped on the bandwagon and filed their own motions for sanctions; their motions were also endorsed by the magistrate judge. Concluding that many of Golden's positions were wholly devoid of legal support, the district court decided to impose sanctions against him pursuant to Fed R. Civ. P. 11(b)(2), in the form of attorneys' fees. But because the sanctions related only to certain parts of the complaint, the district court reviewed the defendants' billing records and ordered Golden to pay just the fees related to the offending claims. Soon thereafter, Golden settled with Nadler, which was voluntarily dismissed from the case. At that point, the district court granted Golden's motion for a final judgment under Fed R. Civ. P. 54(b). This timely appeal followed.

II

Golden has abandoned his civil RICO theory on appeal and instead has concentrated on the district court's dismissal of his §1983 claim against Sigman. This court reviews a dismissal pursuant to Rule 12(b)(6) *de novo*. The district court concluded that Golden's §1983 claim against Sigman was a nonstarter for two independent reasons: Sigman was not a state actor, and she was absolutely immune from suit. While Golden challenges this decision on appeal, in the district court he repeatedly said that his acceptance of "[the district court judge's] ruling without seeking further relief before her or elsewhere" should weigh against the imposition of sanctions. Sigman interprets Golden's words as a waiver of his argument against dismissal of his §1983 claim. "[O]nce a position is announced" in district court, Sigman contends, "backpedaling on appeal cannot be allowed." *Miller v. Willow Creek Homes, Inc., 249 F.3d 629, 631 (7th Cir. 2001).*

In our view, Golden's statement falls short of a waiver. . . . This court has found waiver only when an attorney has unambiguously taken a position irreconcilable with that presented on appeal. *Miller* illustrates the point well. There the court found that the appellants had waived their right to appeal by: (1) withdrawing a motion for reconsideration; (2) notifying the court that "[they were] not going to be appealing" summary judgment; and (3) requesting that any related claims be stricken from the amended complaint. See *Miller, 249 F.3d at 631* (emphasizing appellants' "clear statements of their intent" to waive appeal). In contrast, by framing his statement in the past tense (he "accepted" the dismissal order), Golden did not explicitly forswear the possibility of an appeal. Furthermore, noting that the court dismissed his state-law claims for lack of supplemental jurisdiction, Golden points out that referring to "further relief . . . elsewhere" might allude to pursuing these claims in state court. We are satisfied that he avoided waiver of appellate review.

Turning to the merits, we begin by observing that we recently held that child representatives in Illinois are entitled to absolute immunity. *Cooney v. Rossiter, 583 F.3d 967, 970 (7th Cir. 2009)* (analogizing child representatives to guardians *ad litem* and court-appointed experts). But Cooney left the door open a crack for some suits against representatives. Immunity extends, it acknowledged, only with respect to conduct that "occurred within the course of [a child representative's] court-appointed duties." *Id.* At the time Golden filed his lawsuit, Illinois law made child representatives responsible for acting as the child's attorney, pursuing investigations into the facts, and offering recommendations to the court. 750 ILCS 5/506(a)(3); *Cooney, 583 F.3d at 969* (explaining that a "child's representative is a hybrid of a child's attorney, 750 ILCS 5/506(a)(1), and a child's guardian *ad litem*").

Golden asserts that he raised allegations in his complaint that Sigman engaged in misconduct that fell outside the scope of her statutorily defined role. He focuses on Sigman's allegedly false and misleading communications with the parties on matters related to the custody dispute. According to Golden, Sigman falsely told Dale that Golden was dangerous and misrepresented facts about the proceedings to Golden. Even assuming that this were true, however, Sigman was still carrying out her responsibilities as a child representative; those duties centrally include speaking with the relevant actors about the custody proceedings and investigating the facts. *Id.* (concluding that child representative could not be sued based upon his conversations with a psychiatrist regarding the children in the custody dispute). In this limited capacity, her actions closely resemble those of a guardian *ad litem*. Thus, she functioned as an "arm[] of the court" and "deserve[s] protection from harassment by disappointed litigants, just as judges do." *Id.*

More problematic are Golden's allegations that relate to Sigman's acts as an advocate, such as her preparation of court orders and her efforts to eliminate the role of the court-appointed psychiatrist. Though these tasks are part and parcel of a child representative's statutory duties, they involve a form of advocacy that more closely resembles the work carried out by a public defender than that of a guardian *ad litem*. As the court in *Cooney* did not confront allegations implicating a child representative's actions as an advocate, it did not have the opportunity to comment on this issue.

We, too, can lay it aside for another day, for a different reason. In our case, the *Rooker-Feldman* doctrine bars us from reviewing the question whether Sigman violated Golden's rights when she acted as Dale's advocate. *See Rooker v. Fidelity Trust Co., 263 U.S. 413, 415-16, 44 S. Ct. 149, 68 L. Ed. 362 (1923); District of Columbia Ct. of App. v. Feldman, 460 U.S. 462, 486, 103 S. Ct. 1303, 75 L. Ed. 2d 206 (1983).* The doctrine prevents a party "complaining of an injury caused by [a] state-court judgment" from seeking redress in a lower federal court. See *Exxon Mobil Corp. v. Saudi Basic Industries Corp., 544 U.S. 280, 291-92, 125 S. Ct.*

1517, 161 L. Ed. 2d 454 (2005). Although we recognize that the Supreme Court has warned against a broad reading of this doctrine, see *Lance v. Dennis, 546 U.S. 459, 126 S. Ct. 1198, 163 L. Ed. 2d 1059 (2006)*, our case does not present the risk of expansion that was present in *Lance*. There, the Court disapproved the use of *Rooker-Feldman* "where the party against whom the doctrine is invoked was not a party to the underlying state-court proceeding." 546 U.S. at 464. In our case, the parties are identical, and the only injury that Golden alleges that he has suffered from Sigman's supposedly biased advocacy is the alienation of Dale's affections and a reduction in his custodial rights. These harms flow directly from the fruit of Sigman's efforts: state-court custody orders favorable to Rosenbaum. Golden has not alleged a procedural harm that is separate and independent from the state court's custody determination. See, *e.g.*, *Nesses v. Shepard, 68 F.3d 1003, 1005 (7th Cir. 1995)* (explaining that plaintiff's claim that his state trial was tainted by politics was distinct from a claim that the state-court judgment was erroneous). As Golden's allegations cannot be separated from the state court's judgment, *Rooker-Feldman* acts as a jurisdictional bar. We add for the sake of completeness that even if some aspect of these orders escapes *Rooker-Feldman*, after *Lance*, we would reject Golden's claims on the merits. The federal court would be obliged to give full faith and credit to the state-court judgment, see 28 U.S.C. §1738, and we see no reason why Golden should be entitled to reopen matters that the state court actually resolved or could have resolved.

All that remains of Golden's complaint are a couple of allegations, neither of which has merit. Golden's conclusory claim that Sigman helped Rosenbaum violate court visitation orders lacks the factual specificity required to raise it above the speculative level. Similarly there is nothing to Golden's allegation that Sigman had Dale's school deny him access to Dale unless he was accompanied by a guard. Sigman only informed Dale's school that Golden's visitation rights had to be restricted after the state court had limited Golden to an hour a week of supervised visitation. Sigman's communications with the school, as a practical matter, added nothing to the state court's order, which as we already have explained cannot be re-examined.

Having determined that absolute immunity and *Rooker-Feldman* wipe out Golden's §1983 claim, we conclude that the district court properly granted defendants' motion to dismiss. Thus, there is no reason to assess whether the district court was correct in ruling in the alternative that Sigman was not subject to suit under §1983 because child representatives are not state actors.

III

Golden also takes issue with the district court's decision to impose Rule 11 sanctions and the methodology the court used in calculating its award of attorneys' fees. We review sanction rulings under Rule 11 for an abuse of discretion. See *Fabriko Acquisition Co. v. Prokos, 536 F.3d 605, 610 (7th Cir. 2008)*. Golden objects to the timeliness of Sigman's and Thomas's motions for Rule 11 sanctions; he disputes the district court's decision to grant Rule 11 sanctions; and he takes issue with the amount of attorneys' fees awarded to Sigman and Thomas as recompense for his sanctionable conduct. We address each argument in turn.

Sigman and Thomas delayed filing their Rule 11 motions for approximately a year after they filed their motions to dismiss. Golden submits that this lassitude should have led to a dismissal of the request. Sigman and Thomas counter that Golden forfeited this argument by failing to raise the issue of timeliness until his motion to reconsider the district court's order granting Rule 11 sanctions. We agree with Sigman and Thomas that Golden failed to preserve this line of argument. Nor is Golden's misstep excusable. The question is not a pure issue of law; rather it depends centrally on the facts, some of which are contestable. Moreover, it does not appear as though the district court ever addressed the timeliness of Sigman's and Thomas's motions.

Even if Golden had not forfeited his timeliness challenge, the question whether to grant sanctions would have been one for the district court's discretion. The district court would not have been compelled to accept Golden's characterization of the delay as a full year. Indeed, that assertion turns out to be weak upon closer examination. In order to come up with a year, one needs to rely on the date when Golden's original complaint was filed, in January 2005. But he amended that complaint twice, adding claims against Thomas and altering the claims he had brought against Sigman. The district court would therefore have been well within its rights to look at the time between the date when the defendants filed their respective motions to dismiss (May 20, 2005, for Thomas and July 5, 2005, for Sigman) and the date of the Rule 11 motions. Viewed that way, it appears that Thomas waited only four months to serve her Rule 11 motion and 13 months to file it, while Sigman delayed service for just two months and filed 11 months later. Both Rule 11 motions were filed with the court well before the district court entered final judgment in 2008.

The district court did not abuse its discretion in tolerating this delay. Not only did Sigman and Thomas file their motions before final judgment, they both complied with Rule 11's "safe-harbor provision" by serving Golden with their motions before the case was dismissed. See Fed. R. Civ. P. 11(c)(2); cf. Fed R. Civ. P. 11 1993 Advisory Committee's Notes (tying the need to file Rule 11 motion before the conclusion of the case to respect for the safe-harbor provision). Golden had ample opportunity to withdraw his offending pleadings, as he was served more than a month before the district court dismissed the complaint. Moreover, Golden's claim of prejudicial delay rings hollow given that he had threatened earlier to seek sanctions against Sigman for her *premature* service of a Rule 11 motion.

Even if the motions were timely, Golden contends that the district court erred in granting Sigman's and Thomas's request for sanctions. The district court concluded that sanctions were warranted for everything in the complaint except the §1983 claim against Sigman and two of the state-law claims against Thomas.

With regard to Golden's state-law claims against Sigman, the district court decided to impose sanctions because *Scheib v. Grant, 22 F.3d 149, 157 (7th Cir. 1994)*, clearly granted Sigman absolute immunity under Illinois law. Golden argues that his failure to abide by *Scheib* should not be held against him as he did not uncover the case during the course of his reasonable pre-filing inquiry. Not surprisingly, the district court rejected the idea that poor legal research could amount to an excuse, pointing out that a simple natural language search of "absolute immunity" and "guardian *ad litem*" in Westlaw would immediately have uncovered the case. While Golden might not be expected to have access to the judiciary's research tools, this does not excuse bringing a federal lawsuit in reliance on research tools unable to locate controlling precedent. The district court was on firm ground when it concluded that a reasonable search would have uncovered the *Scheib* decision, which had been out for eleven years at the time Golden filed his suit.

We AFFIRM the judgment of the district court.

A.   Location of a Library

When a firm is establishing itself or moving into new offices, consideration should be given to the placement of a library within the firm. Ideally, the library should be located in a place that's most convenient to access for its most frequent users. The amount of traffic through a library should also be evaluated. Would a firm really want the library to be located on a floor that houses senior partners with a prestigious clientele? Perhaps not, since those entering and leaving the library may well get a glimpse of high-profile clients who have hired the firm. Are clients likely to be given at least partial access to the library? Will the library be featured on tours given to clients and prospective clients to demonstrate the vast capabilities of the firm and to show off the firm's resources? If so, then a location in an office building's basement might not be the optimal choice. Some law firms enter into arrangements with sole practitioners or even with other law firms to allow other attorneys access to the library, sometimes for a fee. Traffic and security should also be considerations when deciding where to site a library within a law firm.

Large firms are likely to have a space dedicated for use as a library. At one time, separate terminals had to be used for Lexis and Westlaw research, and these were often housed in a firm's library. Now, with wireless Internet access and the use of CDs, downloadable books, and online databases, much of a lawyer's research can be done right from her office. Small firms may have a multipurpose library area that doubles as a conference room or as office space for law clerks. To the extent possible, anticipated firm growth—and increased demands on a firm's library—should be considered when planning a firm's library. Increased budgets for more books, periodicals, and database access are likely to be needed as a law firm grows. Will the room accommodate an expanded library?

B.   Contents of a Library

A law firm's library does not contain only legal materials. Lawyers are not necessarily limited in their roles to just providing legal advice; they often are closely involved in a client's business decisions—while also, of course, providing input on the legal implications of any course of action a client might take. Some lawyers play crucial roles in putting together business deals. This being the case, they aren't just conversant about the law; they are intimately familiar with various industries. They need to keep abreast of developments in a field.

Lawyers and staff people also must research prospective clients, so a firm's library should include materials on corporations and industry sectors. Moreover, firms must undertake to gather **competitive intelligence**: They must gather information about the industry and market they serve, anticipate how developments will affect their own business, and then respond accordingly.

Librarians also play an archival role, preserving materials developed by a firm and even preserving its history. Marketing materials often feature brief case studies of a firm's past successes. Long-lived firms sometimes publish firm histories on significant anniversaries (50th, 75th, 100th). A librarian can be instrumental in preserving a firm's institutional memory. One hundred years out, no one at a firm will remember today's successes, but a library can document and preserve them so that future generations at the firm will be able to access and retrieve them.

Librarians must make sure that materials in the library are up to date. The types of materials a library obtains range from print to CD to digital. A librarian also arranges for access to a variety of databases and other online services. While some materials are stored in the library itself, a significant number are accessible directly from a lawyer's computer or mobile device. The costs of various materials, and periodic updates to them, must be factored into a law firm library's budget.

1. Forms of Law

A law library, no matter what its size, stocks both primary and secondary sources of law. **Primary sources of law** are those issued by a law-making body, such as the president, a legislature, and the courts. Examples of primary sources are statutes, executive orders, court decisions, regulations, and treaties. **Secondary sources of law** are those that explain or interpret the law but do not actually create any law. Law review articles are an example of a secondary source.

American jurisprudence relies on the doctrine of **stare decisis,** a Latin term meaning "to stand by things decided." Courts rely on **precedent,** or prior decisions, in reaching conclusions. If a court has previously decided a point of law, later judges follow that precedent when similar cases arise. **Mandatory authority,** such as earlier decisions by the same court, is binding on courts and other lawmakers; it must be followed. **Persuasive authority,** such as decisions issued by courts in other jurisdictions, may be convincing but is not binding on a court or other lawmaker.

Lawyers look to secondary sources of law to help them understand the evolution of the law. These aids can help lawyers appreciate nuances in the law. Lawyers also look to law in other jurisdictions to help persuade a tribunal to make a decision in a client's favor, especially if an area of the law is undecided or somewhat murky.

a) PRIMARY SOURCES

Court decisions (also referred to as **caselaw**), statutes, executive orders, treaties, regulations, and court rules are examples of the primary sources of law a lawyer

competitive intelligence: Information about an industry and the market it serves.

primary source of law: A material issued by a law-making body, such as the president, a legislature, or the courts.

secondary source of law: A material that explains or interprets the law but does not actually create any law.

stare decisis: A Latin term meaning "to stand by things decided"—the principle that courts rely on prior decisions, or precedent, in determining the outcome of a case.

precedent: Prior decisions by a court.

mandatory authority: A source of law that is binding on a court.

persuasive authority: A source of law that is convincing but not binding on a court.

caselaw: Law made by the judicial system.

needs to refer to in her practice. Whether a library stocks physical volumes of these materials on its shelves or provides digital access to them varies by firm. Remember that primary sources of law are issued by lawmakers at the federal, state, and local levels. Additionally, law firms engaged in international law need to refer to sources of law issued in other nations and by intergovernmental organizations, such as the European Communities (European Union). The depth and breadth of a law firm's collection of materials depend on its size and its practice areas.

Law made by the judicial system is referred to as caselaw. A court's decision in a case is called an **opinion.** The first available version of a court's decision in a given case is a **slip opinion.** Slip opinions are compiled in chronological order in published books called **reports,** but most people in the legal field refer to them as *reporters.* **Official reports** are those that are approved by the government. **Unofficial reports,** also called reporters, include more than just the text of cases themselves; they also include summaries, called **headnotes.** The West Group, a legal publisher of case reports, originated a key-number system used to catalog caselaw, with headnotes detailing the points of law that have been addressed or decided by the case. These headnotes are linked to a numbering system that identifies particular points of law.

The Supreme Court's decisions are published in *United States Reports, Supreme Court Reporter,* and *United States Law Week.* Courts of appeals decisions are published in the *Federal Reporter.* District court decisions are published in the *Federal Supplement.*

State caselaw is published in state reports and in regional reports that aggregate the caselaw of several surrounding states. For example, Connecticut Supreme Court decisions are published in the *Atlantic Reporter* and in *Connecticut Reports.* The decisions of Maryland's highest court, the Court of Appeals, are published in the *Atlantic Reporter* and in *Maryland Reports.* Nevada Supreme Court decisions are published in the *Pacific Reporter* and in *Nevada Reports.*

Courts, while issuing written decisions that are published in reports, sometimes designate certain decisions as "unpublished." Jurisdictional rules about citing and relying on **unpublished opinions** vary, but, historically, such decisions were considered to be binding only on the parties to the case. Unpublished opinions may not be as thoroughly researched as published ones.

> The chief argument against the publication of every opinion handed down by a court of appeals is time-based; it is, in other words, an exercise in efficiency. The amounts of hours required to research, write, and pass opinions among judges for approval and publication make it difficult to quickly move cases through the judicial system. Proponents of the unpublished opinion argue that the use of unpublished opinions eases the existing time constraints present in a crowded docket.[5]

In 2006, the Federal Rules of Appellate Procedure were modified to allow the citation of unpublished opinions:

Rule 32.1. Citing Judicial Dispositions
   (a) Citation Permitted. A court may not prohibit or restrict the citation of federal judicial opinions, orders, judgments, or other written dispositions that have been:

---

opinion:
A court's decision in a case.

slip opinion:
The first available version of a court's decision in a case.

reports:
Books containing caselaw published in chronological order.

official reports:
Accounts of cases that are approved by the government.

unofficial reports:
Accounts of cases issued by the government that also include summaries.

headnotes:
Summaries of the legal points covered in a case.

unpublished opinions:
Court decisions designated as unpublished and historically binding on only the parties to a case.

(i) designated as "unpublished," "not for publication," "non-precedential," "not precedent," or the like; and
(ii) issued on or after January 1, 2007.[6]

The Advisory Committee on the 2006 amendments to the rules took care to explain the limited scope of this new rule:

> Rule 32.1 is extremely limited. It does not require any court to issue an unpublished opinion or forbid any court from doing so. It does not dictate the circumstances under which a court may choose to designate an opinion as "unpublished" or specify the procedure that a court must follow in making that determination. It says nothing about what effect a court must give to one of its unpublished opinions or to the unpublished opinions of another court. Rule 32.1 addresses only the *citation* of federal judicial dispositions that have been *designated* as "unpublished" or "non-precedential"—whether or not those dispositions have been published in some way or are precedential in some sense.[7]

State courts also designate opinions as "unpublished." Local rules should be consulted before citing or relying on an unpublished opinion as precedent.

Laws made by legislatures are **statutes.** A **slip law** is a pamphlet-style publication of an individual statute that is printed right after it has been passed into law. Lawyers and others find these slip laws to be very handy documents for easy reference. They are compact and easy to flip through. Federal statutes are published in chronological order in *United States Statutes at Large*. They are then codified, or arranged by topic, in the *United States Code*, which is divided into 50 titles. **Annotated** versions, which include explanations of the law and references to cases and other materials in which the law is interpreted, are published in the *United States Code Annotated* and in the *United States Code Service*. Lawyers who specialize in certain areas of the law, such as environmental law, might use reference books in which all pertinent statutes have been compiled, like Thomson Reuters's *Federal Environmental Laws.*

Sometimes, mistakes creep into printed versions of a statute. The text printed in *Statutes at Large* governs if there is a discrepancy in the language between it and the *United States Code,* as the U.S. Court of Appeals for the Third Circuit explained in *Royers, Inc. v. United States*, 265 F.2d 615, 618 (3d Cir. 1959): "the official source to find United States laws is the Statutes at Large and that the Code is only prima facie evidence of such laws."

In addition to statutes, law libraries might, depending on the type of practice involved, store vast amounts of information about proposed federal and state legislation, committee hearings and reports, and bills introduced—in short, the entire legislative history of a law.

Orders issued by the President are called **executive orders.** They are published in the *Federal Register* and compiled in Title 3 of the *Code of Federal Regulations.*

Rules issued by federal agencies, or **regulations,** are proposed in the *Federal Register* and published there before being compiled in the *Code of Federal Regulations.* Regulations promulgated by state administrative agencies are published in comparable publications at the state level.

Article 2, section 2 of the U.S. Constitution authorizes the President to make **treaties**—agreements with other nations—with the advice and consent of the

statute:
A law passed by a legislature.

slip law:
The first official publication of a statute in the form of an unbound pamphlet.

annotated statutes:
A collection of statutes that includes explanations of the law and references to cases and other materials in which the law is interpreted.

executive order:
An order issued by the President.

regulations:
Rules issued by government agencies.

treaty:
A formal agreement between countries.

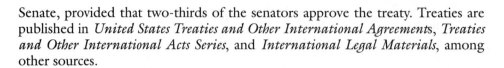

Senate, provided that two-thirds of the senators approve the treaty. Treaties are published in *United States Treaties and Other International Agreements*, *Treaties and Other International Acts Series*, and *International Legal Materials*, among other sources.

b) SECONDARY SOURCES

Secondary sources of law are tools that aid in a lawyer's understanding of the law. They can also be helpful starting points for research on a particular subject. The following are examples of secondary sources of law:

- Legal periodicals, such as *New York Law Journal*, *Legal Intelligencer*, *National Law Journal*, and *American Lawyer*, focus on developments in the law (court opinions, regulations, etc.) and on the legal business itself (law firm mergers, associates' salaries, helpful law firm technology, etc.).

legal treatise:
A scholarly work that covers a particular area of the law in considerable detail.

- **Legal treatises** are scholarly works that cover a specific area of the law in considerable detail. They are likely to be used by practitioners as a refresher or as a starting point for additional research. Examples include *Colorado Criminal Practice and Procedure*, 2d ed., by Robert J. Dieter (2010); *Corporate Criminal Defense: Compliance, Investigation, and Trial Strategies* by Eric W. Sitarchuk, Mark S. Srere, and Kelly A. Moore (2010); and *Federal Money Laundering Regulation: Banking, Corporate and Securities Compliance* by Steven Mark Levy (2010).

hornbook:
A legal text that covers the basics of a particular area of the law, including explanations of how the law evolved and the current status of the law.

- **Hornbooks** are more basic and straightforward than treatises. They cover the basics of a particular area of the law, including explanations of how the law evolved and the status of the law in today's world. Hornbooks are useful to law students who want to understand how the law developed over time and to lawyers who need to review a certain area of the law. Examples are *Principles of Conflict of Laws* by Clyde Spillenger (2010), *Principles of Criminal Law* by Wayne R. LaFave (2d ed. 2010), and *Uniform Commercial Code* by James J. White and Robert S. Summers (6th 2010).

- Nutshells are short introductory books. They are very helpful for law students who are just learning about a given field within the study of law. Lawyers might also refer to them to brush up on basic areas of the law. Examples are *Gaming Law in a Nutshell* by Walter Champion Jr. and I. Nelson Rose (2012), *Climate Change and Sustainable Development Law in a Nutshell* by Patrica Salkin and John Nolon (2010), and *Oil and Gas Law in a Nutshell* by John Lowe (5th ed. 2009).

restatement of the law:
An explanation of the law as it currently is.

- **Restatements of the law** identify and explain the law as it currently exists. Restatements are used by courts and practitioners to understand the current status of a given area of the law.[8] Restatements are developed and published by the American Law Institute in Philadelphia. Examples of restatements are *Restatement (Third) of the Law of Agency* (2006) and *Restatement (Third) of the Law of Trusts* (2003).

legal directory:
A compilation of the contact information of legal professionals.

- **Legal directories,** such as Martindale-Hubbell and JurisPro, list the contact information of professionals in the legal field, such as lawyers and expert witnesses.

- Legal dictionaries, such as *Black's Law Dictionary*, explain legal terms clearly.
- Legal encyclopedias tend to have relatively brief entries on legal topics. Examples are West's *Indiana Law Encyclopedia* (2013) and *The Oxford International Encyclopedia of Legal History* (2009).
- Law reviews and law journals are periodicals in which scholarly papers about various aspects of the law are discussed. Articles tend to be lengthy—from 5,000 words up to 20,000 words or more. The terms *law review* and *law journal* are used somewhat interchangeably, but law reviews are often published by law schools and edited by law students, whereas law journals are often published by bar associations. Examples of law reviews are the *Georgetown International Environmental Law Review* and the *George Washington Law Review*, both of which are edited by students.
- Examples of law journals are the *American Intellectual Property Law Association Quarterly Journal*, a publication of the American Intellectual Property Law Association, and the *Federal Circuit Bar Journal*, a publication of the Federal Circuit Bar.
- Legal newsletters are short publications on particular areas of the law designed specifically for practitioners. Two examples are *e-Commerce Law & Strategy* and *LJN's Product Liability Law & Strategy*.
- A law library will likely subscribe to both general-circulation newspapers (those of interest to the general public) and legal newspapers, which focus on legal developments and often contain court calendars and the text of recent decisions. Examples of legal newspapers are the *New York Law Journal* and the *Legal Intelligencer*.

2. Books

Some lawyers still rely heavily on printed text. Sometimes, a senior partner will make new associates conduct research the old-fashioned way—by referring to casebooks and, to update their results, to **citators** such as **Shephard's**. To the extent that research can even be done this way anymore, it serves as a good lesson on why one would never want to do that again. The process is very time consuming when done by pulling volumes of books from shelves. Today, updating legal research can be done very quickly using a computerized citators available on Lexis or Westlaw.

That said, some law books are still very useful, such as compilations of certain laws. Some books are still not available in electronic media, such as a **loose leaf** (a book bound with rings that open, allowing for the addition and removal of pages) on a very specialized area of the law that is periodically updated.

3. Periodicals

Lawyers must keep up with developments in the business world as well as in the law. Libraries are likely to subscribe to a variety of trade publications (focusing

citator:
An index of legal decisions and related materials that allow researchers to track the history of a case and to locate other cases that have cited it.

Shepardizing:
A means of updating caselaw and other legal materials by using Shepard's Citations, a publication that identifies the history and treatment of a case, statute, or other legal authority.

loose leaf:
A book bound with rings that open, allowing for the addition and removal of pages.

on a specific industry or sector) and general-interest publications, such as the *Wall Street Journal* and the *New York Times*, in print or online.

4. Form Books

Form books contain templates for various forms that a lawyer might use in her practice. Form books may provide general forms for filing complaints, answers, and other documents in court, or they may be more specialized and contain forms for specific practices, such as bankruptcy, real estate, or family law.

5. Online Databases

A number of commercial and free online databases are available to lawyers. Examples include Westlaw, Lexis, Loislaw, and Findlaw. THOMAS (named after Thomas Jefferson) is an online database maintained by the Library of Congress that includes the text of federal bills. Some states now designate the online versions of legal decisions and other documents as official ones. Some states have ceased printing paper versions of their state registers and publish online only.[9]

6. CDs and Other Technological Advances

Books in print are being replaced by materials presented in other formats. Many books are now available on CD, the Internet, or digital readers, such as Amazon's Kindle or Apple's iPad. Law librarians are likely to circulate information about new additions to the firm's library via e-mail notices to the firm's personnel. Working with a firm's information technology (IT) staff, librarians may also be involved in creating internal SharePoint Web sites that allow people within the firm to communicate easily with one another on specific topics. Discussion boards can enable people to have online conversations on a specific subject and for these discussions to be preserved to allow others to see their results in the future. Documents can also be shared via SharePoint. Different departments or teams within the firm might have locations on the site to share information. Many of these activities are useful in creating an "institutional memory"—even after current lawyers have retired or moved to other firms, their work and activity are recorded for future use by firm personnel as needed.

7. Document Library

Much of a law practice involves somewhat repetitive work—creating wills, preparing divorce petitions, or drafting contracts. Lawyers do not create every document from scratch for each client; they are likely to modify documents created for other clients to add pertinent provisions for a specific client. Many documents contain what is called **boilerplate,** or standardized text. Similarly, lawyers involved in litigation are likely to rely on briefs prepared for previous clients for lengthy explanations of the law. Most law firms create their own brief banks and form files,

boilerplate:
Standardized text for use as clauses in documents.

which might be compiled and maintained by the firm's librarian. A librarian might also maintain a collection of lawyers' speeches and other presentations. A librarian should maintain the firm's own history. Such a collection is useful to firm marketers who might look for information on historic "wins" by the firm and who might hope to document the growth and success of the firm over time.

C. Management Systems

A library that is in disarray is of little use to practitioners. A law firm must have procedures for circulating materials, for checking out materials from the library, for tracking them, for locating them, for retrieving them, and for reshelving them. A librarian may develop and implement a system for circulating materials and enforce it as necessary. Sometimes persuading senior-level partners to follow procedure can be dicey. Some may be wont to simply walk off with a helpful treatise. Good communication and persuasion skills are vital to a successful law firm librarian.

A librarian is likely to communicate via a firm's intranet or e-mail system, to circulate materials, to announce the arrival of new ones, and to request the return of any missing items. Specialized lists should be compiled, so that materials dedicated to a specific area of the law are announced to only those lawyers and staff who are likely to need them. Environmental lawyers do not need to know that a new treatise on family law is now available. A law librarian should also monitor legal developments in which the firm might be interested and circulate information on prospective purchases for input from practitioners.

A law firm may have a library committee with which the librarian works to select materials for purchase and to improve operations of the library. A librarian might be involved in negotiating purchasing agreements with vendors and licenses for the use of electronic resources, for online services, and for access to other databases. Costs are always a concern for libraries, so a librarian may periodically review the cost of various databases, periodicals, and other materials to ascertain whether a firm is getting the maximum benefit from these resources. Services that are unused or underused might be canceled or restricted in some way. A librarian may well work with the IT staff to develop and implement tracking systems for materials in circulation.

A librarian should have a system for conducting tours of the library and the materials it offers and for providing training classes for summer associates, new hires, and experienced legal researchers. A process for obtaining feedback about the training and for measuring the effectiveness of the training should be included in the system.

A librarian's project management should include identifying goals, establishing a schedule, identifying deliverables, and monitoring and trafficking to make sure that deliverables are actually received. For instance, in planning a firm's book purchases for the year, a librarian might establish a system for gaining input on which ebooks to purchase, create a purchasing schedule, make sure that ebooks are accessible, and then alert the appropriate people to their availability.

Checklist

- The contents of a law firm's library vary depending on the size of the firm and the practice areas it hosts.
- Libraries must be well organized.
- A librarian's role differs depending on the type of firm, its culture, its size, and the materials in its library.
- A librarian is likely to curate a firm's collection, review and circulate materials, conduct training, and do research.
- Outreach to members of the firm is important so that lawyers and others are comfortable using the library and finding materials there.
- When a firm is establishing itself or moving into new offices, consideration should be given to the placement of a library. Ideally, the library should be located in a place that is most convenient for its most frequent users to access.
- Anticipated firm growth—and increased demands on a firm's library—should be considered when planning a firm's library space.
- Large firms are likely to have a space dedicated for their library. Small firms may have a multipurpose library area that doubles as a conference room or as office space for law clerks.
- With wireless Internet access and the use of CDs, ebooks, and online databases, much of a lawyer's research can be done right from her office.
- In addition to containing legal materials, a firm's library should include materials on corporations and industry sectors.
- Librarians also play an archival role, preserving materials developed by a firm and even preserving its history.
- Librarians must make sure that materials in the library are up to date.

Vocabulary

annotated statutes (p. 339)

boilerplate (p. 342)

caselaw (p. 337)

citator (p. 341)

competitive intelligence (p. 337)

curate (p. 330)

executive order (p. 339)

headnotes (p. 338)

hornbook (p. 340)

legal directory (p. 340)

legal treatise (p. 340)

loose leaf (p. 341)

mandatory authority (p. 337)

official reports (p. 338)

opinion (p. 338)

persuasive authority (p. 337)

precedent (p. 337)

primary source of law (p. 337)

regulations (p. 339)

reports (p. 338)

restatement of the law (p. 340)

secondary source of law
  (p. 337)

Shepardizing (p. 341)

slip law (p. 339)

slip opinion (p. 338)

stare decisis (p. 337)

statute (p. 339)

treaty (p. 339)

unofficial reports (p. 338)

unpublished opinions (p. 338)

Career Preparation Tips

Knowing and understanding and being able to search for and retrieve primary and secondary sources of law and other pertinent materials is vital to those working in law firms. Refine your research skills while you are in school and have access to many databases. Practice the same search on different databases and compare the quality of materials that you receive so you can begin to make assessments about which databases are superior for certain types of searches. Practice, practice, practice: Research skills improve over time. What might be a frustrating and time-consuming activity now will become much easier, and even fun, as you become more adept.

If You Want to Learn More

The American Association of Law Libraries. http://www.aallnet.org

American Law Institute. http://www.ali.org

Association of Legal Writing Directors. http://www.alwd.org

ExpertPages is a directory of expert witnesses. http://expertpages.com

FindLaw Lawyer Directory. http://pview.findlaw.com/

In Custodia Legis is a blog written by the law librarians of Congress. http://blogs.loc.gov/law/

International Legal Technology Association. http://www.iltanet.org

JurisPro is a directory of expert witnesses. http://www.jurispro.com

Law Library of Congress. http://www.loc.gov/law

Legal Writing Institute. http://www.lwionline.org

Lexis. http://www.lexis.com

Loislaw. http://estore.loislaw.com

Martindale-Hubbell is a directory of lawyers. http://www.martindale.com

Microsoft SharePoint. http://sharepoint.microsoft.com/en-us/Pages /default.aspx

Office of the Federal Register. http://www.archives.gov/federal-register /about/

Special Libraries Association. http://www.sla.org

THOMAS is an online database of legislative materials maintained by the Library of Congress. http://thomas.loc.gov

Treaties and Other International Acts Series. http://www.state.gov/s/l /treaty/tias/index.htm

Treaties in Force provides information about treaties to which the United States is a party. http://www.state.gov/s/l/treaty/tif/index.htm

Westlaw. www.westlaw.com

WestlawNext. http://info.legalsolutions.thomsonreuters.com /westlawnext/default.aspx

Wolters Kluwer is a publisher of legal materials. http://www.wolterskluwer .com

Reading Comprehension

1. What are three functions of a law firm librarian?
2. Why would a lawyer undertake competitive intelligence activity?
3. Is a law review article a primary or secondary source of law?
4. Is a decision issued by a supreme court in a different jurisdiction mandatory or persuasive authority?
5. What is the difference between official reports and unofficial reports of caselaw?
6. Can unpublished court decisions be cited as precedent?
7. What is the difference between a statute and a regulation?
8. What is the difference between a hornbook and a treatise?
9. Do law students typically edit and publish law reviews or law journals?
10. Why would a lawyer use boilerplate in a document?

Discussion Starters

1. Suppose you work for a law firm of 20 lawyers. The firm has hired a law office manager, who has recommended that the firm library be dismantled to save money. What arguments would you make for preserving and maintaining the library?
2. Read the excerpt from *Golden v. Helen Sigman & Associated, Ltd.* What was Golden's problem with Sigman? Did the court seem to have a viewpoint about Golden's behavior? Why did Golden have to pay sanctions? Should Golden's inability to locate appropriate caselaw have shielded him from sanctions?
3. Why do law firms have to keep up to date about what their competitors are doing?
4. Suppose your law library must reduce its annual budget. What cost-saving measures would you propose? What expenses would you argue should be maintained?
5. In what ways might a law firm librarian and an IT staffer work together?

Case Studies

1. You are the law office manager for a six-lawyer general practice law firm in Virginia. You have been asked to research and recommend online databases for the law firm to use. Compare and contrast three, and recommend one database.
   a. What factors should you consider when you evaluate databases?
   b. Would your recommendation change if the firm, instead of being a general practice, was an intellectual property boutique?
   c. Would your recommendation remain the same if the firm focused on criminal cases in state court?
   d. What limitations in the various databases did you find?
2. You are the librarian for a small law firm. You have been asked by one of your partners to research treatises on banking regulations. Prepare a list of ten treatises on banking regulations, and make a recommendation about which ones your firm should purchase. Be certain to include the title, author, publisher, date of publication, price, and a brief synopsis of the treatise. Explain why you think your firm should purchase or not purchase each book.
3. Your supervising partner tells you he wants to brush up on bankruptcy law and wants the library to purchase two volumes on the subject. What questions would you ask the partner about the type of book he would

like the library to purchase? Put together a list of ten prospective books along with their publishers and pricing information, and recommend three. Why did you choose as you did?

4. Using an online database, locate a case decided by your state's highest court within the last six months and download a copy of it. Using a second online database, locate the same decision and download it. Which database was easier to use? Are the two downloaded decisions identical, or are there variations in the documents? For instance, are there headnotes or summaries in both documents? If so, compare and contrast them. Do you find that one set of headnotes is more accurate than the other?

5. Locate one treaty that the United States has ratified within the last ten years. What legal practice areas are likely to be interested in the subject matter of the treaty? Why?

Endnotes

1. *See, e.g., Law Firm Leadership During Times of Change: Q&A with LLSDC President Cameron Gowan*, Fastcase, http://www.fastcase.com/law-firm-leadership-during-times-of-change-qa-with-llsdc-president-cameron-gowan/ (last visited Sept. 15, 2013).
2. Bess Reynolds, The Challenges of E-Books in Law Firm Libraries (American Association of Law Libraries and International Legal Technology Association digital white paper), The New Librarian, Oct. 2012, *available at* http://www.aallnet.org/main-menu/Publications/aall-ilta-white-paper.
3. Law Librarian, Law Firm Adoption of eBooks, Law Professors Blog Network (May 20, 2013), http://lawprofessors.typepad.com/law_librarian_blog/2013/05/law-firm-adoption-of-ebooks.html.
4. Theodora Belniak, *The Law Librarian of the Twentieth and Twenty-First Centuries: A Figuration in Flux*, 101 Law Libr. J. 427, 448 (Fall 2009).
5. J. Jason Boyeski, *COMMENT: A Matter of Opinion: Federal Rule of Appellate Procedure 32.1 and Citation to Unpublished Opinions*, 60 Ark. L. Rev. 955, 958 (2008).
6. Fed R. App. P. 32.1 (2013).
7. *Id.* (Notes of Advisory Committee on 2006 amendments).
8. *See, e.g.,* American Law Institute, *Projects Overview*, http://www.ali.org/index cfm?fuseaction=projects.main (last visited Sept. 15, 2013).
9. *See, e.g.,* American Association of Law Libraries Electronic Legal Information Access & Citation Committee, *2009-10 Updates to the State-by-State Report on Authentication of Online Legal Resources*, Feb. 2010, *available at* http://www.aallnet.org/committee/ELIAC/Authenticationreportupdates/2009AALLAuthenticationReportUpdates.pdf.

14

Technology and the Law Firm of the Future

Chapter Outcomes

By the end of this chapter, a student will be able to:

- Demonstrate how technological advances have affected the legal industry
- Assess the advantages of virtual law practice
- Use social networking platforms for promotional purposes
- Identify opportunities to change the way the legal industry functions and to make it more efficient
- Evaluate the impact of technological advances on professional ethics
- Understand economic pressures on the legal industry
- Discuss typical technology used by law firms

Words such as *cables, lithographs, telex,* and *dictaphone* aren't exactly common vocabulary in a law office anymore—but they once were. Similarly, words like *webinar, podcast, voice mail,* and *smartphone* may be obsolete 10, 15, or 25 years from now. Think of technology in your own world that you might already use less than you once did or not at all: answering machines, fax machines, film, floppy discs, even a landline telephone! Technology is really a tool to help lawyers and others work better, smarter, and faster.

Law office managers must anticipate and plan for emerging technology, and lawyers and staff must use current technologies responsibly. Law firms that spend lavishly on the latest technology tools that lawyers or staff find too time-consuming or challenging to learn how to use are not budgeting wisely. Law firms that choose not to upgrade technologically may actually find that they're losing clients. Some prospective clients even specify that information technology capability be addressed when they issue requests for proposals from prospective law firms.[1] Training is necessary for new technology, and managerial support for lawyers and others to attend training sessions is also vital—without it, expensive gadgetry may lie fallow until it, too, becomes obsolete.

A. How Technology Has Changed the Practice of Law and Law Office Management

Fifty or 60 years ago, lawyers largely relied on secretaries for help completing tasks. Secretaries in the days before printers and copiers had to take dictation and then type numerous versions of a document, sometimes making multiple carbon copies as they typed. In the days before answering machines and voice mail, switchboard operators answered telephones and took messages.

Technological advances have changed how lawyers do their jobs. Lawyers and their support staffs need different skill sets today. Lawyers should know how to type, how to conduct legal research electronically, how to communicate with clients and others via the Internet, and how to use different types of software—for word processing, creating documents, tracking time, measuring performance, and handling other tasks and assignments that might arise. Likewise, secretaries must be comfortable using many different computer programs, not just word processing software. Law office managers today might find that much of their work is automated. Spread sheets tabulate income and outgo when data are entered into a computer program, client invoices are generated electronically and may well be transmitted via the Internet, supplies and postage might be ordered online, calendars are maintained on computers, and conflict of interest checks are conducted electronically.

The development of notebook and tablet computers, smartphones, easy and constant Internet access, small and affordable scanners, and lightweight copiers means that workplaces now have more flexibility. Lawyers can work well remotely—whether they're on the road and working from a hotel room near a client or working from a home office or from their car. Legal research need not be conducted in a library with reference books; it can be done using online databases such as Lexis and Westlaw. Secretaries aren't necessarily needed to work on the first drafts of documents; lawyers might be able to pull up templates and forms right on their own computers. Workspaces aren't limited to the confines of a traditional office. According to the 2013 ABA Legal Technology Survey Report, 5 percent of lawyers surveyed have a **virtual law office**,[2] meaning one for which there is no centralized office. Instead, lawyers and staff work from different locations (often their home offices) and generally communicate electronically rather than face to face. Seventy-three percent of lawyers work remotely at least some of the time.[3]

In some ways, although advances in technology mean that lawyers are free to roam, they're actually more chained to their work than in the past. The ease of communication via e-mail, texting, and smartphone means that clients may expect their lawyer to be available and working around the clock.

virtual law office.
A law office for which there is no formal, centralized office; instead, lawyers and staff work at remote locations (often their home offices) and generally communicate electronically rather than face-to-face.

Today, a large law firm may have an information technology (IT) staff or department. A small firm might outsource this function to a contractor. A large firm with an IT staff may well customize software that it purchases or actually have the IT staff develop its own software.

1. Consolidation

Technology has also made the administration of law firms easier. Lawyers in large law firms, with multiple offices in the United States and around the world, are able to communicate easily and efficiently thanks to e-mail; wikis; Google Drive (Google Docs) and SharePoint sites; software such as Skype, which allows voice and video calls to be placed via the Internet; and other communication platforms. A **wiki** is a Web site that can be modified and added to by visitors to the site. The word *wiki* means "quick" in Hawaiian.[4] For instance, visitors might post messages, write lists, post helpful materials, and create Web casts that other visitors can access. Wikis are sometimes described as virtual white boards or notebooks, where thoughts and other ideas can be jotted down and then elaborated on.

wiki:
A Web site that can be modified and added to by visitors to the site.

The convenience of wikis is that rather than trying to track e-mail messages back and forth among multiple addressees, users can alter documents and other materials directly online. Users need not be online all at the same time; they can arrange to be notified via e-mail when a change to a document on the wiki is made. Wikis can be especially useful to large law firms that have lawyers in different offices working on a client matter.

An example of a large wiki is Wikipedia.com, an online encyclopedia where visitors can modify entries to the site. Wikis need not be accessible to the public at large; wiki sites can be limited to only certain visitors. Documents can also be managed and shared via SharePoint sites, which are Web sites that use Microsoft SharePoint's Server Platform. Access to SharePoint sites, too, can be restricted to specified persons. Google Drive allows documents to be shared with specified users and to be accessed remotely.

2. Outsourcing and Offshoring

Technological advances allow law firms to hire others to do portions of their work. **Outsourcing** is the practice of retaining a third party to perform a portion of a business's activities. At a basic level, some firms outsource mail-room activities rather than hiring their own employees to work there. Law firms are not in the business of disseminating received materials in the most efficient fashion; expert consultants can do that better and more cheaply, especially for a small law firm. In addition, certain services that are outsourced are probably done by people who have skills superior to those of the staff the firm itself might hire. For instance, a mail delivery clerk who works for a large organization that firms outsource to has the potential to be promoted. That outsourced clerk will likely be more motivated to do a good job and to make improvements in the service provided. At a small law firm, that person would probably not move beyond the top job in the mail room.

outsource:
The practice of retaining a third party to perform a portion of a business's activities.

Firms might outsource back-office functions such as accounting or technical support. Again, a hired consultant may well have more up-to-date expertise than an employee at a law firm. Moreover, thanks to the ease of electronic communications, those accountants and technical support consultants need not necessarily be located near the law firm's office. They might be halfway around the world in countries where labor is significantly less expensive than it is in the United States and other Western countries.[5]

offshoring:
Relocating a business's
activities to an area in
another country where the
jobs may be done more
efficiently.

Offshoring is the relocation of a business's activities to an area in another country where the jobs may be done more efficiently (typically, lower employment costs). Not only accounting and other back-office functions are outsourced; legal services are outsourced and offshored as well. "Outsourcing relationships are typically governed by an outsourcing agreement that must address and specify things such as: the scope of services to be provided, service levels (i.e., benchmarks), the length of the contract (typically long), choice of laws, and privacy and data protection."[6] A law firm might hire lawyers in another country, such as India, to handle routine legal matters for a client. A large law firm might hire an inexpensive, small law firm located in the United States to handle discovery to appease a client who is trying to keep down costs. A firm or even a client might use temporary lawyers, temporary paralegals, e-discovery services, and other low-cost alternatives to performing functions internally.[7]

Some corporate in-house legal departments are opening offices in remote locations. For example, General Electric uses lawyers and paralegals in Gurgaon, India, for basic contracts work, which is then reviewed by its U.S.-based counsel.[8]

Whether legal work is outsourced or offshored, or both, some concerns arise about the ethics of using cheaper workers, maintaining confidentiality as material is transmitted back and forth between various offices or shared via Google Drive and SharePoint sites or in other ways, and ensuring quality. The American Bar Association, in an ethics opinion, approved the outsourcing of legal work to both lawyers and nonlawyers provided that ethics rules on competence, supervision, and protection of confidential information are met, along with rules barring the unauthorized practice of law and reasonableness of fees.[9] Clients typically must be informed that a lawyer is outsourcing work, especially since a client's confidential information cannot be revealed to another without the client's consent.[10] A lawyer may charge a client only the actual cost of the outsourced work along with a portion of the costs for overhead and for supervising the outsourced services—unless a client agrees to pay a higher rate.

A somewhat elevated inquiry into the abilities of lawyers located in remote jurisdictions may be necessary before a firm outsources legal work. For instance, are those lawyers trained sufficiently in legal matters? Was their education adequate? Are they sufficiently familiar with the requirements of confidentiality and other duties owed to clients?

3. Virtual Law Practices

Thanks to the growth of online databases, the development of ebooks and other resources, and the ease with which technology can be used to access documents, to conduct conferences, and to communicate in other ways, some lawyers find that they can provide more cost-efficient legal services to clients by working from a home office rather than commuting to an office building every day. Clients can be drawn to virtual law practices because their legal fees might be lower than those they would pay to a lawyer with a lot of overhead costs. Lawyers and support staff might be drawn to virtual law practices because they can work more comfortably from home. Some states have expressly allowed virtual law practices to be developed.[11] Other states require that lawyers have a physical address, which can limit the development of virtual law practices. Monitoring the unauthorized practice of law can become more challenging for states when law firms are operating in virtual law offices and clients can be geographically dispersed.

When operating as a virtual office, law firms must take care to protect private client data and must still observe applicable ethics rules in the states in which they are operating.[12]

4. Social Networking

Lawyers should market themselves on various social networking sites such as LinkedIn, Twitter, and Facebook. One survey found that almost 85 percent of law firms are using social media.[13] Such sites allow lawyers to set up accounts and to post information about their experience. Lawyers can post messages and demonstrate their expertise in a particular area of the law. Law firms might also establish a presence on these sites, which can be used for multiple reasons to attract prospective employees, and to keep in touch with firm alumni—who might one day funnel business to the firm or actually become a client. Moreover, lawyers and others in the field can use these sites to gather competitive intelligence about competitors. By assessing the information rival lawyers and law firms are posting, a lawyer might be able to differentiate herself from her competitors or highlight capabilities that distinguish her from the competition.

Even when a lawyer opts not to use social networking sites, other lawyers and prospective, current, or former clients still use these sites for professional reasons. Prospective clients doing online research to locate prospective lawyers are less likely to find a lawyer who does not have a social media presence.

Social networking sites can pose hazards for lawyers, though, even if the lawyers themselves do not have accounts on these sites. For instance, audience members listening to a lawyer's presentation might be tweeting, or posting updates via Twitter, in which they assess the lawyer's remarks. This can happen in real time, thereby limiting the lawyer's ability to respond right away. Similar updates might be posted via cell phone on Facebook, LinkedIn, and other sites. Someone might also be sending text messages via cell phone during a presentation. Even if a lawyer chooses not to participate on these sites, the sites should be periodically checked for mentions of the lawyer or the lawyer's law firm. The lawyer can then decide whether, or how, to respond. Some search engines, such as Google, allow users to set up alerts so that they will be notified when new material with their selected search term (which can be their name) is posted on the Internet.

Lawyers can also make use of the Internet and social media sites to gather information and evidence about parties to a lawsuit:

Whether you're a family lawyer looking for evidence that will affect a custody or property settlement, an employment lawyer discovering that a sexual harassment plaintiff isn't as innocent as he or she purports to be, or a personal injury litigator seeking evidence that a plaintiff isn't as physically limited as he or she claims to be, social networking sites are a virtual treasure trove of information for both sides. Prosecutors have used Facebook . . . photos to impeach murder and drunk driving defendants, and criminal defense attorneys are using everything from YouTube video footage to Facebook status updates to clear their clients.[14]

Lawyers must take precautions not to act inappropriately on social networking sites, such as by adding judges before whom they appear as friends or by engaging jurors on a case. This is an evolving area of the law. A Florida Advisory Opinion warned judges not to "friend" lawyers who appear before them, because it might give the appearance that the lawyer has undue influence before the judge:

> The Committee believes that listing lawyers who may appear before the judge as "friends" on a judge's social networking page reasonably conveys to others the impression that these lawyer "friends" are in a special position to influence the judge. This is not to say, of course, that simply because a lawyer is listed as a "friend" on a social networking site or because a lawyer is a friend of the judge, as the term friend is used in its traditional sense, means that this lawyer is, in fact, in a special position to influence the judge. The issue, however, is not whether the lawyer actually is in a position to influence the judge, but instead whether the proposed conduct, the identification of the lawyer as a "friend" on the social networking site, conveys the impression that the lawyer is in a position to influence the judge. The Committee concludes that such identification in a public forum of a lawyer who may appear before the judge does convey this impression and therefore is not permitted.[15]

In comparison, the California Judges Association found that judges can be active on social networks and be friends with lawyers who may appear before them, although judges should take certain precautions to avoid any appearance of impropriety.[16]

Lawyers must also consider potential ethical repercussions if they establish blogs, Web sites that are, in some measure, a personal journal (even one that addresses professional matters) that typically allows comments on the material to be made by visitors to the blog. A number of lawyers have blogs that focus on their particular practice area. A lawyer's blog is sometimes called a "blawg" because it is a blog involving a legal subject.

Lawyers, when writing on blogs, must remember client confidentiality and other ethical constraints. One lawyer in Illinois faced disciplinary action for allegedly publishing confidential information about a client on the Internet via the lawyer's blog.[17] In a separate matter, a judge was disciplined for having ex parte communications with a lawyer via Facebook.[18]

In certain circumstances, a presence on Facebook or a blog might be considered to be lawyer advertising and thus subject to ethical rules on advertising. For example, the Kentucky Attorneys' Advertising Commission proposed a new amendment on social media:

> "'Advertise' means to furnish any information or communication containing a lawyer's name or other identifying information, and an 'advertisement' is any

information containing a lawyer's name or other identifying information, except the following. . . . Information and communication by a lawyer to members of the public in the format of web log journals on the internet that permit real time communication and exchanges on topics of general interest in legal issues provided there is no reference to an offer by the lawyer to render legal services."

Communications made by a lawyer using a social media website such as MySpace and Facebook that are of a non-legal nature are not considered advertisements; however, those that are of a legal nature are governed by SCR 3.130-7.02(1(j).[19]

This stance was somewhat controversial, and the regulation had not been adopted as of Sept. 18, 2013. In New York, blogs, newsletters, and client alerts are sometimes considered advertising. General information about developments in the law is not considered advertising, but information disseminated by a lawyer or law firm about that specific lawyer or firm is.[20]

Lawyers who use social media sites should be certain to check state ethics rules regarding interactions on and use of these sites. In particular, they should take care not to give legal advice via their blog or form an attorney-client relationship—and they should include disclaimers so that visitors to the blog site are aware that posts do not constitute legal advice or establish a lawyer-client relationship.

5.   *Unbundling Legal Services*

Effective legal representation is unavailable to many people who could not possibly pay the associated legal fees for any counsel they seek. Technological developments, however, have made information about the legal system and pertinent documents far more available to those in need of legal advice than they once were. Some people who need legal help are willing to take a "do it yourself" approach and to buy less expensive materials that can help them. A person might set up her own business and prepare and file appropriate legal paperwork for doing so. Another might represent himself in his own divorce action but get a little help from a lawyer in preparing the underlying paperwork. In-house counsel, in an effort to cut legal costs, may hire a legal services outsourcing vendor to handle some matters rather than going to its high-priced law firms for everything. Computer software can guide users to prospective solutions to their legal problems:

> Technology promises to change the nature of the legal information product niche. Document assembly software that presents different documents based on answers to questions can go beyond the "one size fits all" forms and present tailored documents. Despite a temporarily successful effort to ban it in Texas, Intuit's WillMaker Plus software is now sold throughout the U.S. Online, companies such as LegalZoom offer a wide variety of documents. LegalZoom claims to have created more than one million legal documents, [and] has attracted funding from A-list venture capitalists that clearly see a substantial business opportunity . . .[21]

These do-it-yourself vendors are making a significant impact on the legal industry. More than one million wills have been prepared by users of Legal Zoom.[22] Another do-it-yourself service, Rocket Lawyer, had 70,000 daily visitors as far back as 2011.[23]

Whether and to what extent legal outsourcing services owned by nonlawyers and electronic aids for do-it-yourselfers are violating proscriptions on the unauthorized practice of law is a matter that is still being debated. Some bars have explicitly allowed this unbundling of legal services provided that the client is fully informed.[24] Those involved in these unbundled legal services must also take care not to violate ethics rules prohibiting fee-splitting with nonlawyers.

B.   Market and Generational Shifts

Market pressures and law firm inefficiencies, combined with technological advances, have changed the legal industry significantly in recent years. Thanks to economic recession, clients remain disinclined to spend excessively for legal assistance. Some became disinclined to pay high hourly fees for the work of inexperienced junior associates who have not received much practical training in law school.

Due to technological advances, reasonable alternatives can be had for reasonable prices. Corporate clients are more likely to funnel routine work to less expensive law firms or to use legal services providers at a reduced cost. A client might offshore some legal work or use legal software to generate documents associated with less complex matters. Individuals at modest income levels might choose to represent themselves in court, perhaps with a little assistance from a lawyer who has helped them prepare papers to file.

1.   Price and Performance

Large law firms, especially, have been challenged both by the economy and by their own structures. The trend toward consolidation by merger has meant that law firms are able to offer more services to a broader pool of clients around the world, but the marriage of firms has not always been compatible. Firms might find their resources stretched when they have agreed to compensate highly certain high-visibility, big-name partners. They might also become bloated with expensive nonequity partners whom they have hired because clients did not want to pay less experienced associates. A firm's compensation scheme and pressure to meet billable hour requirements might mean that lawyers do not delegate tasks that could be performed less expensively by others but instead keep them to themselves. Lawyers sensing trouble are disinclined to stay and might jump to another firm.[25]

These developments are bringing about significant changes in the legal field:

> The new law firm model will have a much smaller ownership base. Firms will hire fewer lawyers but keep more as permanent employees, although most will not become equity partners. The size of support staff will also diminish as legal process and knowledge management become automated. Many functions, including basic legal tasks, will be outsourced to individuals and organizations that can provide these functions at lower cost than the firm could if it handled them itself. The physical footprint of the law office will be dramatically smaller as fewer people will actually work at a desk in a traditional office building. A handful of global mega-firms

will dominate the international legal business, and specialized boutiques will replace regional generalist firms in most metropolitan legal markets.[26]

These changes have created opportunities for those in the legal field with an entrepreneurial bent. Increasingly, legal services are being provided by entities other than lawyers or with less direct involvement by lawyers. Legal document preparers, legal software Web sites, and do-it-yourself law books have made the law more accessible to people who are disinclined to pay high prices for legal advice.

Although restrictions on the unauthorized practice of law and professional responsibility rules still pertain, they are evolving in some areas. For instance, Texas explicitly allows the sale of legal forms and other materials via the Internet:

> the "practice of law" does not include the design, creation, publication, distribution, display, or sale, including publication, distribution, display, or sale by means of an Internet web site, of written materials, books, forms, computer software, or similar products if the products clearly and conspicuously state that the products are not a substitute for the advice of an attorney. [27]

2. *Working with Millennials*

Changes in the legal industry and the high price of attending law school mean that some new lawyers are looking for more satisfying alternatives than working for a large law firm. Although the pay at such firms is certainly good, the hours can be grueling. Associates might be disinclined to put in so much time at the office and prefer quality of life to being on the partnership path—especially because so few people allegedly on that path actually ascend to partnership. Cultural differences among generations—with law firm elders insisting that younger lawyers "pay their dues" and more junior associates preferring different work atmospheres where collegiality, plenty of feedback, and a pleasant day-to-day work experience may be more paramount—can create conflicts.

Younger members of the workforce, such as those born between 1992 and 1995, referred to as millennials, grew up in a digital world and have approaches to work that differ from older generations. Millennials have been described as "lazy, entitled, and selfish,"[28] and some older people have been challenged to work with them. Because millennials grew up using computers and cell phones, they are technologically adept and realize that they need not be seated in an office, at a desk, for 15 hours a day to work effectively.[29] They work well collaboratively and are interested in feedback. Many[30] realize they will never make partner, and so refuse to work lengthy hours to meet high billable hour requirements to entertain the fiction that they might. They also realize that they are unlikely to stay more than a few years at any given employer. Law firms have had to adapt as this new generation enters the legal field by focusing more on quality-of-the-workplace issues.[31]

C. Typical Technology Used by Law Firms

Hardware and software are expensive. A law firm should develop a technology plan to assess its hardware and software needs, anticipate future growth, and provide for maintenance and purchases of warranties. Depending on the law firm's needs and budget, the plan may even prioritize purchases.

Hardware is the physical electronic equipment a firm needs (as distinguished from **software,** the computer programs needed to run much of the hardware). A firm's hardware needs are likely to include the following items:

hardware:
The machines, wiring, and other physical components of a computer or other electronic system.

software:
The programs and other operating information used by a computer.

- desktop computers
- laptop computers
- computer server for a networked computer system
- webcam for use in online video conferencing and for the creation of podcasts and Web casts
- USB sticks on which to store documents
- interface controllers (such as USB cords) to connect devices to the computer
- smartphones
- landline telephones
- telephone and voice mail system (for forwarding calls and to allow callers to leave voice messages for recipients)
- digital cameras
- digital video recorders
- digital voice recorders
- printer
- copier
- scanner
- fax machine

A firm's software needs are likely to include these items:

- an operating system, such as Microsoft Windows 8 or Mac OS
- calendaring and docket management program
- time, billing, and accounting program
- case management program
- file management program
- document management program
- electronic spreadsheet program, such as Excel
- word processing program, such as WordPerfect or Microsoft Word
- slide presentation preparation program, such as PowerPoint
- software for handling digital images, such as PhotoShop
- software for creating PDFs, such as Adobe Acrobat
- trial preparation software
- e-mail program
- antivirus program
- firewall and anti-spyware programs to defend against computer intruders
- videoconferencing program such as Adobe Connect
- cloud computing software for document storage and sharing
- Skype or other software enabling voice and video calls to be made via the Internet
- encryption software

- voice recognition software, which automatically transcribes a user's dictation
- text messaging software
- graphics presentation program

Performance, in addition to cost, should be considered when selecting software. Try to find out how often software tends to crash. Think about how much time and effort will be devoted to addressing and fixing problems. Will the original software vendor be able to handle problems? If not, is there off-site and helpful technical support? Will technical problems be handled in-house by the law firm's IT personnel? Whether the software can be easily customized should be taken into account, as should the frequency of upgrades in the software. Training requirements and ease of use should also be considered. How likely are lawyers and others to use the software if extensive training is necessary? Is training free? How committed is the firm to providing training sessions and requiring staff and others to attend?

Given the demands of the modern office and the 24/7 accessibility clients tend to expect of their lawyers, remote access to information must also be provided to attorneys and appropriate staff members. Legal uses of conventional consumer electronics should be considered. For instance, the Apple iPad tablet computer and the Kindle reader are potentially very useful to lawyers as more applications are available for the iPad and more materials, such as continuing legal education documents, are available for the Kindle. Lawyers meeting with clients need not bring boxes of documents with them; they need only upload them to electronic devices such as the iPad and then pull them up as needed. A law firm's IT personnel should stay abreast of developments in the field so they can alert lawyers to useful software that may help them do their jobs better. New programs are often debuting, especially applications for smartphones and the iPad. For instance, Jury Tracker, an application for the iPad, allows lawyers to track jury members and record their observations about juror responses.

What much contemporary technology actually does is allow a lawyer to work in a virtual law office. The lawyer need not be tethered to a desk at firm headquarters. As a practical matter, a virtual law office is really the ability to work from home, to work off-site, such as at a client's office or, if traveling, in a hotel room or airport. Some law firms, recognizing the attraction of low overhead and convenience that a virtual law office provides, are setting up shop as a virtual business, meaning that there is no central office building where the law firm is sited. Virtual law practices are likely to make use of Web-based word processing and document management applications and to invoice electronically. As with brick-and-mortar law firms, however, client communications must be protected and secure.

Lawyers and staff involved in litigation must pay particular attention to changing court requirements and adapt their own technology to that required for litigation. Some courts allow electronic filing of documents; for example, Federal Rules of Civil Procedure Rule 5(d)(3) allows federal courts, in their local rules, to establish electronic filing requirements:

(3) Electronic Filing, Signing, or Verification.
A court may, by local rule, allow papers to be filed, signed, or verified by electronic means that are consistent with any technical standards established by the Judicial Conference of the United States. A local rule may require electronic filing

only if reasonable exceptions are allowed. A paper filed electronically in compliance with a local rule is a written paper for purposes of these rules.

A number of courts use videoconferencing.

Graphics may need to be created electronically for use in the courtroom, and compatibility of the firm's technology with the equipment available for trial must be determined beforehand.

D.   Safeguarding Information

Confidential client information as well as confidential information about the law firm's business itself that is stored electronically must be protected against hacking by outsiders and against unauthorized intrusion by a user. Computers in networks pose a special hazard, because if someone manages to access one portal, it's possible that all of the information in the network might be in jeopardy. Access to networks must be limited, in terms of both who has access and what information can be accessed by a given individual. For instance, a firm's financial records and human resources files should not be accessible by everyone who works at the firm. Access must be limited to authorized users only. Access to a law firm's network should be password-protected.

The Computer Fraud and Abuse Act, 18 U.S.C. §1030, outlaws certain acts related to the unauthorized access to computers. Lawyers who access computerized data inappropriately may be subject to professional disciplinary action. Consider the following case.

Lawyer Disciplinary Board v. Markins
663 S.E.2d 614 (W. Va. 2008)

OPINION

LAWYER DISCIPLINARY PROCEEDING
TWO-YEAR SUSPENSION, WITH ADDITIONAL SANCTIONS
Per curiam.

In this lawyer disciplinary proceeding, Respondent Michael P. Markins ("Respondent") objects to the sanctions recommended by a Hearing Panel Subcommittee of the Lawyer Disciplinary Board ("Board") for violations of the West Virginia Rules of Professional Conduct ("Rules"). Following a disciplinary hearing conducted on July 20, 2007, the Board determined that Respondent violated Rules 8.4(b) and (c) by repeatedly accessing the email accounts of other attorneys, without their knowledge or permission, for over a two-year period. The Board recommends, *inter alia,* that Respondent be suspended from the practice of law for a period of two (2) years. Though Respondent does not dispute the facts giving rise to the disciplinary charges filed against him, he contends the recommended sanctions are too harsh.

For the reasons discussed below, we adopt the Board's recommendations.

I.   Factual and Procedural Background

The facts of this case are not in dispute. Respondent has been a practicing attorney since October, 2001. At all times relevant, Respondent was employed as an associate attorney at the law firm of Huddleston Bolen, LLP ("Huddleston").[1] His wife, also an attorney, was similarly employed at the law firm of Offutt, Fisher & Nord ("OFN"). In late October or early November of 2003, Respondent began accessing his wife's OFN e-mail account without her permission or knowledge.[2] Respondent testified that the purpose of reading his wife's e-mails was to secretly monitor her activities because he believed she had become involved in an extramarital affair with an OFN client. Respondent further testified that, initially, he improperly accessed only his wife's account and later, that of another attorney, an OFN partner.[3] Eventually, however, Respondent's curiosity got the better of him, and he began accessing the e-mail accounts of seven other OFN attorneys. Obviously, Respondent did so without either the knowledge or permission of the account holders.

When an OFN attorney began to suspect that her e-mail account had been improperly accessed, OFN retained Paul Law, a computer systems engineer, and launched an investigation. From Mr. Law's investigation, it was learned that on numerous occasions from sometime prior to November 7, 2003, until March 16, 2006, Respondent gained unauthorized access to OFN e-mail accounts from three IP accounts:[4] Respondent's Huddleston IP account; Respondent's residential IP account; and the IP account at the Hampton Inn in Beckley, West Virginia, where Respondent had been monitoring a trial in which both Huddleston and OFN clients were being represented.

According to D.C. Offutt, Jr., the managing partner of OFN, although they were not able to view the actual e-mail messages read by Respondent, they were able to determine which e-mail accounts were accessed, the date and time they were accessed, and from what IP account. Furthermore, Mr. Offutt testified that if there was an attachment to an e-mail, they could determine whether the attachment had been opened. More specifically, they were able to determine that on one occasion certain confidential OFN financial information sent by the firm's chief accountant to the firm's partners by e-mail attachment was opened by Respondent.

---

[1] It is undisputed that while in law school Respondent was an outstanding student, graduating near the top of his class. While at Huddleston, Respondent was well thought of in the legal community and was on the firm's "Partnership Track."

[2] The password to his wife's e-mail account was her last name. Similarly, the passwords to the e-mail accounts of all OFN attorneys was the individual account holder's last name.

[3] During his testimony before the Board, Respondent described an e-mail between his wife and an OFN partner in which the partner encouraged Respondent's wife to join her and a particular client in an evening out. (It is unclear from Respondent's testimony if this is the same client with whom he suspected his wife of having an affair.) According to Respondent, the partner's e-mail suggested that they would keep the evening a secret from Respondent.

[4] Mr. Law explained that, "[i]n layman's terms, an IP address is basically a phone number for a computer. . . . It's basically Caller ID for computer systems."

It is undisputed that Respondent improperly accessed the e-mail accounts of OFN attorneys on more than 150 occasions. In so doing, Respondent learned personal information about certain attorneys which had been relayed confidentially via e-mail. With regard to confidential client information that had been accessed by Respondent, Mr. Offutt was particularly concerned with the fact that OFN and Huddleston, Respondent's employer, represented co-defendants in a large mass tort case that was in litigation during the time period at issue. In March, 2006, Respondent, along with other lawyers whose firms were involved in the mass litigation, was monitoring the trial from the Hampton Inn in Beckley, West Virginia. While monitoring the proceedings, Respondent gained unauthorized access into various OFN email accounts from the Hampton Inn's IP account. According to Mr. Offutt, Huddleston's mass tort client had a contractual relationship with and a claim for indemnity against OFN's client. Though the claim was not then being litigated, Mr. Offutt testified that information included in the firm's e-mail system would have been "helpful" to Huddleston's client. However, neither Huddleston nor OFN found evidence that any information between OFN attorneys and its client in that case had been compromised.[5]

Following the disciplinary hearing in this case, Mr. Offutt indicated in an affidavit that, since Respondent's misconduct was reported by the Charleston Gazette newspaper and the Associated Press, OFN "has suffered further damage to its image and reputation." Mr. Offutt further indicated that one of the firm's clients expressed "serious concerns" about the security breach and about whether Respondent improperly accessed important information concerning that client. According to Mr. Offutt, this client has put the firm on notice of a potential claim for damages against it. Mr. Offutt indicated that he anticipates that similar concerns will be expressed by other clients in the future and that the negative ramifications and stigma of Respondent's misconduct will be felt for many years. Finally, Mr. Offutt indicated that his firm suffered direct economic losses as a result of Respondent's actions: Mr. Offutt, along with other firm lawyers and staff, spent considerable time and resources investigating and attending internal meetings on the matter and were distracted by the events and their aftermath.

In March 2006, Respondent's wife, who had been completely unaware of Respondent's misconduct, told Respondent that someone had been breaking into OFN e-mail accounts and that the firm was getting close to finding out who it was. Shortly thereafter, Respondent revealed to his wife that it was he who had been improperly accessing the OFN e-mail accounts. The following day, Mr. Offutt, who had learned from the computer expert's investigation that Respondent was responsible for the unauthorized access of the e-mail accounts, inquired of Respondent's wife if she was aware of Respondent's actions. Though she had just learned of Respondent's misconduct, she denied any knowledge of it to Mr. Offutt. Immediately thereafter, Respondent's counsel contacted Mr. Offutt and others at the firm to disclose his actions. Both Respondent and his

---

[5] When contacted by Mr. Offutt about the breach in OFN's e-mail system by one of its employees, Huddleston conducted its own investigation to determine if Respondent had ever saved OFN e-mails or other OFN computer files in Huddleston's computer system. From its investigation, Huddleston found no information improperly accessed from the OFN e-mails on its computer system.

wife were eventually terminated from employment by their respective law firms as a result.[7]

Respondent has consistently maintained that he has never disclosed to anyone any information he obtained from improperly accessing the various OFN e-mail accounts. He testified that he has never used any of the information in an improper manner; did not save any of the accessed emails onto his computer; and did not forward any of the emails to another person.

On December 18, 2006, the Board filed a Statement of Charges against Respondent, alleging violations of Rule 8.4(b) and (c) of the West Virginia Rules of Professional Conduct. The Board alleged violations of Rule 8.4(c) "[b]ecause Respondent engaged in the repetitive unauthorized access of [OFN] e-mail accounts by improperly using various e-mail account passwords assigned to various [OFN] attorneys." Under Rule 8.4(c), "[i]t is professional misconduct for a lawyer to: . . . (c) engage in conduct involving dishonesty, fraud, deceit or misrepresentation."

The Board also alleged violations of Rule 8.4(b) "[b]ecause Respondent's repetitive unauthorized access of [OFN] e-mail accounts was criminal in nature, violated West Virginia Code 61-3C-12,[10] and adversely reflected on his honesty, trustworthiness or fitness as a lawyer[.]" (Footnote added). Under Rule 8.4(b), "[i]t is professional misconduct for a lawyer to: . . . (b) commit a criminal act that reflects adversely on the lawyer's honesty, trustworthiness or fitness as a lawyer in other respects[.]" The Board further alleged there to be "aggravating factors," stating that "Respondent's conduct involved multiple offenses and a pattern of misconduct, was for a selfish motive, and constituted illegal acts."

No criminal charges arising out of Respondent's unauthorized access of OFN e-mail accounts have ever been filed against Respondent.

Following the disciplinary hearing before the Board, the Board found Respondent had violated Rules 8.4(b) and (c), as charged, and recommended the following sanctions:

1. That Respondent be suspended from the practice of law for a period of two (2) years;
2. That, upon reinstatement, Respondent's private practice be supervised for a period of one (1) year;
3. That Respondent complete twelve (12) hours of CLE in ethics in addition to such ethics hours he is otherwise required to complete to maintain

[7] Respondent's wife was initially placed on administrative leave, with pay. When Mr. Offutt learned that Respondent's wife did not answer truthfully when she denied knowledge of Respondent's misconduct, her employment was terminated. As indicated above, Respondent's wife did not know about Respondent's misconduct until he disclosed it to her the evening before she met with Mr. Offutt.

[10] W. Va. Code § 61-3C-12 (1989) (Repl. Vol. 2005) states:

Any person who knowingly, willfully and without authorization accesses a computer or computer network and examines any employment, salary, credit or any other financial or personal information relating to any other person, after the time at which the offender knows or reasonably should know that he is without authorization to view the information displayed, shall be guilty of a misdemeanor, and, upon conviction thereof, shall be fined not more than five hundred dollars or confined in the county jail for not more than six months, or both.

his active license to practice, said additional twelve (12) hours to be completed before he is reinstated; and

4. That Respondent pay the costs of these proceedings.

In the instant matter, we are mindful of the mitigating factors presented by Respondent, including the unique circumstances which motivated his misconduct in the first place. However, there are also several aggravating factors which this Court cannot ignore or minimize. Though Respondent initially accessed his wife's OFN e-mail account with motives very personal to his marriage, his misconduct eventually became more rampant. Out of simple curiosity, he broke into the e-mail accounts of eight of his wife's unsuspecting co-workers on almost a daily basis for over a two-year period. He did not cease or disclose his actions until he learned OFN's computer experts were on the verge of discovering who was behind the unauthorized intrusions. Moreover, in addition to confidential personal information, Respondent viewed confidential financial information intended to be read exclusively by OFN partners. With regard to confidential client information, in one instance, his firm and OFN represented separate co-defendants which had interests adverse to each other because Respondent's client had an indemnity claim against OFN's client.

Finally, we recognize that with the widespread use of computer e-mail as an important method of communication between and among attorneys and their clients comes the potentiality that the communication might be improperly infiltrated. This Court does not take lightly the fact that, in this case, it was an attorney who repeatedly accessed the confidential e-mails of other attorneys without their knowledge or permission. Thus, the imposition of a suitable sanction in a case such as this is not exclusively dictated by what sanction would appropriately punish the offending attorney, but, just as importantly, this Court must ensure that the discipline imposed adequately serve as an effective deterrent to other attorneys, "to protect the public, to reassure it as to the reliability and integrity of attorneys and to safeguard its interest in the administration of justice." *Battistelli,* 206 W.Va. at 201, 523 S.E.2d at 261, quoting *Lawyer Disciplinary Board v. Taylor,* 192 W.Va. at 144, 451 S.E.2d at 445. Accordingly, based upon the foregoing, we are compelled to adopt the recommendation of discipline tendered by the Board.

IV.   Conclusion

For the reasons stated above, we adopt the Board's recommendations and hereby impose the following sanctions upon Respondent: (1) Respondent is suspended from the practice of law in West Virginia for a period of two years; (2) upon reinstatement, Respondent's private practice shall be supervised for a period of one year; (3) Respondent is ordered to complete twelve hours of CLE in ethics in addition to such ethics hours he is otherwise required to complete to maintain his active license to practice, said additional twelve hours to be completed before he is reinstated; and (4) Respondent is ordered to pay the costs of these proceedings.

License suspended, with additional sanctions.

In addition to protecting themselves against unauthorized intrusion, law firms must arm their computers against **viruses,** computer scripts and programs that interfere with the use of one's computer. A virus might slow a computer down, disable it entirely, disseminate information inappropriately, or destroy files or entire programs. Viruses are disseminated via the Internet. They are often attached to documents that are downloaded to someone's computer. Before downloading, a document should be scanned for viruses. New viruses are constantly being disseminated, so a firm must have antivirus software that is frequently updated. Other precautions must also be taken. A firm should have a firewall program installed in its computers. A **firewall** limits access to a computer from outside intruders. An anti-spyware program is also vital for computers that have access to the Internet. Malicious **spyware** is tracking software that disseminates information over the Internet. Spyware is typically unknowingly downloaded by an Internet user. An anti-spyware program will block the transmission of unauthorized data that the spyware is trying to disseminate.

A firm should also establish a policy regarding metadata, information about other data that a computer software program might automatically tabulate. **Metadata** is embedded in documents and tracks information about the creation of and modifications to the document. It is technically defined as "data about data." If metadata is not removed from a document, it may provide information about the changes to a document that were made, how many people reviewed the document, how much time each person spent on it, and specific editorial revisions that were made.

In some jurisdictions, there may even be an ethical obligation to remove metadata before a document is disseminated.[32]

Information should be backed up frequently so that, should a catastrophic destruction occur, data can still be retrieved. In addition, a law firm should have a policy for disposing of computer equipment. It is vitally important that confidential information be removed from the computer's hard drive before the hardware is discarded.

1. The Internet and the Cloud

Lawyers and appropriate staff members must have Internet access to send e-mail messages, to transmit data to clients, to conduct legal research, and possibly to make telephone calls. A firm must plan and budget for its Internet accessibility. Will access to the Internet be via cable and then by wireless connection? Will access be via high-speed telephone lines? A firm may need to be wired with additional cable or phone lines. Wireless routers, which allow wireless access to the Internet within the firm, may also be needed. If a firm does have wireless access, such access must be password-protected. In addition, material transmitted over the Internet should be encrypted. Encryption software scrambles data to protect it as it travels over the Internet. It is then unscrambled, or decrypted, when the appropriate recipient of the data gains access to it, typically by entering a password.

In addition to having a firm Web site for promotional purposes, a firm may need to use document sharing sites (such as SharePoint or Google Drive, home to Google Docs) so that lawyers and clients can collaborate easily on very large files that cannot easily be transmitted via e-mail. In the past, this was done by printing

virus:
Computer code that has a detrimental effect on one's computer by slowing it down, disabling it entirely, disseminating information inappropriately, or destroying files and programs.

firewall:
A computer program that blocks unauthorized access to a computer from outside intruders.

spyware:
Malicious tracking software that disseminates information over the Internet.

metadata:
Information embedded in an electronic file about the creation and modification of that file.

a long document out and shipping it to a client by, for instance, FedEx. Today, documents can be transferred much more easily. Access to document-sharing sites is limited to specified users with a user name and a password.

Increasingly, lawyers and other users are turning to cloud computing, which allows for the storage of documents on a remote server rather than on an individual computer.[33] "The obvious advantage to 'cloud computing' is the lawyer's increased access to client data. As long as there is an internet connection available, the lawyer would have the capability of accessing client data whether he was out of the office, out of the state, or even out of the country."[34] Security of files in the "cloud" is a concern, but some state bars have approved the storage of files in the cloud so long as protective measures are taken to preserve confidentiality.[35]

2. Intranets and Extranets

intranet:
A computer network that allows users within a firm to access information and to communicate with one another internally.

extranet:
A computer network that allows controlled access to information from outside the firm.

A firm should have an **intranet**, its own computer network that allows users within the firm to access information and to communicate with one another internally. Via a firm's intranet, lawyers and others can access forms, standardized language for documents, and other documents stored in the intranet. An intranet is also likely to have a message board for announcements and may feature internal e-mail. An **extranet** allows controlled access to information from outside the firm. An extranet might be used to allow both clients and their lawyers to work on documents.[36]

3. Disaster Recovery Plan

A disaster recovery plan should be in place to provide instructions in the event the firm experiences a catastrophic loss of its own hardware or software. If a law firm's computer servers are destroyed in a fire or in an earthquake, how will backed-up files be located, when, and by whom? How will clients be notified that the firm has experienced a setback? If clients must be contacted because the firm needs their help to reconstruct its databases, how will that scenario be handled? Who will make sure that any necessary insurance claims are filed? If legal action must be instituted against someone because of the disaster, who will oversee and coordinate that effort? A disaster recovery plan should also specify the procedure to be followed if a laptop, smartphone, tablet computer, or other hardware is lost or stolen.

Some states now have statutes requiring certain procedures to be followed if a breach of computer security occurs. Often, notice must be provided to the people whose personal information may have been inadvertently disclosed.[37]

Lawyers and staff members should be apprised of extra precautions they should take when using hardware, such as laptops, outside the office. Computers and smartphones should be password protected. A disaster recovery plan should identify precise steps someone within the firm should take if a laptop is lost or stolen or if some other breach of confidentiality occurs. Who should be alerted first if a laptop is stolen? At what point should the police be notified? At what point should clients be notified, and by whom?

E. The Future of the Legal Industry

This is an exciting time to be working in the legal profession, especially in the realm of law office management. As clients try new means to hire lawyers, by, for instance, using online bidding; as lawyers work more collaboratively with their clients and with other lawyers; as solid law office management principles can help control budgets; and as legal advice and legal products become accessible to a broader audience that needs legal help, one can't help but be enthused about the possibilities for entrepreneurship and innovation. Sure, the industry is changing. Those working the legal field can change with it and find new ways to run the business side of their operations.

Checklist

- Law office managers must anticipate and plan for emerging technology, and lawyers and staff must use current technologies responsibly.
- Some prospective clients specify that information technology capability be addressed when they issue requests for proposals from prospective law firms.
- Lawyers should know how to type, conduct legal research electronically, communicate and collaborate with clients and others via the Internet, and use different types of software—for word processing, creating documents, tracking time, and handling other tasks and assignments that might arise.
- Outsourcing and offshoring legal work has become viable for both law firms and clients.
- Rules allowing the unbundling of legal services allow more do-it-yourself activities and supporting businesses in the legal marketplace.
- The development of lightweight laptops, smartphones, easy and constant Internet access, affordable scanners, and copiers means that workplaces now have more flexibility.
- Social networking sites such as LinkedIn, Twitter, and Facebook allow lawyers to set up accounts and post information about their experience. In certain circumstances, a presence on Facebook or a blog might be considered to be lawyer advertising and thus subject to ethical rules on advertising.
- Lawyers can also make use of the Internet and social media sites to gather information and evidence about parties to a lawsuit.
- Lawyers must take precautions not to act inappropriately on social networking sites, such as by adding as "friends" judges before whom they appear or by engaging jurors on a case.
- A law firm should develop a technology plan to assess its hardware and software needs, anticipate future growth, and provide for maintenance and purchases of warranties. Depending on the law firm's needs and budget, the plan may even prioritize purchases.

- Performance, in addition to cost, should be considered when selecting software.
- Lawyers and staff involved in litigation must pay particular attention to changing court requirements and adapt their own technology to that required for litigation. Some courts allow electronic filing of documents.
- Confidential client information as well as confidential information about the law firm's business itself that is stored electronically must be protected against hacking by outsiders and against unauthorized intrusion by a user.
- The Computer Fraud and Abuse Act, 18 U.S.C. §1030, outlaws certain acts related to unauthorized access to computers. Lawyers who access computerized data inappropriately may be subject to professional disciplinary action.
- A firm should establish a policy regarding metadata and its removal from documents prior to their dissemination.
- Information should be backed up frequently so that, should catastrophic destruction occur, data can still be retrieved. In addition, a law firm should have a policy for the disposal of computer equipment.
- It is vitally important that confidential information be removed from the computer's hard drive before the hardware is discarded.
- A disaster recovery plan should be in place to provide instructions in the event the firm experiences a catastrophic loss of its own hardware or software. A disaster recovery plan should also specify the procedure to be followed if a laptop, smartphone, tablet or notebook computer, or other hardware is lost or stolen. Some states now have statutes requiring certain procedures to be followed if a breach of computer security occurs. Often, notice must be provided to the people whose personal information may have been inadvertently disclosed.
- Economic and technological changes have also contributed to changes in the legal industry and how it operates. Lawyers and others in the field may find more entrepreneurial opportunities open to them.

Vocabulary

extranet (p. 366)	outsource (p. 351)
firewall (p. 365)	software (p. 358)
hardware (p. 358)	spyware (p. 365)
intranet (p. 366)	virtual law office (p. 350)
metadata (p. 365)	virus (p. 365)
offshoring (p. 352)	wiki (p. 351)

Career Preparation Tips

Elders of the legal industry recognize that the market is changing and that startup technology businesses might well post the biggest challenge to the traditional law firm in the future. Embrace your own entrepreneurial spirit. As you review the chapters in this book, think of opportunities to change the way the legal industry has done business in the past. Undertake a bit of competitive intelligence data gathering: Is anyone currently doing this? Could you do this in a better, more efficient way? Would your proposal work within the parameters of your state's professional responsibility rules and unauthorized practice of law statutes? Try pitching your ideas to prospective investors or to prospective employers.

If You Want to Learn More

Above the Law blog. http://abovethelaw.com

Google Analytics. http://www.google.com/analytics

Greedy Associates blog. http://blogs.findlaw.com/greedy_associates/

International Legal Technology Association. http://www.iltanet.org

Jury Tracker. http://www.jurytracker.com/JuryTracker/JuryTracker.html

Microsoft SharePoint. http://office.microsoft.com/en-us/microsoft-sharepoint-collaboration-software-FX103479517.aspx

Virtual Law Practice. http://virtuallawpractice.org/about/

World Legal Information Institute. http://www.worldlii.org

Clio is a client-collaboration, time and billing, and practice management platform. http://www.goclio.com

Rocket Matter offers online law practice management software and document storage. http://www.rocketlawyer.com

Another practice management and client-collaboration platform is Total Attorneys. http://www.totalattorneys.com

Adobe Connect is software that enables online meetings to occur. http://www.adobe.com/products/adobeconnect/web-meetings.html

Axiom Law is a legal services outsourcing vendor that provides legal services to in-house counsel. http://www.axiomlaw.com/index.php/overview

Riverviewlaw also provides unbundled legal services. http://www.riverviewlaw.com

An online legal document service is Legal Zoom. http://www.legalzoom.com/

Reading Comprehension

1. How has automation changed the practice of law?
2. Under what circumstances is the outsourcing of legal work ethically acceptable to the American Bar Association?
3. Why would a law firm be interested in offshoring certain work?
4. How can lawyers use social networking sites to build their business?
5. How can social networking sites be harmful to lawyers?
6. What is the difference between an advertisement and a blog?
7. What factors should a law firm consider when purchasing software?
8. How might an iPad be useful to a lawyer?
9. What is the difference between a computer virus and spyware?
10. How can lawyers transmit very large files efficiently?
11. Why is cloud computing convenient for lawyers?
12. How should confidential business information be protected?
13. What economic pressures do law firms face?
14. Why are rules allowing legal services to be unbundled important for the field?

Discussion Starters

1. Look up and compare *Shurgard Storage Centers Inc. v. Safeguard Self Storage Inc.*, 119 F. Supp. 2d 1121 (W.D. Wash. 2000) to *International Association of Machinists and Aerospace Workers v. Werner-Matsuda*, 390 F. Supp. 2d 479 (D. Md. 2005). In what ways are the decisions similar? How are they different? How can law firms prevent unauthorized access to confidential materials in their own computer systems?
2. Google "Everyone's a Winner at Nixon Peabody," a promotional song released by a law firm. What was the controversy concerning the song

released by the law firm Nixon Peabody? Did the firm receive positive or negative attention because of the song? What does the retrievability of information about this matter even though it took place a number of years ago tell you about a law firm's history on the Internet?

3. Find three law firms that have accounts on Facebook, Twitter, and LinkedIn. What information is posted on each site? Is any negative information posted? How does the type of information posted vary? Why do you suppose the law firm is posting in each of these venues? Do you think the firm's postings are effective?

4. Look up ethical rules on social networking sites in your jurisdiction. Are judges allowed to use the sites? Are lawyers allowed to use them? Do any restrictions apply? Look up the ethical rules in a neighboring jurisdiction and compare them with your jurisdiction's rules. Which set of rules to you think is preferable? Why?

5. Try to find some information accessible on the Internet that focuses on the negative aspects of a firm. How might this affect the firm's business? Do you think the information might alter a client's opinion of the firm? What action, if any, might the firm take to prevent this information from being posted?

6. Find two blog postings by lawyers at a large law firm. Why do you suppose the lawyers selected the topic they did to write about? What was their ulterior purpose in writing about the topic? Is the posting specific, or do you find the information to be somewhat vague? Did anyone comment in response to the blog postings?

7. Using an online legal database such as Lexis or Westlaw, locate a recent court decision involving a blog, Twitter, or Facebook. What was the issue regarding the blog, Twitter, or Facebook? How was the issue resolved? What might future bloggers or users of Twitter or Facebook learn from this decision?

Case Studies

1. You are the law office manager for a five-lawyer firm that focuses on family law. What hardware and software should you purchase? If the firm's budget does not allow for all of the purchases you recommend, which items would you forgo?

2. You are the law office manager for a 700-lawyer, full-service firm with five offices in the United States, one in Asia, and one in Europe. What software might such a firm need that a five-lawyer firm based in Missouri does not?

3. Look up help-wanted ads for IT staff people at a local law firm. What qualifications are required? What job responsibilities are involved? Are salaries mentioned?

4. Suppose you work for an intellectual property boutique based in Washington, D.C., that has 25 lawyers. Draft a disaster preparedness plan for the firm. Are any special considerations necessary given the firm's focus?

5. Suppose you work for a ten-lawyer litigation firm. The firm is thinking of switching from Dell computers to Apple computers. What would be the reason for such a change? Would the switch make the law firm more efficient in some way?

6. Suppose you work for the environmental group of a major national law firm. Your firm is competing for the business of a major client that manufactures pesticides. Find three competing law firms that might be interested in the business, and conduct some competitive intelligence research. What sorts of clients do these firms represent? What kinds of cases have these firms been successful in winning? Might these firms have any conflicts of interest regarding the prospective new client? Do these firms have any weaknesses your firm might capitalize on? How can your law firm distinguish itself from the competition?

7. Research several virtual law firms. In what jurisdictions do they operate? What sorts of services do they provide? Do you notice any special measures being taken to comply with pertinent ethical rules?

8. Research several legal support services providers. What services do they offer? What do they charge? Do they make any claims about the quality of their work or provide notice explaining whether they are providing legal advice?

Endnotes

1. Douglas Caddell, *Selling Your Law Firm's Tech*, Law.com Legal Technology, June 4, 2007.

2. Robert Ambrogi, *Number of "Virtual" Law Practices Shows Decline in 2013 ABA Technology Survey*, Robert Ambrogi's LawSites blog (Aug. 13, 2013), http://www.lawsitesblog.com/2013/08/number-of-virtual-law-practices-shows-decline-in-aba-tech-survey.html.

3. *Id.*

4. Peter Buck, *Wikis Put Lawyers on a Collaborative Path*, Law Technology News, May 8, 2008, *available at* http://www.law.com.

5. *See, e.g.,* Julie Creswell, *Law Firms Are Starting to Adopt Outsourcing*, N.Y. Times (Oct. 27, 2006), *available at* http://www.nytimes.com.

6. Alexandra Hanson, *Comment: Legal Process Outsourcing to India: So Hot Right Now!*, 62 SMU L. Rev. 1889, 1891 (Fall 2009).

7. *See, e.g.,* Nina Cunningham, *Is Outsourcing an Opportunity for Law Firms?*, LJN's Legal Tech Newsletter (May 2013), *available at* http://www.altmanweil.com/Outsourcing0613.

8. *See, e.g.,* Ellen L. Rosen, *Corporate America Sending More Legal Work to Bombay*, N.Y. Times (Mar. 14, 2004), *available at* http://www.nytimes.com.

9. ABA Standing Comm. on Ethics and Prof'l Responsibility, Lawyer's Obligations When Outsourcing Legal and Non-Legal Support Services, Formal Op. 08-451 (Aug. 5, 2008).

10. Peter H. Geraghty, *Recent Ethics Opinion: Outsourcing*, Your ABA, *available at* http://www.abanet.org/media/youraba/200809/article11.html (last visited Dec. 5, 2010).

11. *See, e.g.*, State Bar of Cal. Standing Comm. on Prof'l Responsibility & Conduct, Formal Op. 2012-184 (2012); N.C. State Bar, Formal Ethics Op. 10 (2005).

12. A.B.A. Law Practice Management Section eLawyering Task Force, *Suggested Minimum Requirements for Law Firms Delivering Legal Services Online* (Oct. 15, 2009), http://meetings.americanbar.org/webupload/commupload/EP024500/relatedresources/Minimum_Requirements_for_Lawyers_2009_10_24.pdf-5k-2009-11-19.

13. John G. Browning, *Facebook, Twitter, and LinkedIn—Oh My! The ABA Ethics 20/20/ Commission and Evolving Ethical Issues in the Use of Social Media*, 40 N. Ky L. Rev. 255, 256 (2013).

14. Judge Gena Slaughter & John G. Browning, *The Attorney and Social Media: Social Networking Dos and Don'ts for Lawyers and Judges*, 73 Tex. B.J. 192, 192 (Mar. 2010).

15. Florida Supreme Court Judicial Ethics Advisory Committee, Opinion No. 2009-20 (Nov. 27, 2009), *available at* http://www.jud6.org/legalcommunity/legalpractice/opinions/jeacopinions/2009/2009-20.html. *See also* Florida Supreme Court Judicial Ethics Advisory Committee, Opinion No. 2012-12 (May 9, 2012), *available at* http://www.jud6.org/legalcommunity/legalpractice/opinions/jeacopinions/2012/2012-12.html.

16. California Judges Association Judicial Ethics Committee, Opinion No. 66 (2010), *available at* http://www.caljudges.org/ethics_opinions.vp.html.

17. *In re Peshek,* No. 09CH89 (Hearing B. Ill. Att'y. Registration & Disciplinary Commn. *filed* Aug. 25, 2009), *available at* http://www.iardc.org/09CH0089CM.html. Peshek was suspended from practicing for a couple of months in 2010. Att'y Registration & Disciplinary Commn. of the Sup. Ct. of Ill., https://www.iardc.org/ldetail.asp?id=388941527 (last visited June 20, 2011).

18. *In re Terry*, No. 08-234, at 1 (N.C. Jud. Standards Commn. Apr. 1, 2009), *available at* http://www.aoc.state.nc.us/www/public/coa/jsc/publicreprimands/jsc08-234.pdf.

19 AAC Regulation No. 17: (proposed new regulation) SOCIAL MEDIA SCR 3.130-7.020(1)(j), *available at* http://www.kybar.org/30 (approved by Kentucky Board of Governors on July 30, 2010, subject to review and comment).

20. *See, e.g.*, N.Y. State Rules of Prof'l Conduct R. 7.1 Comment (as amended through Dec. 20, 2012), *available at* http://www.nysba.org/AM/Template.cfm?Section=For_Attorneys&ContentID=152184&template=/CM/ContentDisplay.cfm.

21. Ray Worthy Campbell, *Rethinking Regulation and Innovation in the U.S. Legal Services Market,* 9 N.Y.U. J. L. & Bus. 1, 39 (Fall 2012).

22. AbacusLaw, Don't Let These 5 Big Changes in the Legal Profession Be Catastrophic to Your Law Firm, *available at* http://www.abacuslaw.com/form-five-changes/ (last visited Sept. 18, 2013).

23. Daniel Fisher, *Google Jumps Into Online-Law Business With Rocket Lawyer*, Forbes.com (Aug. 11, 2011), http://www.forbes.com/sites/danielfisher/2011/08/11/google-jumps-into-online-law-business-with-rocket-lawyer.

24. *See, e.g.*, D.C. Bar, Opin. No. 330 (July 2005), *available at* http://www.dcbar.org/for_lawyers/ethics/legal_ethics/opinions/opinion330.cfm.

25. *See generally* Noam Scheiber, *The Last Days of Big Law*, New Republic, Aug. 5, 2013, at 25.

26. Gary Munneke, *When Brahmins Bumble: Dewey Really Care?*, 84-SEP N.Y. St. B.J. 28, 33 (Sept. 2012).

27. Tex. Gov't Code Ann. §81.101(c) (2013).

28. Jeanne Meister, *The Boomer-Millennial Workplace Clash: Is It Real?*, Forbes.com (June 4, 2013), http://www.forbes.com/sites/jeannemeister/2013/06/04/the-boomer-millennial-workplace-clash-is-it-real/.

29. *See, e.g.*, Lawrence J. Centola III, *Bridging the Divide Between Baby Boomers and Millennials*, 61 La. B.J. 18 (June/July 2013).

30. *See generally* Rodney G. Snow, *Baby Boomers Meet Millennials in the Legal Workplace: From Face-Lift to Facebook*, 4-DEC Utah B.J. 8 (Nov./Dec. 2011).

31. *See generally An Anniversary Roundtable: Transformations in Law Firm Management*, 30-SUM Del. Law. 8 (Spring/Summer 2012).

32. See, e.g., Maryland State Bar Association, Inc. Committee on Ethics, Ethics of Viewing and/or Using Metadata, No. 2007-09 (2007).

33. Richard Acello, *Get Your Head in the Cloud*, A.B.A. J., April 2010, at 28-29.

34. Alabama State Bar Ethics Opinions 2010-02, Retention, Storage, Ownership, Production and Destruction of Client Files, at 14, *available at* http://www.alabar.org/ogc/PDF/2010-02.pdf (last visited Dec. 16, 2010).

35. *See id.*

36. *See, e.g.*, Douglas Caddell, *Selling Your Law Firm's Tech*, Law Tech. News, June 4, 2007, *available at* www.law.com/tech.

37. *See, e.g.*, N.Y. Gen. Bus. Law §899-aa (2013).

Glossary

acceptable use policy: guidelines for the appropriate use of technology

admittance pro hac vice: admittance to the bar of another jurisdiction on a temporary basis for the purpose of working on a specific case

alphabetic filing system: a system in which files are stored alphabetically, by last name of individuals, or by business name of corporate clients

alphanumeric filing system: a system that combines elements of both alphabetic and numerical filing systems

annotated statutes: a collection of statutes that includes explanations of the law and references to cases and other materials in which the law is interpreted

associate: a lower-level attorney, typically with only a few years of practice

attorney-client privilege: an evidentiary privilege that allows a client to prevent the release of information given by the client to her attorney

attrition: a reduction in the number of people in a group, such as law firm employees

"back-office" activity: work that deals with the business administration side of the law firm

bar coding: a method that tracks files using a bar code assigned to each file

BCC: blind courtesy copy or blind carbon copy indicating a list of recipients who are not identified in a communication

blended rate: an hourly rate established based on the legal team that will be working on a matter

block format: the layout of a letter in which each line is flush with the left margin and there is an extra space between paragraphs

blog: a shortened form of the term Web log—a frequently updated online diary or journal-type writing that chronicles recent developments; sometimes called a "blawg" in the legal field, a blend of the terms *law* and *blog*

boilerplate: standardized text for use as clauses in documents

boutique practice: a practice that focuses on only one particular area of the law

brand: the associations and experiences that define an entity, person, or service

bread-and-butter client: a steady client that generates a consistent stream of business for a firm

brochure: a marketing tool, frequently in print as well as online, describing the capabilities of a law firm or practice group

budget: an estimate of a firm's revenues and expenses

business casual attire: clothing that is less formal than standard workplace attire but not as casual as weekend wear

business continuity plan: a set of procedures and information for continuing to provide services in the face of a disruptive event

calendaring: the act of recording important information on a calendar

captive law firm: a law firm in which the lawyers are employees of an insurance company

case management systems: law firm management programs that include information about lawsuits involving clients and other client matters, along with other documents, calendars, lawyers' notes, and timekeeping elements

caselaw: law made by the judicial system

CC: courtesy copy or carbon copy, identifying a list of recipients other than the addressee

C-suite: the chief officer positions in an organization, such as chief executive officer, chief operating officer, and chief financial officer

centralized file system: an arrangement in which all the files are located in one file room

chief sustainability officer: a new job description in some law firms for a person who promotes the conservation of resources and seeks to minimize the impact of the firm and its clients on the environment

chief talent officer: a new title for the head human resources director, who focuses on recruiting employees and managing their performance

churning: the inappropriate practice of running up hourly legal fees with excessive discovery requests and other matters to create additional legal work, thus generating more fees

citator: an index of legal decisions and related materials that allow researchers to track the history of a case and to locate other cases that have cited it

client activity report: a description of the activities performed by attorneys and other timekeepers at the firm for a specified client, the hours spent on these activities, and the hourly rate of each timekeeper

client matter: a client's legal problem; the subject of a given law firm representation

client team: a group of lawyers, paralegals, and others within a firm who work together for a given client

cloud computing: use of remote servers for data and management allowing users to access data from any computer with an Internet connection (rather than programs and other materials being stored directly on one's personal computer or internal network)

communications strategy: a plan for controlling the transmittal of information to the public, the press, clients, or the workforce

competitive intelligence: information about an industry and market served

contract attorney: a lawyer hired temporarily by contract for a specified period of time

contract employee: someone hired on a temporary basis and typically with no benefits

convergence: a corporation's practice of consolidating the number of outside law firms it uses

cross-selling: marketing other practice groups within a firm to a client

curate: care for or oversee the items in a collection

deadline: the date on which a specified document is due

decentralized file system: also called a local filing system, an arrangement in which files are in various locations in an office, such as with individual attorneys or specific departments

decorum: behavior that is in good taste and propriety

deep pockets: abundant financial resources

default date: the date an opposing party will be considered to have defaulted if an answer is not filed by the appropriate deadline

disaster preparedness plan: a set of procedures devised for responding to emergency situations

disbarment: revocation of a lawyer's permission to practice law

disciplinary action: punishment taken against a lawyer for violating ethics codes

disclaimer: a statement appended to an e-mail or fax transmission aimed at minimizing liability, such as for breach of confidentiality, when the communication is delivered to an unintended recipient

disengagement letter: a letter from a lawyer terminating her representation of a client

diversity manager: a person who promotes awareness of diversity issues and helps an organization achieve its diversity goals

docket: a list of matters in litigation; caseload

domain name: a unique name that identifies a Web site that concludes with a domain suffix, such as .com or .net; the domain name may begin with www followed by a period

draw: an advance taken by an equity partner against her share of the firm's profits

employment at will: A work relationship that has no contract and can be terminated at any time by either the employer or the employee

equity partner: a partner with an ownership interest in a firm

ergonomics: the study of the relationship between people and their working environment geared toward maximizing productivity while ensuring health and safety of workers by providing appropriately designed tools for work-related tasks

ethical wall: also called a Chinese wall or a firewall, an unbreachable wall built around a lawyer who has a conflict of interest so that others in the firm can still work on the matter

executive order: an order issued by the President

external client: outside entities that hire the firm to perform legal work

extranet: a computer network that allows controlled access to information from outside the firm

facility management: coordination of a business's workspace, involving oversight of buildings as well as services

feng shui: a Chinese term meaning "wind and water"—an ancient Chinese practice of harmonizing the environment and balancing its energy patterns to achieve health, happiness, and prosperity

fiduciary duty: a duty of good faith and trust owed to a beneficiary by a fiduciary

firewall: a computer program that blocks unauthorized access to a computer from outside intruders

firm culture: the personality and tradition of behavior at a law firm

firm history: a written account of the development and experiences of a law firm since its inception

flat fee: a prearranged price for a particular piece of work

"front-office" activity: work that supports the law practice itself

full-service practice: a legal practice sufficiently large and with a depth of expertise to accommodate the vast majority of clients' legal problems

general practice: a legal practice that offers a range of legal services, from business to personal

green building: a structure that uses resources efficiently and is environmentally friendly

grievance: a complaint filed by a client against a lawyer asserting violation of a state's ethical rules

hardware: the machines, wiring, and other physical components of a computer or other electronic system

headhunter: a recruiter

headnotes: summaries of the legal points covered in a case

home office: the headquarters of a law firm

hornbook: a legal text that covers the basics of a particular area of the law, including explanations of how the law evolved and the current status of the law

hourly rate: the amount a timekeeper charges for one hour of work

income budget: a projection of all sources of income

internal client: partners and others in a law firm who dole out assignments to other lawyers, paralegals, and others in a law firm's staff

intranet: a computer network that allows users within a firm to access information and to communicate with one another internally

J.D.:   *Juris Doctor,* or Doctor of Laws, degree earned by most graduates from law school today

knowledge management: the means by which knowledge is provided to allow people to perform their jobs

lateral hire: a lawyer who joins a different law firm after practicing law elsewhere

law clerk: a law student who works at a law firm, typically on a part-time basis, while attending law school

law firm subsidiary: an affiliate business, such as lobbying or consulting, of a law firm

law journal: a periodical (typically a newspaper or magazine) focused more on topics pertinent to actual law practice, often published by bar associations

law office manager: a lawyer or hired nonlegal professional employee who handles the business aspects of a law firm's operations

law review: a periodical edited by law students containing scholarly articles written by practitioners, law professors, and judges; essays; case notes; book reviews; and other topical information

legal directory: a compilation of the contact information of legal professionals

legal project management: the application of project management principles to legal matters to enhance value for clients while maintaining profitability for the law firm providing service to the client

legal treatise: a scholarly work that covers a particular area of the law in considerable detail

leverage: the ratio of nonequity lawyers to equity partners

LL.M.: Master of Laws degree

loose leaf: a book bound with rings that open, allowing for the addition and removal of pages

mailing date: the date on which a document must be sent in order to be received by a deadline

mandatory authority: a source of law that is binding on a court

marketing: the process by which firms promote and sell their services

marketing director: a person who oversees the development and implementation of a firm's marketing initiatives

marketing plan: a guide for promoting a firm's services that identifies business development goals, specifies target markets, and indicates means for achieving the firm's goals

master calendar: a calendar on which important dates for an entire law firm are recorded

megafirm: a law firm that has hundreds, or even thousands, of attorneys

metadata: information embedded in an electronic file about the creation and modification of that file

mission statement: a short description of the law firm explaining the type of work it undertakes and perhaps describing the firm's overall philosophy

multidisciplinary practice: a practice that involves more than one profession, such as law and accounting

multijurisdictional practice: the practice of law in more than one state or country

net profit:　revenues minus expenses

newsletter:　a bulletin sent out periodically that provides updates about legal developments of interest to a firm's clientele and prospective clients

nonequity partner:　a junior partner who does not have an ownership interest in the firm

numerical filing system:　a system in which a unique number is assigned to each client and an additional number is assigned to each client matter

of counsel:　a salaried attorney, typically one with more experience than an associate, who is not on the partnership track at a firm

official reports:　accounts of cases that are approved by the government

offshoring:　relocating a business's activities to an area in another country where the jobs may be done more efficiently

operating budget:　a projection of both revenues and expenses

opinion:　a court's decision in a case

outsource:　to send work to an outside provider; the practice of retaining a third party to perform a portion of a business's activities

paralegal:　a person who assists a lawyer in completing certain legal tasks but who is not trained as an attorney

parameter:　boundary; a factor that determines a range of variations

partner:　a lawyer who jointly owns and runs a law firm with other lawyers

partnership track:　The path of a newly hired attorney who is expected to be promoted to partner after serving as an associate for a requisite number of years

permanent associate:　an associate who is not on the partnership track at a law firm

perquisite, or "perk":　a benefit or special privilege bestowed on an employee in addition to salary

personal calendar:　a calendar maintained for an individual's own use

persuasive authority:　a source of law that is convincing but not binding on a court

precedent:　prior decisions by a court

primary source of law:　a material issued by a law-making body, such as the president, a legislature, or the courts

private client:　an individual client who has a high net worth

profits:　revenue less expenditures

protocol:　a procedure or set of rules

realization rate:　the percentage of actual income paid to the firm from the billable hours of each timekeeper

records management:　the process by which materials containing information are organized, handled, and stored

records retention:　the length of time a piece of information should be kept

regulations:　rules issued by government agencies

reports:　books containing caselaw published in chronological order

restatement of the law:　an explanation of the law as it currently is

retainer: an upfront payment made by a client for work that a lawyer will perform in the future

runner: someone hired to solicit personal injury cases on behalf of a lawyer

satellite office: a branch office of a firm

secondary source of law: a material that explains or interprets the law but that does not actually create any law

secondment: the practice of lending associates to a corporate client so the associates gain an improved understanding of that client's business

sexual harassment: inappropriate advances, requests for sexual favors, or verbal or physical conduct of a sexual nature

Shepardizing: a means of updating caselaw and other legal materials by using Shepard's Citations, a publication that identifies the history and treatment of a case, statute, or other legal authority

slip law: the first official publication of a statute in the form of an unbound pamphlet

slip opinion: the first available version of a court's decision in a case

social networking site: an online community that permits its members to post information about themselves

software: the programs and other operating information used by a computer

sole practitioner: a lawyer who practices law on his own, without partners

spyware: malicious tracking software that disseminates information over the Internet

staff attorney: an attorney hired with the understanding that he is not on the partnership track at a firm

stare decisis: a Latin term meaning "to stand by things decided"—the principle that courts rely on prior decisions, or precedent, in determining the outcome of a case

statute: a law passed by a legislature

statute of limitation: a law barring lawsuits after a certain period of time after the activity (such as a car accident) that gave rise to the legal action occurred

summer associate: a law student hired to work at a law firm during the summer with the understanding that the student will be considered for an associate position at the firm

sustainability: the conditions in which humans and nature can exist in harmony so that social, economic, and environmental needs of current and future generations can be met

telecommunication system: means of transmitting signals for the purpose of communicating via telephone, computer, radio, television, and other devices

template: a model with a standard format

tickler: a reminder about an upcoming deadline

time-to-billing percentage: the amount of time billed divided by the amount of time recorded

timekeeping: the practice of tracking and recording time

tombstone ad: a law firm announcement, typically published in black and white

trade publication: a periodical geared to a specific business or industry

treaty: a formal agreement between countries

trigger date: the date that launches a specified amount of time by which another event must occur

unauthorized practice of law: the practice of law by someone not admitted to practice in a given jurisdiction

unofficial reports: accounts of cases issued by the government that also include summaries

unpublished opinions: court decisions designated as unpublished and historically binding on only the parties to a case

"up or out": the policy that an associate passed over for partnership is expected to leave the firm

variance reporting: a comparison of the projected expenses and income with the amounts actually achieved

virtual law office: a law office for which there is no formal, centralized office; instead, lawyers and staff work at remote locations (often their home offices) and generally communicate electronically rather than face-to-face

virtual world: a computer-based simulated environment allowing a group of people to gather at an online location and interact primarily via the Internet rather than face-to-face

virus: computer code that has a detrimental effect on one's computer by slowing it down, disabling it entirely, disseminating information inappropriately, or destroying files and programs

Voice over Internet protocol (VoIP): a means of transmitting voice communications over the Internet

Web site hosting service: an entity that stores Web pages and makes them accessible on the Internet

"white shoe" firm: an established, highly prestigious law firm (white shoes refer to the white bucks worn by members of the upper class in the northeastern United States)

wiki: a Web site that can be modified and added to by visitors to the site

work product doctrine: an evidentiary doctrine that prevents certain documents prepared by a lawyer for a client from being disclosed during the discovery process in litigation

Index